Gospel Without Borders

Gospel Without Borders
Separating Christianity from Culture in America

JIM ROTHOLZ

RESOURCE *Publications* · Eugene, Oregon

GOSPEL WITHOUT BORDERS
Separating Christianity from Culture in America

Copyright © 2015 Jim Rotholz. All rights reserved. Except for brief quotations in critical publications or reviews, no part of this book may be reproduced in any manner without prior written permission from the publisher. Write: Permissions. Wipf and Stock Publishers, 199 W. 8th Ave., Suite 3, Eugene, OR 97401.

Resource Publications
An Imprint of Wipf and Stock Publishers
199 W. 8th Ave., Suite 3
Eugene, OR 97401

www.wipfandstock.com

ISBN 13: 978-1-4982-0964-9

Manufactured in the U.S.A.   02/27/2015

Unless otherwise identified, all scripture quotations are taken from the Holy Bible, New International Version, Copyright © 1973, 1978, 1984 International Bible Society.

Scripture quotations marked RSV are taken from the Revised Standard Version, Copyright © 1946, 1952, and 1971, the Division of Christian Education of the National Council of the Churches of Christ in the United States of America.

Scripture quotations marked NLT are taken from the New Living Translation, Copyright © 1996, 2004, 2007, 2013, Tyndale House Foundation.

Scripture quotations marked KJV are taken from the King James Version, by public domain.

Scripture quotations marked TV are taken from The Voice, Copyright © 2012 Thomas Nelson, Inc.

Scripture quotations marked GWT are taken from God's Word Translation, Copyright © 1995 by God's Word to the Nations, Baker Publishing Group.

Scripture quotations marked NASV are taken from the New American Standard Version (NASV), Copyright © 1960, 1962, 1963, 1968, 1971, 1972, 1973, 1975, 1977, 1995, The Lockman Foundation.

Scripture quotations marked ESV are taken from the English Standard Version, Copyright © 2001, Crossway Bibles, a division of Good News Publishers.

Scripture quotations marked NET are taken from the New English Translation, Copyright ©1996-2006 by Biblical Studies Press, L.L.C.

Scripture quotations marked HCSB are taken from the Holman Christian Standard Bible, Copyright © 1999, 2000, 2002, 2003, 2009, Holman Bible Publishers.

To my gaggle of beloved siblings
—Becky, Michael, Wade, and Lee—
whose unwavering love and support over the
vagaries of a lifetime means more to me
than words could ever express.

Contents

Introduction | xi

PART I: WHO ARE WE HUMANS?

1 The Nature of Culture | 3
   The Distance Between Us | 4
   Form Versus Substance | 5
   Ethnocentrism | 8
   The Self-Other Divide | 9
   Language | 12
   Human Nature | 16
   Cultural Relativism | 17

2 Human Nature: The Good | 20
   Relational | 25
   Sentient | 28
   Free Will | 29
   Coupling | 30
   Sharing and Giving | 32
   Personality and Experience | 33
   Religious/Spiritual | 35
   Conscience | 38
   Rational | 39
   Ideology and Worldview | 41
   Symbol Using | 44
   Creative | 45
   Aesthetically Sensitive | 46
   Purposeful | 47
   Faith | 49
   Fun and Sense of Humor | 50

3 Human Nature: The Not So Good | 52
   Self-preservation | 54
   Self-centered | 56
   Prideful | 58
   Bent Toward Wrongdoing | 60
   Bent Toward Belligerence | 61
   Scapegoating | 64
   Taboo-Making | 66
   Memes | 67
   Wither Human Nature? | 69

PART II: WHO ARE WE AMERICANS?

4 America's Cultural Origins | 73
   Origins | 73
   Our First Ancestors | 76
   The Pilgrims | 79
   Slaves and Greeks | 80
   Natural and Social Environments | 81
   The Present | 85

5 Early American Cultural Influences | 88
   Individualism | 88
   Religious/Moralistic | 91
   Egalitarianism | 95
   Hard Work and Progress | 96
   Patriotism | 99
   Humans Over Nature | 103

6 Post-Industrial Cultural Influences | 108
   Materialism | 109
   Privilege and Superiority | 112
   Logic and Reason | 114
   Youth and Image | 117
   Fun and Entertainment | 121
   Benevolence | 125

7 Contemporary American Cultural Norms | 130
   Hyper-competitive | 131
   Nationalistic Fervor | 133
   Corporate Dominant | 135

Consumerist | 137
Entrepreneurial | 138
Technologically Infatuated | 140
Litigious and Politicized | 142
Nihilistic and Cynical | 143
Privacy Hoarding | 145
Mobile and Displaced | 147
Casual and Informal | 148
Highly Sexualized | 149
Image Controlling | 151
Gender Bending | 152
Power Struggles | 154
Segmented Pluralism | 155
Democratized Spirituality | 157
Complexly Ineffective | 158

8 **Enduring American Myths** | 161
The Greatest Nation on Earth | 162
The Land Of Equal Opportunity | 164
The Invisible Hand Still Guides Us | 165
Nature Is Stable and Bountiful | 167
The Noble Savage Lives On | 168
Cultural Evolution | 170
America Is Generous | 172
Americans Know Enough About the World | 174
Americans Are Not Racist | 175
It's Our Job to Make the World Democratic | 177
Our Adversaries Are Thwarting Our Progress | 180
Life Should Be Fun and Make Us Happy | 183
Are We There Yet, Mom? | 184

PART III: WHO ARE WE AMERICAN CHRISTIANS?

9 **Christianity in America** | 187
What is Christianity? | 187
Christianity as Religion | 191
Country Club Christianity | 194
Formulaic Faith | 196
Christianity as Power and Influence | 198
Reactionary Faith | 200
Respectable Christianity | 201

Competitive Christianity | 203
Cerebral Christianity | 205
Christianity as Public Service | 207
Post-Christian Christianity | 208
Back to the Future | 212

PART IV: WHO ARE WE MEANT TO BE?

10 The Kingdom of God | 217

Misconceptions About the Kingdom | 218
What is the Kingdom of God? | 220
The Law of Love | 222
God's Word is Truth | 224
Holiness, Power, Goodness, and Grace | 226
The Kingdom is Emerging | 227
The Devil Wreaks Havoc | 228
Redemption is at Hand | 232
God's Economy of Inversion | 234
All the World is Sacred | 236
Whence the Kingdom? | 238

11 Living in the Kingdom in America | 240

Inward-Outward | 242
In God We Trust | 244
The Language of the Kingdom | 247
Personalizing the World | 249
Partners in Transformation | 252
The Freedom of Inclusion | 256
One World | 261
God's Dream for America | 264

12 Conclusion: It's All About Image | 267

The New Nature | 267
Epigenetics | 269
Our True Identity | 271
The High Calling | 273
America the Beautiful | 276
Ready the Bride | 277
Flourishing East of Eden | 279
Welcome Home | 280

Bibliography | 285

Index | 297

Introduction

Culture is doing what feels natural.
—Barry Hewlett

One of the most important and far-reaching issues facing the Christian church today involves grasping the differences between faith and culture. The way our faith and culture intertwine directly impacts everything and everybody around us, including the church's institutions, programs, and role in larger society and the world. Yet the intersection of and interplay between faith and culture is one of the least understood, most veiled and misconstrued dimensions of most believers' lives. Exactly what culture consists of and how it combines with and impacts faith is so obscure to many that they have no idea it even holds the slightest bit of significance. But then that's the nature of the beast. As an anthropology professor of mine so succinctly yet poignantly summed it up, "Culture is doing what feels natural." So natural, in fact, that we fail to even notice it is having a very profound impact on our perceptions and behaviors. And in failing to notice, we often make the critical mistake of thinking that our faith and culture are one and the same—a mistake repeatedly made not only by Christians in this country but by people within every religion and culture around the world. The result is all too often a faith-culture mix that can easily become the Golden Calf we worship and the idol to which we cling in our failure to deal directly with a highly personal and intensely engaging God.

When faith and culture get so entangled that we cannot tell them apart—and if we are not constantly asking what the difference is, you can be most certain we have them thoroughly mixed together—we end up valuing form over substance. And then we find ourselves inadvertently "playing religion" rather than experiencing biblical faith. We become trapped in the myth of a god we have created in our own image—a domesticated deity who, it just so happens, sees things the way we do, supports our political and social agendas, and generally likes the same kind of people as we (see Ps 50:21). When faith and culture intermingle and remain unexamined, the result is comfortable religion that reassures rather than challenges and leads to complacency rather than fulfillment through loving relationship, service, and engagement with the miraculous. It becomes a self-serving religion with a light glaze of true faith on top. "Light religion" always entails self-satisfaction, self-justification, and a worldview that blames others for the ills we perceive in and around us. It leads us into a spiritual and psychological cul-de-sac where we become victims in a world of our own creation—a world far from the elevated beauty of the kingdom Christ came to establish.

In spite of our penchant for ethnocentricity, we American Christians do tend to faithfully proclaim that the gospel is God's gift to all of humanity. We do believe in a universally-relevant Christ who calls all people to God through faith in himself. A fair portion of our time, money, and energy is spent getting that gospel message out to "every nation, tribe, language, and people" (Rev 14:6, NLT), because we believe it is both our calling as Christians to do so and the rightful possession of those who have yet to receive it. But in the process we too often export a watered-down faith-culture mix instead of the pure life-changing gospel, unaware that the simple but powerful message of Jesus Christ is what the world longs to hear and deserves to hear.

But what is that gospel? What exactly is the essence of the message we feel so compelled to proclaim? Can we identify an "essential gospel" that avoids detrimental cultural trappings, one that is appropriate to everyone, everywhere? Or are we doomed to package it in a culture-specific format that risks making the good news either incomprehensible, irrelevant, or at worst, totally inappropriate for those who differ from ourselves? And beyond our proclamation, how extensively has our culturally-generated version of the Christian faith impacted our own lives: the choices we make, lifestyles we lead, values we hold, and influence we yield? These are tough but necessary questions if we intend our faith to be both sound and relevant to our own lives and the world and age in which we live.

The prime difficulty we will face in attempting to shake Christianity loose from any type of cultural mooring is that Christ came to us, and still comes to us, in and through culture. That is, we experience our faith in cultural terms—and there's "nothing wrong with that," as Jerry Seinfeld famously said. As humans we are culture-bearing creatures. It is the skin we wear and the unavoidable way we encounter the world around us. We can no more effectively remove our culture than we can change our personality. It is an integral part of us and makes us who we are. Without culture, humans would cease to exist; that is, we would cease to be fully human. And for that very reason, true objectivity on the part of any human being is an illusion. We can only perceive the world through a worldview that is culturally constructed. But—and this is a very big but indeed—to remain unaware of the values and influence of our cultural heritage and how they shape and affect our faith (not to mention the faith of those with whom it is shared) is to live in a state of unnecessary ignorance that severely limits rather than expands that faith. Cultural literacy, like reading literacy, opens things up in many a wonderful way.

As followers of Christ, therefore, we have something of an obligation to become ever more culturally literate in order to be ever more fully engaged in life and more fully immersed in, guided by, and blessed by a viable faith in the living God. Cultural literacy is a means to an end, a tool by which we seek to apprehend that jewel of great worth that behooves us to sell all else to possess (Matt 13:46). It aids our efforts to shed the burdensome layers of cultural baggage that weigh us down, freeing us to serve and experience the love, grandeur and grace of a God who is so much bigger and benevolent than the limited notions any single cultural perspective could possibly allow. Combining our faith with cultural literacy can help us gain a new perspective from which our view through that "glass, darkly" is significantly less obscured (1 Cor 13:12, KJV). The more universal our faith perspective—the more fully we embrace a "gospel without borders"—the more personal freedom and fulfillment we will experience as Christians, and the more we will be able to understand, love and serve humanity both far and near. And through it all, we can better know and honor the One who has called us "out of darkness into his marvelous light" (1 Pet 2:9, RSV).

My approach to this daunting endeavor is itself cultural (as though there were any other possibility). Our Euro-American way of life, our Christian faith, and the Bible itself will be evaluated through a number of culture-related lenses with the goal of fleshing out the essence of each area while grasping the interplay between them all. To do that requires identifying important cultural influences and biases that tend to be read into the biblical text and attached to our inherited expressions of faith, reinforcing predominantly "culturalized" brands of Christianity. One of the most useful tools for understanding our cultural biases is the cross-cultural perspective. I will employ it repeatedly throughout the chapters to follow, with a keen interest in the way differing Christian communities around the world view and live out their faith. Their perspectives will not only illuminate the biases in our own Euro-American framework, but help bring out the essence of our shared faith.

Culture history is another instructor, though it is always subject to the preconceptions of the historian. As Napoleon once purportedly stated, "History is the version of past events that people have decided to agree upon."[1] The people of whom he spoke were those who wielded the social and cultural power to define for others what was considered true, regardless the historic facts. We will, therefore, examine a number of foreign and historical perspectives on our faith that derive from "the powerless," while applying those perspectives as a grid to help frame a more universally relevant Christian faith and gospel message. We will also attempt to examine the scriptures in a fresh way, applying as culturally-neutral a perspective as possible through inductive approaches to interpretation. Understanding one's own cultural framework and how it has been applied to interpreting the message of the Bible is an important and necessary first step toward letting the scriptures speak for themselves by not forcing a preconceived theological framework upon them. Ultimately, we hope to arrive at a place where we can distinguish the essential differences between our faith and our culture, and determine which features of any culture accords with or works against that singular and universally-applicable standard of experientially-realized biblical truth.

The book is divided into four parts. The first is "Who Are We Humans?" I begin this section with a chapter that offers an understanding of culture and its role in our lives, followed by two chapters on human nature—"The Good" and "Not So Good"—and its pivotal role in shaping and understanding any and all cultures. In part II ("Who Are We Americans?"), the first chapter delves into the culture history of America by identifying the social, political, and environmental influences that played dominant roles in cultural formation in the country's early years. This is followed by a chapter listing the cultural values that became established in early America, and then a chapter on values that developed as a result of the Industrial Revolution and carried into modernity. Next I offer a chapter that identifies a number of contemporary American cultural norms that are rooted in the collective cultural values espoused by the dominant culture. I conclude the section with a chapter on the myths that bind together and perpetuate these values and norms in contemporary American life.

The third part of the book, "Who Are We American Christians?" seeks to draw parallels between the church's distinctive expressions of Christian

---

1. Bonaparte, Goodreads, http://www.goodreads.com/quotes/47684-history-is-the-version-of-past-events-that-people-have, accessed October 25, 2014

faith and the cultural values from the previous sections that define the culture-at-large. In this section's only chapter, "Christianity in America," I question what Americans consider Christianity to be, and identify different culturally-derived influences on the faith while discussing the ways those influences shape the competing versions of Christianity we see in America today. To help with the task, I occasionally refer to both Christian and non-Christian religious traditions from around the world, with a particular emphasis on non-Western, low-income countries, to provide an overall context to better understand the unique cultural characteristics that make up the American church.

Part four is titled "Who Are We Meant to Be?" and transitions into a culturally-informed study of the life and teachings of Jesus and the early Apostles. The first chapter in this section pays special attention to the concept of the kingdom of God and the universal nature of its appeal. From these sources I derive a set of "kingdom values" whose principles are employed as a framework by which to evaluate the dominant values represented within both the church and larger culture in America. In the chapter "Living in the Kingdom in America" I provide some examples of ministries and faith communities that illustrate those kingdom values. The book ends with a summary chapter that ties together the various threads of the book into a singular biblical perspective on the believer's true identity, noting the cultural implications that derive from that identity for American Christians.

There is much to learn and much to gain through this undertaking. However, it will be necessary for the reader to keep his or her hackles down, for it will involve some soul-searching and self-examination that may at times feel quite uncomfortable for some Americans who feel their faith and identity threatened. Yet there is no other way to go about the undertaking than to critique every important facet of our culture as it applies to our faith and the larger world in which we live. My intention is to offer a constructive critique that will lead to positive outcomes. I have no particular bone to pick, only a little drum I like to beat tenaciously. I hope the end goal of arriving at a faith and lifestyle less encumbered by the superficial and extraneous constraints of our culture will be more than worth any discomfort experienced along the way.

I readily admit that I speak not as one who has "arrived" or attained some sort of enlightened view of things; for that perspective, too, is culturally-generated by our obsession with things scientific (none can claim absolute clarity about the nature of our world and our place as Christians in it). Although absolute truth exists in the person of Christ Jesus, who proclaimed himself "the way, *the truth*, and the life" (John 14:6), we can only partially and imperfectly reflect that truth, relying on God, through means that defy all logic, to then birth what is ultimately true—which is nothing less than his Spirit of love, grace, and wisdom resident in our hearts. My starting point, then, is to admit that I (we) unavoidably and often inaccurately present God's truth in culture-laden packaging—what the Apostle Paul calls bearing our "treasure in jars of clay" (2 Cor 4:7). Any effort to reduce that packaging, which derives its only significance through association with its contents, can only result in more room for the real goodies inside.

I confess to being but a humble student of culture and the Bible, a novice made aware of the ungainly cultural baggage I have personally and needlessly lugged about for too many years. But like all who seek to know God more intimately and serve him more faithfully, my goal is to jettison all that proves superfluous to historic biblical faith that it may more freely grow and flourish. The process of unfettering that faith, we will find, is not so much a matter of attaining anything at all, but rather identifying what already exists and letting go of all the detritus we have unknowingly accumulated alongside the real treasure. It is a matter of emptying so that God might fill, not setting oneself apart as possessing special knowledge (an element present in most religious traditions). It rather involves identifying with others whose differences in this life are typically considered less important than our own. A faith perspective informed by some degree of cultural literacy does not lift one above the fray as much as it puts one right into the middle of it, shorn of unnecessary impediments, free to love and serve in joy, humility, power, and grace. To the degree that we can liberate ourselves from the constraints of a limited faith-culture perspective—whatever our particular configuration of "culturalized" Christianity may be—the universally-relevant Christian faith we espouse and proclaim will be free to blossom into the truly "good news" the world in all its diversity longs to hear and see lived out—often for the very first time.

PART I

Who Are We Humans?

1
The Nature of Culture

Culture is a little like dropping an Alka-Seltzer into a glass —you don't see it, but somehow it does something.
—Hans Magnus Enzensberger

After all the introductory talk about the importance of understanding culture, it must be stated that there is no such thing as culture per se. One can certainly find numerous elaborate definitions of culture in social science texts. But at the end of the day, culture is only a cognitive handle; it's little more than an agreed upon abstraction with which we investigate the incomparably vast array of human behavior, cognition, and material objects. Culture is an amorphous designation that refers to the totality of the human endeavor, from what we use to wipe ourselves to the symbolic conceptions that attend the hand that does the wiping. Culture even determines our sense of whether or not it is appropriate to mention such things in print. In other words, every dimension of human life—the whole shebang—is either directly or indirectly included in the field. If humans think it, do it, or seek to represent it, then it's culture. That all-encompassing characteristic is both its strength and its weakness, and why so many people have trouble grasping what culture is and how it applies to their everyday lives. I hope we can facilitate some change in that perception in the sections to follow.

THE DISTANCE BETWEEN US

These days the term "culture" is thrown around so much that it is has become more than a little ambiguous—similar to the term "love." Popularly understood, culture means either the arts—often designated "high culture"—or the values people carry around in their "hearts and minds."[1] But technically speaking, it is more like the soil from which both the arts and ideas emerge. As such, most cultural expression emerges from the unconscious, where it is deeply rooted in a sense of identity. The typical example used is the distance we are comfortable putting between ourselves and another person with whom we are speaking. Most South Americans prefer a foot-and-a-half or two, while North Americans can feel threatened unless the distance is closer to three or four feet. If you watch a conversation between representatives of these two different regions, the one will continually move closer and closer as the other repeatedly backs up—both completely unaware of the issue that causes them to dance their way toward what feels normal to them. "Close talkers" feel rebuffed when their counterparts back up, while the counterparts feel their personal space being violated through imagined aggressiveness on the part of the other. We absorb the bulk of such behavioral guidelines as children and develop life-long preferences that are so deeply ingrained in our perceptions that any other way of doing things feels not just strange, but downright wrong.

To take things a step further, the very interest some of us have in analyzing the distance between speakers is also an element of culture. We Euro-Americans are not only oriented toward caring about such matters, we are consumed with anything that can be measured and analyzed. We love our numbers! It is one of the cultural offspring of scientific rationalism, the worldview paradigm that has invaded all dimensions of contemporary Western life, commandeering virtually every cultural niche it encounters. Yet science and its methodologies are, in the final "analysis," just another way of trying to understand, control and manipulate the world in which we live—no different in principle than fortune-telling or voodoo. The desire to understand, control, and manipulate our environment is itself rooted in human nature, a matter to be taken up in the next chapter.

All worldviews are expressions of cultural adaptations; for culture is at essence a means of coping with and adapting to the world as we perceive and experience it, and is thus constantly changing right along with the changing world we encounter. More on culture change later, but the important point here is that since change is becoming more and more rapid

---

1. Hunter, *Change the World*, 6.

in modern life—so much so that constant change is the new normal—our cultural values are now in a permanent state of flux. We must therefore continually renegotiate our worldview and its attendant values if we are to successfully engage the world around us. The implications of this trend for Christians are enormous in terms of understanding our faith and our ability to make that faith relevant to the times in which we live. The Apostle Paul well understood this critical need when he said, "I have become all things to all people so that by all possible means I might save some. I do all this for the sake of the gospel . . ." (1 Cor 9:22–23).

Does this mean Christians need to be mercurial in the values we espouse, changing colors like chameleons to fit the changing cultural landscape? Absolutely not . . . but then . . . absolutely so. Our basic faith, of course, doesn't change nor need we fret over the expression of that faith with which we are most comfortable (e.g., praying in tongues, reading the King James Bible, or singing hymns as Pakistani believers do to the accompaniment of tablas and the harmonium as they sit cross-legged on the floor). But it is critical to recognize that the forms that bear our faith are just forms and themselves not inherently sacred. They are but the luggage within which we carry the only thing of ultimate value—a vibrant faith in the living God. To give priority to that faith, we must be ready and willing to discard all extraneous baggage the second we perceive that it doesn't adequately serve the purposes of the One who has called us into a vital relationship with himself. If we get caught up in the vain attempt to sanctify the cultural forms through which our faith is expressed, defending those forms as though all things sacred are at stake—we could call it "Crusader Syndrome"—then we lose our bearing and end up with an inappropriate, impotent, or even destructive version of biblical faith. It is futile and even silly to expend energy attempting to defend mere religious culture.

FORM VERSUS SUBSTANCE

We Christians would surely benefit by refocusing our attention on the differences between cultural preferences (the forms) and true faith (the substance), for that is the necessary starting point from which we can then proceed to successfully live out the gospel of Christ. No one is privy to such discernment by virtue of birth, brains, or culture of origin. It must be consciously pursued and conscientiously applied on a daily basis. The discernment of which I speak is, in essence, what the Bible refers to as wisdom—the prudent and practical application of knowledge. Biblical wisdom gives us the ability to discern the differences between culturally-generated religiosity and sound, biblically-based faith. Scripture tells us that such wisdom is acquired through reverence toward God, who then bequeaths divine wisdom as a gift to those who diligently seek it (Prov 2:1–6; 9:10; Ps 111:10; Jas 1:5). In a world run rampant with dry data and pointless facts—a glut of superfluous information—wisdom is sorely lacking.

If we who claim to be followers of Jesus do not seek the wisdom to understand the lines of demarcation between faith and culture, as culture-bearing creatures we will simply emulate the masses of good-hearted but unenlightened religious folk who are hard-wired to follow their own particular set of inherited conventions, which too often entail arrogance, bigotry, and even animosity toward those who are different. Without discernment we end up adopting values of convenience from those who have unquestioningly taken them from their predecessors, thereby perpetuating a superficial Christianity that can say more about inherited Western culture than it does about a contemporary and universal message of divine love and redemption. The gospel that Jesus and his disciples promulgated was undeniably universal in scope, and we have been entrusted with the task of sharing that precious treasure with each and every one of our fellow human beings (2 Tim 1:13–14).

I suspect that no believer consciously wishes to misrepresent a globally-relevant gospel message by offering an irrelevant localized version of it—as one might attempt to give flip-flops to Eskimos in need of *mukluks*. Yet that is exactly what we do when we insist that others think, act, and live out their faith with the cultural forms we ourselves inherited and find most comfortable, throwing around religious jargon to authenticate our inclusion among the "true believers." For example, to insist that all believers should belong to a certain political party is no less misdirected than missionaries who not so long ago insisted on dressing naked Papua New Guineans in Western garb in order to attend church in a "proper" manner. Seems silly now but we unwittingly continue to do such things out of a combination of naiveté and ignorance—meaning only that we haven't bothered to learn better. In the process, we have certainly failed to heed the Apostle Paul's words to Timothy to "... correctly handle[s] the word of truth" (2 Tim 2:15).

If you press a Christian from the developing world for his or her real opinion on the depth of Western Christians' faith, don't be surprised to hear that they think we are a rather shallow lot. Many of them patiently put up with our fast-food faith, which can look enticing from the outside but too often lacks real substance. Because most of us have never really suffered for our faith, we tend to value it accordingly. We take it for granted, just as we do our next meal. As Heidi Baker put it in *Compelled by Love*,[2] the poor are always hungry and that hunger translates into a desperate longing for God; while our state of physical satiation too often translates into a lukewarm spirituality. We Western/American Christians often view our faith as an add-on to the rest of our lives—a serving of nourishing greens alongside the main meal of artery-clogging steak and fries. In the words of Jim Wallis, "Modern conversion brings Jesus into our lives rather than bringing us into his. We are told Jesus is here to help us to do better that which we are already doing."[3] It is unfortunate that we have allowed our faith to be so emasculated by our self-pleasuring, consumer culture. We've seemingly traded a wholesome, life-giving protein-rich meal for mere sugar water, leaving us in a state of spiritual hypoglycemia.

But self-condemnation is not biblical and certainly not part of the message and life of Jesus, who came not to condemn the world but to save it (John 3:17). Condemnation of any sort, whether of self or others, is yet another cultural add-on that has served many a fire-and-brimstone preacher quite well. Red-faced and hostile sounding, many traditional American preachers scare the Hades out of their listeners but fail to draw them into the love and comfort God offers through a compassionate Savior. Too often those very tactics get exported to the "mission field" (an antiquated concept at best) where indigenous preachers emulate their Anglo counterparts by delivering a culturally inappropriate message in an ineffective and alienating manner.

How in the world did we Americans become so obsessed with judging and criticizing ourselves and others—insisting on conformity to mere cultural forms? However it has come about—and I suspect it is partly rooted in the competition that ethically-unbridled free market capitalism unwittingly generates—we have suffered for it as a society. Evidence the many believers who carry around heavy and unnecessary burdens of guilt, and the tragically growing legion of young women (Christians equally represented among them) who struggle for their very lives with anorexia nervosa, unable to accept any image of themselves but a hopelessly emaciated one that matches the Twiggy-like cover models popular magazines brazenly parade before us.

The bottom line is that we need biblical wisdom to understand the important distinctions between our faith and our culture. That wisdom, paradoxically, comes to us as a pure gift from God to those who ask (Jas 1:5). A humble, prayerful diligence takes us a long way toward making that search

2. Baker, *Compelled by Love*, 1, 10.
3. Wallis, *Call to Conversion*, 27–28.

fruitful. And it helps us to fulfill Paul's admonition to continually work out our salvation (our spiritual growth and development) through "active reverence and a singleness of purpose in response to God's grace."[4] It is actually God at work in us, according to Paul, shaping our hearts and minds "to will and to act in order to fulfill his good purpose" (Phil 2:13). To me this means that God is actively guiding us in our efforts to discern the intersection of faith and culture, for by doing so we are in a better position to conform to his plans and purposes which, as previously stated, are focused on the world as a whole and every one of its wonderfully diverse array of peoples.

ETHNOCENTRICISM

The natural tendency to judge other peoples and cultures by our own standards and values is inevitably absorbed from those around us through a process of enculturation. It is no secret that we unconsciously copy others, whether it is their way of speaking, behaving, or thinking. Every parent can see this in his or her own children, who sometimes say and do the very things we wish they didn't learn from us (ever heard a five-year-old curse like a sailor?). In the same way, people within groups copy one another, leading to shared values that distinguish them from other groups. Inevitably those distinctions are viewed ethnocentrically; that is, from a single cultural perspective.

"Ethno" is derived from the Greek word for race or people. Also from the Greek, "centric" is an adjective that means "pertaining to or situated at the center." Thus, ethnocentrism means to view other peoples and cultures from our own group's cultural center—our given cultural perspective—and carries with it a strong connotation of bias and sense of superiority. The curious thing is, every culture does it to one degree or another, making ethnocentrism one of many panhuman traits. Those of us from the Western world, Americans in particular, have become notorious for our ethnocentric views of the rest of the world. Others can see it in us, even if we cannot. As a nation, we actually believe ourselves, and regularly proclaim ourselves, to be the "greatest nation on earth"—thereby following in the steps of every haughty empire down through the ages (see Isa 10). More on that theme later, but for the present suffice it to say that ethnocentrism has infected the American church in ways that very much harm its life as well as its relevance in the world. From narrow-minded denominationalism at home to patronizing programs abroad, we sometimes foster more resentment than goodwill, more harm than healing. Rather than fulfill our high calling as

4. Barker et al., *NIV*, 1806.

ambassadors of Christ (2 Cor 5:20), ethnocentrism limits us to occupying futile posts as emissaries of self.

Perhaps the best way to grasp the importance of ethnocentrism for us as both Americans and as Christians is to see its role in other nation-states and religions; for it is always easier to see the speck in another person's eye than the log in one's own (Luke 6:41). A prime example of ethnocentrism at work abroad is among Islamic Jihadists who vilify Americans and Christians together in one fell swoop (such people generally don't distinguish between the two because they do not separate their own religion and nationality, and they misconstrue what makes one a Christian, assuming birth and heritage alone to be sufficient). When we hear the intimidating language and destructive threats coming toward us from Jihadist quarters, we immediately recognize that they do not really know us as real persons but have imposed a set of alien and inappropriate categories onto us and our situation. We feel misunderstood and perhaps a bit angered to be portrayed and manipulated in such a way, all of which can easily lead to less than loving intentions toward those who some might call our "enemies" (who, even if they were, are the very people Christ has called us to love and serve in Matt 5:44).

In order for Christians to avoid responding in kind—that is reciprocally, "eye for eye and tooth for tooth"—we must learn to identify and set aside any ethnocentrism on our part that would inhibit our ability to fully reflect the love of God and the message of the gospel. It is important to realize that the evil we see in others is generally little more than a reflection of our own dark side, our unredeemed nature that has yet to be submitted to the life-enhancing light of Christ. And it should go without saying that when we do project evil onto others, we are no longer mirroring him; for at that point we have fallen prey to one of the most common and destructive tendencies we exhibit as human beings—vilifying those outside our natal family, culture, or nation.

THE SELF-OTHER DIVIDE

No discussion of culture can proceed without understanding the critical role of group identity. In fact, cultural studies assume the group to be the center of focus, in contrast to disciplines such as psychology that focus more specifically on the individual. The individual always reflects his or her culture, but that culture can never be understood through the individual alone. No one person adequately represents the wider culture; rather, the individual and the collective culture inform one another in a self-reinforcing, self-perpetuating manner. For example, early on infants begin the important process of distinguishing self from others—a stage well established long before those defiant two-year-old "No!"s become standard fare. Prior to that, both self-identification and self-distinction is with the mother or other immediate caregiver. Yet once the ego begins to be actively expressed, an individual moves on to broaden his or her sense of self through identifying with a group or a set of groups. Those who fail to take this important step are considered abnormal, even pathological, in their social and psychological development. The need for group identification is enormously powerful precisely because, historically speaking, no individual can survive and thrive except as part of a protective network of tightly-knit people. We are built on numerous levels to be in relationship (see chapter 2).

From family to friends to community and beyond, all of us find our identity in the concentric social circles that radiate out from ourselves. We absorb the values of each expanding group as a means of building our own sense of self/ego and also as a means of finding security for that self in the wider world. And as we do, we not only absorb the culture of the group, we contribute to strengthening its collective expression. A healthy individual is one who has found a wholesome balance between self and group identity. Those lacking on either score are vulnerable to some form of social pathology that can undermine their own welfare and that of others. Ergo, beware the loner.

Within American culture (and many other Western cultures) there is often a dilemma we face as individuals, because individualism itself is a cultural value we absorb via the group! That leads to the constant need to "express our individualism" as a by-product of identifying with others. It can get to be hard work, as the American actress Tallulah Bankhead humorously noted when she said "Nobody can be exactly like me. Sometimes even I have trouble doing it."[5] The result of constantly negotiating our way between self and group identity is always interesting and sometimes very entertaining, as evidenced among contemporary youth who nonchalantly wear their pants so low that underwear and butt-cracks make unwanted public appearances. They (and we've all done it in one form or another) end up conforming to supposed non-conformity in the ego's desperate effort to simultaneously be both a distinct individual and an accepted member of a valued group. It's a clumsy dance we all perform as part of the maturation process.

Somewhere along this path of forming one's self identity, every human being in every culture learns to draw lines of distinction between self and others, my group and not-my-group, us and them, our people and not our

---

5. Bankhead, Goodreads, http://www.goodreads.com/author/quotes/373651, accessed October 23, 2014.

people. And the placement of those lines is inevitably absorbed along with the subcultural values of the groups with which one has most closely identified. In other words, we absorb a sense of who does not belong within our group from the preexisting values of that group. Racism, in all its inglorious forms, is rooted in this dimension of culture formation. Yet the self-other divide has flexibility according to circumstances. We may embrace someone who plays on our church softball team who we otherwise consider an outsider to our social clique. Meanwhile, the self-other divide is always a key determinate of our ethics and behaviors toward others. We are, for example, most often kind and understanding toward our self-identified group while justifying less than edifying behavior toward those we consider outsiders. Race, ethnicity, gender, age, religion, and social standing are the standard criteria by which any one group determines where other people and groups fall on a continuum between "our people" and the despised (or at least dubious and untrustworthy) "not our people."

There is a fascinating situation in Ethiopia that illustrates the power of group identification and the compelling influence on human behavior effected by the self-other divide. Among the eighty plus ethnic groups in that East African country, in the remote southwestern part of the country there live a number of cattle-herding cultures that belong to the Surma language group. Among them are two "tribes" that are known to be related in the distant past by virtue of shared history, language and culture. Yet these two tribal groups do not acknowledge one another as kin, and have historically engaged in mutual acts of theft and violence.

Conversely, in the north are the Falasha, or "black Jews" of Ethiopia, who consider themselves (and are officially considered by the nation of Israel) to be one of the lost tribes of Israel, and thus ethnic Jews through distant blood links. However, there is no historic, linguistic, or genetic evidence to substantiate any such links. Rather, the opposite appears certain to be the case. Yet because of the mutually accepted categorizations that depict a shared blood relationship between the two groups, they behave congenially, and even sacrificially, toward one another. For that reason many thousands of Falasha were airlifted out of Ethiopia by the Israeli military and "repatriated" to Israel in a covert "rescue" operation that occurred while I lived in Ethiopia in 1991.

In the case of the Surma, the exact opposite response is apparent. The two groups are indeed related in the not too distant past by common ancestry, but do not now acknowledge that shared lineage. The situation may have started as a family split, an East African version of the Hatfields and the McCoys. Regardless, the distancing eventually became cemented into cultural traditions that now affect contemporary behavioral norms. The reality of a common past became lost in a reformulated present that has led to animosity, recurrent cattle raiding, and tit-for-tat style murders on both sides. Whether speaking of the Surma, Falasha, or Israelis, the behaviors of one group toward another—and by extension one individual toward another—is predicated on whether the "other" is categorized as "one of us" or not. This processing is replicated in the perceptions and behaviors of all human beings worldwide and the respective culture groups to which they belong. We do it on a daily basis with little awareness of its presence and influence, such as when we use the term "non-Christian."

The implications for Western churches and their home cultures are enormous; for we all inherit cultural values that place virtually all foreigners in the "other" category. And once that happens, all kinds of unredeemed behaviors can, and often do, follow. They may not be on the same scale as that of the German Nazis whose cultural values allowed them to so depersonalize the Jews, Romani (Gypsies) and other "outsiders" (non-Aryans) that those groups were seen as sub-human and expendable, but some level of loveless behavior generally follows. Christians are, by definition, people who are committed to structuring their lives around the words, life, and person of Jesus. And in so doing, a new set of values supersedes, or at the very least redeems, whatever one's inherited values may be.

To claim to follow Jesus yet not to experience a reformulated cultural sense of self and other is contradictory at best. When that failure happens—and a persistent theme of this book is that it happens all too often—it means a person or a group has simply repeated the same moral blunders that animated the Nazis and World Trade Center bombers, who blindly expressed the unexamined values of their native cultures to justify hideous actions that first distanced and then dehumanized their victims. Part IV will revisit this issue when we explore what a reformulated set of Christian values might look like, and how such kingdom values are meant to reform our view of and behavior toward those who lie beyond our culturally-inherited self-other divide.

LANGUAGE

Language is an integral part of culture; likewise, cultural values are readily expressed and apparent in language. For that reason, language is one of the most powerful weapons in the arsenal of those who wish to denigrate any individual or group that lies outside an arbitrarily drawn category of "our people" (it can also be an important means of inclusion). The ancient Greeks coined the term "barbarians," and their sense of superiority has remained attached to the word ever since. They used the term to describe those ethnic groups outside the urbane Greek city-states whose language had a nonsensical "bar-bar-bar" sound to them. Today, when we label and call someone a "foreigner" or "immigrant," for most Americans that means we, like our Greek forbearers, have already placed them on the other side of a divide that delineates those we trust from those we don't. To go further and label a person or nation as our "enemy" (e.g., Iran or North Korea) is to open the door to abuse and even violence, justified, as many think, by some unspoken culturally-sanctified moral imperative. Labeling others with negative and highly-charged names and categories takes us in the opposite direction from the nature of God and the healthy Christian worldview we are called to espouse. Of course, we have to use categories and labels to negotiate our way through life. But our choice of words and terms directly reflects the attitudes and values lurking behind them (even as they shape our own attitudes and values, along with those who hear them), clearly communicating any associated biases or disapproval.

Our words reveal our intentions and agendas because words function symbolically—standing for something beyond themselves while possessing great power to elicit emotions. It is rather fascinating to realize that sounds emitted through our vocal structures—mere compressed air shaped by tongue, teeth, and palate—carry with them shared meaning and values. The power behind the symbolic use of language is its ability to immediately and evocatively draw upon associated cognitive structures, including images and emotions. Think, for example, about the associated images and emotions that are conjured up by the follow string of sounds: "o-sa-ma-bin-la-den." They are *only* sounds—a simple string of vowels and consonants. Yet they are so much more to every American.

Thus, the words with which we choose to communicate are incredibly powerful at shaping the way we and others think and act. As the writer Oliver Wendell Holmes aptly put it, "Language is the blood of the soul into which thoughts run and out of which they grow."[6] Proverbs 18:4 declares that our words are "deep waters." They come from our innermost beliefs, attitudes, and values, and they go just as deeply back into both ourselves and those who hear them (Prov 12:18). Indeed, they go so deeply that neuroscientists tell us that the words we speak and the thoughts we associate with them actually shape the physical structures of our brains—the dendrites where emotion-stirring memories are stored—resulting in either toxic or healthy emotional states that drive our behaviors toward both ourselves and

6. Holmes, BrainyQuote, http://www.brainyquote.com/quotes/quotes/o/oliverwend152697.html, accessed October 23, 2014.

others.[7] This means that, in essence, we are what we speak—for better or for worse. And that is why scripture warns us in the book of James (1:19, 26) to be highly selective of the words we use. Jesus took the matter a step further, declaring that the words we employ can be the means of defiling us because they reveal and multiply the dark places of the heart (Matt 15:17–18). Conversely, they can also reveal the good (Matt 12:35).

But speaking circumspectly is not customary within modern American culture, as evidenced by television's "talking heads" who blather away intransigent opinions about everything under the sun. As Americans, we are taught early on to have an opinion on everything, and to broadcast it tirelessly—as though that somehow proves it true, displaying our intellectual prowess, or lack thereof, in the process. In our rush to be quick to be heard and slow to listen, most of us are generally unaware of the power of the words we use; power to do good or evil, to build up or to tear down (Prov 18:21). Yet this power is both recognized and skillfully employed by many with self-serving agendas. Notice how governments, no matter how oppressive they may be, label insurgents with terms such as "terrorists" or "rebels," whereas those same people are called "patriots" and "liberators" by themselves and their supporters. All of us justify our actions by the labels we place on ourselves and others. The World Trade Tower bombers called their victims *infidels* ("ones without faith"), the worst of insults in their highly religious Islamic culture. The Nazis called Jews *Judenschwein* ("Jewpig"), while Hitler often used the term *Judenscheisse* ("Jews**t"). Americans, too, have historically used demeaning names and labels for those we have opposed—the Japanese, Vietnamese, Germans, and Iraqis. I need not list those names here, for we have heard them too many times before.

At the heart of such labeling is the dangerous yet diabolically effective act of dehumanizing others. Dehumanization is, by definition, placing another person or group in a subhuman category (i.e., animal-like). Once done, all manner of violence and wickedness can be justified. However, the act of dehumanizing is but the far end of a continuum that begins with simple depersonalization. To depersonalize another person or group is to deprive him/them of their God-given intrinsic value, their very personhood. It is to think of and treat other human beings in a detached manner through the use of categories rife with negative connotations, rather than treating them as individuals created in the sacred image of the God we love and serve. The labels we apply will differ, but it is of utmost importance that we understand the intentions of our own hearts whenever we apply them. No one can show the love of Christ to another person while categorizing

---

7. Leaf, *Switched Off*, 22, 95.

her by way of negative stereotypes. Those of us who call ourselves Christian should make it our goal to echo David's prayer in Psalm 19:14, where he humbly recognizes the importance of both words and thoughts: "May the words of my mouth and the meditations of my heart be pleasing in your sight, O Lord." Later we will see that God's calling entails personalizing each and every human being we encounter, for that act helps insure that our thoughts, words, and deeds are appropriate to the faith we represent.

We use language as a sieve to determine who is in or out of our group because shared language or dialect is an immediate indicator of shared culture. There are many historic examples of the way shibboleths have been used to distinguish friends from enemies. The term shibboleth, as biblical sleuths well know, derives from the twelfth chapter of Judges, where the Gileadites were able to capture and slay their adversaries, the Ephramites, whose own dialect did not include the "sh" sound contained in the Hebrew word shibboleth, thereby revealing their true identity. In WWII there were many examples of Allied soldiers using shibboleths to identify German and Japanese infiltrators—and Axis soldiers to identify Allied ones—including the famous use of the word *lollapalooza*, which, due to their mispronouncing "l"s as "r"s, Japanese soldiers immediately gave themselves away.

Ask yourself this question: When I hear someone speak with a foreign accent or an unfamiliar dialect of English, how do I unconsciously categorize that person? Is that category positive or negative? Do I feel cordial and at ease with the emotions that categorization entails, or does it make me feel distrustful and threatened? The mental slots into which we put others *always* reveal much more about ourselves than it does about those others. If we look for it, our language will reveal to us much about our own cultural values. And unless those values align with the values inherent in the message of the gospel, they will need to undergo radical alteration. Otherwise, we fall prey to hypocrisy by claiming one truth but living another. And though we may not recognize the inconsistency within ourselves, it is glaringly obvious to others—especially those from foreign lands and cultural backgrounds that differ from our own. In addition, we ourselves will suffer psychologically and spiritually from an unconsciously-perceived lack of integrity that results from any disconnect between our words and the feelings and beliefs behind them. Our words are to be honest—our "yes" is to be yes, and our "no" to be no—according to Jesus (Matt 5:37). We can do no better than to follow Paul's admonition, seeking always simply to "speak the truth in love" (Eph 4:15).

HUMAN NATURE

One may ask if a bias toward our own is not only natural (and therefore, *de facto*, a good thing) but an inescapable inheritance of our human nature. Does it not also provide a survival benefit for both the individual and the group? Indeed, both are true. But Christians are called to be transformed to such an extent that our lives no longer conform to the mandates of either our inherent natures or to any cultural heritage that conflicts with the gospel (Rom 12:2). To possess a preference for our own—whether family, friends, or culture—is perfectly fine according to biblical ethics, so long as it doesn't come at the expense of loving others outside those parameters. It is not an either/or scenario but rather both/and. As the incomparable Spanish cellist Pablo Casals put it, "The love of one's country is a splendid thing. But why should love stop at the border?"[8] The same can be said for any naturally occurring group and the demarcations it draws. Christians are, by definition, adopted into a new social order that supersedes our natural and cultural affinities (Matt 10:37; Gal 3:26–28), a matter to be more fully explored later.

The dimensions of human nature are vitally important to the purposes of this book; yet it is a highly disputed concept, the reality of which is disparaged by some. Still, no Christian theology or worldview can be sustained without reference to the existence and influence of human nature. For that reason I will devote the next two chapters to an examination of human nature and its fundamental role in shaping culture. That inquiry will help to establish the working definition of culture that forms the framework of my entire discourse. That definition is as follows: culture is the functional interplay of a coherent and distinct set of beliefs, experiences, perceptions, behaviors, and artifacts—involving both the conscious and unconscious and derived from both past and present—that directs a self-identified group in its efforts to flourish within the particulars of its given environment through adaptive expressions of human nature. If that sounds way too cumbersome and unwieldy (of course it does!), try this alternative on for size: Culture represents a self-defined group employing its human and natural resources to promote its own idea of success. As such, culture boils down to group-sanctioned expressions of human nature. Before trying to unpack the matter further, we first must address a concern that always seems to surface among some Christians.

---

8. Casals, Goodreads, http://www.goodreads.com/author/quotes/198277.Pablo_Casals, accessed October 23, 2014.

CULTURAL RELATIVISM

For many believers, suspicions generally follow hard on the heels of any mention of the word "relativism." It is predictably associated with the idea that there are no absolutes and all forms of ethics and, therefore, behaviors and lifestyles are equally valid. Technically speaking, that view is part of what is referred to as "moral relativism," and derives from philosophical inquiry into the nature of truth and our ability as finite human beings to perceive it. Cultural relativism, however, derives from the field of anthropology and makes no such judgments as to absolutes. Rather, it is simply a method for studying other cultures that attempts to set aside one's own cultural frame of reference—an endeavor that is inevitably ethnocentric to some degree and thus impossible to fully accomplish—in order to better comprehend the logic and integrity inherent in other cultural configurations. No matter how weird and random some dimension of another culture may appear to us, each component of every culture makes sense within its own cognitive schema. Each has internal consistency. Hindus allowing cows to freely roam the streets of major cities, pooping and urinating wherever they please, is consistent with Hindu beliefs in the sacredness of cows. And when one considers the cow's historic role in largely rural India—providing milk products, dung for fertilizer and fuel, urine for natural pesticides, draft animals, and dowry for brides among other things—it is no wonder they are elevated to near divine status. The very life and livelihood of rural Indian people has for millennia depended upon that one critically important animal.

There is an anthropological term for this internal perspective: the *emic* (from the inside). Much social science research into foreign cultures attempts to utilize an *emic* perspective in order to understand the various aspects of a culture as seen by those native to it. Thus, native/indigenous perspectives (via native "informants") are utilized as a starting point for researchers. Once that perspective is understood, the researcher will then usually attempt to frame the knowledge gained into an *etic* (from the outside) perspective—one that applies to the researcher's goals and interests, such as comparing cultures to arrive at universal theories that attempt to explain various behavioral norms.

For the purposes of this book, cultural relativism is an important tool in the tool kit. If we can see the logic inherent in different cultures and worldviews, we are in a better position to respect and not react negatively to them, and thus better understand how Christianity can be organically relevant to any and all cultures. In addition, the exercise itself puts us in a better position to stand outside our own cultural heritage and worldview and constructively critique it from an *etic* perspective, which the Bible and the gospel provide when we don't read too many of our own cultural limitations into them.

For example, it is important to understand that moral relativism is alive and well in the modern Western world and has within the last century become a cultural norm under the rubric of secular humanism. It is, however, not new, dating back to the early Greeks and the Sophist philosopher Protagoras whose statement (bequeathed us through Socrates), "Man is the measure of all things . . . ,"[9] leads to the common assertion today that "What anyone believes is true for that person. What you believe is true for you; what I believe is true for me,"[10] reverberate in many of today's secular Euro-American worldviews. Recognizing that all such worldviews—religious and secular alike—have an internal consistency that derives from a specific culture history is a necessary first step toward removing the negative knee-jerk reactions we sometimes have when encountering perspectives that differ from our own. As the Good Book says in James 1:20, "God's righteousness does not grow from human anger." If discovering the universal application of the gospel is one of our goals, it is imperative that we find an all-encompassing biblical perspective (or as close as we can come to one) from which to evaluate the pros and cons within each and every cultural configuration.

Before we can do that, however, we must acknowledge a presupposition that derives from our Christian faith. It is that every culture and every subculture (such as motorcycle gangs in Houston or Hindus in Belize) is comprised of three categories of cultural values: those that, in principle, are harmonious with the gospel and the kingdom of God, those that exist in opposition to it, and those that are essentially neutral. Obviously every culture and subculture has all three types, and it is our job to find a way to discern one from the other. In order to do so, it is necessary to lay out those faith principles that give us a measuring stick by which to gauge each dimension of any culture, no matter how wild or weird it may seem on the surface (see part IV). We would be foolish to think that logic and some enlightened, modern theoretical perspective alone could do the job—each such perspective being inevitably skewed by its own cultural biases. So it will be necessary to dig beneath the outward patterns that so easily entrap our judgment and attempt to get at the underlying issues that drive our perceptions and motivations as Americans. As much as is humanly possible, we want to see human behavior as God sees it, which requires acknowledging first and foremost that "Man looks at the outward appearance, but God

---

9. Protagoras, *Theaetetus*, http://classics.mit.edu/Plato/theatu.html, accessed October 25, 2014.

10. Wood, "Relativism," para. 1, http://www.stanford.edu/~allenw/webpapers/Relativism.doc, accessed October 23, 2014.

looks at the heart" (1 Sam 16:7). Later we shall see that the presence of God's Spirit within cultural forms is key to determining which of those forms is in alignment with the gospel and the kingdom it boldly announces.

2

Human Nature: The Good

What lies behind us and what lies before us are small matters compared to what lies within us.

—Ralph Waldo Emerson

HUMAN NATURE IS REFLECTED in the social, psychological, and spiritual characteristics that all humans share. Not all of those characteristics are unique to humans since we share many of them with the animal world. But a number are uniquely human and reflective of a divine personality that is not similarly imprinted elsewhere in creation. Although we are quick to note that God is evident in every dimension of the natural world (Romans 1), in intriguing ways he is even more uniquely manifest in what the Bible presents as the cumulative act of his creation—the much maligned human race. Thus, the biblical claim that mankind alone is formed in the image of God implies that at least a modicum of God's character and personality is exclusively reflected within the human dimension of the created order. Our nature, though not unique in it's entirely, none-the-less uniquely displays the nature of God.

Most educators and practitioners of the natural sciences do not take kindly to the idea of a nature unique to humans, as one might guess. As traditionally taught in the West, the natural sciences are paradigmatically constrained to logic consistent with naturalism, a logic that can only acknowledge that which is confined to the material world through measurable processes of cause and effect. The so called "soft sciences" such as sociology and psychology more readily allow for cognitive and behavioral traits unique to humans, but they too are unable to consider those traits independently of biophysical causation—meaning that our biology and behavior are ultimately nothing more than expressions of our genetics. The bulk of contemporary anthropologists refer to a biogenetically-derived human "capacity for culture and language," but no distinct human nature outside of a genetic expression under the manifest influence of specific environments.[1] The result, according to this line of reasoning, is that no way exists in contemporary anthropological theory to approach the subject of human nature outside of culture-bound inquiries that bring with them the inevitable imposition of ethnocentrism and subjectivity, rendering the whole enterprise "a fool's errand."[2] Thus, for most anthropologists, culture alone *is* human nature.

Given the paradigm under which the social sciences operate, issues relating to morality are always linked to cognitive structures and their capacities—often described as the evolved biological potential to conceive ethical systems via cultural means. The two areas of genes and morals can never be separated under this model. So according to this line of reasoning within the social sciences, not only is there no independent human nature, even if there were, we as culture-bearing creatures could never discover it! For many social and moral theorists, humans are conceived as "blank slates" upon which culture is subsequently imprinted, and that imprint includes concepts of faith and ethics. Still, a minority of academics dissent from this politically-correct but rather myopic view, recognizing that something critical is missing in the equation—namely, how to explain the uniformity of cultural expression around the world. The sum appears to be more than the total of the parts.

The British anthropologist Maurice Bloch has stood against the gale of post-modern reductionism by arguing that a distinct, innate human nature simply cannot be ruled out given the ethnographic record,[3] while the linguist Steven Pinker insists that those who deny human nature—academics at the fore—none-the-less live their day-to-day lives as though it does exist, "common sense" guiding their behaviors contrary to their intellectualized theories.[4] However, even for these "renegades," whenever human nature is discussed it is always linked to genetics and evolutionary adaptations that fall back on naturalistic causes. There is no room for God and, indeed, according to the theories, no need for him. It is clear that no other logical

---

1. Antrosio, "Human Nature," §1.1. http://www.livinganthropologically.com/anthropology/human-nature/, updated 31 July 2012.
2. Marks, "Biological Myth," 154.
3. Bloch, *Cultural Transmission*.
4. *Blank Slate*, 422.

conclusion can be reached through a scientific materialist approach because presuppositions determine outcomes. Thus, both the natural and social sciences as practiced in the West are, by *their* nature, necessarily limited when it comes to understanding human nature. It is a limitation that lends them strength in some areas of inquiry, but leaves them incapable of adequately addressing any potential metaphysical association with human nature.

Logically speaking, even if one allowed for the position that God works through genetics and evolutionary processes alone (which many Christians believe), there is still the need to explain exactly how and at what point he intervenes to affect these areas—a position that still requires a supernatural imposition no different in principle from God intervening every moment in every dimension of the created order. For naturalists who attempt to explain *everything* through evolutionary principles, there is the *enormous* problem of how one derives the gene and its blueprints in the first place, because in any cause and effect process there must be an initial cause which remains unexplained.[5] From my perspective, it appears grossly inconsistent to posit something arising from nothing, even if that something is only energy encapsulated in a pre-expanded universe (as Varghese points out, we don't even know what energy is or where it came from[6]). That's where faith comes in—faith in science, that is. What else can we call it? It is a faith whose adherents' fervency often outshines that of religious folks.

The supposition of any science-based worldview is that humans are not substantially different from the rest of the natural world, except in terms of our biological and cognitive capacities that express themselves through culture, which then alters our genes and biology in a never-ending feedback loop of co-evolution. According to this paradigm, humans are circumscribed within a material world that functions under the auspices of the immutable laws of physics, chemistry and biology. Of course, we must ask who or what set the pattern for such natural laws to exist.[7] In addition, it must be pointed out that from a cultural standpoint, modern Western science and its methodologies, though functionally unmatched in the utility of

---

5. In *Wonder of the World*, Varghese details the logical shortcomings of naturalism, and its absolute inability to explain the existence and origin of the natural world or the rational self-conscious mind in humans, both of which require intelligence only attributable to God.

6. Ibid., 35–42.

7. Varghese states that "The existence of the laws of nature is the single greatest mystery uncovered by science . . ." (p. 24). He elaborates this theme throughout the book, devoting one section to "Intelligence in Nature," (pp. 48–52), which he argues can only be attributed to a divine Creator who is beyond nature itself.

its paradigms and applications within the physical realm, is but one cultural construct among many.

Science itself is but one way of seeing and knowing reality—and in no way a comprehensive one. If one follows the logic, science has determined the rules through which it can never access a metaphysical realm, even if that realm exists as the preeminent dimension of the cosmos. In so doing, it has accurately reflected its cultural roots in the materialism and rationalism of Enlightenment thinking. Thus, in terms of human nature, scientific approaches cannot enlighten us regarding the possibility that there are dimensions beyond its circumscribed definitions of reality. But then one cannot expect a computer to process the meaning of love. Those worlds never collide, and they are not meant to. We must look elsewhere to gain an understanding of human nature to see if some dimension of it lies within the non-material realm.

Importantly, without a holistic understanding of what is entailed in being human, it is simply not possible to accurately determine all the dynamics and parameters of culture. In other words, if there is a non-material aspect to human nature—a divine imprint, however derived—science, despite the sophistication of its methodological approaches, will be blind to it. That will undoubtedly sound both laughably arrogant and hopelessly naïve to those who do not share a faith-based perspective. But by virtue of the very logic that naturalism proclaims foundational—that no reality exists outside of a materialistically-circumscribed one—how could one arrive at any other conclusion? That is not to say that a faith-based perspective is necessarily comprehensive or holistic, just that it allows for another important layer of understanding to be accessed beyond that which science is able to offer. And every layer is important.

The writers of the Bible assume the existence of human nature, but do little to define its components because isolating and compartmentalizing human beings (and their environments) is very much a post-Enlightenment phenomenon linked to a science-based worldview. Yet unearthing a biblical basis for human nature has great utility, and that is exactly what we will attempt to do. The process will be indirect, for we must extrapolate inferences to human nature from pertinent scriptures. The list of human characteristics compiled below is overlapping and interrelated, and could easily be constructed differently. The categories chosen and the order given is for purposes of clarity (mostly my own!), and I do not claim it is either immutable or exhaustive. In its totality, which includes the next chapter, the list will prove pivotal to our goal of properly understanding the intersection of culture and faith, particularly as it pertains to life in America.

Human nature as I present it falls into two categories that, for the most part, mirror one another—the one side is a direct reflection of what we traditionally know of God's personality and character, and the other a corrupted "dark side" of the same. This paring, of course, corresponds to the biblical teachings regarding Creation and the Fall, the latter having severely deleterious effects on humankind. Interestingly, the existence of many of these characteristics is acknowledged outside of theological circles—most notably in the aforementioned social sciences—but are almost never linked to origins consistent with a conventional biblical worldview. One of the objects of my inquiry will be to show that a proper study of human nature (which is, to be fair, far from what I can claim to offer here) provides fruitful insights into the existence and nature of God.[8] For human nature, as far as I understand that complex entity, represents a set of patterned universals that can never be adequately explained through naturalistic causes alone. If true, then one can justifiably surmise that non-naturalistically existing patterns within humans necessarily point to a pattern-maker beyond nature, or at least that's what unbiased logic and common sense seem to indicate—apparent to common folk the world over but somehow beyond the comprehension of many among the intellectual elite.

Personally, I've yet to work out how a gaggle of scuffling monkeys, given eons of time banging on a piano, could ever compose a Mozart sonata. Yet the idea that rational self-conscious human beings and their complex morality-laden cultural systems could evolve from the random combination of basic elements (whose initial origins are still left unexplained) is of a much higher order of probability than even our precocious monkeys producing Mozart. One mathematician has calculated the odds to be less than one in a billion trillion (that's twenty-one zeros!)[9]. Of course, no sonata even comes close to the incredible intricacy and absolute wonder of human nature, or even a flower for that matter. Yet however one looks at the issue, rational inquiry alone proves insufficient. Some degree of faith is required—in the agency of God or in selfish genes copying themselves into fantastically complex machinery that, despite the impressive if noisy output of some of the machines, can't seem to eradicate human beings contemplating realms beyond themselves. Perhaps a faith gene mutation slipped into the mix somewhere along the line! One thing is for certain, human agency

---

8. This line of reasoning is found in the works of the seventeenth-century French mathematician, physicist, and Christian philosopher Blasé Pascal, who argued that human nature directly supports the truth of the Christian revelation. For an in-depth study of Pascal's apologetics on the topic, see Groothius, "Deposed Royalty," 297–313.

9. Morris, "Mathematical Impossibility," para. 14, http://www.icr.org/article/mathematical-impossibility-evolution/, accessed November 1, 2014.

alone can never logically prove—or disprove—either side of what tends to be a highly-charged and often fruitless debate.

RELATIONAL

There is no part of human nature more reflective of God's own nature than humankind's fundamental orientation toward meaningful relationships. This one dimension alone can account for virtually all of human behavior beyond that of basic survival. So deep is our need to engage with others (including a spiritual "other" which, for some cultures, means deceased ancestors and other spirit creatures) that nearly every other aspect of human nature can be traced back to it. We are made to be in relationship, just as God's basic nature is relational within the Trinity and with all of his created order. To be without meaningful, loving relationships and thus feel unwanted, is to suffer what Mother Teresa called a different kind of poverty—just as destructive and dehumanizing as the heart-rending physical needs she daily confronted among those she sacrificially loved in Calcutta's pitiless streets. We're learning that loneliness, a destructive and growing blight within modern Western societies, is profoundly dehumanizing in its effect, leading to numerous physical and psychological maladies including early death among the elderly who lose the will to live in a world without love and relationship.

The contemporary Christian artist Toby Mac sings, "I was made to love and be loved by You."[10] This understanding is simple, profound, and utterly fundamental to a Christian understanding of human nature and our relationship to God. The orientation for loving relationship with God not only defines our basic orientation as human beings, it is there precisely because God is also oriented toward loving and being loved, and we are made in the *Imago Dei*. Thus, loving God (and as it turns out, other human beings) is being *fully* human. It is an absolute expression of our deepest nature that wonderfully reflects the very nature of God, whose very essence *is* love (1 John 4:8).

Yet the relationship between God and mankind is deeper still; for human beings are made to worship the Almighty. Our hearts are fashioned to love and adore Someone with every fiber of our being; and if God is not the one upon whom we focus our worship, then we substitute some lesser person, group, set of ideas, or thing(s). But worship we will, for it is our deepest nature to do so. To worship God is actually our highest calling and the state of being in which humans are most fulfilled. We recognize that truth most

10. Mac, "Made To Love."

fully when we are in the act of worshipping "in spirit and in truth" (John 4:23–24). Yet when we are not, we are constantly seeking through other means—often unawares—to get back into God's presence and the elevated state of abandonment to loving worship.

Beyond love, worship, and the spiritual realm, there is simple relationship. We are "wired" to engage other people—geared to be socially interactive, and designed for satisfying relationship. Prior to any possible influence of culture, babies will intuitively focus on human faces in their vicinity. In fact, they cannot help but do so. It is in their nature and they cannot do otherwise. Those who fail to display this behavior are suspected of pathologies such as autism. So utterly relational is our makeup that we imagine human faces in nature's patterns (e.g., rocks, clouds, the moon). Our entire being is hyper-sensitive not only to human images, but to human touch, sounds, movements, smells, and presence, as the blind and deaf can attest. The existence of different levels of human society, from the family through ethnic groups and nations (the latter two involving a great deal of social construction), represents a tangible expression of our intensely relational nature.

Of course, the rest of the animal kingdom is similarly designed for each species to interact with its own kind; and some species are even wired to interact with other species within their environments. Some co-evolve, such as Ecuador's incredible symbiotic relationship between the four-inch beaked Swordbill hummingbird and the equally long tubular flower blossoms that depend on them for pollination. Other hummingbirds also have uniquely curved beaks to take advantage of the curved blossoms they feed on. So what makes human relations within their social and natural environments different from the plant and animal kingdoms? God and culture. Our relational nature extends from and to God (see "Religious" below) and is almost exclusively expressed through culture.

Our orientation toward relationships with other people is a critically important dimension of our human nature. Our emotional makeup is not designed for us to be alone, cut off from others. Whenever that happens—whether it be widows living in isolated loneliness or hermits who have withdrawn from society—it represents a cultural imposition on our basic human nature. This is because human beings, by virtue of our psychological makeup, are inescapably social. Without healthy social intercourse, and especially without access to intimate relationships, our health and emotional well-being badly deteriorate. Neuroscientist Laura Leaf tells us this is especially true of our need for affectionate touch, which allows us to tap into a divinely-designed "natural pharmacy" that releases health-inducing chemicals into our systems.[11] She points out how frequently Jesus touched those he healed, while always engaging those he encountered in the most personable terms. He knew that humans are hard-wired to respond to such personal engagement because we are made in the wondrous image of an intensely personal and highly responsive Creator.

Culture exists because of the shared relational nature among all of humanity. We form families, communities, and nations—layers of social engagement—as a direct expression of our need to interact with others. Sadly, modern life often fails to deliver the healthy social networks we need to thrive, leaving many alone and lonely, often in the midst of strangers who themselves feel alone. Yet when those social connections function properly, it can be truly breathtaking—as when communities bind together to deal with serious problems. One inspiring example was the effort of those from Louisiana who experienced Katrina's wrath coming to the aid of New York and New Jersey communities devastated by Hurricane Sandy. When people bind together, they are always stronger and more effective at whatever they decide to do, whether good or evil. Either way, our nature compels us to be actively among one another.

We know that positive relationships stem from our birth families, with parents playing an almost God-like role in the lives of their children. As the Franciscan writer Richard Rohr insightfully observed, each of our personal conceptions of God—from loving and benevolent to harsh and judgmental—takes shape in the form of our parents and our relationships to them.[12] In addition, our homes set the stage for our relations with the outside world. Children's interactions with parents and siblings (and parents' interactions with spouses and neighbors) form the templates that determine how we will interact with others upon reaching adulthood. An anthropologist once told me that his research among death row inmates with a history of violence toward women showed they all had one single factor in common—the tragic perception that their mothers didn't love them. Sadly, it was the lack of the deepest relationship need embedded in our human nature that triggered those psychologically-damaged men to project all their brokenness onto their victims, seeking in the most unimaginably twisted ways to find the loving relationships they never knew.

---

11. Leaf, *Switched Off*, 23.
12. Rohr, *Jesus' Plan*, 116.

SENTIENT

We humans are extremely emotional beings, and that includes men who are acculturated to appear otherwise (a shout-out here to my fellow Texans!). Why? Because emotions make relationships work. Pathos is the stuff of human interaction, the fuel that ignites the fire. Ask any woman whose man is unable to express his emotions because he has absorbed the cultural value that it is "unmanly" to do so. Perhaps the worst relationship is a nonexpressive one. "I wish that you were either cold or hot!" (Rev 3:15, NET). Perhaps women are more obviously and outwardly emotional *in general*—a design function likely related to their critical and sacred role in childrearing and holding families together (remember the death row inmates)—but men are equally sentient in their own way. Just mention sex or sports to kickstart that process!

Here again, we are feeling creatures because God himself is sentient. As Heschel's "most moved Mover,"[13] he is the opposite of the passive, detached deity who emerged from Aristotelian philosophy—passionless and unconcerned with the petty pursuits of lowly mankind. The Enlightenment added yet another layer of misconception—that of the mechanistically-minded divine watchmaker who, once having fashioned and set the creation in motion, receded to an impenetrable realm beyond time and space from which he could coolly observe the futile goings on of mortal human beings relegated to a cruel and uncaring universe. Men and women always have and always will project their clumsy and myopic worldviews onto the God they perceive but have yet to find, thereby rendering him fallaciously comprehensible and thus safely distant. Better a remote and dispassionate deity than an intensely intimate engager who engulfs us in his utter holiness and omnipotence, requiring a response from us. The unknowing heart assumes that the more distant God is made to be, the more secure one ought to feel from his feared and fearful presence (see Ex 20:18–20)—as one would prefer that a massive asteroid pass well beyond earth's atmosphere. But such people do not know that God's true nature radiates with absolute goodness and love.

Fear, a distinct dimension of human nature, is the basis of most religious sentiment across cultures and through time. Religion has for eons been the established means to control an unhealthy fear of God which, quite naturally, arises when a consciousness of wrong crosses the path of a keen perception of a deity concerned with moral behavior. And so would it have remained for all time were it not for God's self-revelation—his surprising

---

13. Heschel, *Prophets*, 12.

disclosure that his true nature is neither dispassionate nor diabolical, but loving and compassionately engaged in the affairs of every strand of his creation. In Jesus we see holiness and omnipotence—the very thought of which would logically engender fear—clothed in sacrificial and all-embracing love. Given our inbuilt human capacity for intimate relationship, Christ's "packaging" elicits the most intense and highest form of emotional response—wildly abandoned love and adoration of God. Our love of God sets our emotions ablaze as nothing else can, bringing them into the fullness of expression for which they were designed. It was God who created the means by which his own loving and relational nature could be expressed and returned in a mutuality meant to spiral into endless joy on the part of both partners.

But an element was still missing . . .

FREE WILL

If naturalism is correct, then there is no such thing as free will. We are slaves to our genes and the behaviors they necessitate. Even the choice to go against the most intensely natural impulse and commit suicide is only a rare but inevitable expression of gene-induced behavior—animals do it at times—or aberrant psychological behavior ultimately tied to biology. Referring to humans, the eminent biologist E.O. Wilson put the matter succinctly, declaring, "Genes hold culture on a leash."[14] By that reasoning, all conscious and unconscious behavior—every thought, impulse, and action—is predetermined by our biology, which then gets shaped by our culture. We cannot escape determinism's unyielding grip no matter how hard we try. It's not exactly the kind of news that makes one want to jump for joy.

Yet scripture doesn't exactly clarify things. We are told that believers were predestined before the foundation of the world to follow Christ (Eph 1:4), and that God is perfectly omniscient, knowing precisely what humans will and will not do and think. Yet, paradoxically, we are also told that we must personally choose to follow Jesus, and decide each and every moment if we will live our lives faithfully toward God—or decide not to live them, as might be the case. Thus, within the constraints of a divinely-controlled universe, the Bible tells us we exercise the free will to conform to or rebel against the pattern and pattern-maker. Our choices will not ultimately change the shape or direction of God's purposes, in that he can use and alter any and all human choices to promote his own designs, but it will provide real options on our part and a choice on God's part as to how to react to them. This

---

14. Wilson, *Consilience*, 127.

theological perspective places the focus on an active relationship, whereas naturalism puts human choice within the confines of genes reacting to an impersonal and immutable environment. Which accords better with our sense of what is involved in day-to-day choices in life? Our very dependence on intentionality provides the answer. Human behavior often reveals what theory alone can fail to illuminate.

Free will choice, whether to become a Christian or to watch a movie with one's spouse, is critical to the health and integrity of any relationship, and most especially one with the eternal God. Love demands the free exercise of the will, otherwise it is not love at all. Everyone knows this is true on the level of lived experience. A forced relationship is a fractious relationship within which neither genuine love or respect can take root. Those who espouse naturalism act in ways that refute its basic premises whenever they choose to act willfully toward others (or expect others to act willfully toward them). They *believe* they are exercising free will whenever a choice is made to be supportive of or antagonistic toward others, their actions contradicting their deterministic paradigms. Additionally, non-believers exercise free will in choosing to reject this very argument.

It is the exercise of our free will that makes our relationship with God and one another viable; for free will represents the heart of true love and friendship, as everyone unconsciously knows. God chose to love us and gave us the means to choose to love him and others. Moral choice is a distinctively human characteristic that sets us apart from all our furry fellow creatures, and the very one that allows us Christians and non-Christians alike to resist and oppose the love and presence of our free will maker. By exercising our free will to love and serve God, we not only participate in a mutually encouraging relationship, we also appropriately engage our emotional and spiritual hardware in a way that brings joy and promotes wholeness—the natural state we are designed to experience. How many therapists and pharmaceutical companies would go under if we Christians regularly made that ever so important choice?

COUPLING

In Genesis we read, "It is not good for the man to be alone, so I will create a companion for him, a perfectly suited partner" (2:18, TV). Like their creator, humans reflect an intimate relational nature that, the world over, is almost exclusively expressed in a committed coupling of one man and one woman. This characteristic of human nature drew the attention of some of the most noted ancient Greek philosophers, including Aristotle, who spoke of man as "a conjugal animal." There are, of course, plenty of exceptions to the norm of one man and one woman joining together in a conjugally-based relationship. Many cultures have polygynous arrangements and a few exhibit polyandry (see below), but both types can easily be explained through cultural imposition. The occurrence of multiple wives (polygyny) is always found in heavily male-dominant cultures where women have low social status and little say regarding their prescribed roles in society. Often there are other factors as well, such as traditionally high death rates among birthing mothers and young children whose labor is critically important to an agriculturally-based livelihood.

At the same time, the occurrence of multiple husbands (polyandry) is always found in regions such as Tibet where unique economic factors are deterministic. In this case yak and sheep herding takes men away from home for months at a time, leaving their wives and children alone to work scarce cropping land. The conditions make it adaptive to have more than one man committed to a household. Still, in almost every case the men are brothers, revealing a concerted effort to keep resources within the extended family. Thus, the exceptions to coupling represented by polygyny and polyandry can be understood as cultural adaptations to unusual circumstances—adaptations that run contrary to normal human behavior.

The human psyche is such that one intensely intimate relationship with a person of the opposite sex is fulfilling in a way that any number of close, more casual relationships could never be. It provides a wholeness that is complimented by and supportive of raising children—creating, interestingly, a trinity of relationships within one family. Homosexuality, though present around the world in many cultures both ancient and modern, is rare enough that it could never be said to represent the general expression of human nature within any ethnic or racial group at any time in history. Although well-established in the Western world, its numerical infrequency clearly emphasizes that heterosexual coupling is by far the typical expression of human nature. But more importantly, both heterosexual and homosexual relationships display a shared drive to couple within one intensely intimate and personal relationship.

Thus, despite the lack of attraction to the opposite sex—a matter that will almost certainly in time prove to have at least some genetic basis, with culture being the means through which it finds expression—the basic drive to couple is still present within homosexuality as a panhuman characteristic of human nature. And that is what is germane to the discussion. The fact that one-night stands are now commonplace in modern Western culture (whether bi- or homosexual) is entirely consistent with fallen aspects of human nature (see next chapter) and a science-driven reductionist worldview wherein much of life has lost coherence, isolating desire from purposeful relationship and sex from love. The loss is symbolically evidenced in pornographic photos showing faces turned away or edited out entirely, dehumanizing and objectifying the subject into mere body parts. For many, sex has unfortunately become little more than a mechanical act of consumption, no different in principle than grabbing a burger to satisfy one's noontime hunger.

But what of those who remain celibate and never choose marriage? For such persons, certainly many different factors are involved, such as personality, religious commitment, and even economic priorities that override the drive to couple. Yet one can surmise that, especially for religious celibates, human coupling is an unpursued social expression of an even deeper drive to "couple" with God in an intimate, life-long bond. And by that token, religious celibates are expressing the same coupling drive, only not in its most frequently expressed form. If a common drive to couple underlies both human-to-human and human-divine relationships, it leads to the delightful understanding that marriage is but another channel through which a person can experience God's abiding and intimate love. One's spouse, by these lights, becomes God's immediate incarnational expression of himself. That is, his presence is practically and immediately available in and through one's partner, through whom we are loved and cared for as unique human beings. Furthermore, we can love God in return through loving and honoring our spouse, which Ephesians 5 encourages us to do as an expression of our faith. Jesus became flesh because incarnational love is undeniable love. His love can be seen as continually and incarnationally present in the marriage relationship, for those determined to look for it.

SHARING AND GIVING

The desire and capacity to love our spouse is related to another dimension of our human nature. We have a need to *give* of ourselves, which is a remarkable imprint of God's own nature borne out of the expression of his love in Christ. But the divine design that motivates us to love our spouse and family—those most intimately involved in our lives—also extends outward toward friends, neighbors, and even strangers. The level of intimacy may decline as we move from family outward, but the basic drive to share and give does not, thereby fulfilling a divinely-fashioned channel to wholeness and joy. Jesus could say that it was more blessed to give than to receive (Acts 20:35) because he knew that our nature was designed in just that way. It may need to be awakened through cultural cultivation (see "Memetics" in chapter 3), but giving and sharing exist as a fixed part of our divinely-endowed hardware. That being so, we have to be taught to ignore it. We have to learn to choose selfishness, which will not "feel" natural unless we are enculturated in that direction.

Some may not think the desire to share with or give to others could possibly be an innate dimension of our human nature, especially parents who must struggle so mightily to counter what seems to be our real nature—that of selfishness (which I categorize as the antithetical, fallen side of sharing, and will discuss in chapter 3). But it makes perfect sense, given the previously mentioned traits. Our orientation toward intimate relationships full of positive, energizing emotions based on free will and mutual support naturally leads to sharing and giving in ever-expanding circles. Love can never be idle. It simply cannot exist without expression because it is inherently active and generates ongoing exchange with others. Like the magnetic energy between opposing charges, love is by definition perpetually dynamic. Unexpressed love is not love at all, even if love's only expression is inward, to negatively manifest as worry or jealously within a relationship. Neither human nor divine love is complete in itself. Both find wholeness in fully giving of themselves. Such an understanding adds a new layer of insight to the most quoted of New Testament verses: "For God so loved the world that he gave his only begotten Son . . ." The mutuality of love is one of its greatest strengths.

The subject of sharing and giving will be discussed further in chapter 6 under the heading "Benevolence."

PERSONALITY AND EXPERIENCE

It is nothing less than remarkable that every human being has a distinct personality, apparent in the unique vocal signature of every person who has ever lived.[15] Billions have inhabited the planet, but no two have ever been the same. We've come to take this marvel for granted without realizing that it removes us from the category of replicated flesh—mere genetic photocopies of an evolved prototype—to uniquely designed creations, each with a distinctive arrangement of genes, thoughts, emotions, and behaviors. It is this distinctiveness as utterly unique individuals that represents yet another universal characteristic of our human nature. Although we have categories

---

15. In *Healing Sounds*, Jonathan Goldman states that each person is endowed with a distinctive sound signature made up of the combined frequencies of all the bodily systems. Goldman describes it as a vibratory signature that represents the totality of each individual's unique personality (p. 13).

into which personality types are cast and criteria by which to measure different character traits, what binds us all together as human beings is the exclusive combinations of types and traits that distinguishes every last one of us. It is our *differences* that unite us! We are unified in our individually configured characteristics, and that is cause for celebration.

The importance of this understanding is that it can free us from typecasting one another through the use of staid categories and past associations. (Ever heard someone say, "It's people like you who . . .".) And for that matter, it should also help us to put away the useless casting of cultures into categories relevant only to preconceived notions (the essence of ethnocentrism), realizing that not only are all cultures refreshingly unique but every one of the individuals within each culture is an amazingly distinctive human being in his or her own right. Therefore, to treat individuals from different cultures as though they share the same outlook on life sets the stage for misunderstanding and its ugly cousin, mistreatment. But if we focus on each individual as matchless, celebrating diversity in all its forms, we are in the best position to understand people for who they really are—utterly unique individuals God has meticulously designed—and avoid falling prey to the negative judgments Jesus warned against (Matt 7:1-6).

We actually already have an innate knowledge that others possess unique personality profiles and moods that can shift like the wind. We know this because humans have a keen sense for reading the personalities of others. It is a form of discernment that arises from the cumulative perceptions of those we encounter. Problems generally follow when we perceive but one or two traits—or misperceive them as is very often the case—and jump to conclusions. Yet we have to "read" others in order to know where we stand in relation to them, first discerning whether they are a threat and then determining if there is individual or mutual advantage at stake through interaction—our brain and gut busily doing intricate calculations of gestures, body language, inferences of speech, smells, and dozens of other sensory inputs. What is intriguing about each encounter is the realization that not only does each person display a distinctive personality continually altered by shifting moods, but each person has a unique experience of perception based on his own distinctive personality, current mood, and unique (sub)cultural background. In other words, each of us perceives the same person differently at different times, with every single encounter becoming a once-in-a-lifetime experience.

Yet given the fact that all our perceptions are filtered through our own subjective experience, there can be no perfectly objective perception of anyone. That is not to say that our perceptions are useless or inaccurate on a practical level, but only that our own personalities and experiences necessarily color our ability to totally and accurately perceive another person, who has no fixed personality anyway. Can we tell if someone is insincere or threatening? Of course. Can we tell if another person has ulterior motives? Sometimes. Can we tell if someone else is right with God? Not without divine knowledge, which is not at our disposal as often as we would like to think. The bottom line is that we ought to approach each person we meet with the realization that we are prone to misread and thus misjudge at least some dimensions of their character and motives.

Our uniqueness as individual personalities, each one perceiving the world and everyone in it in absolutely exclusive terms, can open us to the possibility that God is actively present in one another in the very areas we are prone to misperceive or overlook, mysteriously dwelling in the distinctives we all share. If we look for God there, we might be surprised to find him lurking about in the very places our impositions normally occupy. But if we never bother looking for the divine image in one another, allowing stereotypes and preconceptions to rule our consciousness, we're almost guaranteed to miss the subtle beauty of his glorious presence in one another and the blessing that entails.

RELIGIOUS/SPIRITUAL

The social sciences have always found it convenient to explain religious sentiment as merely an expression of psychological necessity; that is to say, folks are scared of the unknowns in life and find it comforting to devise a supernatural world that gives some sense of order and purpose in an otherwise intolerably grim and impersonal universe. And that line of reasoning is certainly valid to a degree. Religion does provide comfort, and humans have concocted an extremely bizarre array of religious rituals and beliefs to cope with realms unseen. Religion also has significant impacts on social stability and the ability of those in authority to maintain the status quo, thereby protecting their accumulated wealth, power, and status. From ancient rulers who were considered divine (e.g., the Inca, Romans, Egyptians) to Europe's "divine right of kings," religion has always served the empire and protected its elites. So far, so good for social theory.

But social theory becomes strained and contradicts its own principles when it tries to explain why *all* peoples in *all* places at *all* times have been religious in the broadest sense of that term. Culture alone cannot satisfactorily explain how even the most isolated of tribes in the most distant past (unaffected by empires and ruling elites) have a spiritual realm firmly embedded in their worldview and culture. No group has ever been identified at any time that is non-religious. Post-Renaissance Europeans revived the Greek-derived concept of a purely material universe, and it has persisted in numerous manifestations ever since. Still, the most vigorous of efforts by materialisms' successors have still not managed to eradicate the world of the "silly" notion of God. That leaves us with a one-hundred percent rate of belief among every sociocultural group that has ever existed—a rate that for any other social, cultural or psychological characteristic would be considered a definitive indication that it is innate to what we are calling human nature. And if it is innate, from where did it emerge? If every other human characteristic is determinate of a reality to which humans are responding, why is religious sentiment not accorded the same status? Why must it be explained away as a purely imaginative phenomenon—a pathological one at that—involving fear? To claim that religious sentiment is a universally-present adaptive behavior based on fear of the unknown is to miss the rather obvious—that God exists and people perceive him—and to impose one's preconceptions in such a manner that would not be tolerated with any other topic.

People are religious today, as they have been in ages past, because they perceive the reality of God and a spiritual realm. They perceive *what is* and respond to it like all other realities in life, because they are both sentient and relational. God has not been an abstraction to all people at all times, and the spiritual realm a mental trick to avoid worry. In fact, people worry *more* believing there is a spiritual realm that must be placated through human effort. It would be much more adaptive to be naturally atheistic and live one's life here and now without concern for what lies "out there" or beyond the grave. Why would every known historic grouping of humanity invent scenarios that made their lives more difficult and less adaptive? Where is the logic and precedent? The only reasonable explanation for universal religious belief is that it reflects a reality that exists and is exceedingly apparent to all but those whose "great learning" (Luke 10:21; 1 Cor 1:27) has, in fact, become a psychosocial trick by which *they* try to convince themselves not to worry. Atheism, in fact, represents an adaptation to human sin and pride in the form of an intellectualized worldview which is essentially a cognitive Tower of Babel. Atheism makes its proponents feel better by denying and avoiding what the rest of humanity *knows* is real. Thus, to write off religious sentiment as mere adaptive behavior toward life's uncertainties represents, in essence, a classic case of projection.

Humankind is universally oriented toward the spiritual realm simply because it exists. It is our "God hole," if you will; the "God-shaped vacuum in the heart of every person [that] can never be filled by any created thing.

It can only be filled by God, made known through Jesus Christ."[16] In modern parlance, Pascal reasoned that all humans have ingrained within their deepest being the drive to seek a reality that lies beyond their social and material world; it is a reality found only in the person of Jesus, who exists throughout, yet beyond, all social and material realms. It is the theme echoed in Ecclesiastes 3:11, which states that God has "set eternity in the human heart." And without fulfilling that desire for the eternal—without finding God—we can never be completely whole at any level of our existence. Without God, human nature remains fragmented and incomplete, leaving a broken humanity.

All cultures in all times have exhibited an orientation toward the spiritual, from the shamanistic beliefs of the forty-thousand-year-old San Bushmen of South Africa to modern-day Japanese, among whom researcher Andrea Molle observed that, despite their reluctance toward organized religion, all social levels of Japanese regularly engage in spiritual practices. Molle's research among modern Japanese reflects ethnographic research across cultures around the world, confirming a panhuman orientation toward spirituality.[17] Even the vast majority of contemporary Americans, battered by a decades-long onslaught of scientific materialism, refuse to give up what they perceive as real, despite the social stigma that now accompanies religious belief. Americans cannot help but be drawn to a spiritual dimension precisely because it exists—just as our stomachs long for food, lungs for air, and emotions for interpersonal relationships (Romans 1:18–20). Americans would do well to remember this common denominator whenever we are tempted to look disparagingly at native and foreign religions we don't comprehend. They are all following their God-imbued nature to seek him, no different than we. At the end of the day, we are all pilgrims traveling through perilous times, utterly dependent upon grace. And God is equally inviting us all to partake of his goodness and the abundant life he alone provides (Ps 36:7–8).

---

16. Although this quote is widely attributed to Blasé Pascal, it is in fact a transposition of Pascal's original statement, which follows: "What else does this craving, and this helplessness, proclaim but that there was once in man a true happiness, of which all that now remains is the empty print and trace? This he tries in vain to fill with everything around him, seeking in things that are not there the help he cannot find in those that are, though none can help, since this infinite abyss can be filled only with an infinite and immutable object; in other words by God himself," *Penseés*, 75.

17. Molle, "Spiritual Life," 131–39.

CONSCIENCE

What is the conscience? Some claim it is only a sense of guilt or innocence regarding what we have been taught about morally equivocal cultural values. Certainly it involves that, but thinking that a learned set of morals and appropriate behaviors shapes the conscience is putting the cart before the horse. Human societies—every single last one of them—develop elaborate systems of morals and right behavior *precisely because* of a conscience that is keen to express itself. No other species has such a faculty. You can certainly make your poor dog feel guilty for eating food off the counter (ours got a plate chock full of freshly-baked muffins!) when he bloody well knows better, but the poor beast is only reacting to you and not an ethically-oriented conscience. Its instincts are to please the master because *its nature* is to follow an alpha-leader in an intensely social pack relationship. There are no "bad" dogs, even when pit bulls do the unthinkable because of bad judgment on the part of their owners who, despite all the public warnings, somehow fail to recognize the dangers inherent in that breed.

Though not explicitly mentioned in the Hebrew Scriptures where the focus was different—what has been described as a right "relationship between God and a covenant community rather than an autonomous self-awareness between a person and his or her world"[18]—the New Testament clearly teaches the universal existence of the conscience (Cor 2:14–15). The conscience consists of a morally-oriented self-awareness that is absolutely unique to humans, but is not itself the moral voice of right and wrong. Rather, the conscience is the capacity to apply self-reflection to the moral values to which one has been exposed. For Judaeo-Christians, that means the relevant scriptures plus teachings about them, whether orthodox or otherwise. Other religious traditions and even non-religious systems of morality provide a different set of guidelines. Interestingly, all religious and moral traditions have roughly similar sets of codes to that of the Ten Commandments, roughly divided into categories of "doing good" and "doing no harm."[19] The lists all display a desire for harmonious relations between people and their environments, which are logical prerequisites for any community to flourish. The conscience, we can say, is the God-instilled capacity for healthy self-awareness that directs the will to choose that which benefits the group over the individual, which of course has indirect benefits for the individual.

---

18. Meadors, *BEDBTO*, s.v. "Conscience," para. 2, http://m.biblestudytools.com/dictionaries/bakers-evangelical-dictionary/conscience.html, accessed November 7, 2014.

19. Keith, *Natural World*, 42.

The Ten Commandments, and Jesus' summary of all the Law of Moses (Mark 12:30–31), emphasize an additional dimension beyond social harmony. It is the command to love, honor, and respect God as part of a covenant relationship. But how can we be commanded to love God and still exercise the free will that, as mentioned above, is crucial to any healthy relationship? The answer surely lies in the understanding that love is more than the emotional sensation that our contemporary culture has come to associate with the term. Love involves exercising the will and free choice. We can choose to love just as surely as we can choose to hate, and must, in fact, make a free-will choice to do either. Neither love, hate, nor indifference arise without some level of inward assent, whatever emotions are involved.

The command to love God is coupled with the command to love one's neighbor by Jesus, revealing the fact that God's desire is that we choose to do both, knowing we are perfectly free to do neither. The two obviously go together and reinforce one another. That tells us there is more at stake than just social harmony. There are eternal consequences to our moral choices. Through the *command* to love God and neighbor, the self-reflective aspect of the conscience is sufficiently appraised of the eternal importance of the matter that the will is then in a better position to choose to do just that. It would be unloving of God to fail to give such a command, given the consequences. Freedom is not the lack of guidelines; it is the informed opportunity to choose what is right. Only when a conscience has become jaded, as Paul tells us it can certainly become (1 Tim. 4:2), would one willfully choose behavior that is not only wrong but ultimately self-destructive. Of course, the Bible tells us there is more to the equation because there is, in fact, a destructive side to human nature that forcefully broadsides the conscience (a subject to be dealt with in the next chapter).

RATIONAL

Rational thought is a central pillar within human nature. It represents a capacity that certainly relates to our highly-evolved brain size and the IQ it generates. It is part of human nature because rationality is universally present, central to our identity as humans, and a distinction between us and the rest of the animal kingdom. Though some animals definitely display the ability to use some rudimentary forms of rational thought—African chimps, for example, have been observed deftly using sticks to extract protein-rich termites from mounds—there is no higher-order logic or self-refection involved, which as we have just seen, allows for a moral dimension to be present as part of rational decision-making. In addition, it is important to recognize that every dimension of human nature functions in an interdependent manner that, taken as a whole, constitutes what it means to be human.

In the Western world we have almost completely focused on the mind as the center of human life and consciousness—the body being seen as primarily a set of biological systems animated by the brain—and lost a more holistic view of ourselves as multi-dimensional beings with intelligence centers embedded in several areas of the body (e.g., the gut and peripheral nervous system). We cannot function as human beings through the workings of the brain alone. Body, mind, and spirit form a unified whole. To separate them is to deconstruct our humanity, leaving us soulless machines—which is just what contemporary scientific worldviews seem to have done.

In his impressively researched book, *The Blank Slate*,[20] MIT psychologist Steven Pinker outlines a number of reasoning faculties that are part-and-parcel of his version of human nature. Though he is keen to point out that their origin is found in the evolutionary structures of the physical brain, it is none-the-less instructive for the breadth of categories it unveils. According to Pinker, research has identified a number of cognitive faculties: an intuitive understanding of physics, biology, engineering, spacial sense, numerology, probability, economics of exchange, informational databases applied through logic, language based on a memorized vocabulary, grammar, and other rules of speech. In addition, Pinker lists other ways of knowing that involve both emotion-based intuition and rational assessments pertaining to a wide variety of real life situations, such as assessing danger. For Pinker these comprise our "core intuitions," which applied to band-level, hunter-gatherer lifestyles but are not necessarily adaptive to modern ones. Proper education requires going beyond these intuitions and "unlearning" the "primitive" ones like engineering, "which attributes design to the intentions of a designer" instead of evolution.[21] His own impeccable logic in building an argument against humans beginning life as blank slates onto which culture is imprinted, inadvertently reveals that rational thought can never outdistance the presuppositions that accompany it.

Rational thought and logical processes, whether accessed through intuitive cognitive structures or learned systems of knowledge, is a necessary but insufficient step toward an understanding of God and his reflected nature in humankind. Logic and reasoning alone can never explain why people do completely irrational things, like drink themselves into a stupor or lie on tanning beds with full knowledge that it will turn their skin

---

20. Pinker, *Blank Slate*, 220–23.
21. Ibid., 223

leathery and cancerous. The illogical, self-destructive side of human nature that Paul spoke of in Romans 7 is only explicable through the rationale of sin and a fallen nature—an understanding that science-based reasoning, for all its insightful contributions toward knowledge and learning, can never adequately grasp.

IDEOLOGY AND WORLDVIEW

Humans possess a unique capacity to look at the world in a coherent way, developing an overarching worldview that makes sense of its totality—at least in their own minds. Our worldview is comprised of an amalgamated set of ideologies: political, social, religious, and philosophical among them. Together these ideologies form a particular functional perspective, an integrated way of viewing and living in the world-at-large. Each individual possesses his or her own worldview, yet individual worldviews overlap in concentric circles shaped by culture. For example, a person may be a Democrat, a human rights activist, a conservationist, and Jewish, while his Republican neighbor may be Christian and think global warming is a left-wing inspired hoax (let's hope not). Their worldviews differ because of their differing ideologies. One will be more liberal and activist, while the other more conservative and adverse to change.

But whatever our particular worldview, those with whom we share the majority of ideological positions are most likely to share our cultural background as well; for it is shared culture which presents us with a fixed set of ideological options from which we then incorporate our own configuration. We don't make up our ideological beliefs *ex nihilo*. Rather, we choose them—largely unconsciously—from among the vast inventory afforded us through the culture groups we engage. For Christians, it is our job to continually realign our culturally-generated worldviews with a faith-based, biblical worldview—an endeavor best described as a perpetually ongoing, never completed process.

Religious ideologies are perhaps the most powerful and scariest of ideologies because they can dominate and directly influence every other type. Take, for example, the nineteenth-century religious ideology that undergirded our country's belief in Manifest Destiny. It was, in essence, a Christian Caucasian vision of a divinely-authorized continental expansionism. We justified a war with Mexico and the violent and ruthless subjugation of numerous Indian tribes, appropriating their lands and indiscriminately taking hundreds of thousands of lives without regard to any concept of basic human rights, because "God willed it." Perhaps a modern-day Manifest

Destiny lives on in America's present political and economic ideologies, through which we uphold the largely unacknowledged belief that it is this country's God-given role to bring democracy and free market capitalism to the rest of the world (see chapter 8).

Yet we Americans are certainly not alone in the way we impose our religious ideologies onto the rest of the world. Our European forebears—the British in particular—bequeathed us the notion that Christianity and nationalism could be (inappropriately) packaged together for export. The British, to be fair, were not the first or the last to do so. Religious majorities today continue to justify their nationalistic policies through the power wrought of dominance. Modern-day northern Nigeria is a good example, with its implementation of a regionally controlled Islamic government that has institutionalized *Sharia Law* in that part of the country—following similar movements in other countries with Islamic majorities.

Wherever they are present, religious ideologies hold great power to do good or to do evil. Bible Belt Christianity has produced those who work tirelessly on pro-life issues (a good thing according to my personal religious ideology) while also occasionally producing individuals who have found it conscionable to take human life through bombing abortion clinics—crossing over the fine line between religious activism and mindless fanaticism. In the same vein, Egyptian politics and policies have, until quite recently, been heavily influenced by the Muslim Brotherhood, which has an admittedly commendable history of building hospitals, promoting literacy, and assisting the poor. Yet there is a dark side, seen in the Brotherhood's religious ideology and their historic intimidation of any who do not share their brand of faith. The organization's official credo involves this chilling declaration: "Allah is our objective. The Prophet is our leader. Qur'an is our law. Jihad is our way. Dying in the way of Allah is our highest hope"[22] How comforting to be among the minority Christian population living under such threatening slogans. If only they were *just* slogans. Islamic religious ideology in Egypt spawned numerous radical Islamist groups that actively promoted an agenda of church bombings and mob killings of Christians. Largely unnoticed by the outside world, this same type of religiously-inspired violent hatred

---

22. Until recently the official Muslim Brotherhood English language website, http://www.ikhwahweb.com, prominently displayed the quoted pledge, but has since removed it. Yet the pledge remains intact for the Brotherhood and the Muslim Student Association's Pledge of Allegiance, as referenced in the online video "Muslim Student Association Pledge of Allegiance: Jihad is my spirit, I will die to establish Islam (video)," posted March 19, 2011, accessed October 26, 2014. See also, Helbawy, "Muslim Brotherhood," 65.

goes on in many other predominately Muslim geo-political regions, such as Northern Nigeria, Sudan, Somalia, Syria, Pakistan, and parts of India.[23]

Muslims promote Islam as a "religion of peace," and I have known many peace-loving and kind Muslim people (one of whom jeopardized his own safety to intervene on my behalf when I was a youth in a life-threatening situation in Pakistan). But Islamic religious ideology, *like all religious ideology*, can be a far cry from the tenants of one's faith. We Christians are shackled with our own unsavory and bloody history spawned by religious ideologies that have veered 180 degrees from the life and teachings of Jesus—from the Crusades in the Middle East, to Jewish pogroms in Europe during the Middle Ages, to the not-so-long-ago brutal subjugation of African slaves. All of these aberrations lead us back to the dire need to discern the differences between our precious faith and the cultural attachments that can, and often do, lead to the most unChristlike behaviors.

Whatever a person's worldview, whether religious or secular in nature, it is driven by myth. By myth I do not necessarily refer to fiction, as the term has come to mean in popular culture, but rather to the stories and beliefs regarding one's origins as a people (often considered sacred); stories that then serve to shape ideology, a sense of identity, collective behavior, and a notion of group destiny. Labeling the origins of a particular ideology or worldview as mythological makes no judgment as to its veracity. We may speak of the Judaeo-Christian creation myth or with equal accuracy speak of the myth that an invisible hand (a la the nineteenth-century economist Adam Smith) guides free market economies toward the good of all without government oversight and intervention.

Bruce Lincoln, a University of Chicago Divinity School professor, provided a good working description of myth when he called it "ideology in narrative form."[24] The point here is that our ideologies and worldviews arise from our culture history and deserve attention when we question the role our culture plays in our faith. In spite of the modern trend toward a spirituality in which it is only God and me (or me and "the universe" for some non-Christians), our religious experience and practice as American Christians is rooted in the experience and practice of those who came before. We need to understand something of our own culture history in order to make sense of the culture that surrounds and reverberates through us today. Chapter 4 will delve into the importance of understanding America's

---

23. Current information regarding persecution of Christians is available on several websites, among them: Christian Freedom International, www.christianfreedom.org; Opendoors, www.opendoorsusa.org; and Voice of the Martyrs, www.persecution.com, accessed October 26, 2014.

24. Lincoln, *Theorizing Myth*, xii.

culture history and chapter 8 will go on to considering the contemporary myths that continue to influence us as Americans.

SYMBOL USING

Symbols are absolutely integral to human social interaction. We use them all the time unaware, and learn their meanings and associations from childhood through complicated processes of enculturation. We use language symbolically to refer to abstract ideas and events, past and present, all of which carry meaning (constantly changing) that has relevance only through learned and shared culture. The importance of symbols and symbolic language for this study is the fact that symbols are highly affective; that is, they stir up our emotions. In the words of the incomparable religious philosopher Joseph Campbell, "A symbol is an energy evoking, and directing, agent."[25] Whenever our emotions are accessed through symbols, we become energized to definitively act in response. According to Campbell, the symbol itself sets the direction for the emotion-laden energy—but that direction is culturally determined.

The cross provides an example of the affective power of symbols. It was an instrument of the worst kind of torture and humiliation under Roman rule, where it symbolized the power of the Roman Empire and the horrible fate of any who dared to challenge it. That diabolical instrument of death and human subjugation has become just the opposite for Christians over the last two thousand years—a symbol of life and the power to overcome tyrannies both internal and external through faith in Christ. No one who has been exposed to the story of Jesus can look at the cross without some emotional response, even if it is only irritation or a sense of pity and consternation for those of us "foolish" enough to believe in such things. Its meaning, however, is fluctuating rapidly as celebrities now regularly wear ostentatiously large crosses as "bling," eliciting a whole new set of associations. Some folks think it offensive that "their" symbol is being usurped in such a way. Again, we see the power of culture at work in their response.

The reason the cross and other symbols are so affective relates to the values that get associated with them by various groups. When those values conflict, so do the emotions triggered by any given symbol. In America, the symbolism now associated with the cross is so strong that law suits are constantly being filed as to who can display it and where. It certainly is an "energy evoking agent." Given the values of some Americans, the cross is emotive because for them it represents the worst kind of intolerance and they

---

25. Campbell, *Wild Gander*, 143.

are tremendously energized to remove it from any and all public venues in order to promote their own supposedly threatened set of values. The point being that it is in our nature to employ symbols as a means of furthering our goals in the world because symbols are extremely powerful and integral to the way all humans relate to one another. Likewise, we are constantly being manipulated by others through the symbols they employ to attain their own particular ends. One can imagine an ongoing battle using symbols as weapons, which is exactly what has happened with the ichthus and Darwinian fish bumper stickers over the past decade or so (soon enough we will all tire of the hubbub and move on to other symbols with which to do battle).

CREATIVE

Whether or not one appreciates the accessorized use of crosses in the entertainment industry, it shows the creative side of human nature. Creativity is a close accomplice to purposefulness (below), for it allows us to find new and effective ways to reach our goals. And it is certainly not the sole domain of artists, for all of us use creativity daily in many of our endeavors, including our speech. The way we unconsciously individualize language to communicate to different people in differing contexts—changing word order, prefixes and suffixes, inflection, etc.—shows that creativity is innate to our nature. Some of us may be more creative than others, but as a species we are all extremely so.

Like most of the dimensions of human nature listed in this chapter, creativity is a direct reflection of our divine image. Not only did God create the universe, he seems to have done a rather artistic job of it. Science is really just our best effort to unravel *how* and *what* God created so we can take advantage of that knowledge to further human goals. And we do that by creatively employing our understanding and skills to improve life; or, in some cases, to take advantage of one another. Creativity flourishes when it is hitched to getting ahead in life. For our predecessors, that meant replacing stone tools with metal, domesticating wild animals like the horse and dog, and growing crops to supplement hunting and gathering. In America today creativity is booming in virtually every field of human endeavor because the monetary repercussions of novel products and processes are incredibly motivating to most. But, again, that is largely due to the cultural value we have placed on wealth and the things it can provide. Thus, human nature and culture get inextricably linked, and to properly understand either one requires that we get a firm grip on both.

AESTHETICALLY SENSITIVE

Because all humans are attracted to beauty, it is only appropriate to recognize that aesthetic appreciation is an important characteristic of human nature. We are magnificently hard-wired to see, hear, taste, smell, and touch that which is beautiful. Of course, standards of beauty differ greatly from culture to culture. The Surma of Ethiopia, for instance, find irresistible a woman whose lower incisors have been knocked out to accommodate a 6" ceramic lip-plate that extends her lower lip well out from her face. In China, until the early twentieth century most men were extremely attracted to a woman who had undergone "foot binding"—a painful process whereby a woman's foot was literally shaped into a point by years of purposeful deformity that left her unable to walk. Sexy!

Though modern Americans may not find a triangular-shaped foot all that enticing, we all share an appreciation for various forms of symmetry, which is central to any definition of beauty. Thus, we dance, sing, paint, and even write with a sense of joy in that which is patterned and harmonious as opposed to random and dissonant. Yet even dissonant music, such as compositions by the infamous composer John Cage, have some patterned format by which the dissonance is expressed. The most egregious-sounding rock music in America will adhere to traditional Western timing to lend form and symmetry to the supposed bedlam. "Beauty is in the eye of the beholder," it is said. But the beholder always possesses an internal template that displays some element of regularity and proportion because that's our divinely-imbued nature.

Our ability to discern what is beautiful within our own culture involves the use of abstraction. We carry around in our heads idealized versions of beauty (which advertisers cleverly prey upon) and recognize those versions in the people, places, and things we encounter. Then we create with those idealized versions of beauty in mind. Artists are persons who imagine that which is not and work to bring it into being according to an idealized pattern that previously exists only as a mental-emotional abstraction.

Wonderfully, this inclination is also part of what it means to be created in the image of God, who first imaged the worlds and each of us before bringing the universe into being (Eph 1:4). Whenever we fashion something good of the world in which we live, we participate with our maker in an ongoing act of creation.[26] Yet when coupled with the darker side of human nature—our collective bent toward evil, in particular—our aesthetically-oriented talents can be turned into the most destructive tools imaginable. Whether directed

---

26. Crouch, *Culture Making*, 35–36, 268.

at human beings (e.g., diabolical forms of torture such as waterboarding), nature (e.g., mountaintop strip mining), or culture (e.g., pornography and glorified violence) we are more than capable of destroying what we are meant to love and protect. Our attraction to beauty and the desire to create it is quite easily thwarted by the unsavory aspects of human nature.

PURPOSEFUL

Underlying all of our efforts, whether good or bad, earth-shaking or mundane, is an interesting dimension of human nature—that of purposefulness. Human behavior, however weird and misdirected it may appear on the surface, is always driven by some degree of purposeful motivation. No one gets out of bed or eats a meal or even scratches his head without purposefulness playing a role. However grand and glorious or pathetically selfish our daily activities, they are directed by inward motivations that are personally meaningful as part of a larger purpose we seek from life. This may sound unremarkable on the surface, but purposefulness represents our amazing capacity to provide order and coherence to individual acts which otherwise would be nothing more than random events. Without purposeful behavior, chaos and insanity rule. To understand human nature and its impact on human behavior, it is necessary to recognize that each person is motivated by an unseen vision of where his or her efforts will lead. We all march forth purposefully toward our unseen goals, often frustrated by apparent obstacles in the way—usually in the form of other people or insufficient funds.

The focus on purposefulness gains added importance when we consider that many people are unaware of the larger purposes that drive their choices and behaviors. Psychologists tell us that a great many of those who succeed to reach the top of their professions are driven by a need for acceptance that was missing from childhood. The overriding purpose that drives their often impressive efforts is to find that missing love and acceptance in the imagined approval and admiration that success supposedly provides. But, of course, it never really does. By contrast, the Westminster Shorter Catechism declares that "Man's chief end [in life] is to glorify God, and enjoy him forever."[27] That may seem rather limiting and self-indulgent until we remember that God most often comes to us in the guise of other people. If and when loving and celebrating God becomes our primary purpose in life, it alters all lesser goals with their self-serving and generally futile

---

27. BPCO, http://www.shortercatechism.com/resources/wsc/wsc_001.html, updated July 28, 2008.

aspirations, making worthwhile every effort no matter how tedious or unappealing it may initially appear.

The primary means by which we seek to attain our chosen purposes is through shaping and managing whatever environments surround us. Whether it be trimming nose hairs or repairing ozone holes, we seek to achieve our larger goals by attempting to manage the social and material worlds within our reach. But humans are not alone in this methodology. Environmental management can be seen throughout the natural world, from Lyme spirochetes disabling the immune systems of their hosts to grizzly bears tunneling snowcaves in mountainsides in preparation for hibernation. We humans follow suit, disabling the financial networks of drug cartels and tunneling under waterways to extend our system of highways, hopefully with more than survival in mind. Even tattoos and ear rings are forms of environmental management with purposeful intent. One may not think highly of the purposes driving such behaviors (impressing friends and attracting mates), but understanding that purpose can make sense of them. We all engage in manipulating our environments in one way or another, and would do well to recognize it.

Many of our collective efforts to manage our environments raise questions regarding the real purposes lurking behind them. The power we are able to bring through technology can be devastating to the natural world. Hand axes could only do so much to fell forests when humans first mastered the art of metallurgy. Now commercial fishing trawlers scrape entire ecosystems right off the ocean floor in minutes while entire mountaintops are easily removed by blasting them to kingdom come in pursuit of coal reserves. The technological sophistication of our environment managing tools has grown to absolutely staggering proportions. We're now splicing genes, creating life-saving medicines from deadly snake venoms, and fashioning robots with such sophisticated artificial intelligence that some ethicists worry robotic intelligence might someday impose its self-determined rule on humankind. What would robot nature look like?

All of this leads us back to the importance of purpose. If we get that right, we can proceed to create and manage in ways that accurately reflect the nature and purposes of God. By our design and nature, humans are meant to be "world-makers," in the words of sociologist James Hunter.[28] We are purposeful because God is always purposeful. We express it through going about the job of shaping our environments—making and remaking our inhabited worlds. Our creative impulses are fueled by innate curiosity and concentrated purposefulness, all of which can be employed for either good

---

28. Hunter, *Change The World*, 1.

or evil. Human will is the determining factor in the equation, directing our energies to either reflect or mar the divine image we bear.

American culture reflects the purposeful side of human nature by way of the values we hold dear. The section "Hard Work and Progress" in chapter 5 will return to this topic.

FAITH

It would seem reasonable to include faith under the religious heading above. Certainly they are interrelated. But I have set it aside to focus on the fact that faith is not some esoteric and mysterious component of the religious person's psyche, but a universal expression of human nature that relates to most of the traits listed above, including reason. In Western culture faith is generally contrasted with reason and even considered antithetical to it. But this understanding is itself culturally imposed by the worldview that has come to dominate pubic discourse—scientific materialism. There is nothing inherent in faith that divorces it from reason, or vise versa.

In fact, those who promote a faith-reason dichotomy are exercising faith in their own powers of reasoning and in the intellectual positions to which they adhere. Theirs is not faith in a person (although it often involves that) but in a systematic understanding of reality which people "believe" they are privy to. Pride and ego—other dimensions of human nature that will be explored in the next chapter—easily get woven into the mix of faith and intellect, further obscuring the matter for all involved. Inflammatory rhetoric and emotion-charged debates only entrench proponents in their various positions, often revealing more about their given personalities and the cultural values they hold than the subject matter under debate.

Of interest to our inquiry into human nature, however, is the fact that humans display a strong propensity to believe that their particular view of reality is the right one. It is rather alarming to realize that each of us goes about our day feeling as though we see what's really there. It doesn't matter where you stand in regard to the philosophical question regarding our *ability* to perceive objective reality, because the pertinent focus is on the fact that we *act* as though we do. Even post-modernists who posit that all is subjectively perceived *believe* their take on the issue is the right one. The implications of this self-confirming dimension of our human nature are enormous in terms of understanding culture and behavior. And it has immediate application for Christians and our engagement with others, as we shall see later on. In part IV we will seek to comprehend the perceptions of

Jesus, which entailed a reality he called the kingdom of God; a realm most of us, Christians included, seem unable to notice in our midst.

Faith is intertwined with many other aspects of human nature, forming an interactive matrix of interdependent parts. For instance, faith entails a relational component, whether that is God or an evolutionary history of gene-bequeathing predecessors. It, of course, engages our sentient side and employs our free will. Each person's personality and subjective experience help comprise the quality of her faith, which also draws upon the conscience, reasoning, and an ideology-infused worldview. We employ our creativity and aesthetic sensibilities in our expressions of faith, and we purposely manage our accessible environments in order to fully and satisfyingly express it. In sum, faith is a basic, integrating component of human nature, one that cannot be ignored without causing irreparable damage to our understanding of who we are as human beings.

FUN AND SENSE OF HUMOR

Not all our human traits are so serious. We have a lighter side that helps balance things out. It comes in the form of fun, entertainment, and adventure. Although each culture defines and cultivates these areas in unique forms and combinations, they are omnipresent in human societies far and wide. Folks like to enjoy themselves and do so everywhere through dancing, music and singing, festivals, competitions and poking fun at one another. The latter strategy entails our ability to possess a sense of humor, which thank God we do—at least most of us.

In chapter 6 under the heading "Fun and Entertainment" I will discuss the role of humor in contemporary America, relating it to our seemingly endless capacity to entertain ourselves as a necessary release value for the stresses under which we live. Humor's important role in maintaining mental health means that it is most adaptive wherever stress and hardship abound. As Henry Ward Beecher said, "A person without a sense of humor is like a wagon without springs. It's jolted by every pebble on the road."[29] Life in America, for all its affluence (or perhaps in large part *because of* all its affluence) has plenty of pebbles in the road. Humor helps us cope with things we can't control, giving us at least a sense of some power through being able to laugh at our circumstances. Just as struggle is universal, so is humor; only its frequency and form differ across cultures. One person's humor is another's offense, as some Nepali friends of mine once found out when they

---

29. Beecher, IZquotes, http://izquotes.com/quote/14539, accessed October 31, 2014.

broke into side-splitting laughter after seeing me slip off a muddy path and take a thoroughly inauspicious tumble down the hill (negotiating muddy mountain trails was mere child's play for them).

As far as we know, humor is a distinctively human trait because it involves abstraction and projection, which require more than a modicum of brain power. It certainly has a functional purpose in the complex array of traits we call human nature. Yet some animal researchers are convinced that they have observed chimps, macaws, and parrots display behaviors that indicate a sense of humor, believing they have seen these creatures actually laughing at other animals in compromising situations.[30] One wonders if being watched so closely by gawking humans put the poor animals under undue stress, eliciting behaviors they otherwise would never display! With that ponderous thought in mind, its time to move on to the next chapter where I will consider a few of the grittier dimensions of human nature. We'll need to take along a sense of humor to help keep things in perspective.

---

30. AWI, "Sense of Humor," §1, https://awionline.org/awi-quarterly/2011-winter/do-animals-have-sense-humo, accessed October 24, 2014.

3

Human Nature: The Not So Good

Two things are infinite: the universe and human stupidity; and I'm not sure about the universe.

—ALBERT EINSTEIN

IN ONE WAY OR another, the characteristics described in the last chapter were all reflective of the character and personality of God, whose image is ineffably stamped on human nature. Yet, as pointed out in the descriptions, any and all of those characteristics can be employed for either good or ill. By contrast, the characteristics of this chapter directly represent the dark and fallen side of human nature. In them we see the divine image corrupted and disfigured into various shades of evil that range from simple acts of self-interest to hideous acts of unspeakable violence. This "underside" of man's inherited nature goes well beyond self-deception, which is widely recognized by both secular and religious circles alike to be one of humankind's most practiced cognitive aptitudes. Self-deception tends to emerge alongside willful expressions of wrongdoing which, at some stage, involve predetermined choices to think and act in a self-serving manner that comes at the expense of others. Once that critical determination is made through the will, a course is set and the mind finds plenty of justifications through which to filter out the voice of conscience and all higher moral authority.

Human nature's nastier side represents the antithesis of the divine image stamped upon our personhood through conception's deepest mysteries.

The scriptures tell us it is a direct manifestation of the Fall and its catastrophic repercussions, not only for mankind, but for the whole of creation (Gen 3; Rom 8:19–23). Like a small bruise on an apple that spreads to encompass the whole fruit, the fallen side of human nature has the power to usurp all vestiges of God's goodness imaged in humanity and despoil whole persons in short order.

No commendable aspect of our humanity can withstand the onslaught of human nature's dark side once it metastasizes—a fact well documented by Elie Wiesel in his searing accounts of Nazi atrocities toward the Jews during the Second World War.[1] Every person, no matter how sweet and loving she may appear to be, is capable of the most despicable acts committed by the worst of tyrants and their henchmen down through history's darkest corridors. Until we realize that fact, we haven't grasped the full dimensions of human nature and the effects of the Fall upon it. Our proclivity toward evil is an uninterrupted continuum, where no qualitative moral difference exists between hateful thoughts and murderous violence (1 John 3:15). They are but a singular sentiment with differing expressions. Christianity posits that humanity's fallen nature is a ferocious beast that, given the right circumstances (e.g., someone threatening what is most dear to another), can escape its cage to wreak heartless havoc on any who stand in its way.

Yet just as the divine image is so easily disfigured, so is it possible to redeem the most diabolical side of human nature through the efficacious work of Christ upon the cross—itself the penultimate demonstration of evil redemptively transformed. Nowhere in scripture is this possibility more evident than in the life of the Apostle Paul, whose murderous ways were reformulated into the indefatigable efforts of one through whom God brought incalculable good into the world. Paul proved that, through God's all-sufficient provision of a transformed heart and mind, the beast can be tamed and made to serve the divine image-maker and his express purposes for humankind and the rest of his beloved creation.

The redemptive process, however, rightfully begins with casting a harsh light upon the various dimensions of our fallen nature in order to gain some perspective on their subtle, yet powerful impact in our lives. It is a rather disagreeable task to catalog our human faults, and probe some of their worst dimensions and expressions. Yet it is a necessary first step

---

1. Wiesel's most famous work about Nazi atrocities toward Jews is *Night*. Among Wiesel's many awards are the Nobel Peace Prize and the Presidential Medal of Honor. He established The Elie Wiesel Foundation for Humanity, whose mission is "to combat indifference, intolerance, and injustice through international dialogues and youth-focused programs that promote acceptance, understanding, and equality." http://www.eliewieselfoundation.org, accessed October, 27, 2014.

toward recognizing both the power and possibilities of God's redemptive work in our lives, and the potential impact of divinely-wrought transformation on our hurting world.

SELF-PRESERVATION

It's no secret that all people are imbued with a deep-seated drive to protect and save their own lives. That drive is the essential bedrock of both human nature and the nature of every living creature. It takes but a nanosecond for the self-preservation mechanism to kick in if one gets dunked underwater, after which both man and beast will frantically engage every resource available to regain the surface. We've all experienced that uncomfortably panicked impulse and know it to be a good and necessary one. Don't leave home without it. So what's the point? Just this: Christians are at times expected to counter this deepest compulsion within our human nature; for Jesus told his disciples they must willingly give up the natural inclination toward self-preservation in order to follow him (Matt 10:39). That's scary stuff; but then he also set the example—joyfully we are told (Heb. 12:2)—laying down his life for others (John 10:11). Every disciple is instructed to follow his example by being willing to do no less (1 John 3:16), encouraged by the promise that those who lay down their lives for Christ's sake will actually gain true life in the process (Matt 16:25).

This means that the most basic and unconscious aspects of our human nature are to be under the control of the will, which enlists areas such as faith, purposefulness, relationship, and rational thought to form a conscientious, overarching worldview. There is no part of our nature that is not affected by our faith and commitment to follow Jesus. The deepest level of our humanity, where the impulse to simply stay alive dominates all others, is also the dwelling place of the Almighty and the place where both faith and the power to express it reside. No wonder people cry out to God when their lives are in jeopardy, for we intuitively know him to be right there—"an ever-present help in times of trouble" (Ps 46:1, GWT).

Suffice it to say that this issue of denying the most powerful of our natural impulses reveals the absolutely radical implications of the Christian faith. For it is a faith that on occasion calls us to live in direct opposition to the most deeply ingrained feature of our very nature—the innately-placed mechanism to stay alive. Unless we are able to grasp that Christianity is not only countercultural but at times also *counter-natural*, we have yet to realize the true dimensions of the faith we espouse. No wonder Jesus asked his disciples if they were ready to drink the cup [of suffering and death] he was to drink, when they boyishly inquired as to the nature of their future rewards for following him (Matt 20:20–23). I doubt that many of us believers are ready to answer that probing question in the affirmative.

I've always found such talk unnerving because I do not feel myself cut from the same cloth as heroes of the faith such as William Tyndale or Dietrich Bonhoeffer. I'm just an ordinary, easily tempted bloke who, like the Magi of old, have seen a blazing light that I cannot help but follow (Matt 2:1–12). Fortunately, the source of that light knows all things and has lovingly set a course that, through his constant grace and empowerment, I *can* follow through life's inevitable ups and downs. Still, it's not about my strength; it's about how strong God is in me. And there is a world of difference between the two.

It is the case that most believers' denial of the impulse to preserve self will come in benign forms, such as countering a bias toward one's own group or culture—a bias with roots in the culturally-enhanced natural inclination to preserve ourselves and our ilk, first and foremost. Yet on a daily basis we can symbolically lay down our lives each time we choose to hold the door open for another person to pass through first, or to give generously to assist someone in need who has no means to repay us. And if we can lay down our lives in the seemingly inconsequential areas of life, then there will certainly be the grace to do the same whatever level of self-denial is asked of us.[2]

The natural bias toward preserving one's group ahead of all others is but one of a number of secondary traits associated with self-preservation. Self-protection generally entails some level of fear. It most often issues from a deep anxiety over preserving and defending all that is associated with self. Of course, fear is at times a good thing, the necessary means to swing us into action to get off the tracks before the train roars by. But it is also unleashed when our priorities get convoluted and pride or possessions appear threatened, taking a huge toll on bodily systems designed only for the occasional emergency. Unfortunately, we learn through culture to fear all sorts of people and circumstances that we *perceive* to be a threat to our health and well-being, when in fact they are far from it. Then folks make a bad habit of projecting their fears onto others. Xenophobia, the fear of foreigners so well portrayed in Flannery O'Conner's tragically humorous short story set in the old South, "The Displaced Person,"[3] is all about fear of the unknown and those who appear different. Precisely because culture and nature so powerfully combine to promote fear of the unknown within the unsuspecting,

---

2. Tom Howard, formerly a professor at Gordon College, first pointed out to me that the simple act of holding open the door for another person represents the spiritual symbolism of willful self-sacrifice.

3. O'Conner, "*Displaced Person*," 195–251.

a wide-ranging education should be a life-long endeavor for everyone who can access it.

We Americans are also enculturated to mistakenly believe that our material possessions are a necessary part of self-preservation—insuring our well-being—and we tend to worry ourselves sick over how to acquire and hang onto large quantities of them. Yet one of our biggest fears as Americans is the loss of control over our circumstances, since we live under the illusion that we can and should control every aspect of life—from the germs on our countertops to the democratic principles (or lack thereof) practiced in distant countries. Despite the many biblical injunctions to live lives free of fear and anxiety, most of us tend to worry over just about every detail of our overly-complicated lives. By constantly expressing that worry to others through words, deeds, and the attitudes that accompany them, it becomes a self-reinforcing cultural norm that gets passed around like the flu. Thus, we often preserve the less desirable aspects of our culture through a misdirected attempt to preserve self.

SELF-CENTERED

The difference between self-preservation and self-centeredness is that the former involves basic physical survival, while the latter involves preserving and even indulging a culturally-spawned *sense* of self that contrasts with the biblical view of who we are as human beings created in God's image. Yet one can easily see that there are linkages between self-preservation, self-centeredness, and the issue of fear previously mentioned. Although acting in the interest of self is ubiquitous among all peoples, many Americans seem particularly adept at it, clueless to the fact that other viable perspectives exist outside of their own limited experiences. But America is not alone among the industrialized nations of the world, wherein there seems to have arisen a modern-day "cult of self" that promotes attitudes and actions that scream "It's all about me!" Rick Warren recognized this collective pathology through his decades of pastoral work, and thus began his best-selling book *The Purpose Driven Life* with the biblical rejoinder, "It's not about you."[4] In order to fully get his point—that God has a plan and our job and joy lies in conforming to it—we must consciously counter the culturally-reinforced natural inclination to put ourselves and our concerns ahead of God and his kingdom.

Not surprisingly, we often put self first under the guise of doing what we think is best for our children, community, ethnic group, or country—those extensions of self with which we most closely identify. In ideal

---

4. Warren, *Purpose Driven Life*, 21.

circumstances, that is a good and necessary orientation. It helps parents to properly care for their children and communities to adequately address the needs of the needy among them. But under the influence of the dark side, it inevitably leads to an indifference and intransigence toward the concerns and needs of those who lie outside a tightly-guarded sacred circle. Jesus pointed out that loving and doing good to friends and family gets us no further spiritually than the level of "scoundrels" (Luke 6:32, TV), who happily do as much. He insisted that his followers circle of concern and benevolence should be cast wide enough to include everyone, even our adversaries or "enemies" (Luke 6:35). That's about as wide as a circle gets.

This verse is typical of others in the Bible that assumes self-centeredness to be part of human nature because each contains admonitions to avoid it. The detailed laws given through Moses, such as those forbidding exploitation of aliens, widows, orphans, and poor neighbors, presuppose a natural orientation toward engaging in selfish behavior (Ex 22:21–27). We also see the same assumption in the prayer of Psalm 119:36—"Turn my heart toward your statues and not toward selfish gain." Self-seeking, selfish gain, and ambition are the focus of numerous New Testament scriptures (e.g., Rom 2:8; 15:1–2; Phil 1:17) directed toward believers and identified by Paul as behaviors associated with "the sinful nature" (Gal 5:19–21). Meanwhile secular-oriented researchers are engaged in fascinating baby studies prompting ongoing debate over whether our true nature is inherently selfish or altruistic.[5] Some of the research seems flawed by what I call "anthropocentrism"—belief in the superiority of human-centered perception and reason.

Unjustified self-assurance is also a panhuman dimension of our nature. We humans walk about actually believing that the world we perceive and our particular individual understanding of everyone in it is, in fact, accurate. We have within us the proclivity to discount the perceptions of others in favor of our own, which we have convinced ourselves are true and correct. As the nineteenth-century philosopher Bertrand Russell put it, "Every man, wherever he goes, is encompassed by a cloud of comforting convictions, which move with him like flies on a summer day."[6] The "know-it-all" perspective is largely unconscious and does have adaptive application in terms of getting things done in this world. But ultimately it is egotistical and self-serving to assume that somehow the way one see things is the "right" way (i.e., the way things *really* are).

---

5 Tucker, "Are Babies Born Good?" http://www.smithsonianmag.com/science-nature/Are-Babies-Born-Good-183837741.html, accessed October 27, 2014.

6. Russell, *"Dreams and Facts,"* para.5. http://www.users.drew.edu/~jlenz/br-dreams.html, accessed October 27, 2014.

By this view, a person's individual worldview, politics, theology, and other convictions are, in his estimate, the only correct way of seeing things. "If you agree with me, you too are correct," or so the thinking goes. "If you don't, you are misperceiving reality, and I am obligated to correct your erroneous perceptions (i.e., to bring 'enlightenment' or 'awareness' to you)." Rare the person who admits his perceptions are necessarily limited (see Cor. 13:12); or someone who is actually open-minded toward a different take on life, possessing a genuine desire to listen and learn. And sometimes things aren't right or wrong, but just different or paradoxical. As Christians we have to learn to live with pluralism and paradox within our own faith or we will surely find ourselves both frustrated and befuddled by contemporary life. Jesus' solution for "know-it-all-ism" is simply not to judge others negatively (Matt 7:1)—a liberating resolution we've somehow managed to discount as quaint, New-Agey, and unworthy of our elevated spiritual status. Hello pride!

PRIDEFUL

There is confusion over the dual meaning of pride which, on the one hand we are taught to avoid and even despise, and on the other to embrace (e.g., "Take pride in yourself"). Linguistic, philosophical, psychological and religious perspectives all conspire to obfuscate the matter which, for our purposes, can simply be differentiated by substituting the distinguishing terms "hubris" and "self-esteem." Yet there is a point at which a healthy self-esteem goes sour, turning to hubris—one of the original "seven deadly sins" identified by the early church. That is the point at which egotism and arrogance enter the picture, leading to an overestimation of one's self-worth, opinions, and abilities. When I speak of pride in this section, it is hubris alone to which I am referring. I include pride as part of human nature because it exists across all cultures as a manifestation of a panhuman orientation toward a tendency to misjudge one's importance, accomplishments, worldview, and religion vis-à-vis "others."

There seem to be two kinds of hubris-laden pride. The one involves a genuine arrogance based on the simple, culturally-generated delusion that a person or group is superior to others. Some would refer to this as simple egotism or arrogance, but it's all the same beast. I have seen it flagrantly manifest among certain high caste groups in India and Nepal, especially in their attitudes toward lower castes (which included *all* foreigners). The other avenue to pride for both individuals and groups is through an unconscious sense of inferiority that employs pride as a tool of denial, projecting one's own imagined inferiority onto others. Both are ugly, whether manifest in a single individual or a whole society, and both emerge from a pathologically unhealthy self-image. The Olympics and political conventions are good fora to see them both in action.

Though pride tends to perpetuate itself through memes (see below) and acculturation to group values, it represents a seed within human nature that only needs a little watering to sprout and grow vociferously. Humility, on the other hand, though naturally apparent in the personalities of some people, generally must be cultivated through religious and moral influences. Yet so insidious is pride that many (myself included) who have sought to cultivate humility have, at the bitter end of their efforts, only discovered that they have become more than a little proud of just how humble they now are. "The heart," declares Jeremiah, "is deceitful above all things and beyond cure. Who can know it?" (17:9).

Yet children long to hear and need to hear their parents say the words, "I'm proud of you." (in addition, of course, to the magical phrase, "I love you."). Nothing wrong with that, is there? It seems to depend on the context and the message conveyed. We all know that children need their self-esteem built up through genuine parental love and attention, just as adults need positive feedback from the authorities under whom they function. All Christians long to hear, "Well done, thou good and faithful servant" (Matt 25:21, KJV). But children need to know unequivocal parental love in order to get the template correct for understanding and embracing God's unmerited and unconditional love. The essential message children (and all of us) need is one of approval—not simply for doing what's right, but simply for being who we all are—the Creator's image-bearers. Given that kind of approval, children *want* to do what's right.

Still, a parent can tell a child she is proud of her in such a way as to convey a sense of superiority over others, generating and perpetuating hubris. The meaning lies beyond the words themselves, and humans at every stage of life are equipped with keen facilities to discern that meaning through the facade that words often create. That's why a hug can at times communicate far more than mere words. The inherent power of our actions is well captured in the wisdom-laden traditional Amish proverb, "You can preach a better sermon with your life than with your lips."[7]

---

7. Fisher, *Amish Proverbs*, 69.

BENT TOWARD WRONGDOING

Another obvious dimension of fallen human nature, even conceded by many who lack a faith perspective, is mankind's bent toward wrongdoing. Though some philosophies posit that human nature is intrinsically good, while science takes the position that it is neutral or non-existent (the politically-correct "Blank Slate" argument), both positions are hard-pressed to explain rampant evil in the world except through an unjustified reliance on the "nurture" argument—wherein all wrongdoing is either learned behavior or an environmentally-induced expression of non-adaptive genes. Most Christians embrace the concept of "original sin" to explain humanity's bent toward wrongdoing, even though a conscious attempt to do the right may exist. The Apostle Paul famously describes the propensity for evil as the fruit of a sinful nature that, apart from the Spirit's redemptive work, perpetuates itself in spite of the most fervent of human intentions (Rom 7:14–25; Gal 5:17). Solomon also arrived at the same conclusion after employing his famed wisdom to understand the mysteries of life. In Ecclesiastes 9:3 (TV), he uncompromisingly declares that "Human hearts are inclined toward evil . . ."

The human bent toward wrongdoing becomes embedded in culture through behaviors, attitudes, and institutions reflective of it. America's unattractive record on racism is a prime example—a problematic but elusive issue that is alive but generally sublimated in the twenty-first century. Culturally-sanctioned wrongdoing allows "descent" folks to engage in questionable acts simply because others are doing the same. The "foundations of evil," in the words of Richard Rohr, "[are] in cultural assumptions."[8] We tend to assume things are the way they are because that's the way they are meant to be. In the words of the nineteenth-century French physician and anthropologist Paul Broca, "The least questioned assumptions are often the most questionable."[9] No one is motivated to change laws, institutions, or attitudes that remain ethically unexamined, especially if they benefit from them in some way (e.g., gerrymandering legislative districts). Those who do wish to change unfair laws and practices are almost always those harmed by them; yet they are not always in the position to do so without outside help.

Knowing that humans have a tendency to act contrary to the conscience, and even at times contrary to the will, makes it easier to conceive the origins of schoolyard bullies and lynching mobs. Both are forms of a

---

8. Rohr, "The World," http://myemail.constantcontact.com/Richard-Rohr-s-Daily-Meditations-The-World-The-Flesh-and-The-Devil-Ecumenism-June-25-2013.html?soid= 1103098668616&aid=8TQcogt_nuU, accessed October, 17, 2014.

9. Broca, ThinkExist, http://thinkexist.com/quotation/the_least_questioned_ assumptions_are_ often_the/184203.html, accessed Nov. 2, 2013.

"pecking order"—the stronger (chickens) ganging up on the weakest among them. Human nature, in this regard, is no different than animal nature. If someone else is the object of hatred and violence, then people tend to feel safer themselves—or so the natural mind reasons. And if someone personally feels secure, he or she can more easily participate in wrongdoing, either directly or through willful omission—that is, failing to act on behalf of what's right when there is the opportunity to do so. Perhaps the "flaw" of omission goes a long way toward explaining why white Americans (and the U.N. for that matter) have had less than robust responses to disasters in places like Rwanda and the Congo than was the case in European Yugoslavia, where people looked more like us Western Europeans and mainstream Americans. Evil often comes in subtle packages.

The bent toward wrongdoing certainly explains why so many Americans in high positions—from pastors to presidents—jeopardize their careers and reputations with boneheaded one-night stands. The best-intentioned are vulnerable to the voice of unreason, and no amount of counseling or tinkering with moral and legal systems will eradicate that weakness. It's within human nature and not something "out there" that needs fixing. To think that the inclination to do wrong either doesn't exit (as most humanistic philosophies maintain) or can be hidden under a religious cloak is hubris of the highest degree. The bent is bent until the new nature emerges and is given full reign. Religion works overtime to hide or compensate for the shortcomings of human nature ("do not go near the door [of temptation]," warns Prov 5:8). But according to Paul, we are no longer under its diabolical control; rather, we are controlled by the Holy Spirit (Rom 8:9). Yet a beast lurks in the shadows (1 Pet 5:8), and I've yet to meet a single soul who is safely and permanently out of reach of its fearsome claws. Thus does Peter warn us to be on the alert and sober-minded (ibid.).

BENT TOWARD BELLIGERENCE

Human nature has a belligerent side that is apparent in America's culture of violence, both at home and abroad. I have purposely chosen to use the term "belligerence," which can entail violence, because belligerent words and attitudes alone do not sufficiently express the human tendency I am trying to describe. For behind belligerent words and attitudes is always the implied threat of aggression or violence. That's why Jesus could say that the person who angrily called another, "You fool!" does so from the same inward place that also gives rise to murder. War and violence are merely the collective expression of belligerent cultures, or at least a group of belligerent leaders, which belligerent cultures tend to cultivate and follow.

Some may argue that belligerence is merely cultural and point to Buddhist societies such as Bhutan to prove the point. Certainly Buddhist nations and cultures are far and away the least belligerent groups of people on the face of the earth—a hopeful example for the rest of the world to follow in that regard. But the pacifism promoted through Buddhist teachings only makes the point that culture can vastly modify the belligerent impulse in any direction without ever fully eradicating it. Personal and collective violence persists in countries where Buddhism is the norm, such as Thailand and Myanmar. That is, in part, admittedly due to the cultural imposition of foreign values spread through a hegemonic political history and the dominating influence of contemporary global economics.

Yet violence and war have existed throughout the long histories of Buddhist countries, especially during the Middle Ages when violent clashes characterized relations between Southeast Asian nations where differences between Theravada and Mahayana branches of Buddhism often led to warfare.[10] Cambodia, historically an isolated country with the world's second highest percentage of Buddhist citizenry, generated one of the most bloodthirsty regimes known to man. Although Communist-Marxist in philosophy, the Khmer Rouge murdered three million of their own people in the nineteen eighties under a regime that drew inspiration from its own violent culture history. Over the last fifty years there have been numerous violent indigenous nationalist movements in Southeast Asian countries, such as the monk-led "969 Movement," which has targeted non-Buddhists, and particularly Muslims.[11] Though promulgated by practicing Buddhists, ethnic conflict is usually the primary causative factor behind those violent confrontations—providing yet another example of faith and culture becoming so tightly bound together as to become indistinguishable, to the detriment of both.

Buddhism's Noble Eightfold Path clearly reveals the inherent belligerence in the human heart. Right speech, right action, and right livelihood all call for "non-harmful" actions toward others *precisely because* of the human capacity and proclivity to act otherwise. Were there no inherent belligerent tendencies, there would be no need to promote actions contrary to them. And although the end goal of Buddhism is to attain enlightenment through *nirvāna*, awakening to the "true nature of the self"—that divine

---

10. Jerryson and Juergensmeyer, *Buddhist Warfare*.

11. Jerryson and Juergensmeyer, *Buddhist Fury*; Tikhonov and Brekke, eds., *Buddhism and Violence*.

nature free of all desires, including belligerent ones—the fact that all Buddhists are locked into "the cycle of death and rebirth" means belligerence is on some level alive and well as part of the lived nature (behavior) of its adherents. Thus, if it is all but ubiquitous in individual Buddhists, it will be found in all Buddhist cultures, however sublimated in form. For that very reason, anthropologist Donald Brown lists aggression and violence as one of hundreds of human universals, for it is "found among all peoples known to ethnography and history."[12]

Men, of course, are much more prone toward belligerence and violence than women, for reasons, we are told, to do with hormonal and other genetic differences. But again, it is culture that determines acceptable levels for both sexes given their prescribed roles in society. It seems that American culture is now intent on drawing aggression and belligerence out of women, who have little trouble meeting the *macho* challenges they face in the military, as mixed martial arts experts, or in the highly competitive and aggression-cultivating worlds of business, law, and politics. Interestingly, in many cultures where men can be notably aggressive in demeanor, such as certain countries in the Middle East, Latin America, and Asia, women are conversely yet notably meek and submissive. There's no doubt that, in general, any belligerence on the part of women in these cultures has been turned inwardly because no acceptable channel exists for its outward, social expression. Violence toward oneself is still violence, whether it comes in the form of burqa-clad suicide bombers or anorexic Western teenagers. Even the most bellicose and aggressive males can, at times, also turn their violence inward—as did Japanese men under Imperial rule who sometimes resorted to *seppuku* (*harakiri*), and, tragically, as sickeningly large numbers of Indian farmers are doing today by way of rat poison and suicidal hangings to escape impossible economic difficulties they currently face in that country.[13]

Most often, however, the human tendency toward belligerence is expressed in the form of retribution. We humans seem to posses a deep-seated need to meet out punishment, often violent, toward those whom we perceive to have offended or abused us. It issues from a tit-for-tat, eye-for-eye mentality that is all but ubiquitous among individuals, groups, and nations. Fallen human nature deems that if we suffer, we want others who caused it to suffer in return. It may not always take the form of a the vengefully murderous genocide that engulfed Rwanda in 1994, or even the fist-a-cuff

---

12. Brown, "Human Universals," 47–54.

13. CHRGJ, "Every Thirty Minutes," http://www.chrgj.org/publications/docs/every30min.pdf., accessed October 17, 2014; Shiva, "Seeds of Suicide," http://www.globalresearch. ca/ the-seeds-of-suicide-how-monsanto-destroys-farming/5329947, accessed October 17, 2014.

scuffles that occasionally break out in Parliamentary arguments in the Ukraine and the Philippines, but widespread litigation by individuals and economic sanctions by governments are also efforts to punish those we perceive to have done us harm.

Indeed, in most societies—America at the forefront—individuals feel they have the *right* to pay back in kind (or worse) those who have harmed them. That right lies deeper than the laws of the land, on a moral level that seems to be natural to us all. Kids have it, and regularly express it in schools or on playgrounds; but adults perfect the many ways it can be expressed in *socially-acceptable* terms—that is, what one can get away with and not suffer recrimination from peers or public officials. Jesus, of course, offered a different response when he told his followers to "turn the other cheek" and "love your enemies, do good to those who hate you, bless those who curse you, pray for those who mistreat you" (Matt 5:38–41; Luke 6:27–30). Were retribution not so deeply ingrained in fallen human nature, his teachings would not sound so radically alternative, going well beyond the teaching in Leviticus to leave revenge to the God of justice (Lev 19:18)—itself a radical departure from the legal and cultural mores of its day.

SCAPEGOATING

Scapegoating, a fascinating and illuminating means of expressing belligerence, is seen in every known culture, from ancient to modern, and band-level to post-industrial. It involves directed violence toward an animal, person, or group that has been rendered the symbolic substitute for the whole society. As popularized by French-born social science philosopher, Réne Girard, the theoretical underpinnings of scapegoating are to be found in all human societies' collectively-expressed violence toward a person or group that has been vilified and marked for symbolic sacrifice in order to keep violence under control and outside of the main social group. In his classic book, *The Scapegoat*,[14] Girard details the plight of many such victims, including European Jews targeted under *pogroms* by the majority Christian populations during the Middle Ages. In that instance, The Plague was blamed on the Jews, who were targeted and killed in a sacrificial manner by citizens of a number of northern Mediterranean countries who were desperate to blame someone for the dire events that seemed to lie outside their control. Thus, the vilified group always exists as a *perceived* threat (the Jews had economic power and represented a non-Christian entity within a "christianized" society). But for violence to actually break out, according to

---

14. Girard, *Scapegoat*.

Gerard, there generally needs to be a specific trigger that threatens to undo social order and stability, as was the case with the Black Plague.

Students of the Bible will recognize the origin of the scapegoat theme from the Book of Leviticus. And that is the source from which Girard developed his theory. The sixteenth chapter of Leviticus describes the process by which the sins of the Israelites were imputed to a goat once a year, thereby allowing the people to escape the punishment God would have otherwise meted out for transgressing the prescribed laws of Moses. In fact, two goats were involved. One was sacrificed on the alter of the Tabernacle, and the other led outside the camp to be freed—symbolically bearing away from the Hebrews the sins that had been paid for through the sacrificed animal. Propitiatory animal sacrifice has been practiced since time immemorial, and continues today in small-scale cultures around the world where chickens, goats, and other domesticated animals are regularly used in ritualized sacrifices that are believed to benefit those involved. According to Girard, however, Jesus permanently broke the scapegoat pattern (and our felt need for sacrifice) through his innocent and willful self-victimization—thereby offering humankind a way to end collective violence and the irrationality of sacrifice.

Regardless as to whether Girard's biblical and theological interpretations seem *kosher* to most Christians, the important take away is that scapegoating is a real, panhuman behavior that remains functional in contemporary societies around the globe—including America. The targeting of Muslims for hatred and violence since 9-11 (in which, shamefully, an American Sheik was killed by an unstable white American male who thought he was gunning down an "Arab") is a form of scapegoating that needs to be called out for what it is. Christians are called to be supportive of people and groups that the larger society irrationally targets as an inappropriate means of coping with collectively-sensed stress and insecurity. Individuals who represent antithetical values to mainstream culture (and, sadly, traditional forms of Christianity) are still dying today through modern versions of scapegoating. Homosexuals, minorities, and even the homeless and elderly are sometimes singled out for victimization by segments of society that feel they cannot control the social, economic, and political direction of their lives and the country. Collective scapegoating, according to Girard, begins with individual desires, and spreads through behaviors and attitudes copied by others (see "memes" below). The gospel bids us Christians to break down barriers and borders, and welcome all of God's children into his love, mercy, and full acceptance. Like Gerard, we should do no less than proclaim that *there no longer exists any need* to vilify and punish anyone. Jesus took care of the matter once and for all (Heb 10:10).

TABOO-MAKING

Taboos are culturally-sanctioned prohibitions against behavior considered too sacred or too profane for the average person to engage in. If they do, it can precipitate some form of retribution upon both the individual and the group. Specially-appointed intermediaries such as priests or shamans—often considered to be divinely-endowed—must negotiate the spirit realm and facilitate the good of the people in light of the dangers surrounding a taboo. Traditional Christianity, and Catholicism in particular, considers handling the host properly to be the domain of the pastor or priest, who has the authority to insure that it is not desecrating to those who handle or take it.

Although every culture grouping has taboos of some sort, no single taboo is universal. This means that although taboo-making is found the world over, the particular form the taboos take is culture-specific. Common ones include incest, infanticide, and dietary laws. Yet most are unique to their cultural milieu. Among Muslims, for example, touching the Koran with one's foot is considered taboo, as is defaming the Prophet Mohammad. No one, *including imams*, is permitted to do such a thing. In the Bible there are many taboos outlined in the Mosaic Law, including who could enter the Tabernacle, when, and under which circumstances to avoid the treat of divine punishment. Beside communion, Christianity also has a taboo associated with blaspheming the Holy Spirit—that unpardonable, if somewhat controversial, sin Jesus warned against in his exchange with Jewish scribes who accused him of demonic empowerment (Mark 3:22–30).

But taboos are not limited to the religious realm or to tribal culture. The concept is applied both popularly and within the social sciences to all prohibitions against behaviors considered to be morally reprehensible by the society-at-large. Using the "N-word" is now taboo in America, unless you are an African American (though its slang use among youth and comedians is soundly criticized by the larger black community). Use of the word "God"—and most definitely the name "Jesus"—in public is quickly becoming taboo within American cultural life, except within an officially-sanctioned invocation or closing (e.g., the generic phrase "May God Bless America" commonly used at the end of public speeches). Eating one's pet dog or cat is taboo in our country, just as eating pork is prohibited among Orthodox Jews and eating beef forbidden for high-caste Hindus. But the most enduring American secular taboo may well be desecrating the flag, against which there is currently no law, but very intense and effective social pressure. Many other countries do have laws against desecrating their national flags, and will prosecute offenders. But in 1989 the U.S. Supreme Court ruled that this country's First Amendment Rights take precedence, and it is legal for citizens to do so. Still, the taboo remains in effect through the raw power of social sanctioning.

The very word "desecrate" reveals that taboos invoke a conception of the sacred—that which is sanctified, holy, or venerated. For something to occupy that category, it must do so in opposition to all that is commonplace or contaminating (e.g., using the toilet). This distinction is part-and-parcel of any religious worldview, but not overtly recognized within secular culture. Yet its implied presence indicates a spiritual/religious orientation within human nature, as described in the previous chapter. Although most agnostics and atheists would not admit to creating a sacred/common divide, it is none-the-less revealed in the culturally-sanctioned taboos to which they adhere. One can see this in the unspoken taboo among adherents of atheistic and naturalistic philosophies, which stipulates that no credibility should be afforded to the beliefs held by religious people. God is taboo, as is any serious allowance for a creationist position of any sort. To allow it would be crossing the revered line-in-the-sand drawn by scientific materialism—the worst transgression a modern, "rational" person could possibly commit. To cross that line, even in search of common ground for the betterment of humankind and the environment (as the eminent biologist E.O. Wilson did in his book *Consilience: The Unity of Knowledge*,)[15] is to incur the condemnation, not of God or ancestral spirits, but of one's erudite friends and colleagues. Wilson took a lot of flak for his perceived accommodation of religious perspectives, though a few well-meaning critics applauded his intent.

Sometimes individuals allow their egos to elevate their opinions to a venerated realm where they unwittingly worship their own haughty prognostications. At that point they are constrained to guard their opinions closely—their sacred ground inundated with taboos against trespassing—because their very identity has gotten so tightly wrapped up in their beliefs and opinions. It is not dissimilar to the way some culture groups stand ready to fight to the death any who besmirch the honor and reputation of family, clan, or tribe. Yet I have noticed that the whole matter is often hidden from the eyes of those who are otherwise so very perceptive in their areas of expertise. We humans are certainly an interesting, if curious, lot. May God bless us every one.

MEMES

The manner in which human beings decide that a theory or opinion is something worth defending, whether in America or the deserts of the

---

15. Wilson, *Consilience*.

Middle East, is through a method of cultural copying called "memetics." First popularized by the brilliant but acerbic faith-basher Richard Dawkins in his book *The Selfish Gene*,[16] memes represent a theoretical attempt to explain in evolutionary terms the way cultural transmission occurs from one individual to another, eventually affecting an entire culture or society. Memes represent "units of culture" such as ideas, beliefs, behaviors, and artifacts that function within culture in an analogous manner to the way genes function within biological organisms, adaptively evolving over time. That is, memes get copied from one individual to another, represent some degree of variation in the copy, and succeed over other meme options through an adaptive mechanism based on the "survival of the fittest" model. Examples include Copernicus's heliocentric model of our solar system, which displaced its earth-centered predecessor, and the ubiquitous use of credit cards instead of hand-written checks to go shopping. In both cases, a unit of culture got copied between individuals until it became successfully established as the primary expression of culture within the larger society.

Not without controversy and its detractors, memetics none-the-less provides a working model across disciplines for understanding how cultures change over time based on innovative thoughts, beliefs, behaviors, and material innovations. Its significance to this study is through the insights it provides into how the components of culture—the norms, values, and myths to be addressed in the chapters to follow—emerge from human nature to become the variations we see in cultures and subcultures within America and around the world. In terms of religion, memetics allows a better understanding of the processes involved in the widespread disparity of beliefs and behaviors within Christianity, as well as within religious and spiritual traditions everywhere. It provides a handy tool to help us Christians understand our own cultural heritage, and how that heritage conforms to or conflicts with the dictates of an historic, biblically-based faith.

Although memes are not part of human nature, but a mechanism by which human nature gets variously expressed through culture, I have placed the topic toward the end of this chapter to provide a conceptual bridge between the sections that have come before and those to follow. The modus operandi remains the same: The various and sometimes conflicting facets of human nature are expressed through culture by way of individuals who copy one another (children from parents, neighbor from neighbor, and so forth) in ways that are informed by the past yet altered enough to be adaptive to changed circumstances in the present. All of contemporary

---

16. Dawkins, *Selfish Gene*.

American culture, including the forms our religious beliefs have currently taken, came about in this way.

The knowledge of God that Jesus brought to humanity began as a meme, and subsequently spread from one individual to another over two millennia until it became established as the predominant religious norm in America—a norm that must constantly adapt to stay relevant to ever-changing circumstances. The important question is: How much has American Christianity mutated or evolved away from that original meme? And is that original meme still appropriate to the circumstances that define modern America and the world?

WHITHER HUMAN NATURE?

Before leaving our reflections on human nature, it is perhaps necessary to ask just where human nature might be located. Is it in our genes and cognitive structures, as some maintain? Or is it lodged in our viscera alongside the "second brain," with its rich neural network? The reason for asking is to free ourselves from the reductionist thinking which essentially all scientific and theological paradigms require—both of which are specifically Western approaches to understanding ourselves and the world in which we live. Determining how knowledge is legitimately acquired is ultimately a game of power in which certain factions attempt to control all others by defining the terms of engagement. Scientific materialists are playing that game with all their might, attempting in hegemonic fashion to supersede all other epistemologies. Although logic and rational thought certainly have a legitimate and needful place in the methodology of Christian inquiry, we participate in a realm that reaches far beyond the mind and its cognitive abilities. We must, therefore, be in a position to embrace and appreciate experiential and faith-based ways of knowing that expand our understanding of ourselves, our world, and the spiritual realm that animates it all. And, hopefully, the holistic understanding that the combination of our faith, human experience, and intellect provide will translate into a state of consciousness and engagement that is as elevated as the reality it allows us to perceive and participate in.

So it was a trick question—Whither human nature?—and a silly one at that. Human nature exists as an aspect of the whole person, just as does the personality, our perceptions, and the soul—none of which the microscope will ever find. Searching for the location of these dimensions of our humanity reminds one of Nikita Khrushchev's overly-confident declaration made in 1961 after the Soviet Union first orbited the earth: "Gagarin [the cosmonaut] flew into space, but didn't see any god there."[17] Secular paradigms don't find anything beyond our genes and the massive brain it purportedly single-handedly spawned, and they are attempting to define and circumscribe reality accordingly for us all through cultural and intellectual hegemony. Yes, human nature could be tied to biological structures such as genes (one thinks of the Old Testament declarations that the sins of the fathers will be manifest in their offspring for three or four generations),[18] but human nature is best understood as a descriptive attempt to present human beings in a holistic manner that includes our lived experiences, inclinations, intuitions, aspirations, and common sense—among other areas. All of the various dimensions of our humanity lead us to the conclusion that the whole is so much more than the sum of the parts. In order to see that whole we must lift our gaze beyond our culture-bound limitations, and especially beyond the myopic views of science, however wonderful and useful it is for so many worthwhile human endeavors.

Yet even with that widened gaze our understanding represents but an infidesimally tiny particle within a universe of knowledge that stretches into an incomprehensible eternity. Such thinking will sound like nothing more than self-delusional sentimentality to those who have not met the One who fills that eternity—the very One who also lovingly chooses to dwell within those possessed of humble hearts (Isa 57:15). True understanding, however limited in breadth, comes from reverence for God (Ps 111:10; Pr 9:10), whose love is as vast and limitless as eternity itself, whose grace and goodness are utterly boundless, and whose presence lends joyful purpose to each and every dimension of life.

It is his nature that is embedded in ours and has transformed the disfigurement of the temporal effects of the Fall. Yet in the fullness of time, when all knowledge is engulfed in pure Presence, that divine nature will emerge fully within us in all its glorious splendor; and then we shall know genuine wholeness in both our persons and our every perception (1 Cor 13:9–12; 1 John 3:2). Although scripture informs us believers that we possess the mind of Christ here and now (1 Cor 2:16), it is imperative that we diligently seek to remove all the impositions of self and culture that constantly threaten to limit such an utterly marvelous and transformative gift.

---

17. Danick, "Didn't See," http://roadsfromemmaus.org/ 2009/10/04/he-didnt-see-any-god-there/, accessed October 27, 2014.

18. See, for example, Exodus 34:7, Deuteronomy 5:9, and Numbers 14:18.

PART II

Who Are We Americans?

4

America's Cultural Origins

America is not just a country, it's an idea.
—Bono

ORIGINS

The dominant culture in America, like any national culture, is the end product of a number of formative factors that together have molded it into the configuration we see today. To understand who we are as Americans and why we think and behave the way we do, it is necessary to appreciate the influential factors that played a major role in shaping us. Notable among those formative factors is our adaptation to our unique environments (social and natural, both past and present), our inherited culture history (which is an amalgamation of numerous histories, mostly European), and the influential facets of our human nature. Once we have outlined our geocultural origins as Americans, we will then be in a better position to understand our unique values and cultural characteristics, and how they apply to the expression of Christian faith in this country.

It is, of course, no secret that America is one of the most multicultural and multiethnic countries in the world. So it is somewhat misleading and presumptuous to even speak of the dominant culture in America as a distinct entity. But I employ the concept as it is commonly understood, even though the dominant aspect of our culture is undeniably changing from traditionally white, middle-class values. Although that traditional segment is shrinking relative to growing minority populations—Hispanics in particular—it none-the-less embodies the values that continue to dominate much of the political, institutional, and commercial life of America, thus retaining the "power" to define cultural norms.

One of the best ways to gauge the influence of any particular culture group in America is to take note of its interest to the advertising world. Most ads still target a white, middle-class audience, although minorities are now more often included in specific commercials, depending on the product being advertised. Yet, over time, even minority and immigrant populations within America come to reflect many of the values of the dominant, mostly white middle-class through the process of acculturation. This is most clearly seen with minorities who are younger, and among second and third generation immigrants. Television/mass media and public school education have combined to make America the proverbial "melting pot" of peoples and cultures, despite its multi-ethnic makeup (sometimes referred to as an ethnic "salad bowl"). Thus, an identifiable mass culture still exists—basically white, but steadily colorizing—even as many minority groups (and Anglos of differing backgrounds) seek to rediscover and identify on some level with their own unique cultural heritages.

Although white, middle-class values most heavily influence American popular culture, it is more productive to think of that culture in a generic, non-racial/ethnic form—as an amorphous, all-inclusive expression of the mainstream. That is the direction popular culture is headed as it continually absorbs minority cultural values into its once nearly all-white center. It is probably most accurate to speak of a process of two directional change occurring simultaneously, as the dominant American culture absorbs minority values from among its subcultures while reconfiguring those minority values into the dominant cultural configuration.

It is important to note that changes in culture always involve some conferred advantage to both the cultural center and the cultural periphery, such as the economic benefits that derive from "hip-hop" cultural values being incorporated into mainstream American culture. Language, as has been stated, is a very good indicator of the presence of subcultural values within the mainstream culture. Black, urban slang words like "bling," "chill," and "yo," are now heard so often in mainstream settings—most notably among youth—that we tend to forget their distinct origins. Yet the very presence of that subcultural language in mainstream culture indicates the presence and acceptance among mainstream Americans of at least some of the values of the urban subcultures that produced it—indicating more melting in the pot. It is instructive to recognize that language shapes and reflects culture even as it is reflective of and shaped by it. Put differently, language changes culture while being changed by it. Language and culture always simultaneously evolve as integral elements of one another. Technically, language is considered a dimension of culture, but it is so important a component that when a people's language dies (and around the world, roughly one dies every two weeks) the entire culture dissolves in response.[1]

The absorption of black, urban cultural values into mainstream culture is an example of a process social scientists refer to as "culture change." Yet it is important to realize that there is no such thing as static culture; there is only a cultural center with its representative values evolving through time as an adaptation to its changing social, cultural, and natural/built environments. In our example, mainstream American culture is constantly undergoing reconfiguration as an adaptation to the social and cultural (black, inner-city) environments that spawned hip-hop culture. Rural, black culture has its own influence, as does the urbane and well-educated black subculture in America that gained national attention with the election of the country's first African-American president (actually, he is no more black than white, African than Anglo. But the values of mainstream American culture long ago determined that someone of mixed race whose outward appearance is that of a "person of color" will be identified according to his or her minority race.[2] But stay tuned, for that too is changing!).

It is important to note that since cultures are constantly in flux, it is futile to try to maintain some illusory traditional culture in America, or anywhere else. Those who attempt to hang onto and prop up a traditional notion of American culture—inevitably the people who benefit economically or socially from the status quo—are fighting a losing battle. Equally futile is the attempt to control the precise direction of culture change, which always occurs as an unconscious, collective process of adaptation to unforeseen alterations in the social, political, and natural environments. Who, for example, could have ever predicted the endless changes wireless technology has wrought on American culture (and cultures worldwide). Culture change, like genetic mutation, is for all intents and purposes, a random, non-directional process (there is actually a logical process behind both types of change, but we simply are not intelligent enough to comprehend all the complex variables involved, and so we must label them "random"). Therefore, those who expend their energies trying to control the particular direction and tenor of culture change usually end up getting crushed by those unbridled changes—a process repeated again and again by political

---

1. Harrison, "Languages Die," 58–61.
2. See Rotholz, *"What Makes Obama* Black?" http://scholarsandrogues.com/2008/11/02/what-makes-obama-black/, posted November 2, 2008.

leaders around the world who fail to succumb to populaces that insist on moving toward democratic reforms.

Christians in America should take heed. Our job, in my humble opinion, is not to attempt to preserve some imaginary notion of a Christian culture or nation (as though *any* culture or nation-state deserves that title). Rather, beginning with ourselves and our own interior life, it is to facilitate deep change from within—change that will emanate the love of God and allow the gospel of Jesus to express its inherent relevance to the changing world and times in which we live. Humans are by nature resistant to change, both inwardly and outwardly. The gospel, by its very essence, is quite adaptive to any and all changes in human societies and cultures. It always provides a universal fit. Rather than try to micro-manage the details of our ever-changing culture—unpredictable because the behavior of any single individual anywhere can have such wide-ranging effects on the whole—we would do better to make certain that our lives and gospel message, over which we do have control, remain relevant to whatever cultural changes are occurring.

If you differ with me on this point of focus, don't spring a leak. I know the "culture wars" University of Virginia sociologist James Hunter first described in his 1992 book by that name rage on unabated in America.[3] Yet we Christians of every stripe are obligated by the love and sacrifice of our Savior to find a way to bridge our differences (1 Cor 1:10; Eph. 4:1–3)—a task we can only do by fully embracing the person and teachings of the One to whom we've all devoted ourselves (including our egos). In part IV we shall attempt to get at the heart of our common faith, so that all differing opinions can be evaluated in the light of that singular perspective. My hoped for goal is that the essence of the gospel can be distinguished from the cultural forms that labor mightily to bear it, to the glory of its magnificent author.

But before we delve into the contemporary forces shaping American cultural values, it is essential to first consider the historic social, cultural and environmental forces that laid the initial foundation for our system of beliefs and values; for they will help us to better grasp our contemporary cultural values and the distinctive cultural norms that derive from them. All cultural values have a firm foundation in history, and ours is by no means an exception.

OUR FIRST ANCESTORS

All Americans are immigrants, including the so-called "First Americans" who, according to most archeologists, departed Asia via a frozen Bering

---

3. Hunter, *Culture Wars*.

AMERICA'S CULTURAL ORIGINS

Straight to arrive on a pristine North American continent toward the end of the last Ice Age (ca. 13,000 BP). Waves of other Native Americans followed. But were they really the first immigrants? There is a fascinating theory that posits an even earlier migration of Ice Age Europeans, the Solutrean people, who are thought to have made their way along the North Atlantic archipelago by island-hopping in small boats, arriving in North America over twenty thousand years ago. Period artifacts found in Pennsylvania and along the East Coast suggest a link with the Solutrean culture that existed in France and Northern Spain from 17,000 to 24,000 BP.[4]

Another "First American" theory emerges from research of Kenniwick Man, whose nine-thousand year-old skeleton was discovered in Washington State in 1996.[5] Just before his remains were to be buried by Native Americans local to the area in which he was found (who claimed him their direct ancestor), it was discovered he was not of Native American heritage. Rather, he was of Polynesian descent, though not directly related to any living populations anywhere in the world today (the Maori of New Zealand and the Ainu of northern Japan being the closest). Researchers theorize that Kenniwick man represents the earliest group of migrants to North America (ca. 15,000 BP); a people who died out or were genetically absorbed by later waves of Asian migrants who, over time, gave rise to Native Americans (who lack the genetic evidence to claim direct ancestry to Kennewick man—evidence which they currently discount).[6] Thus, we do not really know who our earliest ancestors were, or any certainty about their ethnic heritage.

Later came the Vikings, whose North American voyages put them on the continent about a thousand years ago, half a millennium before Columbus even set sail. Although the Vikings made no permanent settlements here—Greenland being the closest known long-term settlement of that period—evidence suggests they did make forays as far south as Canada's Gulf of St. Lawrence, where they likely traded with the native Iroquois of the area (a Viking coin minted around the time was discovered at an Indian dig site in Maine). Although the Vikings as a distinctive people disappeared over time, their genetic heritage lives on among millions of Americans today, due, in most part, to later Scandinavian migrations to North America.

Modern Euro-American history in the U.S. mainland, however, begins with the 1513 landing of Ponce de León in Florida—a once celebrated occasion that, along with Columbus's 1492 landing in El Salvador, is quickly falling out of favor with many Americans sensitive to the plight of indigenous

4. Stanford et al., *Across Atlantic Ice*.
5. Douglas, "9,000 Year-old Man," 52–63.
6. Ibid., 60.

people who were negatively impacted by these early *conquistadores* ("conquerors"). The first recorded American settlement dates to 1565 when the Spanish established a fort at St. Augustine, Florida. Within a few decades, Spanish colonizers had settlements in New Mexico and had already explored the coast of California, which remained unsettled by Spanish emissaries for another two centuries. Although Spain's colonial empire would be strongest from Mexico south, its cultural and genetic imprints remain in North America to this day, representing the earliest and most enduring contribution of our European heritage (some people assume the Brits hold that honor).

But the Spanish were not the only explorers in North America during the sixteenth century. The French made many attempts to establish permanent settlements from Quebec to Florida, and even in Texas, only to have them all fail. The French were tenacious, however, and a century later began exploring and eventually settling areas from the Great Lakes to Louisiana's Gulf Coast. The English, not to be outdone, began their North American empire building at Jamestown, Virginia in 1607, and subsequently acquired territory all the way up the Eastern seaboard from Florida to Canada. The Dutch, Swedes, Scotts, Germans, and Poles were also all involved in establishing settlements during the seventeenth century, either as colonists or as craftsmen and mercenaries for nationalities other than their own.

These early settlers were all lured to America by economic pursuits initiated from their European homelands. Companies such as the Virginia Company of London and the Dutch East Indies Company were seeking lands around the globe whose resources could be exploited for the benefit of their empires back in the Old World. They, along with the Spanish, came to the Americas primarily for the *entrepreneurial* opportunities they accorded. It was a land grab reflective of European expansionism in the rest of the habitable world: viz., the Caribbean, South America, Africa, South and East Asia, Indonesia, and the islands of the Pacific. At one point in the late fifteenth and early sixteenth century when Spain and Portugal were the two leading colonizing European powers (Portugal tried to found colonies in Newfoundland and Nova Scotia but failed, finally settling in Brazil), they actually signed treaties to divide between only themselves all newly discovered lands found anywhere in the world outside of Europe! These first waves of Europeans beheld a mysterious world full of treasures to be had for king and country, and America was seen as just another sparkling jewel in the pile.

THE PILGRIMS

That all changed with the Pilgrims. They represented the first group of European settlers who came to America as *refugees*—in this case fleeing the religious persecution they suffered under the authoritarian power of the Church of England. The Puritans followed their path to the New World a decade later, followed by Roman Catholics and Quakers who were also fleeing persecution from the intolerance of England's church-state hierarchy. America was a land of a different kind of opportunity for such groups. It was a land where they hoped to freely practice their religious beliefs without government or church-imposed interference. In pursuing that vision, they set the stage for peoples from many nations who over the course of the next four centuries would come to American shores to flee persecution and oppression of all kinds. From seventeenth and eighteenth century Anabaptists to Hmong and Sudanese Christians of late, America has been a place of refuge for people of faith since the Pilgrims first landed. And it is not so for Christians only, but Jews, Sikhs, Baha'is, Buddhists, and even atheists whose beliefs are considered a crime in countries such as Iran. Yet freedom of religion also means *freedom from* religion, and many have come here for that purpose alone. Finally, there is a seemingly endless list of those who immigrated to America to escape ubiquitous forms of political persecution in their countries of origin. We are all "pilgrims" in a way.

The culture history of America represents a continuum of reasons effecting immigration. On one side are the early empire-building Europeans who brought with them a condescending, exploitative mindset accompanied by a tainted religious ideology that justified exploitation of men and resources. On the other side were the religious and political refugees whose past experiences made them more distrustful of authoritarian structures and more tolerant of dissent. Both are part of our cultural makeup today. Yet in between these two extremes came wave after wave of immigrants who journeyed to America mainly to escape economic hardships back home. "The land of opportunity" was a new start in a land where they hoped to flourish economically, and thus socially, having escaped the confining social, economic, and religious structures of their native lands.

Among these numerous groups of "economic refugees" were the Irish, who fled the potato famines of the mid-nineteenth century, the Poles who escaped war and famine in Europe during the late nineteenth century, and poverty-stricken Chinese of the same period who came to labor in America's growing industrial sectors. The waves continue today among Latinos who perform menial tasks in agriculture and other industries, but also include highly skilled and educated professionals in the fields of medicine, education, and technology. All of them (us) came to America through a combination of push-pull forces. Problems back home pushed them away, while opportunities (real or perceived) attracted them here. For all of them, America was a kind of "Promised Land," where the shortcomings and oppression of "Egypt" were left behind for what was hoped to be a land flowing with "milk and honey." Thus, unlike many of the traditional lands they left behind, America and its culture would come to represent *hope*—a forward-looking, positive orientation that helped spawn and perpetuate values, norms, and myths associated with progress and prosperity.

SLAVES AND GREEKS

Of course there are many who came to America entirely against their will. Between the sixteenth and nineteenth centuries, some three-quarters of a million slaves arrived in the United States, mostly of African origin. By 1860 nearly four million slaves were on the official census registers in the U.S. They were to have an enormous influence on the country and our collective culture and worldview. Yet two areas of influence stand out: first, slavery raised undeniable moral issues that would shape our history and culture in untold numbers of ways, from its intrinsic denial of biblically-based human rights to the abolition movement and subsequent Civil War; and secondly, through widespread racial mixing between plantation owners and their female slaves. The latter influence, something of a taboo to speak about openly, is quite fascinating.

The genetic testing research of Harvard professor Henry Louis Gates has established that many, if not most, black Americans now have some degree of white ancestry, in addition to a small percentage with Native American ties. Some whites also share genetic links with African Americans. And all this despite various state laws that prohibited racial mixing ("miscegenation") from 1691 to 1967, after which the Supreme Court finally ended the charade and ruled all such laws unconstitutional. Thus, slavery in America set us on a course toward what Gates terms "deconstructing race"[7] because, according to his well-founded research, there is no longer any basis to the notion of racial purity in the U.S. If we let that fact sink in fully, it will certainly change the way we think and thus act toward those we now consider racially different from ourselves. God has a habit of taking something awful (e.g., slavery) and turning it into something good (tolerance and understanding toward others).

7. Gates, "A Conversation."

The fact that racial mixing is not only common in America, but becoming more and more so, leads us to a final important issue regarding our culture history—our Greek inheritance of dualistic thinking which guides us toward seeing things as either/or, good/bad, "black or white." Beginning with Plato, the tendency to see the world in dualistic terms permeated all of Western Europe and, thus, the way our immigrant ancestors thought about and acted within their world. Hebraic thought, by contrast, presented a more holistic cosmology in which God, humankind, and nature were intertwined and not separated into opposing factions. The Hebraic mind had its own dualism between the sacred and profane, but fostered an overarching unified worldview in which the spiritual and physical worlds were inseparably bound to one another—closer to Eastern and Native American systems of thought than those we have become accustomed to in the West. Although many Jewish immigrants from Europe would eventually come to America, they would not alter the dualistic thinking trend for the country because they had already been acculturated into Western patterns of thought from living in Europe for generations. For all our ancestors with European links, a dualistic way of seeing the world was a huge conceptual endowment that would have tremendous impacts on the early settlers and the social and natural environments they encountered—an endowment that has remained strong ever since.

NATURAL AND SOCIAL ENVIRONMENTS

The Old World cultural values that our European immigrant ancestors brought to America greatly impacted the unique natural and social environments they encountered. Yet at the same time, those environments had their own power to significantly impact the values and worldviews of its new arrivals. Culture and nature always exist in a relationship of mutual constitution. In America, both have continuously altered one another—from those first settlers on America's wild shores to many of today's inner city minorities who never set foot away from the paved urban environments they inhabit, resulting in a sad lack of appreciation for nature. Our ancestors began a dance with the natural world whose steps we continue to follow, a love-hate affair that has helped and harmed both partners. It's a relationship whose outcome is still as uncertain today as what lay beyond the foreboding forests upon those newly encountered Plymouth shores.

A central tenant of the worldview our European ancestors brought to America derives from the Christian theological position they inherited, believing that humans live between a paradise lost and a paradise to come.

Paradise lost could never be regained by going backward. Eden's gates were seen to be shut tight and guarded by angels and a flaming sword (Gen 3:24). Paradise was only to be had by going forward toward the New Jerusalem that lay at the end of time. This teleological orientation encouraged an ideology of spiritual progress that, in turn, promoted an analogous concept of social progress. The early Welch historian, Giraldus Cambrensis (ca. 1146–1220), reflects this orientation in his statement, "In the common course of things, mankind progresses from the forest to the field, from the field to the town, and to the social condition of citizens."[8]

With a progress-oriented worldview, the first settlers looked upon both the American landscape and the Indians who dwelled there as needing improvement. Many Europeans considered the Indians of the New World to be "on a low scale of savagery . . . worthy of nothing better than serving their Christian masters."[9] After their original encounters with aboriginal peoples, debate had arisen among Europeans as to whether the New World inhabitants were fully human or represented a different race from the descendants of Adam and Eve. A papal bull eventually pronounced Indians to indeed be fully human, although most settlers continued to view them as an inferior breed of humanity that was closer to the animal world than to "civilized" society.

The Spanish explorer Coronado exemplifies this perspective in his 1540 description of the Pueblo Indians of New Mexico, whom he described as "a people without capacity," "stupid," and "of poor intelligence."[10] This view accorded with European explorations on other continents, where indigenous people were engaged by early explorers and settlers. In 1609 the English writer Robert Gray surmised that most of the earth was "possessed and wrongfully usurped by wild beasts . . . brutish savages, which by reason of their godless ignorance, and blasphemous idolatry, are worse than those beasts."[11] An English clergyman described the Hottentots (known today as the click-speaking Khoisan of southern Africa) as "beasts in the skin of man," whose speech was "noise rather than language, like the clucking of hens or gabbling of turkeys."[12]

Virtually all written records of this time show that Europeans considered their culture and traditions to be the apex of civilization (a notion that apparently has great lingering power; see "Cultural Evolution" in chapter

---

8. Glacken, *Traces*, 280.
9. Ibid., 360.
10. Gutierrez, "Pueblos and Spanish," 50.
11. Keith, *Man and Natural World*, 42.
12. Ibid.

8). Although Native Americans were generally seen to be inferior and in need of civilizing (which for Europeans of the time entailed Christianizing), some settlers and missionaries did come to recognize positive characteristics in native peoples and their cultures. Jesuits who lived among tribes of the Northeast were among them, as well as Rhode Island Colony's founder, Roger Williams, who described the Narragansett Indians as "exquisitely skilled" in navigation and able to perform their collective work with joy and great accord.[13] Yet despite a degree of cordial relations with Indians reflected in the first Thanksgiving they shared, the Pilgrim settlers in general viewed native peoples as part of what the eminent historian Bernard Bailyn called "a barbarous environment" that elicited "elemental fears . . . in which God's children were fated to struggle with pitiless agents of Satan, pagan Antichrists swarming in the world around them."[14] The Pilgrims had come, in part, to spread the gospel and to convert the Indians—whom Robert Cushman, the Pilgrims' agent to England and "ancient friend" of William Bradford, the first governor of Plymouth Colony, referred to as "these poor blind infidels."[15]

Bailyn, after meticulous study of original documents from the period, determined that the Pilgrims and Puritans struggled with a dual threat: their own austere spirituality alongside a frightening new environment. "The two [kinds of struggle, physical and metaphysical] were one: threats from within [to the soul] merged with threats from without to form a heated atmosphere of apocalyptic danger.[16] One of those threats, the New England forests, was unlike anything the Pilgrims had ever seen before. And although it is now well established that those forests were not the untouched, old-growth wilderness some have imagined (Indians had long since altered the natural environment into an "anthropogenic" landscape, more-or-less sustainably engaged but far from "pristine"), the early settlers viewed the forests and inland reaches ominously—"a hideous and desolate wilderness, full of beasts and wild men," in the words of Bradford.[17]

But the settlers were amazingly industrious and began to slowly but steadily cut the forests for housing, heating, and cropland. The pastoral lifestyle they knew from Europe, which entailed crops and domesticated animals, functioned best among fields fringed by groves of trees. The fewer

13. Merchant, *Major Problems*, 75.
14. Rosenbaum, "First Blood," 29.
15. Young, "Chronicles," https://openlibrary.org/books/OL7084938M/Chronicles_of_the_Pilgrim_Fathers_of_the_colony_of_Polymouth_from_1602_to_1625, posted August 17, 2009.
16. Rosenbaum, 29.
17. Merchant, 68.

tracts of deep forestland, the more secure the colonists felt, especially from Indians. What is estimated to have been an original New England forest cover of around 95 percent on the eve of colonization was, incredibly, reduced to around 10 percent in some rural farming areas by 1850.[18] By that time, Boston's rapidly expanding urban areas required great quantities of wood for both building and heating. The seemingly endless forestland had been completely transformed, leading settlers to set their sights on the "wild West," a new frontier with another apparently endless supply of natural resources.

Paradoxically, it was the Eastern urban centers that would soon thereafter produce the earliest conservationists, who lobbied to preserve the American West. As Easterners found their own natural resources rapidly shrinking, forward-thinking citizens began to value that which had at first seemed so threatening—the wild forests and animals that dwelled there. This phenomenon led the historian Roderick Nash to make the profound, if seemingly incongruous statement, that "Civilization produced wilderness."[19]

It has always been a minority of Americans who have taken pause at the plight of nature in the face of progress. The nineteenth-century Industrial Revolution that made for prosperity in the urban areas delighted many, despite the toll it took on natural resources, because those resources were still viewed as more-or-less inexhaustible by most Americans. Not only was the New England landscape permanently altered, the Appalachian forests were virtually destroyed by mining interests owned by tycoons from Eastern cities. The problem, however, was not confined to the East. Settlers out West also triggered environmental destruction in their wake, virtually wiping out game such as the buffalo, while denigrating once virgin farmlands in a process that culminated in the Dust Bowl debacle of the 1930s. Few people traveled widely enough to see the effects of an industrializing economy on the hinterlands, and images of the West were often fantastical in nature—embellished by opportunists with a stake in resource extraction or land sales to wide-eyed settlers. Capitalist economics won the day from the original Puritan approach to business, which was infused with humility, piety, and moderation. In fact, according to Bailyn, the Puritan concept of "fair price" trading entailed soul-wrenching deliberations over just how much a devout Christian should profit in any transaction, including those with Indians.[20]

Despite this long and multidimensional culture history, America is still, it seems, primarily defined by the same two polar opposite ideologies.

---

18. Ibid., 195.
19. Nash, *Wilderness*, xiii.
20. Rosenbuam, 34.

On one end of the spectrum are those who are predominantly driven by exploitative interests, as were the early Spanish and nineteenth-century industrialists. On the other end are those who, like the Pilgrims, came to America to establish a better world for themselves and those they encountered (a point lost on some Native American groups and others who see only deleterious effects from European settlement). The net result of these two opposing views of life and economics—maximizing profits without due consideration to the environmental and the social costs involved, versus piety-inspired interactions based on ethically derived circumspection and moderation—has fostered a kind of collective ambivalence within us as a nation. America has a split personality in this regard.

We are now deeply conflicted as a nation. The so-called "culture wars" engage opposing segments of the population which, given their individualized psychological and subcultural inheritances, are more comfortable lining up on one side of the original colonial divide: viz., the status quo-promoting traditionalist with an eye toward self-gain or the morally sensitized progressive oriented toward a notion of the collective good. Add to the picture the unresolved issues of slavery that haunted—and continue to haunt—those who considered themselves "good Christians" (or at least good moralists and Deists), and it is no wonder our cultural inheritance is one of variance. We have two vastly differing ideological legacies informing our collective sense of self. And it seems we are not just divided as a people; we are also divided as individuals—desiring a morally shaped world but all too often acting immorally in our treatment of nature and one another. This discrepancy in our persons and national culture will show up in the issues, values, and characteristics listed in the chapters to follow, much of which can be directly traced back to the culture and context of early America. Beneath this dual cultural model and internal personal conflict is what one Christian philosopher terms our "dual nature"[21]—a human nature that simultaneously reflects the perfection of the original creation and the image of God, conjoined with marred and dysfunctional personalities effected by the Fall.

THE PRESENT

As mentioned previously, culture is always in the process of change. Today's America, and who we consider ourselves to be as Americans, is constantly being renegotiated through a large number of influential factors. And although the precise direction of culture change cannot be predicted due to

---

21. Groothius, *Christian Apologetics*, 427.

the inherently fickle nature of the beast, it is possible to name and understand some of the driving forces behind that change. The formula for culture change is rather simple: it is human nature expressing itself as an adaptation (or attempted adaptation, for some culture change is obviously maladaptive) to contemporary social, political, economic, and natural/built environments. In other words, modern culture is the collective attempt of society to flourish and find relevance in today's world, driven by the undercurrents of human nature.

We flourish when our culture is a good fit for the world in which we live. Yet the dark side of human nature insures that too many of our cultural changes are maladaptative. Too often we seem to make choices that lead us away from human flourishing, as when the value Americans place upon freedom of expression results in a proliferation of pornography. Yet even yesterday's successful adaptations—those that promoted widespread human flourishing—are generally not adequate for the novel configurations that make up today's world. New circumstances require new adaptations; and we must be ready to choose anew what is good. Still, our culture history, both the good and the bad, is always the repository from which all our choices regarding future change are taken—many of them unconsciously present in our every thought.

One of the main problems we face as a nation is the lack of obvious guidelines by which to measure the worth of any adaptation. We expend a lot of time and energy floundering about in trial and error mode, the pendulum swinging back and forth from conservative to progressive approaches to problem solving. For the Christian, scripture provides an unequivocal guide to all of our actions. But it is necessary to let it speak to our current circumstances rather than impose upon it archaic cultural interpretations that may only be appropriate to the past. When we get stuck in those cultural interpretations, we fall into the pit Irish playwright George Bernard Shaw referred to when he said, "No man ever believes that the Bible means what it says: He is always convinced that it says what he means."[22] Chapter 8 will seek to further elucidate this thorny issue.

Meanwhile, it is important to identify the deep-seated cultural values that underlie the expression of new adaptations in American life; for cultural values have a longer half-life than mere cultural expressions. For example, individualism as a cultural norm is expressed in different ways through time, yet has remained central to American culture throughout our history. One can see this reflected in the leading roles of movie actors over

---

22. Shaw, ThinkExist, http://thinkexist.com/quotation/no_man_ever_believes_that_the_bible_means_what_ it/169760.html, accessed November 5, 2013.

the past century, from the first silent films to today's blockbusters, in which the rugged individualist (the protagonist) always stands against overwhelming opposition—and wins! It is a theme that dates back to Pilgrim days and can be traced right through the Colonial period with its Washingtons and Jeffersons, the westward expansion with its Davy Crockett and Daniel Boone-like heroes, and in today's urbanized world where the latest incarnation of James Bond 007 regularly saves the world against all odds.

What follows in the next two chapters are a list of the basic cultural values that define us as Americans, followed in chapter 7 by contemporary cultural expressions in the form of normative behaviors. At times the values will appear contradictory for one of two reasons. First is the contradictory character of human nature, which Paul addressed in Romans 7:15, where he describes an internal struggle between the human will and human desires and behaviors. Because culture is but an adaptive expression of human nature, one can expect to find contradictory culture traits in any given culture. The second reason relates to the first. Our culture history, which we draw upon to facilitate current cultural adaptations, is comprised of moral and behavioral contradictions because it was formed through human choices directed by the conflicts inherent in human nature.

We are the product of that culture history, and so our cultural inheritance will reflect values that, on occasion, are at loggerheads with one another. There is, however, always an overarching harmony in any given culture despite the existence of some opposing values, just as there is a unified personality for any individual despite any incongruence in his or her psychosocial presentation. Each person and each culture is to some degree *functionally* adaptive (except in cases of mental illness and social collapse), but that does not mean the adaptations are optimal. Humans manage to live and work despite serious health problems from poor diets and lack of exercise, while governments carry on despite inadequate support structures to deal with alcoholics and homeless citizens who regularly perish on their streets. Fallen human nature too often dictates that our personal and collective journeys through life are more of a painful hobble than a carefree stroll. Our culture simply reflects whatever disharmonies and imperfections exist within the dark recesses of unredeemed human nature.

5

Early American Cultural Influences

One hundred years before the Pilgrims landed at Plymouth, the Spanish government issued a decree authorizing the enslavement of the American Indian as in accord with the law of God and man.
—NELSON A. MILES

THE SIX FORMATIVE AMERICAN cultural influences listed below are distinguished from the six to follow in the next chapter by virtue of their being rooted in our early culture history. In other words, they were either cultural values our ancestors brought with them from the Old World, or values that developed early on in American history. Each has survived into modernity, evolving, and in many cases strengthening, over time. Though they will be easily recognizable as part of our modern sensibilities, it is important to realize that these six cultural influences flourished prior to the Industrial Revolution and the remarkable changes which followed that watershed event. For that reason we can consider the cultural influences below to represent the bedrock of American culture as we now know it, in that the contemporary values and cultural norms to be discussed in the next two chapters are firmly and inextricably erected upon them.

INDIVIDUALISM

If you ask Americans what makes them unique, most will give a list of characteristics that include being strongly individualistic. We value the notion of going against the grain, the singular individual standing out in the crowd. As Eleanor Roosevelt put it, "Remember always that you not only have the right to be an individual, you have an obligation to be one. You cannot make any useful contribution in life unless you do this."[1] So while we sit in traffic jams or line up at MacDonald's for the same burger a million other people are eating that day, we carry around in our heads the prototypical image of the lonesome cowboy riding solo through the majestic mountains of Wyoming, or the strong-willed pioneer woman (think Dr. Quinn, Medicine Woman) who overcomes all odds to succeed. It is part of the myth whereby we tell our children to be themselves and never give up on their dreams. And it is not hard to see why we think that way.

The early explorers, viz., the Pilgrims, the Colonial Patriots, and the settlers of the American West, all had to be self-reliant. In addition, many of them stood against something—the English Crown, for example—forming their identities as a people who broke away from the establishment. It is a theme that runs right through American pop culture history, producing in each generation those who go their own way (e.g., the flappers of the twenties, the beatniks in the fifties, and a succession of hippies, yuppies, gen Xers, and millennials). It is no secret that the value we Americans place on individualism stands in stark contrast to most cultures throughout the world (the Australians representing a clear exception, their own culture history as exiled prisoners making them quite independent-minded—perhaps more "American" than Americans in that regard), where the individual finds his or her identity in the group, not outside it. African and Asian cultures are well-known for a strong emphasis on group identity.

Many Africans, for example, hold to the traditional concept of *Ubuntu*, a Zulu-derived term inspired by the maxim, "A person is a person through other persons."[2] The philosophy behind *Ubuntu* derives from a worldview in which social unity is paramount and the self is always defined in terms of one's relationship to others. It reflects a worldview in which standing out from one's people and culture is something shameful and to be consistently avoided.

Ubuntu is a value that has been said to have negative consequences where individual initiative and responsibility could otherwise help foster change for the better, as in the case of averting ethnic conflict and the proliferation of HIV/AIDS. But *Ubuntu* can also facilitate positive outcomes in these very areas when coupled with a sense of individual responsibility that

---

1. Roosevelt, GoodReads, http://www.goodreads.com/quotes/45956-remember-always-that-you-have-not-only-the-right-to, accessed November, 5, 2013.

2. Kockalumchuvattil, "Crisis," http://www.kritike.org/journal/issue_7 /kochalumchuvattil _june2010.pdf, accessed March 31, 2013.

builds on traditional culture to achieve solutions to contemporary problems.[3] The significance of *Ubuntu* for us is in understanding that it derived from a unique culture history in which group unity meant survival itself in a very threatening environment. Like American individualism, its applicability to contemporary life and problems lies in its adherents' ability to adapt it to new and larger sociopolitical contexts, thereby making it a force for positive change, rather than an obstruction to it.

Individualism certainly has the potential for good or ill. Like *Ubuntu*, it is in itself neither good or bad, moral or immoral. Individualism is simply human nature expressing itself in a form that was an appropriate adaptation at particular stages of our culture history. When coupled with a moral framework, such as the progressive Christian convictions of Martin Luther King Jr., individualism produced the most remarkable fruit, changing a whole society (and world) for the better. However, that same sense of individualistic, anti-establishment thinking can also produce mayhem or destruction, as when anti-government extremist groups cultivate individuals who carry out domestic acts of terror. One can see how different aspects of human nature, such as fear and self-centeredness, combine with the cultural value of individualism to produce people and movements whose values are far from those taught by Jesus, who, unbelievably, such people often appeal to as part of their warped ideologies. The Ku Klux Klan, for example, consider themselves to be good Christians! (Of course, who would consider himself a "bad" Christian?).

For this reason, I can state with some assurance that the devil is an anthropologist! And it is not because anthropology is inherently evil, as some are tempted to think. The devil, however one defines that dark and malevolent spiritual entity, knows that one of the most effective ways to foster evil in the world is to manipulate cultural values. We humans are quite vulnerable in this way, easily confused into thinking we are doing right by blindly following the dictates of groupthink—the values of our subculture, ethnic group, or nation. We are vulnerable because we are wired to conform to the group from which we gain our sense of acceptance (because of the relational orientation of our human nature). That makes us "easy-pickins" if we fail to evaluate our cultural values in accordance with a moral framework that supersedes all cultural values by providing a transcultural standard against which to measure each and every value (and in my view, only Christianity can provide such a moral framework). Individualism, then, is one highly charged value in this regard, for it can deceive a person into thinking that she is expressing a moral good in an individualistic manner, when she is

---

3. Ibid.

only expressing the hatred and biases she has absorbed from group culture. "Culturalized" Christians are as vulnerable as anyone to this blind spot.

RELIGIOUS/MORALISTIC

Religion was in many ways the centerpiece of early American life, drawing to our shores those Europeans who were disaffected with the lack of religious freedom they suffered in their countries of origin. There was no separation of religion from the rest of life for the first Colonists, which is precisely why there was eventually a provision in our Constitution to separate church from state (to keep the state from encroaching upon freedom of religious expression in colonialists' lives as it had in Europe). Religion became an integral part of the culture of the day, just as it is now in many Muslim and Buddhist countries, and among tribal societies around the globe. That integration included political and economic life, and all socially-sanctioned behaviors.

Early documents such as the Mayflower Compact of 1620, the Cambridge Platform of the 1648, and the 1649 Maryland Toleration Act formally established Christianity as part-and-parcel of Colonial life (according to the latter two documents, Jews and Unitarians were liable to punishment as non-Christians and non-Trinitarians!). Some degree of religious tolerance emerged from the diversity among dozens of Christian denominational communities that immigrated to America to establish the original thirteen colonies and beyond. Although diversity would continue to increase along with westward expansion, eventually bringing non-Christian immigrants from many backgrounds, American culture would never completely loose the Christian-infused values that formed the basic fabric of early Colonial life. Today we continue our journey as a nation, uncertain where our culture begins and Christianity ends, and vise versa. We continue to have a high degree of cultural religiosity despite an obvious and growing trend toward secularization. The Christian religion is simply part of our cultural DNA.

Many believe that not only were early Americans more religious than the Europeans with which they parted ways, but that contemporary Americans continue to be more religious than their Continental cousins (the same can't be said for the nation's African forbearers, for whom religion/spirituality was central to all social and cultural life). But Elizabeth Lemons, a Tufts University Lecturer in Religion, questions the surveys upon which conclusions about America's current state of religiosity are based, arguing that research indicates only half of those Americans who report that they go to church actually do so.[4] Certainly Americans are, in general, religious—though not as uniformly religious as our European ancestors who settled this country. But some European countries are more religious than others (take Italy, for example, as compared to Denmark), and the definition of religious is a rather loose and slippery category ranging from those with nominal to fanatical commitments.

But the interesting implication of Lemons research has to do with what it reveals about the *value* we place on "being religious." This is indicated by the fact that most Americans report that they go to church, synagogue or mosque without the data to back up the claim. The discrepancy is likely due to the fact that we know religion was historically a very important part of our identity as a people, and so most of us have come to associate being religious with being good Americans—similar to the way that being a religious Jew makes one a good citizen of Israel. Religion has therefore become cognitively and culturally fused with patriotism for many Americans, a matter to be discussed later in this chapter as well as in the next. The point here is that the majority of Americans still value religious sentiment, whether or not they themselves are religious in any discernable way. This attitude is commonly seen among parents who are happy to send their children to Sunday School and Bible Camp, but don't otherwise go to church or openly practice the Christian faith.

Time was when being religious, or at least belonging to a church, was a necessary social adaptation. In my parents' generation (the early to mid-twentieth century) it was expected that each family would belong to an organized church—preferably Protestant! If someone did not, they were suspect within the community. Thus, to "get ahead" in life, it was beneficial to be on the church roles, whether or not one actually attended (the case with my family). That adaptive value is rapidly shrinking in modern life as secularism makes inroads into popular culture, and religious affiliation becomes more closely associated with a person's cultural heritage and identity than with personal conviction. Thus, to be Jewish or Catholic is often perfectly acceptable today so long as it only defines one's heritage. But to go further and profess actual convictions of faith is, in many social and work settings, now becoming maladaptive; that is, it puts one at a disadvantage relative to one's non-professing colleagues and competitors. Thus, religious faith is being driven more deeply into the private sphere where, for some segments of the population, issues of personal faith have long been cloistered from public scrutiny (think Ronald Reagan). This trend in America

---

4. Luna, "Secular Europe," http://issuu.com/tuftsdaily/docs/2011-2-16, posted February 16, 2011.

stands in opposition to many societies and cultures where people openly speak of their faith as easily as we speak of the weather. Faith has in part become such a hot-button issue in the U.S. because, as we will see below, it appears to conflict with the highly esteemed value of egalitarianism.

In modern America there also exists a vocal segment of the population that counts itself among the "religious majority," and takes pride in being recognized as such. This self-identified group of Christians often speaks of the religious convictions of the Founding Fathers (there is ongoing debate as to how many were "believing" Christians and how many nominal Deists). They famously point to the nineteenth-century French political thinker and historian Alexis de Tocqueville who, after visiting America in the 1830s, supposedly wrote these oft-quoted words in his highly-acclaimed work, *Democracy in America*:[5]

> I sought for the key to the greatness and genius of America in her harbors . . .; in her fertile fields and boundless forests; in her rich mines and vast world commerce; in her public school system and institutions of learning. I sought for it in her democratic Congress and in her matchless Constitution. Not until I went into the churches of America and heard her pulpits flame with righteousness did I understand the secret of her genius and power. America is great because America is good, and if America ever ceases to be good, America will cease to be great.

Alas, the quote has never been found among de Tocqueville's writings and is decidedly not in *Democracy in America*.[6] Yet fabrication aside, repeated use of the quote in a Christian context establishes an important link between religiosity and Americans' sense of morality. Religious people have historically been seen as good people, but not all "good people" now consider themselves religious. Religion and morality have become uneasy bedfellows in America today, and we're very busy (at least subconsciously) trying to figure out their tenuous relationship.

Many Americans who are not overtly religious fail to recognize that they are none-the-less deeply moralistic, and their sense of morality stems, in large part, from the Judeo-Christian roots of our collective culture history.[7] Although all cultures reflect moral values that roughly reflect the Ten

5. de Tocqueville, *Democracy in America*.

6. See Pitney, "The Tocqueville Fraud," http://www.tocqueville.org/pitney.htm, posted November 13, 1995.

7. Amanda Porterfield traces the historic interplay between Christianity and culture in North America, concluding that Christians have been "highly influential agents" in shaping all aspects of modern life (including its ethical values), even as modernity has in turn shaped North American Christianity. See Porterfield, "North America," 20.

Commandments, the specific value Americans place on character traits such as truthfulness, honesty, industriousness, humility, compassion, giving, and service, to name a few, are based within the biblical, Judeo-Christian tradition. That people value such traits without knowledge of their source is quite common and understandable, though it brings to mind the analogy of a fish admiring its own fins and scales without an awareness of the presence of water all about it. In *Mere Christianity*, C.S. Lewis states that "though Christianity seems at first to be all about morality . . . yet it leads you on, out of all that, into something beyond."[8] Many contemporary Americans have not only failed to go "into something beyond," they have dumped the Christianity for what is equivalent to "mere morality." Today a unique form of cultural morality (i.e., non-religious) has been birthed in America. It is a secular morality that fervently attempts to divorce itself from its Judaeo-Christian roots—and seems to be succeeding quite well.

The morality that many Americans end up espousing is a pick-and-choose affair. A sizeable segment of Christianity and other established religions in the U.S., buffeted by wave after wave of secular humanism and scientific rationalism, are slowly morphing into one of two forms: secularized morality without reference to any spiritual tradition, or an ill-defined, customized spirituality. In the first case, morality is embraced as a standalone guide to life ("We are good people without God"). In the second, individualism and our religious culture history have combined into a grab-bag of personalized spirituality—much like one collects a unique wardrobe to "express oneself." Many spiritually-minded people have outright rejected the Christian notion of God's self-revelation in Christ for a self-determined spirituality wherein spiritual reality is seen as an entirely relative matter.

In both instances, the cultural value placed on individual choice is elevated to a level higher than either collective belief or religious revelation. These contemporary manifestations of morality/spirituality provide an adaptive advantage that makes them attractive to anyone who wishes to advance within contemporary society; for they avoid the unpopularity of narrowly identifying with traditional Christian faith, while garnering social approval for embracing morals of some sort. Furthermore, the individualistic underpinnings of both positions make them feel quite natural to Americans, who have become accustomed to satisfying individual tastes in everything from food to family composition. ("My Significant Other wants skim milk with his double-shot hazelnut latte!")

---

8. Lewis, *Mere Christianity*, 132.

EGALITARIANISM

The fact that individualized spirituality has become normative in America today, despite a steady trend toward secularism, involves issues beyond our cultural identification with a religious past. It incorporates other American values, foremost among them egalitarianism. And although egalitarian concepts in America derive from a multitude of sources—Judaeo-Christian, Greek and Reformation democratic principles, and anti-aristocratic sentiment from feudal Europe—it has become a "stand-alone" value. Egalitarianism is canonized in the collective American psyche through one single phrase in the Declaration of Independence: "all men are created equal." The right to equality is such a powerful cultural value among Americans that we have developed a sixth sense for detecting an air of superiority or arrogance in the speech, mannerisms, and attitudes of one another. We can "sniff out" a snob a mile away, or so we think (different regional accents are easily misconstrued as arrogance, especially Northern accents in the South).

Yet egalitarianism is a value that conflicts with other American values, and thus remains unfulfilled except as a national ideal. Even Thomas Jefferson, who first penned the inspirational phrase, "all men were created equal," owned hundreds of slaves during his lifetime and fathered children with at least one of them, Sally Hemings. It is hard to imagine that he was not conflicted over the issue of proclaiming one truth while living another. And that conflict remains today as Americans try to hold on to the ideal of equality while competing in political, economic, and social institutions that reward those who employ purely individualistic means to put themselves in front of others. Fallen human nature intrudes, allowing us to look down on those we compete against. So although we give lip-service to the inherent equality of all people, we do a poor job of showing it in the way we deal with continuing discrimination of all sorts: racial, ethnic, religious, age and disability-related, to name a few.

To fully embrace an egalitarian ideal is not really adaptive in modern-day America, if ever it were. For we live in a fiercely competitive society in which it is seemingly necessary to push others down in order to "climb the ladder of success." Our kids are taught early on to excel in school and exams—to set themselves apart from the crowd in order to get into exclusive universities and, thus, fast-track their way to "success." We regal them with the idea that anyone in America can become President—that a person can become anything he or she wants simply by setting a goal and diligently pursuing it. However, when someone fails to reach the goal we told them was theirs for the taking, it can lead to embitterment (blaming others) or thinking a personal defect was responsible for coming up short.

We fail to reveal that the cards are firmly stacked against those who grow up without access to wealth, education, and social networks that confer privilege—so-called "social capital." The people who refuse to acknowledge the existence of a stacked deck are inevitably those who have grown up enjoying the perks and support systems of the well-to-do. A minority child raised by a single mom in the slums of Chicago has virtually no chance of "succeeding" when compared to a child born into the privileged life of a suburban, upper-income, Anglo family. Yet we continue to broadcast the notion that by sheer will-power each individual can "pull himself up by his own bootstraps." The disadvantaged in America often have no bootstraps and many are just plain barefoot by comparison. Those of us who inherited the advantages of good homes, schools, and preferential social categories of race, religion, and even looks have little idea how different life would be if we had to make a go of things without that inheritance. It is, in the end, little more than arrogance or naivety to think that we succeed in life on our own. No one does. We succeed only by standing on the shoulders of a vast array of people, past and present—which is the way it is meant to be.

A very important side issue is that our definition of success needs some serious revamping—a topic to be touched on later.

HARD WORK AND PROGRESS

Americans have been hard-working and progress-oriented since first hacking out a foothold in the New England wilderness. We value the idea of hard work so much that one of the worst of insults in America is to call another person lazy. The matter, however, is a relative one. Compared to Europeans (with the exception of the highly-industrious Germans) we do put in more hours, get less vacation time, and are expected to be impressively productive. But if we evaluate our work ethic to that of the Japanese, we can look somewhat slovenly by comparison. Japanese workers are expected to give virtually everything to their jobs, devoting themselves to their work and places of employment ahead of all other commitments, family included.

Still, the important issue is the *value* Americans place on hard-work, because there is no universally-applicable standard by which we can accurately measure just how hard-working we actually are, given differences in technologies and workloads across countries and cultures. For example, how would we compare the work of a Detroit autoworker to a barefoot Nepali rice farmer who uses a wooden plow and oxen to till his fields—a labor-intensive effort that requires planting and thinning by hand, building and repairing canals for water, collecting fodder to feed and maintain oxen, and much more?

Closely related to the value we place on hard work is the high value we place on achieving our goals. Americans are groomed to progress toward tangible results. We differ from many other cultures in this way, especially traditional cultures that value *the process* and not just the product. In such societies, it is expected that socializing takes place during work, sometimes involving group singing and meal-sharing to make a communal task go easier. African slaves brought this collective work focus to America and employed it in the notorious chain gangs that helped establish our country's rail system in the nineteenth century. Classic songs like "Working on a Chain Gang" came from that shameful period. The goal of those slaves and prisoners was, first and foremost, to survive the brutal conditions under which they lived and worked, which a communal approach helped facilitate; whereas chain gang "bosses" had a certain amount of rail to lay each day, and tolerated a collective approach to work so long as the work got done. Although such work gangs are forever gone from the U.S. landscape, they live on in many parts of the world in forms such as child labor factories in developing countries.

"Just get the job done" is an oft-repeated refrain in the American workplace. We are outcome-oriented people and do not tolerate well those who don't "pull their weight." In order to get the job done we value things like punctuality, efficiency, and the ability to creatively "problem solve," and we tend to reward directness, risk-taking, and even aggressiveness. We've employed the social and behavioral sciences to analyze workers and the workplace in order to identify and fix anything that inhibits progress. Fast-food restaurants and call-in centers time their employees' interactions with clients, pushed by "efficiency experts" whose sole goal is to streamline operations and maximize production and profits. The system can easily become impersonal for both workers and clients.

Although some point to the "Protestant work ethic" as a source of being hard-working and success-driven, there are at least two other factors to be included in the discussion that relate directly to one another. One is the mechanized view of the universe that is part of our culture history stemming from the world-changing contributions of Copernicus, Galileo, and Newton during Europe's Renaissance and Enlightenment periods. The other is America's induction into the Industrial Revolution in the late eighteenth and nineteenth centuries, which created a seismic culture shift that mechanized industry in the U.S. and created mass production. In many instances that shift resulted in workers functioning as nameless cogs on impersonal assembly lines. Once highly productive mechanized industry became coupled with capitalist economics, the inevitable goal of industry was to maximize production and offer remunerative rewards for hard-work and entrepreneurialism. Intense competition developed between employees and among companies to wring the most out of workers and achieve maximum profits. Our collective culture has never been the same.

The ability to be highly competitive, success-driven, and even aggressive is certainly adaptive in today's workplace where those who produce more are rewarded commensurately for their efforts. Sometimes workers are even goaded into self-competition, inferred in the motto "Be the best you can be." Many job salaries are now tied directly to output, with commissions, bonuses, and incentives used to maximize both worker output and overall profits. Two professions in which this trend is growing exponentially are coaching and stock trading. The former profession now pays successful college coaches (i.e., those whose teams regularly win) massive salaries that can amount to many millions per year. Though he coached well before salaries ballooned at the college and professional levels, the long-time Green Bay Packers coach Vince Lombardi reflected the country's view of both working hard and reaching the apex of one's professional goals in his poignant statement, "[The] Dictionary is the only place that success comes before work. Hard work is the price we must pay for success. I think you can accomplish anything if you're willing to pay the price."[9] He was known to have been brutally demanding of his players, but won five NFL championships that included victories in the first two Super Bowls. He died of cancer at age 57, but is considered a bonafide "American success story."

What ever happened to the idea that sports has a higher calling that entails mentoring young men and women so they can become well-adjusted citizens? What about learning the invaluable life-lesson of graciously accepting defeat—more valuable than winning by far? Christians must always ask if the means justifies the ends. Certainly winning at all costs is unbiblical, but so is our cultural concept of success—entangled as it is in the pursuit of wealth, power, and status. The hard work it takes to get there is not necessarily virtuous. The current American cultural concept of success is a far cry from the biblical concept of success, in which faithfulness to God is the emphasis. And God seems to employ a sliding scale to determine that.[10]

Many success-driven behaviors are maladaptive at the individual level. Stress, high-blood pressure, heart disease, depression and sleeplessness are rampant in America today, often because our workplace values are so

---

9. Lombardi, ThinkExist, http://thinkexist.com/quotation/dictionary_is_the_only_place_that_success_comes/15116.html; accessed November 6, 2013.

10. See Vanderzalm, *Finding Strength*, 175; Rotholz, *Chronic Fatigue Syndrome*, 96–97.

terribly askew. Our seemingly innocuous goals to succeed at our jobs and careers often drive us "rat race" style into dangerous spiritual and emotional bankruptcy. In interviews with the elderly asked to evaluate their lives, inevitably they express regret at having been so worried about jobs and money, material things, and the opinions of others—public image issues. Instead, these people whose futures promise only decline and death emphasize that if they had the chance to live their lives again, they would put much more time and energy into loving and valuing people, and taking time to "smell the roses" by celebrating life and family. As we all know, men are especially prone to blind devotion to vocation at the expense of family life, too often missing the precious and formative years when their children are growing. But as women fill more and more professional positions within the workplace—attempting to "have it all"—they are now also falling prey to societal norms that require the sacrifice of a traditional, wholesome family life in order to "succeed" professionally.

There is, of course, intrinsic value in hard work. It is a necessary part of our calling in this world in which we have been delegated to eat "by the sweat of our brow." But there is wisdom in the advice of King Solomon, "Do not wear yourself out to get rich; have the wisdom to show restraint" (Prov 23:4). Working hard and succeeding at one's vocation only has meaning within the context of a larger set of values that put kingdom matters first (Matt 6:31–33). It is up to each believer to keep his or her priorities in order, otherwise the culture will happily dictate them.

PATRIOTISM

Without wishing to sound unpatriotic, it must be said that from a cultural perspective, patriotism is little more than an extended version of tribalism; for patriots (a.k.a., compatriots) comprise a geopolitical tribe into which members are either born or immigrate. It involves fervent devotion to a way of life associated with a nation-state whose boundaries often have been arbitrarily drawn through past circumstances with spurious connections to the people who currently live within them. The empires that ruled various regions of the world have, for the most part, drawn national boundaries that serve the rulers' interests. Demarcating borders to secure and enrich empirical interests are most famously exhibited by the empires of Rome, Persia, China and Great Britain. Often ethnically related groups became separated into countries with vastly differing cultures and politics. The Kurds are a good example, today spread between four countries in the Middle East: Iran, Iraq, Syria, and Turkey. Such cultural groups give us perspective on the different emphases any particular people group places on patriotism as a value. For an ethnic Chinese, patriotism is a cultural value of almost sacred dimensions, easily discernable in public venues such as Olympic competitions. But their fellow countrymen, the Tibetans, share no such emotional attachments to the nation-at-large by virtue of the oppressive history they have endured under Chinese rule.

One must admit that patriotism is a bit of an odd sentiment. It is greatly admired within one's own country, but then we find it hard to extend a similar appreciation to citizens of other countries—especially those with whom we don't get along. Venezuelans or Iranians who hold their countries and values in the same high regard as we Americans do are generally thought to have fallen prey to misguided fanatical devotion that has been whipped to fever pitch by oppressive and manipulative leaders—a charge that is no doubt true for many citizens in a country like North Korea. Yet we Americans even find it hard to understand how the British can feel so patriotic toward their royal family who, to our way of thinking, take a lot out of the imperial coffers without doing much to help the average bloke on the street. We love patriotism . . . when it stays within the country.

Americans have a very high regard for patriotism as a home-grown value despite the fact that not every ethnic group shares equally in the value associated with it. Disenfranchised peoples such as Native Americans tend to be much less patriotic than Anglo-Americans—though Native Americans and other minorities in the U.S. have at times been as patriotic as anyone, paying the ultimate price of sacrificing their lives in the wars we have fought. It is a value we officially inculcate through public oaths and ceremonies, but not always successfully. Those who fail to show the kind of respect that norms dictate, such as thrusting a fist into the air instead of placing one's hand over the heart during the Pledge of Allegiance (as happened during the 1968 Mexico City Summer Olympics), are through time subtly shamed into compliance by the larger society. Being unpatriotic is not illegal, but then you don't hear many people publicly claiming to be so because of the unappealing stigma attached to it.

One reason for compliance is that patriotism is very highly adaptive within one's own country. It helps one forward with his or her personal goals to succeed within society. That is because every society needs the devotion of individuals to achieve its collective goals, which is exactly how it became a core cultural value early on in American history. The country needed devoted patriots to counter the British overlords and free itself from exploitative circumstances that entailed, among other things, taxation without representation (similar legitimate grievances are behind many revolutions around the world today and down through history).

Research has confirmed what common sense already indicated, that societies with environmental and/or historical threats—think "howling wilderness" and British rule—develop the strongest cultural norms with the least tolerance for deviation from group behavior.[11] In other words, those from societies under the most stress bind closer together through a greater unified devotion to well-defined norms. Thus did patriotism become a necessary and valued part of the early American cultural landscape. Since that time one can trace its periodic resurgence through our history of wars and natural disasters (as with WW II, 9-11, and Hurricane Katrina). Today's national stressors—from economics to domestic terrorism to foreign wars—keep patriotic sentiment high on the list of American cultural values.

Yet patriotism produces an inherent conflict for religious people in America, unless they are Christians who associate their faith so closely with their country that the two are regarded as indistinguishable (no other faith could ever do that in America). But all religious adherents—devout Christians in particular—must sooner or later ask themselves where their devotion to country might end should it ever conflict with their faith. Where might it conflict even now? Do drone strikes on innocent civilians raise any red flags? Perhaps we should all pray it will never become a major issue as it has for many Christians in other circumstances over the centuries, Dietrich Bonhoeffer and his life-ending anti-Nazi stand notable among them. But Muslims in America have already had to face the issue when the U.S. invaded the "Muslim nations" of Iraq and Afghanistan. Their perspectives can give us great insight into the issue.

To understand their plight, we should ask ourselves what we would do as Christians in the Iranian military (there are, incredibly, reports of a growing number of such believers)[12]—were we ordered to attack Israel or U.S. naval vessels in the Persian Gulf. Does patriotism entail Christian soldiers obeying an order to attack other Christians, as British troops were ordered to do in North Ireland and the Falkland Islands? To bring it closer to home, should a Christian soldier drop bombs on populations among whom it is known that innocent Christians would be killed, as they most certainly were in Iraq during the U.S. invasion in 2003? We cannot avoid the question—Where does patriotism end and faith begin?—though the answers may not be neat and tidy ones.

11. Gelfand et al., "Differences," 1100–1104.

12. *Mohabat News*, "Trend towards Christianity," http://mohabatnews.com/index.php?option=com_content&view=article&id=4439:trend-towards-christianity-among-iranian-armed-forces-on-rise&catid=36:iranian-christians&Itemid=279, accessed October 18, 2014.

If pushed hard enough, most believers will admit that no one can be fully devoted to Christ and also unwaveringly patriotic—no matter the country with which their affections lie. Although we are enculturated not to discuss such touchy matters, deep inside most Christians know that Christ's kingdom is "not of this world" (John 18:36, KJV) and can never be closely aligned with any nation on earth. It is easier to see the disparity of values within other countries than it is within our own. Yet the clarion call of the gospel is to be God's loving expression to the *entire* world, North Koreans included! We are to be ambassadors of a kingdom that knows no boundaries, emissaries of a gospel without borders.

So what does it mean, then, when we pledge allegiance to our country using an oath first written in 1892 by Francis Bellamy—without the phrase "under God"—a socialist Baptist minister who accompanied the pledge with a Nazi-like salute toward the flag?[13] I've never heard an official explanation of what the pledge actually means. We are in large part left to impute our own meaning, hopefully resolving the matter before a serious conflict arises, however miniscule it may be in comparison to Bonhoeffer and so many others like him. Ultimately, each of us must decide what it means to "render to Caesar the things that are Caesar's, and to God the things that are God's" (Matt 22:21, ASB). The only real position that I can say is definitely wrong for Christians is an unexamined one.

Scripture, of course, instructs us Christ-followers to be good citizens whatever our country may be (Rom 13:1–2; Titus 3:1). And we are to be identified as his disciples within our countries by the love we show one another, and all persons by extension (John 13:35). Is this the same love and devotion that patriotism calls us to exhibit? Of course not. Within American culture, love is a term that we now readily apply to objects and situations that are bazaar and mundane ("I love my Toyota!"). We cannot really love objects or even countries. We can only really love God and one another, whether those others are patriots or dissidents, Americans or Cubans. We can only fully devote ourselves to God and one another, whether those others are in uniform or wearing dreadlocks, sitting in the Oval Office or sleeping off a drunken binge on a park bench.

We can be proud of our culture and way of life and devoted to those we love around us, but that kind of commitment is never meant to rival the commitment we have to that other king and kingdom. Our dominant culture will never tell us there is a vast difference between the two, for it is not in the interest of a given sociopolitical structure to do so. The country

---

13. Hallowell, "Did You Know?" http://www.theblaze.com/stories/2013/07/04/one-nation-under-god-the-odd-complex-and-socialist-history-behind-the-pledge-of-allegiance, created July 4, 2013.

needs our devotion to remain functional and maintain whatever position of dominance it may have gained in the world. The real patriot is the one who knows he or she is a sojourner called to genuinely love everyone along the path toward that "better country" (Heb 11:13–16), and lets nothing usurp that love and become a distraction along the sacred journey. We are to be good citizens on earth for the sake of our citizenship in God's kingdom (Eccl 8:2; 1 Cor 10:31; 1 Pet 2:12). We are not called to give our deepest affections to any lesser, temporal cause (1 John 2:15–17). At least that's what I read in my Bible.

If this issue has stirred you up as a reader, bringing to mind slogans such as "America—Love It Or Leave It" (a favorite from my youthful hippie days), then I've succeeded in showing that patriotism is indeed a core cultural value, and one that has a lot of power to trigger emotions. I hope it will help the reader to grasp the effect of culture within each of our lives, and prompt us to ask both how we came to embrace such values and whether or not they should align with those we find in scripture.

HUMANS OVER NATURE

Many Eastern worldviews are inclined toward a harmonizing view of man and nature, thereby seeking to facilitate harmony within self and society. Japanese gardens are designed with this theme in mind, and represent the meticulous attempt to create synchronization between culture and nature. Yet many traditional cultures go well beyond the harmonized view of human-nature relations, such as the native peoples of the Bajo Urubamba River in eastern Peru, who envision their kinship structure extending out into the tropical forests in which they live.[14] For them, the world of nature is engulfed in the world of culture, and vise versa. The Aborigines of Australia also have traditional views wherein the natural environment is inseparable from their sense of identity, both past and present. Specific geologic formations and animals are associated with clan descendents and creation figures in a mystically-imbued world where humankind and nature are utterly interdependent in the overall scheme of life. A viable environmental ethic naturally issues from their worldview.

Many other hunter-gatherer groups on different continents around the world also view their environments in very personal terms, as subject to subject. Anthropologist Nurit Bird-David describes the shared conception that human-nature relations are understood by such groups in terms of a child's relationship to a caring adult. The "forest-seen-as-parent" metaphor

14. Gow, "Land, People, and Paper," 43–62.

carries with it the understanding that the forest will provide unconditionally for the needs of those who live within it. As such, many hunter-gatherers are said to have "confidence" toward their local environment, relating to it in personal, "subjective" terms.[15] Their perspective is one which also extends the social relations of their intimate, band-level society to the forests in which they subsist.

By contrast, Westerners endorse the viewpoint that culture and nature are distinctly separate entities, with humans holding the upper hand as rulers over the natural world. It is an endowment that is thought to derive from the biblical mandate given in Genesis, wherein humans were purportedly given "dominion" over nature. However, that interpretation is itself derived from our Greek-inherited dualistic thinking and fails to take adequate account of the partnership that both humans and nature share in God's larger design. The latter is a position that coincides with today's models of sustainable ecology and will be more fully dealt with later.

As mentioned previously, we have inherited a culture history in which wild nature was equated with danger and uncertainty—the "howling wilderness" of Pilgrim days—fostering the view that the sooner nature is domesticated the better. For those intrepid early settlers and explorers, and for the industrialists and wild West pioneers to follow, it was convenient to take the position that nature was meant to be subject to humanity and to be used as needed to further the goals of human civilization. At the time this ethic was being solidified into a fundamental American cultural value, natural resources seemed so plentiful as to be boundless. As mentioned previously, that view began to change in the nineteenth century when forests started shrinking, water sources started drying up or becoming polluted, and available land became scarcer; but the "nature-is-here-for-our-betterment" ethic persisted. And today many Americans still believe that we have a divine mandate to "lord it over nature." Coupled with the unredeemed side of human nature that tends toward self-aggrandizement, the man-over-nature ethic has led to deleterious consequences for the natural world. There is, fortunately, change in the wind, so to speak, as Hurricane Sandy and other unusual natural phenomena are convincing more of us that global warming is a real threat that, sooner or later, will negatively affect each of us personally unless appropriate action is taken.

The endeavors of science and technology, activities at which Americans greatly excel, both rely on controlling nature. Whether splicing genes, using stem cells for disease eradication, or producing the latest wireless devices, today's scientists and engineers are simply following our forebearers'

---

15. Bird-David, "Tribal Metaphorization," 112–25.

footsteps by attempting to domesticate the natural world. The sophistication with which we approach and apply nature's designs has changed dramatically (e.g., reproductive genetics), but we are still doing the same thing those Pilgrims did when they cleared the forests to heat their homes and plant their crops. And, in general, the same ethic lies behind our endeavors as did theirs; for we believe that humans are superior to and in control of the natural world, and should manipulate and utilize it to further our civilization and its goals. Few seem concerned at this point with the repercussions of "monkeying" with nature, as we now do through genetic research that has, incredibly, advanced to the point where scientists now feel they are able to recreate extinct species of animals through genetic engineering.[16] One wonders if there is not a cautionary lesson for us in the environmental devastation that followed industrialization in America.

The fact is that we are somewhat addicted to our own technological advancements and the practical applications of math and physics that got us to this point. We are a formulaic people who deeply value the knowledge systems that have produced so many modern marvels in the fields of science, medicine, and technology. We got his way through a Western heritage that distinguished itself through its mechanistic view of the world. Nature was often described as a machine, as was the human body, and treated accordingly. Modern technology, especially computers with their binary functions, only further the misconception that all of life is a machine to be driven wherever we fancy going. We only need to punch in the correct formula and, *voilá*, the machine bears us forward toward our desired destination.

If the formulas produce the desired results, we generally consider them ethical by virtue of their effectiveness. We're prone to think that our man-over-nature endowment legitimizes the formulations we use—once again, the means justifying the ends. There are few voices cautioning that we ought to proceed slowly so we can keep our science and its formulations humane—which certainly has not been the case with many military weapons (e.g., landmines, Sarin gas), and likely is not the case with genetically-modified foods (a "breakthrough" that threatens to create numerous irreversible changes in nature as it enriches a few at what appears to be the expense of the poor agrarian masses around the world).

Nature has given us many wonderful formulations of its own. The Amazonian forests are now among the premiere sites of modern scientific exploration because of the vast wealth of medicinal plants and animals found there. Native peoples have taught themselves over millennia which plants and animals have healing properties and which toxins can be harnessed for

---

16. Zimmer, "Bringing Them Back," 28–41.

utilitarian purposes. There is a virtual gold rush of pharmaceutical entrepreneurs from the developed world, Americans at the forefront, laboring to "discover" these native resources and create lucrative wonder drugs to treat modern ailments such as hypertension and heart disease. However, in the past it has not been possible to patent naturally occurring substances in their original state (a situation that is, incredulously, now being jeopardized), leading pharmaceutical companies to genetically alter plants to make them patentable and thus profitable. So we busily apply our formulas and technologies to alter natural substances in order to produce novel chemical formulations—modifying nature for our profit, driven by the same man-over-nature paradigm. But we are learning that altering nature's own formulas at the molecular level can create unforeseen consequences. The human body can rebel, producing life-threatening allergic reactions to the very drugs meant to restore health. Allergies and sensitivities to the thousands of human engineered chemicals to which we currently expose ourselves and our children are reaching epidemic proportions in the U.S.[17]

Yet because we are so intent on controlling every aspect of nature, harvesting it for our use and "advancement," we have also become a hyper health and hygiene conscious people. No one can argue that Americans are living longer as a result of the amazing array of advancements over the past century, perhaps foremost among them the lifesaving discovery of antibiotics in 1928 (another naturally-occurring formulation). But, once again, we are now discovering that nature's grand designs—of which antibiotics are but one—exist in wondrous configurations even in the human gut, where "microbiomes" consisting of many thousands of microbes interact in critical ways we know very little about.[18] Overuse of antibiotics has created a number of problems itself, from stripping the human body of the probiotics necessary for intestinal health, to strengthening disease-causing microbes that persistently modify themselves as an adaptation to the drugs we use to treat them.

Today Americans have a tendency to see germs everywhere, and like the wild animals that seemed so threatening to our Pilgrim ancestors, we feel a compelling need to eradicate them. Germ phobias haunt many in our country. So we are encouraged to spray, wipe, and continually disinfect every surface we touch, fearful of falling prey to unseen malevolent microcreatures. They *are* out there, noxious microbes of every sort waiting for an

---

17. According to environmental health expert and researcher Claudia Miller, M.D., twenty-two percent of Americans with a chronic health issue also suffer from some degree of chemical sensitivity disorder, while Danish research shows that twenty-seven percent of the general Danish population has a noticeable degree of chemical intolerance. See Neimark, "Allergic to Life," 44–51.

18. Conniff, "The Body Eclectic," 40–47.

unassuming host within which to prolong their own lives and agendas. Ironically, hospitals are one of the worst places to catch the nastiest of these critters, especially the flesh-eating, antibiotic-resistant "superbugs." Yet our best hope is to learn to work with, rather than against, every dimension of nature.

This ideology-altering strategy, which requires a reformulation of the man-over-nature paradigm, is now informing us that maybe "germs" too have an important place in God's overall scheme of life, and constantly warring against them can be both futile and self-defeating.[19] Research underway in Scandinavia and Russia indicates that children exposed to fewer germs while still infants end up with weaker immune systems that are more likely to succumb to serious allergies and life-threatening autoimmune diseases.[20] Meanwhile, mounting research within the U.S. strongly indicates that, "The absence of species from the human biome [parasitic helminths "worms," in particular] leaves the immune system in a hypersensitive state that, when combined with environmental triggers and genetic predisposition, leads to allergic and autoimmune disease."[21]

In our headlong efforts to conquer nature, we may, ironically, only be defeating ourselves. Surely nature is not something "out there" to be ignorantly manipulated for our pleasure and material progress, but rather a realm within which we are interactive and interdependent participants under God's providential decree. Even the microbiomes in our guts, it turns out, are incomprehensibly complex "ecosystems" in their own right, existing in a perpetuate state of adaptive flux.[22] In part IV we will highlight the biblical principle that we are meant to be partners with—not lords over—nature in all of its forms, however inglorious we may currently consider them to be.

---

19. Ibid., 47.
20. Curry, "Secret Life," 40–45.
21. Parker and Ollerton, "Evolutionary Biology," 90.
22. See Yong, "No 'Healthy' Microbiome," http://www.nytimes.com/2014/11/02/opinion/sunday/there-is-no-healthy-microbiome.html?ref=opinion&_r=0, posted November 1, 2014.

6

Post-Industrial Cultural Influences

All progress is based upon the universal innate desire on the part of every organism to live beyond its income.

—Samuel Butler

Although the values elaborated in this chapter build upon those in chapter 5, they are distinct from those early American values in that they either arose from or flourished after the Industrial Revolution. Certainly these values existed in some nascent form during our early culture history—some more than others—and this is especially so with the category of logic and reason. But after the Industrial Revolution all of the values listed below came into a degree of fullness that otherwise would not have occurred, resulting in the forms we recognize today. The six cultural values below, along with the early American values, have strengthened and evolved over time into the unique constellation we call American culture today. In some cases, the values in this chapter serve as counterpoints to one another. For example, our penchant for fun and entertainment is, by and large, an adaptive release value for our ethic of hard work and progress. Likewise, our materialistic bent is counterbalanced by the high value we place on benevolent giving. All of the values bleed into one another, and each more accurately represents a sphere of behavior rather than a concrete entity. Keeping in mind the importance of their dynamic inter-relatedness, it is none-the-less beneficial to analyze each value as a separate category in order to better understand the whole.

MATERIALISM

Materialism has been wittily described as "buying things we don't need with money we don't have to impress people we don't like."[1] Americans do seem to love the things money can buy. And it is not hard to see how we come about it, given the fact that one of our culture's measures of success—wealth—is enjoyed and displayed by way of the material effects it can procure. We are under cultural constraints *not* to talk openly about our wealth for reasons that, as far as I can understand, have to do with either fear of being taken advantage of or fear of being seen as elitist (thereby conflicting with the egalitarian value we hold so high). But we are permitted to indirectly display our wealth via the goods and services it can provide. We are, in fact, encouraged to do so. And we learn early on how to judge another person's wealth through the size of his house, year and type of car(s) he drives, social standing of his associates, and which schools his kids attend. "Stuff" announces our income bracket like a bullhorn, and has much to do with Americans' sense of self-identity and self-importance. Material possessions are very much our caste system—the means by which we stratify ourselves and in large part determine one another's social standing and, thus, personal worth to society.

But there seems to be an inverse relationship between our material wealth and our happiness because, at the end of the day, the time and money we expend acquiring things always comes at the expense of something else—investments in relationships, volunteerism, humanitarian giving, spirituality, or just quiet refection. Although this information is no secret, being consciously associated with our Judaeo-Christian sense of ethics, we Americans have somehow managed to ignore it. We have conveniently disregarded the Bible's widely-heralded teaching that we are to orient our lives toward acquiring treasures that outlast this passing world (Matt. 6:19–20), and find our true fulfillment in the process.

Happiness is not biblical, as that concept is understood culturally in America today. Joy, peace, and right relationship with God and others—the biblical ideal of *shalom*—are the defining characteristics of biblical "happiness." And that ideal is repeatedly set against the excessive build up of wealth and possessions our culture equates with being successful and, thus, happy. "Happiness," as Presbyterian minister Tim Keller said, "can always and only be found by seeking something other than happiness [the kingdom of God].

---

1. Morley, "America Entangled," http://www.charismamag.com/life/men/16655-materialism-comes-with-a-dark-side, accessed March 31, 2013.

Aim at heaven," declares Keller, "and you get earth thrown in. Aim at earth, you get neither."[2]

So how did our country get so materialistic? How did the "American Dream" become little more than a laundry list of possessions and a bucket-list of self-gratifying desires? The answer is rooted in a number of factors going back centuries; perhaps too many factors to list. Alexis de Tocqueville was struck by our materialistic obsession during his visit here in the 1830s, deducing the following: "I know of no country, indeed, where the love of money has taken stronger hold on the affections of men."[3] Yet the Industrial Revolution was the marquee event that facilitated every materialistic impulse that lay beneath the surface of our collective culture history. And ever since that water-shed event we have been getting progressively more materialistic as a nation, evidenced by the growing number of terms we now have for and associate with wealth. De Tocqueville would likely be stunned to see how "the love of money" has become something of a national obsession since his statement nearly two centuries ago.

Our yearning for things has proliferated because it is now firmly hitched to our consumption-driven economy and its strategies to maximize growth, thus enlivening a culture of increased and perpetual acquisition. (Perspective can be gained by contrasting our system and its values with non-market driven strategies such as Bhutan's more human-oriented economics based upon that country's intriguing "Gross National Happiness" index).[4] Some religious proponents blame our materialistic aspirations on secularism and an overall direction of moral decline. But that theme is as old as the country, and the church is complicit in the practice. Regardless its origins and means of perpetuation, we now measure the country's well-being almost entirely by way of economic growth indicators, with the stock market viewed as a national pulse that we must anxiously monitor all hours of the day, ER style. The media plays along, telling us that the country is courting disaster if areas such as new home construction and new car sales don't continually show a steady increase, as if the proposition of unlimited growth was actually possible in a world of dwindling resources.

The message we are getting is clear: The only way to move in the direction of the desired steady increase is to sell more and more goods and

---

2. Keller, "Grand Demythologizer." The second part of Keller's statement, "Aim at heaven . . . you get neither," is originally attributed to C.S. Lewis in *The Joyful Christian*, 138.

3. de Tocqueville, "Social Condition," para. 17, http://xroads.virginia.edu/~Hyper/detoc/1_cho3.htm, accessed November 1, 2014.

4. CBS & GNH Research, http://www.gross nationalhappiness.com/, accessed November 6, 2013.

services both at home and abroad. Never mind if we really need those goods and services (remember Paul's quaint words to Timothy about being content with a simple meal and enough clothes to wear?—1 Tim. 6:8). We are constantly indoctrinated with the idea that what's good for the economy is good for the nation. In the process, spending has unfortunately now become irreversibly entangled with patriotism. And Christmas, when we count on sales to soar, has become the most patriotic day of all (the Christmas sales season has now been stretched from before Thanksgiving to well past New Year's Day). The writer Edward Abby, who loved the untrammeled places of the American West, captured the essence of the pathology afflicting our national psyche with his brief and insightful quip, "Growth for the sake of growth is the ideology of the cancer cell."[5]

To perpetuate the deception of a compulsory need for growth, we Americans subject ourselves to a continuous, demeaning bombardment of advertising that often uses the subliminal to instill in us the unmistakable message that it is always good to buy and consume more.[6] We have perfected a consumer mentality that we unquestioningly pass on to our children, who blindly but happily follow suit. (It is heartening that some younger adults are now resisting the indoctrination, evidenced in the annual and increasingly popular "Buy Nothing Day" held on Black Friday in the U.S.) Meanwhile, the masses continue their consumerist mantras: "You deserve a break today;" "You deserve only the very best;" "You work hard, so treat yourself to . . ." At some point resistance fatigue sets in and even disciplinarians can begin to believe the self-indulgent rhetoric.

Feeling ourselves somehow privileged (a cultural value to be discussed below), we don't think it odd that at just 5 percent of the world's population we greedily consume one-quarter of the world's energy output through producing and consuming all our goodies. That's over three hundred times as much as a person consumes from a developing country such as Tanzania. Meanwhile, nearly half of the food we produce in this country is either thrown out or spoils. A planet with finite resources simply cannot support economies such as ours that are based on unbridled growth. (We have now welcomed to our swelling ranks the industrializing and heavily populated countries of India and China, determined to get their own sizable piece of the imaginary pie.) Unfortunately, rampant materialism is something of a

---

5. Abbey, *Journey Home*, 189.

6. The manufacturers of sugary children's cereals have been accused of preying upon kids riding in shopping carts by purposely drawing the eyes of the cartoon characters on cereal boxes to look slightly downward so their tantalizing gaze is not directed at the parent (adult cereal figures tend to look straight out), but at the more vulnerable kids who are yet to learn the dangers of too many sweets. See Tal et al., "Eyes in Aisles."

soulless blight that seems to be infecting the whole world, and the distress is obvious in our rapidly warming planet.

PRIVILEGE AND SUPERIORITY

As previously mentioned, many Americans feel themselves entitled to massively high levels of consumption. After all, we have progressed through our own diligence, hard work, technological advancements, and democratic principles. "Supersize me; I earned it," is the all too prevailing sentiment. And why shouldn't affluence be the reward for our notable accomplishments? Aren't the Tanzanians so far behind because they simply aren't as clever and industrious as we? (Some think there merit to the racist theory that peoples from cold environments have been forced to advance more socially and technologically as a necessary adaptation, whereas the climate of warm-weather peoples has promoted laziness and underdevelopment.) Is there anything wrong with taking pride in the mighty industrialized nation we have become—the "greatest nation on earth"?

Only perhaps that pride comes before a fall, and many a prideful empire past now lies in desolate ruins. The fact that many Americans think moderation shouldn't apply to them is somehow shameful, but many find it hard to admit—like an alcoholic who refuses to face his addiction. A large percentage of Americans have apparently been convinced that our modern-day Manifest Destiny is to dominate the global political and economic structures and skillfully engineer them for our national benefit. There is not only a spirit of entitlement and arrogance behind such an aberrant economic ideology, but also pure and simple greed. We've missed the important distinction between the biblical notion of prosperity, which comes from God and always entails an obligation of generosity toward the less fortunate (Cor 9:11), and the cultural goal of an overabundance slated for self-consumption. The culture tells us more is always better and we should "grab all the gusto" we can get. Its strident voice is hard to resist for those with no higher moral ideology to frame the issue.

Those who feel privileged and superior tend to incorporate whatever is at hand to support their worldview. American political leaders have done this with the words of Jesus from Matthew 5:14, applying them to the United States and its role in the world. Jesus called his followers to be the "light of the world" and a "city on a hill [that] cannot be hidden." The fact that politicians would portray America as a "shining city on a hill" that stands as a beacon of hope and inspiration for the rest of the world reeks of hubris at a number of levels, even as it denigrates the role of the church by equating it with the aspirations of a single nation. Indeed, this country offers unheard of opportunities when compared to many underdeveloped nations around the world, but we are not that light offering *true* hope and inspiration. If we're honest, at best we can only faintly reflect it through selfless concern for others both within and beyond our borders.

Some Americans may find this rendering hard to swallow, but we simply are not a special people in God's sight. A haughty perspective always makes it appear as though everyone and everything evolves around oneself. But the reality is that we are special only in the same way that *everyone* is special to God. We do, however, have a special calling to share our wealth and scientific-technological know-how with a needy world; but that is the call to servanthood, not the call to lead from a privileged position of economic, political and cultural domination. The words of Christ in Luke 12:48 apply: "Much will be required from everyone to whom much has been given. But even more will be demanded from the one to whom much has been entrusted." Americans have been given and entrusted much through divine providence, but it is certainly not given for our own indulgence.

The Pew Research Center has given us a ray of hope about the matter by confirming that Americans' sense of cultural superiority is slowly but steadily waning as the next generation comes of age. In a 2011 poll, 49 percent of Americans agreed with the statement, "Our people are not perfect but our culture is superior to others."[7] That figure is down from 60 percent in 2002. The Germans came in a close second at 47 percent, while Britain and Spain were at 32 percent and 27 percent respectively. Those Americans over fifty years of age were twice as likely to think of themselves as culturally superior when compared to those younger than thirty. The same survey distinguished American values vis-à-vis Europeans when 58 percent said it was more important that we be able to pursue our individual life's goals free of government interference than to have the state insure that no one was in need, with which only 35 percent agreed. The European percentages, not surprisingly, were exactly reversed on this point.

The two values mentioned above—a sense of superiority and freedom to pursue individual goals at the expense of others having their basic needs met—are inextricably linked to one another. In addition, a sense of superiority naturally flows from ethnocentrism because the less we know about those who are different, the easier to depersonalize and thus depreciate them. But how does the American sense of superiority coexist with the noble value of egalitarianism? In a word: *uneasily*. It is an instance of two

---

7. PRC, "American-Western European," http://www.pewglobal.org/2011/11/17/the-american-western-european-values-gap/, accessed March 31, 2013.

values standing in opposition to one another and thereby creating a conflicting sense of identity and purpose. For although Americans genuinely hold to the egalitarian value that all people, irrespective of nationality and station in life, deserve equal dignity and respect, we don't tend to practice what we preach. And that can only mean the egalitarian value remains largely unrealized as more of an ideal than a practical ethic. This reiterates what was said before, yet bears repeating: Americans are egalitarian to a point—the very point at which we perceive a significant level of personal sacrifice will come into play.

Of course, there are many Americans who do not conform to these cultural norms regarding a sense of privilege and superiority—people of faith at the fore. They stand out from the crowd and distinguish themselves by refusing to pursue self-interest ahead of the needs of others, whom they truly consider their equals, or at least worthy of their respect. It is such persons' quality of being different that notifies the rest of us that we hold lesser values. That is why we honor such people—the Dorothy Days, Martin Luther King Jrs., and Mother Teresas in our midst. We recognize in their lives a vision for a better humanity, and it resonates deeply within us, though we may not follow suit for various and sundry reasons of convenience. Often the culture seems to pull us one way while our Judaeo-Christian cultural heritage and worldview pull the other. For many, the culture is by far more compelling—a virtual hurricane of clamor beside that "still, small voice" (1 Kgs 19:20) that bids our allegiance to kingdom matters.

LOGIC AND REASON

Like most Westerners, we Americans value reason and logic over emotion and intuition. We are a left brain-dominant society that uses mathematical and analytical approaches to comprehend and interact with our world. Education, economics, medicine (allopathic), politics, and agriculture are all practiced by America's dominant culture in non-integrative ways that isolate and fragment inherently interrelated systems. The Western medical approach, for instance, isolates and synthesizes chemical compounds and introduces them into the body (which is essentially viewed as a machine) to address disease and discomfort. That approach often fails to address both symptoms and causes precisely because the body is an integrated whole that includes emotional, psychological, spiritual, and social components. By singling out symptoms such as reflux and indigestion, traditional Western medical approaches often fail to get at the complex source of problems, leaving patients dependent on drugs that simply mask symptoms and can cause serious side-effects. NSAIDS (non-steroidal anti-inflammatory drugs) alone account for tens of thousands of deaths a year in the U.S., with many thousands more hospitalized with serious intestinal, kidney, and liver damage. Yet doctors regularly prescribe them as if they were perfectly benign and effective.

Vitamins are utilized in the same way, as isolated compounds that supposedly fit into our body chemistry in a one-to-one manner, replacing depleted and missing nutrients like worn-out parts on a car. Little is known about the interactions between vitamins and minerals within the foods where they naturally occur. Food as medicine is not widely promoted by medical practitioners, not only because they are woefully ignorant about the possibilities, but there is no profit in it. And that is one of the major reasons we are a drug and chemical-dependent society. Our market-based economy, driven by a lucrative and powerful pharmaceutical industry, has successfully promulgated a linear, health-through-medicine paradigm. A shallow logic wins for want of knowledge.

The generally poor track record of allopathic medicine in the U.S. (it is most effective with acute illness, but virtually useless with chronic problems) is perhaps the reason behind the emergence of alternative and/or complementary medicine, an industry that began a few decades ago and continues to grow by leaps and bounds. Because alternative medicine is inherently more holistic, many Americans are drawn to it not only to deal with medical problems but to enhance or maintain whatever health they have remaining. Yet its real success lies in the same arena as conventional medicine—it is amazingly lucrative when driven by market-based forces, which usually entail exploitative costs because alternative medicine is generally not covered by insurance. In 2009 alone alternative medicine accounted for $34 billion in sales, and one in three Americans had tried some form of it. The rule seems to be that if something is lucrative, the culture will find a way to incorporate and perpetuate it.

What alternative medicine has that conventional medicine lacks is the ability to consider alternate ways of understanding human health. Conventional medicine is more or less one-dimensional and logic based, so when the paradigm is faulty or incomplete, so is the effectiveness of the treatment (doctors sometimes resort to telling patients their problems are "all in their head" rather than admit their medical knowledge is possibly limited). This issue of linear thinking underlies many of the failures we see in other areas of private and public life mentioned above. Left-brain dominant approaches are always incomplete, for they do not incorporate other ways of knowing and being in the world. The logical, analytical approach works terrifically in areas such as technological innovations in computing, which are based on binary, mathematical formulations. Americans are unparalleled at making impressive gizmos, from cameras that pass through the digestive tract to drones with precision laser-guided missiles. But we're not so good at social progress, because we underemphasize right brain functions that include intuition and synthesis.

We've been enculturated to rely primarily on one kind of intelligence—the logical-analytical, left-brained type reflected in our educational system's traditional "three Rs": reading, writing, and arithmetic. Our testing systems are heavily dependent upon this one mode to the exclusion of other types of intelligence, including spacial, musical, and interpersonal (see Harvard psychologist Howard Gardner's theory of multiple intelligences).[8] Decades ago American psychologist Robert Steinberg separated analytical intelligence from creative and practical intelligences, a triune system that he believed must function in an integrated manner for people to succeed on both personal and professional levels.[9] But such "whole brain" approaches to education are woefully deficient in our schools today, which inevitably reward left-brained learning that perpetuates the myopic cultural trend.

We would do well to teach that there are many different ways of gaining knowledge other than the science and mathematics-based approaches that dominate the Anglo-American tradition. For example, traditional Native American ways of understanding the world and their place in it come primarily through experiential learning. All traditional cultures use direct and personal encounters with the human and natural worlds to subjectively comprehend their subject matter, rather than attempting to know it through abstract, theory-based, non-participatory methodologies. Our Western/American knowledge base is heavily weighted toward abstract learning that distances the learner from the subject at hand. We therefore consider it more intelligent and advanced to approach the world from a separate, dispassionate position—deriving information ("objective" data) about our subjects through scientific research or abstract reasoning which is then disseminated in detached, controlled environments (e.g., the classroom or lab). By contrast, Native knowledge is passed down from one generation to the next through oral traditions that include participatory cultural events such as interactive storytelling and sacred dance. They rely on a learning-by-doing-and-inclusion approach—one in which learning is not an isolated event from the rest of life. The classroom is all of life.

Who's to say one system is better than another? Can we really "know" and understand a flower without directly and subjectively encountering it?

---

8. Gardner, *Intelligence Reframed*.
9. Steinberg, *Successful Intelligence*.

What about love? Or God? Obviously, all ways of learning and knowing have something to offer, and if we intend to know something fully, we are most likely to do so if we incorporate all available approaches to gain a more holistic result. And we do that not only with our whole brain but with all other parts of our being. When Christianity is approached as a left-brained religious system, it ends up as dry and often controversial theology—leading in many cases to dying, irrelevant churches such as one sees in much of Europe today. "If you take away the elements of experience and revelation," writes Randy Clark, "you are left with religion—perhaps an admirable system of ethics and rules, but not much of a relationship."[10] However, when embraced through a more holistic encounter, as is currently being done in much of Africa and Latin America, Christian faith tends to flourish and grow as an organic component of life and community.

YOUTH AND IMAGE

America distinguishes itself culturally from the rest of the world in many ways, but perhaps none more so than our focus upon youth and image. Grey has become the new black—meaning there exists a cultural bias toward it. Ageism is now blatantly present in our youth-infatuated culture, just as overt racism once was before it morphed into more subtle and institutional forms hidden from pubic view. The modern quest to remain young and "attractive" is, at its heart, just another way we attempt to control nature—that is, the natural progression of our own looks and lives. Many Americans are battling aging as stridently today as our ancestors once battled their own feared environments, pumping ourselves full of hormone-altering substances that make us warriors in the bedroom and, according the ads, happier, better-adjusted, and just plain better-looking individuals—in short, our anti-aging agents make us "hot!"

Immigrants to the U.S. are inevitably stunned at the way we treat our elders. Age and grey hair is an honored and highly-valued life-stage in traditional cultures, where the elderly are treated with great deference and respect (also reflected in the ancient cultures referenced in the scriptures—Lev 19:32; Prov 16:31). For them, elders are valued members of society, whose accumulated wisdom is seen to be essential to the well-being of the community as a whole. By contrast, in America and much of the West older people are often seen as problems with whom younger Americans must reluctantly cope. We are told that the surging population of older Americans is now straining the federal coffers through massive social security payouts

10. Clark, *There Is More*, 101.

(we live so darned long now!), even as they disrupt the lives and livelihoods of our children with apparently incurable conditions such as Alzheimer's and Parkinson's disease. To top it off, old folks drive too darn slow, gumming up the roads for the young and productive members of society who need to get places and get things done.

Although there is a growing market targeting the needs of the aged, their ever-lengthening lives mean a longer percentage of those lives will be spent with the inability to contribute economically to society. In short, old people are non-contributors in a progress-driven and profit-obsessed society—thus an insidious, though still politically-incorrect, resentment toward the elderly has crept into the national consciousness. Yet perhaps the bigger reason our culture struggles with subtle antipathy towards the elderly resides in the fact that older folks are constant reminders that our faces will fall, our ailments increase and, ultimately, death will spoil the party for each and every one of us. We may find ways to put off the inevitable but we will not find a way to control the natural trajectory of life as decreed by the Creator (Ps 103:15; Job 14:2). Therefore, every stooping, hard-of-hearing, disheveled denizen we pass in our busy circuits through life is a stark reminder that we are not ultimately in control of things—and that cuts right against the grain of much we value in America today.

It's instructive to identify the path that led our society to venerate youth and view old age with antipathy. It is a value that can be traced back to the eighteenth century and the Industrial Revolution, when the mass production of goods began to steadily erode the extended family structure as the central unit of production and social interaction. Rural self-employed, extended family life gave way to urban factory work done by younger, unrelated individuals who lived isolated from parents, thus eroding the authority and decision-making role of the family matriarch and patriarch. In addition, health and medical advances led to longer life-spans, increasing the ranks of retirement-age Americans who were no longer a viable part of the American workforce (that trend continues, with the percentage of Americans over the age of 65 expected to more than double by 2060, according to the U.S. Census Bureau).[11] Thus, an inverse relationship developed between the country's growing economy and the declining status of older Americans. The status society accorded younger Americans increased in proportion to the growth of a rapidly industrializing economy. The stage was thus set for shunning old age and idolizing youth.

---

11. Blow, "Radical Life Extension," http://www.nytimes.com/2013/08/08/opinion/blow-radical-life-extension.html?_r=0, accessed November 6, 2013.

Interestingly, the trend toward a market-induced break up of the traditional family structure temporarily reversed itself during the Great Depression, when jobs were scarce and families once again banned together in single housing units as a survival technique. A similar reversal has accompanied the economic downturn of the present decade, leading to "mulitgen" housing developments where two or three generations of a single family live together and share expenses. Many feel it is a reversal that is here to stay, given projected world economic trends and the fact that the percentage of non-Anglo population growth is on the rise in the U.S. (many immigrants are from cultural backgrounds that already prefer multigenerational housing arrangements). It remains to be seen if the recent multigenerational housing phenomenon will have any significant effect on the status of the elderly in our country, but those of us attempting to grow old gracefully are certainly keeping a close watch!

My guess is that the cultural value we place on youthfulness is unlikely to be challenged precisely because it is so highly adaptive in the competitive environment of any market-based economy, let alone a struggling one. Although there are laws in place in the U.S. against discrimination based on age, they are easy enough for employers to get around. And to be fair, who wouldn't want a young, energetic, and teachable young person to represent their company or brand? They usually come with less baggage and are more compliant, if less experienced and wise. Virility and sex appeal have always equated well with sales, and that is why young, attractive twenty-somethings are preferred advertising models to rumpled schoolmarms and wrinkly old codgers. Those factors also helps to explain the sometimes bazaar appearance women's fashions take in the workplace, in particular the pain-inducing and health-compromising compulsion to wear high heels (has there ever been a more ludicrous convention in the history of civilization?).

It is because the culture loudly proclaims that youthfulness is highly valued over age that so much effort goes into looking young and hip despite one's advancing years (and why we are so reluctant to disclose our real age). When image is virtually everything, as it seems to be in much of modern American culture, reality can become a dirty word. Perfectly healthy people are putting their lives in jeopardy to look younger. A Yale Cancer Center study showed that among melanoma-type skin cancer survivors, a full 27 percent reported that, post-treatment, they never bothered to use sunscreen when outside, while 2 percent actually admitted to continued use of indoor tanning beds.[12] Other than having a screw loose, what could possibly ex-

---

12. Dodson, "Melanoma Survivors," http://news.yale.edu/2013/04/08/melanoma-survivors-still-forego-sunscreen-and-use-tanning-beds, accessed June 10, 2013.

plain such behavior except the extremely high value our culture now places on *looking* healthy and attractive through sporting a golden tan? "Image is everything," as the adage goes.

Image-consciousness is a cultural value the marketplace both generates and happily perpetrates because it sells so many goods and services. We are encouraged to micro-manage every zit and gray hair by purchasing products that promise to varnish our image and make us feel better about ourselves. The "selfie," made possible through digital cameras and mobile phones, allows each of us to now capture the most attractive portrait of ourselves humanly possible, photo-shop and then instantaneously post it on Facebook and other social media outlets (and change it as often as our mood dictates). We are thereby better able to control our presentation to the world—self-promoting what we imagine to be our best or most attractive self. And we've made it something of a duty to present an image of ourselves that we think others want to see. Apparently everyone, including married people, is supposed to do whatever necessary to "look sexy." As the undeniably attractive actress Sophia Loren once put it, "Sex appeal is fifty percent what you've got and fifty percent what people think you've got."[13]

Humor aside, there is something tragic about seeing a perfectly fine-looking young man or woman who feels the need to alter their appearance to gain acceptance. Tattoos are all the rage and more complex an issue than a mere attempt at acceptance, but many young women feel an unhealthy need to alter their looks surgically to comply with media-generated images of Barbie-dollish celebrities (who themselves keep an army of cosmetic surgeons busy sculpting their falling flesh). One feels sorry for young women and the battle they must fight to overcome such powerful cultural forces in a vain attempt to conform to impossible standards. Those born with great physical beauty—certainly a culturally relative matter—are quite vulnerable to such forces precisely because it is so easy for their self-image to become closely associated with their looks—which can lead to a desperate battle to maintain as the flower fades and the years exact an inevitable toll. "Such a pretty girl," we hear people innocently say, imparting the unmistakable message that pleasing others is somehow linked to maintaining one's attractiveness. There is a double standard, however, because men are mostly off the hook. But more and more guys—especially those going through the dreaded mid-life crisis—are succumbing to the pressures and going under the knife, justifying their vanity with the argument that it makes them more employable. And in today's world, they are probably correct.

---

13. Loren, BrainyQuote, http:// www.brainyquote.com/quotes/authors/s/sophia_loren.html, accessed June 10, 2013.

But modern life is not all sour grapes. There is something refreshing about our youth culture in spite of its tendency to cultivate narcissism. Sports and fitness have an intrinsic goodness about them, and it is encouraging to see so many Americans, young and old alike, going to great lengths to take good care of their bodies. Trendy or not, healthy activity produces its own rewards, even as it saves everyone money through reduced health-care costs. It is heartening to see that a growing number of companies now provide exercise venues for their employees to utilize during the workday, realizing that healthier employees (and not just those that appear healthy) are more productive by far. Insurance companies apparently concur, another case in point where profitability drives cultural preference.

Health and fitness are certainly adaptive in today's unhealthful environments. Fitness better enables a person to cope with inevitable exposures to the typical American diet (high in saturated fats and starchy foods but low in nutrient-dense fruits and vegetables), while it helps counteract the plethora of toxic chemicals we ingest through virtually every imaginable source: viz., our food, water, air, medicines, topical solutions, clothing, and housing. The Harvard School of Public Health informs us that the average American now carries over 100 synthetic chemicals in his or her bloodstream (the "body burden"), many of which are known toxins and carcinogens.[14] Incredibly, the majority of those chemicals have yet to be tested for human safety. But it is not surprising, considering that over 70,000 synthetic chemicals are in use today in America, with a couple of thousand more added each year. In that we now know that toxins tend to accumulate in fat tissue, there is a long road ahead to bring the 60 percent of overweight Americans to a place of real health and fitness.

The body which we Christians proclaim to be the temple of the Holy Spirit (1 Cor 6:19), is in many cases in deep danger of being culturalized into a façade-flanked warehouse full of toxic chemicals. One can't help but wonder just how happy the Holy Spirit is with the accommodations.

FUN AND ENTERTAINMENT

If American culture values youthfulness, it is no wonder that it also values fun and entertainment; for who can think about youth without also thinking about laughter and having a good time? Yet it is important to realize that our love of fun and entertainment has a deeper function in our culture. It stands as a counterpoint to some of the more austere values mentioned

---

14. Stevenson, "Toxic Chemicals," http://www.advancedhealthplan.com/toxic-body.html, accessed July 2, 2013.

above: viz., logical, hard-working, moralistic. We take ourselves so seriously most of the time that we need a culturally sanctioned outlet by which to maintain some sense of balance. So we've cultivated a niche that permits us to "officially" have a good time. Because Americans work so hard, we allow ourselves to play equally hard—and play we do.

Much of our fun-loving orientation derives from a singular dimension of human nature: the capacity to comprehend life's ironies, and express them though a sense of humor. American culture (and life in general) is full of contradictions—individualism vs. nationalism, religious values vs. materialism (both kinds), elitism vs. egalitarianism—which we often resolve through recognizing the inherent irony of conflicting values and putting a lighthearted spin on the situation. As Mark Twain put it, "The human race has only one really effective weapon and that is laughter."[15] Beginning as a rhetorical devise in ancient Greece, the use of irony and humor is embedded in America's culture history in the form of Old World court jesters, Colonial Era political satirists, nineteenth century theatre, medicine shows, rodeos and circuses, and onward to Hollywood's long lineage of comedians and sitcoms—among them the incomparable Charlie Chaplin, the zany Marx Brothers, Lucille Ball, Seinfeld, and a host of late-night comedians.

Fun and entertainment is a distinct psychosocial survival mechanism in an otherwise taxing environment. It fulfills a need that, in America, has gotten firmly hitched to the penchant we have for monetarily capitalizing on anything with mass appeal. The culture of entertainment that emerged in the U.S. first took hold in the post-Civil War years in the form of touring Vaudeville and Buffalo Bill-style Wild West shows. From there America never looked back. Entertainment of every type was marketed to a growing number of Americans who benefited from Industrialization's cash economy and found themselves with an increase in both fee time and extra spending money. The country learned well the lesson that affluence perpetrates leisure, and that both easily become addictive.

Today the entertainment industry has created an array of theme parks, vacation resorts, media industries, comedy and music venues, and sports and outdoor recreation opportunities that highlight an almost endless list of what has become a seemingly indispensable staple of American life—having a good time. In 2008, nearly 6 percent of the average American's income went toward entertainment. That's the same amount as was spent on healthcare, half as much as food, and twice the amount spent on education. We now "consume" entertainment in the same way we consume other

---

15. Twain, ThinkExist, http://thinkexist.com/quotation/the_human_race_ has_ only_one_ really_effective/156393.html, accessed June 10, 2013.

commodities in our economy. It has become an essential form of sustenance, and we've come to expect that, like fast-food joints, it will always be available to us, 24/7.

In America and other developed nations, entertainment is generally consumed at a small-scale level. It may be through an individual purchasing a music CD, a group of friends purchasing a pay-per-view television event, or a family vacation to DisneyWorld. Most of these types of entertainment are segmented away from the rest of life with its more "serious" concerns, such as work and school. By contrast, traditional cultures incorporate "entertainment" into the totality of life at the community level. Whether storytelling around a traditional Mozambican village campfire at night, or participating in a game of *buzkashi*, Afghanistan's national sport of horseback "goat polo," the entertainment is always a community affair in which other important social and cultural functions take place. Mozambican storytelling always involves teaching children moral lessons and oral history, while "goat polo" is a forum where community leaders are established and young men learn to train and ride horses—an important economic skill among herding pastoralists. Matches can last for days, involve every person in the community, and facilitate social and political interaction on many different levels.

Though one might say these traditional activities involve fun and laughter—certainly a universal human cultural trait—they are not really entertainment in the sense that we use the word. It is more accurate to describe such events as shared enjoyment that serves to reinforce a culture's way of life. It is not an isolated event that stands out from other endeavors, but a pleasurable participation in an occasion that flows seamlessly into every other part of life. Certainly carrying water, chopping firewood, or tilling fields is still brutally hard work, but a non-segmented culture means that song and social interaction help establish a sense of enjoyment for even the most onerous task. One is left to wonder if the great appetite Americans have for entertainment inversely corresponds to the lack of satisfying social interaction and meaningful work that is the hallmark of modern life. There are, however, still subcultures in America where social engagement, work and chores, and entertainment are not yet fragmented, as among an Amish barn-raising events or in a daily gathering of retired African-American men at the local barber shop. Yet, by and large, traditional venues for communal enjoyment of life in America have lost ground to a high-speed culture that whirls us toward ever-more-titillating forms of individualized entertainment that we enjoy in isolation from our families, communities, and traditions.

But we must revisit the issue of happiness. We Americans are happy . . . aren't we? Happiness has seemingly become the primary gauge by which we judge the worth of everything else, from our self-image to our jobs and relationships ("Are you *happily* married?"). One could surmise that if we were as happy as we might wish, we could spend a bit less time and money on entertainment. Maybe our need to pursue a lot of fun and games is something of an indicator that we aren't doing so well on the happiness scale—not getting in enough laugh-reps during the day or attaching so many happy faces to our E-mails at work. Research does show that Americans who go to church are happier than those who don't, but that's a tangent we haven't time to explore.

In his 2008 book *The Geography of Bliss*,[16] correspondent and author Eric Weiner traveled the world assessing populations' subjective sense of happiness while visiting countries listed on the World Database of Happiness compiled by Ruut Veenhoven at Erasmus University Rotterdam.[17] America came in at number twenty-two on the list—no joke! Weiner determined that in America the pursuit of happiness is seen as an individual quest that contrasts with the collective orientation represented in the happiest countries (among them, Scandinavia, Switzerland, and New Zealand). The reason is due to a sense of connection with one's family, community, and nation (the latter through effective social support systems in the countries listed—the "socialism" so many Americans fear). He determined that happiness did not come from digging into one's individual psychological issues, which is basically another individualized endeavor. Thus, for Americans, going to church always trumps reading that promising self-help manual because, as we learned in the chapter on human nature, we are wired to be in relationships.

These conclusions help us grasp the fact that happiness is not a commodity that can be purchased and consumed. The culture has led us astray in this matter. The direct pursuit of happiness is a maladaptive norm. Happiness is best sought as an integrated component of an inclusive social network in which the individual is a valued and interactive member. In that context, the abstract idea of happiness is itself transformed into a broader sense of contentment and belonging which is closer to the biblical state of *shalom* than to any other cultural value found in America today. To the extent that some of our American values promote *shalom*, they represent a redeemed expression of human nature, or, if you prefer, our collective reflection of the image of God. Those values that do not promote *shalom* will in some way or another reflect the darker side of that same nature. Culture, whatever its

---

16. Weiner, *Geography of Bliss*.

17. Veenhoven, *World Database*, http://world databaseofhappiness.eur.nl/, accessed October 28, 2014.

local or national configuration, is always and only the collective expression of human nature—from its most elevated to its most base aspects.

BENEVOLENCE

One of the noblest expressions of human nature involves sacrificial giving. It has become a value in American culture that we hold in very high regard. Volunteerism, charity work, and just lending a helping hand to one's neighbor are tried and true traditions with a long history in this country. They hearken back to our Judaeo-Christian heritage and the unquestioned scriptural basis for giving generously to those in need. Moses commanded the Israelites to give to the needy in their midst and thereby gain God's favor and blessing (Deut 15:10), for God is said to be deeply concerned with the poor and disenfranchised; so much so that Proverbs tells us that when one gives to the poor, that person is actually loaning to God (19:17). What an intriguing idea! But the Israelites were also simply to help their neighbors as part of a righteous lifestyle that promoted *shalom* within the community (Prov 3:28; 21:26b).

The New Testament goes even further, encouraging believers not only to give to those in need but to see the person of Jesus in the needy (Matt 25:34–45). The words of Jesus and Paul portray giving as a natural outcome of a life devoted to God (Luke 10:30–37; Phil 2:4), the outward expression of a heartfelt orientation. Both the Hebrew Scriptures and the New Testament make loving one's neighbor a commandment (Matt 22:39; Rom 13:9; Lev 19:18). Obeying and loving God entail loving one's neighbor and showing it through selfless generosity. And in the Parable of the Good Samaritan, Jesus defines the neighbor as anyone in need who crosses one's life path (Luke 10:25–37). With the breadth of modern communications and the range of contemporary travel, that definition of neighbor would seem to include just about everyone on the planet.

There are, of course, many traditions of giving in other cultures and religions. Almsgiving is virtually universal. Offering hospitality, especially to strangers, is another form of giving. An ancient custom in the Middle East, hospitality is apparent in the deferential manner in which both Abraham and Lot hosted their angelic visitors (Gen 18–19). The tradition carried forward into the New Testament, expressed in the word for hospitality, *philoxenia*, a Greek-derived term meaning "love of strangers." Islam too absorbed the custom, enshrining it as a Qu'rānic code of right conduct, according to which the host had an obligation to God in the person of the stranger and/or traveler, who was considered vulnerable and in need of protection.[18] Pleasing God meant caring for such a person through offering munificent hospitality.

In some cultures giving outside the extended family or local community is not customary. Japan is one such example, where a sense of obligation is limited to those one knows and with whom one regularly interacts—the idea being that persons from other communities should be aided through their own local networks. Many other cultures limit assistance and hospitality to relatives and native villagers, toward whom one has an almost mandatory obligation. I've seen this in Nepal where villagers drop in unannounced to the home of a city-dweller originally from their home village, expecting food and housing as a form of civic duty. The Benjamin Franklin quote, "Guests, like fish, begin to stink after three days,"[19] does not apply to the situation. Hospitality is expected among Nepalis as long as it's needed.

In some cultures charity towards those in need is a religious practice done, in large part, for the good karma it brings to the giver (One *sahdu* in Nepal, sporting a huge grin, informed me that he was doing me a favor by asking for money). Yet in other cultures, such as Native Americans of the Pacific Northwest, giving is an institutionalized form of redistribution. Historically, Indian tribes of the Pacific Northwest did this through the *potlatch*, a multi-day feast that served as a means of redistributing wealth within the community, thereby reducing exploitative social relations and preserving stability within the community as a whole.[20] The rich had an obligation to divest their wealth for the good of the tribe, keeping any one person from gaining too much power over others. Ostensibly, Americans do the same through taxes, though there are seemingly plenty of ways to "game" the system, and few of us consider the human side of where our taxes go.

In the U.S., benevolent giving has been unbridled from its historic cultural roots and now functions as a stand-alone value. Doing "charity" work is admired and encouraged whatever form it takes. Presidents have enjoined citizens to become actively involved in volunteer community service, as did George H. Bush in his 1989 inaugural address when he appealed to Americans to be "a force for good" as willful participants in his figurative

18. Qur'ān, Surat An-Nisā', 4:36–37, http://quran.com/4, accessed October 18, 2014.

19. Franklin, BrainyQuote, http://www.brainyquote.com/quotes/quotes/ b/benjaminfr 151622.html, accessed July 2, 2013.

20. Other Native American tribes had unique cultural traditions that benefited the community as a whole by dissuading individual hoarding. Bear Heart Williams, a medicine man in his Muskogee Nation Creek Tribe and an ordained Baptist minister, recalls the traditional role of the tribal leader: "Traditionally the chief was the poorest man in the tribe . . . He was there to serve the people and he did it without resentment, with a sense of duty." See Amsden, "Bear Hear Williams," 24.

"thousand points of light." Bill Clinton and Jimmy Carter both held high the torch of volunteerism after their presidencies, establishing non-profits that have tackled social problems "both down the street and around the world," in the words of Clinton in his 2007 book *Giving: How Each of Us Can Change the World*.[21] The Carter Center is unique in its broad-based impact around the world, promoting peace and democracy, eradicating preventable diseases, and alleviating human suffering through numerous well-organized and far-reaching programs.

As of 2010, the U.S. had over 1.5 million non-profits with expenditures of 1.45 trillion dollars for that one year alone, according to the National Center for Charitable Statistics.[22] During the previous year, one in four Americans over the age of sixteen volunteered through or for a non-profit, including many celebrities whose high-profile efforts attracted the kind of media attention that spawned ever more volunteerism through the process of memetics. It is a beneficial fad that has inspired many young people to join the ranks of those who give. A 2012 survey titled "The Millennial Impact Report,"[23] showed that 75 percent of those between the ages of twenty to thirty-five had given money to a non-profit in the previous year. Giving and volunteerism is now common among even very young people—including elementary and middle-school age students who actively impact local, national, and international causes through encouraging and innovative efforts.

One of the most impressive ways we give is through altruism that brings together total strangers, often through a tragic event. The Boston Marathon bombing in April of 2013 brought forth such altruism. Absolute strangers risked their lives to aid those who had been injured in the explosions—whose interventions saved the lives of a number of the hapless victims. Similar acts occur regularly around the world whenever there are earthquakes, floods, and automobile accidents—triggered by some deep-seated human drive to drop all social pretenses and treat complete strangers with the empathy and compassion normally reserved for loved ones. Times of crisis have a way of drawing people together in ways normal life never does.

The phenomenon is reflective of a custom observed among the traditional Nuer of Sudan, famously described by the iconic American anthropologist Marshall Sahlins.[24] Sahlins detailed the way Nuer tradionally lived in a loosely knit, lineage-based society without permanent leaders or formal

21. Clinton, *Giving*.

22. NCCS, http://nccs.urban.org/, accessed July 28, 2013.

23. Achieve et al., http://www.themillennialimpact.com/research-2012, accessed October 20, 2014.

24. Sahlins, "Segmentary Lineage," 322–45

political organization. Their "segmentary lineage" system evolved around kinship links in ascending order from family through clan and outward to the whole tribe. The independent, dispersed units only came together to face a serious threat or undertaking, such as an attack on a neighboring tribe like the Dinka. On such occasions the separate segments of the tribe banded together into a cohesive and effective unit that successfully addressed the situation at hand. Afterward the tribal unit disbursed into its original independent family and clan segments, with no desire to maintain an integrated structure of any kind. In fact, the flexible, accordion-like social units *were* its political structure—with unification only existing latently as needed.

Similar segmentary lineage systems have been studied elsewhere among tribal-based societies in North Africa and the Middle East. One can recognize the influence of this phenomenon in the traditional Arab proverb from the region: "I against my brother; I and my brother against my cousin; I and my brother and my cousin against the world."[25] The point here is that a crisis reconfigures both an individual and group sense of identity and responsibility, eliciting more altruistic and self-sacrificial behavior than is otherwise expected. This same type of response occurred in Boston, calling forth a sense of unity and altruism that is normally absent in American culture, where there is typically little sense of obligation toward absolute strangers. Perhaps that is why gangs in backyard brawls and soldiers on distant battlefields act sacrificially for the group—risking life and limb when faced with a crisis. In this regard, perhaps we are all the same, whether illiterate nomadic herders or sophisticated white-collar urbanites.

But is sacrificial giving ever completely free of self-interest? Is there ever a circumstance in which pure altruism exists? Or do we always give with some sense of reward to motivate us? Sociobiology would tell us that we never act in a purely altruistic manner; that there is always a motivation to get one's genes into the next generation, whether in the form of one's own children, a distant member of one's tribe or ethnic group, or a complete stranger whose well-being helps to create a social environment conducive to the benefit of one's own offspring and relatives. It is an interesting perspective, but it seems that humans are driven by more complex concerns than merely sex and reproduction—at least once we outlive our twenties.

Applying the question of self-interest to Americans, it is clear that giving does have its rewards. Benevolence is valued by society and therefore psychosocial rewards attend those who give. If there were no personal and social perks to be had, the level of giving would undoubtedly drop off

---

25. See Kurtz, "I and My Brother," §17, http://eppc.org/publications/i-and-my-brother-against-my-cousin/, accessed October 31, 2014.

precipitously. Certainly many people give simply for publicly-acknowledged benefits, whether social acceptance, self-promotion, or simple tax write-offs. On the personal side, giving produces a sense of emotional well-being regardless of publicity, since we are not only enculturated to feel good when we give, our nature is so constructed that giving is extremely fulfilling. The Bible clearly states that those who give can expect a blessing in return (Luke 6:38). And why not? Why should the giver not benefit from her gift? Jesus, knowing that motivation is critical to the spiritual well-being of the giver, told his followers to give in such a way that the right hand didn't know what the left was up to (Matt 6:3), removing the temptation to let self-interest rule the giver.

Either way you look at giving in America—with or without self-interest attached—it can be considered adaptive behavior. For those whose motivation is simply to do what is honorable to God (or their conscience) and follow the religio-cultural tradition of giving freely, psychospiritual health follows. On the other hand, those who give for self-serving reasons still find themselves better off socially than if they had not given, and their gift itself creates goodwill among others, prompting those others to give in return—to "pay it forward."[26] According to the Bible, self-interested givers receive their reward in this life (Matt. 6:2), whereas those who give out of the goodness of their hearts are rewarded both now and in the world to come. But all are rewarded, for that is the inherently beneficial nature of giving.

Yet there is yet another cultural level to giving in America. As mentioned previously, giving serves as a very important cultural counterweight to the individualistic, self-aggrandizing, materialistic side of life that creates such an uninspiring social environment. Imagine a world where no one does anything for anyone but himself. Depressing to say the least. Thus, we need giving to offset the downward spiral that self-centered cultural norms produce. And this too is adaptive, for it allows us as a society to better cope with the uglier side of human nature and its cultural manifestations. Society better tolerates the local strip club, with its parking lot full of rowdy hooligans on pimped-out Harleys, because down the street is a church from which volunteers reach out to the homeless and needy. Giving is a cultural and spiritual necessity in a world where self-interest thrives; and America is undoubtedly one such place.

---

26. Singer, *The Life*. See also Singer's non-profit website, www.thelifeyoucansave.org., accessed October 20, 2014.

7

Contemporary American Cultural Norms

Americans ... are forever searching for love in forms it never takes, in places it can never be. It must have something to do with the vanished frontier.

—Kurt Vonnegut

Behavioral norms are socially-sanctioned expressions of the values of a society. They are context specific and legitimized by the culture or subculture to which one belongs. For example, we often express the shared American values of egalitarianism, progress, and friendliness through the socially-sanctioned act of shaking hands with colleagues and business partners at work. Group culture has endorsed the fact that in the specific context of the workplace, shaking hands establishes the necessary sense of trust, respect and commonality necessary to successfully declare our shared values as a precursor to proceeding with the business at hand. Our culture history, however, has also determined that a more intimate greeting, such as a hug or kiss, is the appropriate means with which to greet a family member in a more private setting. Mix them up by kissing your business associates at work and shaking hands with your spouse at home and you might find yourself in a rough spot on both accounts.

Like cultural/social norms everywhere, American behavioral norms are unique because the values from which they arise are uniquely American. The kiss in public that can get you into trouble in America is the very one you need to stay out of trouble in the Middle East, where it is an expected public display of trust and affection. The list of cultural norms given below is specifically American, although different manifestations of each can be found in other cultures as part of their own distinctive configurations. What makes this list important is the combined impact it has on our behaviors as Americans (and Christians). As always, the question dogs us: Do these social/cultural norms and the values they reflect conflict with or conform to biblical values and the behaviors they encourage, and are such norms and values currently expressed in the church and its presence in the larger world?

The inventory below is far from exhaustive because the norms guiding our daily behaviors are essentially innumerable. I have, therefore, listed categories representative of the major social norms that apply to our task of understanding the effect of culture on our faith. The categories given are necessarily generalized, and I have offered for purposes of clarification specific examples of normative behaviors where appropriate. It should be kept in mind that these categories are reflective of the dominant culture, yet not necessarily applicable to each and every subculture within it. White Anglo-Saxon Protestant students at Ivy League schools will express different norms than Native Alaskan fishermen. But on the whole the list should serve as a fairly accurate cultural template for the behavioral norms evident today in American society-at-large.

HYPER-COMPETITIVE

Our highly competitive orientation has already been mentioned under the early American cultural values section titled "Hard Work and Progress."[1] That orientation is also derived from other values we hold dear, such as individualism and materialism. What is perhaps hidden to many Americans is the extent to which we are competitive relative to other countries, as well as the types of behaviors that can be linked to that intense competitiveness. What is also important to note is that the same super-competitive drive can in one context be useful and encouraged (e.g., the football field) but in another detrimental and off-putting (e.g., an intimate relationship). Part of

---

1. Competitiveness is commonly listed as a value, and even a core value, among Americans. It all really depends on how one wants to slice the cake, and certainly it can be sliced that way. I simply find it easier to list competitiveness as a cultural norm that supports the more foundational values of "hard work and progress" that are clearly traceable to America's early culture history. Certainly the longer competitiveness is normative, the more it takes on the characteristics of a cultural value. But because it is so closely associated with modern business practices, I find it more helpful to categorize it as I have. The distinction is in no way germane to the thrust of the chapter or the book.

our cultural knowledge is understanding when and where to express norms such as competitive prowess—knowledge that obviously has adaptive value if we wish to succeed socially and professionally.

Like most norms and values, competitiveness is ethically relative, in principle at least, in terms of its correspondence to biblical principles. The circumstances make the difference, along with the need for its expression to be subsumed within a larger, overarching ethical framework such as that provided by a Christian worldview. Many professional Christian athletes are extremely competitive in their given sports, but they won't allow their competitive drive to become primary and affect others negatively because it is circumscribed within the larger life goal of honoring God. At least, we hope that is the case; it certainly is a possibility and the intent of most athletes of faith.

Many Americans apparently think that competition is inherently good because it promotes a marketplace where efficiency and innovation thrive, allowing the best producers, innovators and products to rise to the top while cutting prices for consumers. Not doubt that is true, but there is a lot more to the equation. The price we pay personally and socially to continuously live with a competitive mindset is heavy indeed. In fact, it is soul crushing. Unbridled competition necessarily orients a person, group, or country toward winning or gaining prime position vis-à-vis the "other," which entails an orientation that requires beating out another person or group. Aside from the propensity to view the competitor in negative terms—If you mean to beat someone at all costs, can you really have his best interest in mind?—the need to be the best creates its own stress and tension. Research has shown that happiness decreases in direct portion to increased levels of competition in societies.[2] Also, winning never leads to a sense of permanent satisfaction, because one must continually stay on top to "be a winner."[3] Finally, the need to win against one's competitors creates a condition where personal validation lies outside oneself in life's fickle circumstances. The competitive person—many people define themselves as competitive "by nature"—is always fixated on comparing himself with others to gain a sense of self-worth, rather than oriented inwardly where the only real sense of self-worth can reside.[4] For the Christian, inward can be equated with Godward, in this regard.

It is a given that all-out competition defines the natural world. Plants and animals are locked into a constant battle to own their niche and outdo

---

2. Van de Vliert and Janssen, "Competitive Societies," 321–37.

3. Duina, *Winning*.

4. Williams, "Obsession," http://www.psychologytoday.com/blog/wired-success/201208/why-do-we-have-obsession-winning, accessed April 6, 2014.

competitors both within and outside of their particular species. Without an innate competitiveness, each living organism would perish in an uncaring nature "red in tooth and claw," in Tennyson's explicitly descriptive phrase.[5] Therefore, not surprisingly, our impulse toward competitiveness can be traced to our fallen human nature ("whatever is not of faith is sin," according to Rom 14:23), where it functions as an adaptive survival mechanism. It is directly linked to a number of the baser dimensions of that same nature already discussed in chapter 2: viz., self-preservation, self-centeredness, and fear. And, of course, competitiveness is unmistakably linked to a person's hormonal composition, especially prominent among younger males noted for testosterone levels that often overwhelm other behavioral influences—including rational decision-making! Yet competitiveness is also heavily influenced by cultural forces, and American culture seems to have excelled at its cultivation, outdistancing other industrialized countries in terms of how highly we value its presence.[6]

Christians, however, are called to live on a higher plane that rises above mere fallen human nature. We are called to base our lives on principles that are far from the "reptilian brain" that always seeks its own advantage. Those who live by the dictates of nature alone, however sophisticated their cultural backgrounds, are inevitably reactionary and retributional—natural outcomes of competitive self-interest. We will see in part IV that biblical principles lead us toward behaviors displaying cooperation and collaboration—desperately needed norms in a broken and hemorrhaging world—and away from personal or in-group advantage. That cooperative orientation has, in fact, proven to be more productive and conducive to higher levels of personal and group achievement than unrestricted competition, which necessarily stifles human flourishing with its mandatory winner-loser mentality.[7]

NATIONALISTIC FERVOR

If the dominant culture in America promotes competitiveness, it is no wonder that we are also highly nationalistic. It stands to reason that competition on the individual level is easily and naturally extended to the national level given the right circumstances. Crises are particularly adept at promoting nationalistic fervor, as mentioned in the previous chapter. Our citizens bound together after the World Trade Center attack, circling the wagons,

5. Tennyson, "*In Memoriam*," canto 56.
6. WVSA, http://www.worldvaluessurvey.org, accessed November 28, 2013.
7. Kohn, *No Contest*.

so to speak, at our national borders. Differences among us, particularly the ubiquitous partisan bickering that attends national politics, were set aside in the interest of the country as a whole. Unfortunately, the lull was short-lived and quickly reemerged with a vengeance soon after. Our "segmented" society came together to face our "common enemy" (ill-defined as they were and still are), similar to the way traditional Nuer banded together to face their own crises. And ever since the attacks we have been waving and displaying flags more prominently than ever, as the new post 9-11 world of unrelenting terrorist threats has apparently become a permanent fixture in our collective lives.

Of course, Americans are not alone in displays of nationalistic fervor. It is an almost omnipresent phenomenon around the world—at least among the dominant ethnic groups that control the politics of each country. In America, as in most countries, nationalism is inculcated to the point that it is often used as a gauge by which to measure a citizen's moral character. Support for our military is seen as the most direct way of pledging allegiance to our country and its ideals—the measure of a "good American." "Support the troops" slogans are pasted everywhere, voicing the position that, apparently no matter where they may be or what they may be up to, we are totally behind the military and its far-flung endeavors. So strong is this voice among the majority of Americans that support for the military has attained an almost sacred dimension. It has become a hallowed tenant of secular culture, dressed in quasi-religious garb, especially attractive to Christians. Needless to say, there is an obvious conflict between a quasi-sacred view of the military and the kingdom of God proclaimed by the Prince of Peace.

Questioning the cultural role of the military will not sit well with most Americans, be they flag-waving Christians or not. But the emotive capacity that attends the topic is a sure-fire sign that it is *cultural* in nature and not necessarily scriptural (remember that our task is to the separate the two). Nationalistic fervor taps into the patriotic value discussed in chapter 5, using symbols and symbolic behaviors such as flags and rousing national anthems sung by celebrities to evoke group conformity to a particular national ideal—unwavering devotion to the country and its economic, political, and ideological interests around the globe.

Yet it is incumbent upon Christians, and all thinking people, to ask the unavoidable question: What is the price of that devotion to those outside our borders, such as supporters of the Guantanamo Bay prisoners held for over a decade without formal charges? And is that price morally justified? If your answer is yes to the latter question, then what moral basis supports that justification that is any different from any other nation and its own rationalizations, be it populated by Christians, Muslims, or Hindus? Should there not be a distinctively Christian moral position? Or put in a different light, should a Christian from Iran share the same nationalistic fervor for her country as does an American Christian, based on a shared biblically-derived belief or ethic? There should be such an ethic if our faith is truly unique in character and universal in scope. If we can't identify one, then all our displays of nationalistic fervor must necessarily be culturally based and in need of a biblically-sound revision.

CORPORATE DOMINANT

Much of life in America today is dominated by corporations and the financial elites who own controlling interests in them. So prevalent is corporate culture in America that, as both individuals and local communities, we have unwittingly embraced most of the values that support corporate over private and local interests. Douglas Ruskoff traces this devolution in *Life, Inc: How Corporatism has Conquered the World, And How We Can Take It Back*,[8] from the first monopolistic arrangements among European feudal lords to contemporary American corporations that dominate financial, political, economic, and media sectors of our country. For example, only six corporations now control 90 percent of everything we read, watch, or listen to on the radio—down from 50 companies in 1983.[9]

Evidence that we embrace corporate ideology as a cultural norm can be found in a number of attitudes and behaviors: viz., The way a majority of Americans view the natural environment as a legitimate resource for personal enrichment over that of the collective good; The way economic growth indicators are now seen as the only true measure of our nation's state of health and vitality; The way we now view our homes and properties first and foremost as investments; And the way we now measure success in life in terms of healthy 401ks and other investments.

Apparently corporations now own human DNA sequences and bits of nature itself in the form of medicinal plants patented with future profits in mind. The dominant ethic behind corporate ideology, which most Americans have slowly absorbed over the past few decades, is that if a profit can be made through a business endeavor, whatever its nature and scope, then it is a legitimate undertaking. That is why corporations can, in effect, do with impunity what individuals cannot. The social constraints that normally apply to individual human behavior are not, in most cases, extended

---

8. Ruskoff, *Life, Inc.*

9. Lutz, "These 6 Corporations," http://www.businessinsider.com/these-6-corporations-control-90-of-the-media-in-america-2012-6, accessed September 10, 2013.

to corporate interests, thus allowing self-aggrandizing behavior to flourish with virtual anonymity.

It is easy to feel helpless in the face of the power and influence of corporate structures in our lives—insignificant and powerless individuals next to enormous institutions and structures with the capacity to crush dissent. The culture of corporate domination is such that those of us who are even aware of the matter find it easier to "go with the flow" rather than "kick against the pricks," and our behaviors reveal as much. Those who are not conscious of corporate culture's insidious power are hardly to blame: the transition has occurred so imperceptibly and inexorably over the course of the last fifty years that it has come to seem absolutely normal to most Americans, especially younger Americans who've grown up with no other perspective.

An example to which we can all relate is the emergence of Wal-mart and similar "big box" stores and their impact on local economies. A study done by University of Chicago economists Merriman and Persky[10] showed that in the two years after Wal-mart opened in a Chicago suburb, nearly a quarter of all local small businesses were forced to close, sales tax revenues for the community dipped sharply, and jobs lost equaled jobs gained in the areas in and around the store. The closer the proximity of the small businesses to the Wal-mart, the increased percentage of closures there were. Persky argues that his research shows the falsehood behind the belief that Wal-mart generates economic growth wherever it opens a new store—insisting that just the opposite is the case.

Similar negative community impacts were documented in the 2005 film by Robert Greenwald, *Wal-mart: The High Cost of Low Price*.[11] Its conclusions apply to all large business corporations that compete against, and inevitably take over, local markets—offering lower prices based on larger volume that undermines smaller businesses with larger overhead and less capital to invest. But most Americans have become enculturated to reflect the values that support corporate interests over traditional, small-scale interests, despite knowing on some level that corporations exist primarily to create wealth for the few through capturing a corner on their respective market(s). Our behaviors reflect this bias every time we shop. It is certainly an area where Christians should give pause to find our ethical bearing, rather than naively "consume away" unaware of the powerful impact corporate ideology has on our system of values and the norms they generate. If we care about our neighbors, particularly the poor, then we cannot ignore this issue.

---

10. Merriman and Persky, "The Impact," 321–33.
11. Greenwald, *Wal-mart*.

CONSUMERIST

One of the most ubiquitous elements of modern American culture is its orientation toward consumption. It is a norm that seamlessly emerged out of a number of cultural values mentioned in chapters 5 and 6—most notably materialism. Add in a healthy serving of corporate ideology that has helped convinced us that consumption is tantamount to being fully alive (our country's unofficial *rasion d'etre*) and it is no wonder that we think nothing of participating in excessively consumptive lifestyles. Sadly, we do this despite the fact that most of the world languishes in poverty and each of us could, through moderation and generosity, choose to significantly impact the welfare of any number of people and projects[12]—but often choose to remain uninvolved for any number of uninspiring reasons (see "Privacy Hoarding" below for a few).

I will not reiterate the points made in chapter 6 regarding materialism, the practical outcome of which is over-consumption, but rather focus here on the more interesting topic of the mindset that attends such behaviors. Not only has consumerism apparently become the primary cultural expression by which we participate in society-at-large—"I consume, therefore I am"—but it has pushed many Americans into an actual buying addiction. Our malls are bursting with those who venture into their gleaming labyrinths of excess to purchase items not needed and soon enough discarded as substitute therapy for problems they are facing in their personal lives. Some distressed people turn to comfort foods, some to drink and drugs, and some to the mall—condoned and even encouraged by values and norms that too easily generate and perpetuate what, for all intents and purposes, can only be categorized as sadly pathological behavior.

In his critique of the film *What a Way to Go: Life at the End of Empire*, writer Charles Shaw[13] concludes that "industrial civilization—and its end product, consumerism—has disconnected us from nature, the cycle of life, our communities, our families, and, ultimately, ourselves. This unnatural, inorganic, materialistic way of living, coupled with a marked decline in society's moral and ethical standards . . . has created a kind of pathology that produces pain and emptiness, for which addictive behavior becomes the primary symptom and consumption the preferred drug of choice." In support of the film's message, Shaw quotes a public health researcher's remark, "Addiction is really a hallmark of our era [referring to modern Western civilization], and I think it reflects that we don't have culturally promoted kinds

---

12. Singer, *The Life*.

13. Shaw, "Are You Unhappy?" http://www.alternet.org/story/82013/are_you_unhappy_is_it_ because _of_ consumeraddiction, accessed July 28, 2013.

of other deeper forms of meaning and purpose in our lives. So we make up for it by consuming more." Shaw then draws upon the work of Carl Jung, who theorized that addictions always "address a spiritual loss or deficit," which is certainly the case in modern-day America. Quoting a Christian psychotherapist who has treated addictions for twenty years, Shaw then ties addictions to injury—"some violation of the self, a deep wounding or trauma." Trauma is, at the cultural level, nothing less than "a collective wounding . . . that has left society suffering from a mass form of PTSD," according to "primitivist" writer-activists interviewed by Shaw for his critique.

If Charles Shaw is correct, and I believe the evidence proves he most certainly is, then America suffers from an acute form of twenty-first century addiction in the form of over-consumption—a pathological condition in which deep human and spiritual needs are being falsely and inadequately addressed through a market-driven, culture-approved substitute of material possessions. Surely this is an area where the church not only has something to say, but an obligation to say it. Unfortunately, much of the church is complicit in the problem, mindless participants in and perpetrators of consumerism.

ENTREPRENEURIAL

Americans today are driven to create new and innovative markets by an entrepreneurial spirit that is virtually unrivaled in the world. Certainly countries like China, Japan, and India are also aflame with entrepreneurialism, but none-the-less it is a distinguishing feature of contemporary cultural norms in America. A highly-entrepreneurial focus, both on the individual and corporate levels, is certainly not unexpected given the values we hold and the consumer-driven market economy to which we give virtual free reign. The cultural values of individualism, hard-work and progress, materialism, and highly-educated minds commanding logic-based systems of thought set the stage for entrepreneurs to flourish within a capitalistic system that rewards innovation and expansion within every type of profitable endeavor.

Yet behind much of our entrepreneurial drive is a "get-rich-quick" ethic that is perhaps unequaled in the world. America is known around the globe as the "land of opportunity," which is, for the most part, understood to mean economic opportunity. Because few people can reach their financial goals working at McDonald's or other minimum wage jobs, many immigrants, youth, and the economically-strapped from every sector of socio-economic life are motivated to launch forth and establish new and lucrative undertakings—provided funds for investing are accessible. We are a land of dreamers; most of those dreams involving schemes to enrich us and, thus, theoretically free us from the all-too-often demeaning nature of our menial jobs in the work-a-day world. It is an impulse that is greatly encouraged by a dominant culture that honors and admires those who successfully (almost always defined as financial success) create new business ventures launched through individual creativity, foresight, and good old-fashioned hard work. It has become culturally normative to applaud virtually every type of entrepreneurially-driven behavior with little concern over the ethics of the enterprise.

Yet entrepreneurialism in America is, alas, often the victim of a morality-challenged marketplace that will produce and promote nearly any service or product that can show a profit. And given the addiction our country now has for unnecessary and wasteful consumption, a lot of entrepreneurial ingenuity results in products of highly questionable worth—goods and services that feed our insatiable desires for more stuff we don't need and would be better off without. "Dollar" stores, acre upon acre of factory-outlet malls, and pornographic internet sites lie at one end of entrepreneurial efforts gone wild, but it's getting harder and harder to identify businesses that offer things we *really need* to flourish in mind, body, and spirit. In fact, we would undoubtedly thrive more without being tempted by the host of superfluous enterprises that primarily exist to perform what a friend of mine referred to as a "walletectomy."

Still, no one can deny that entrepreneurialism in America has also produced spell-binding innovations in the fields of medicine, communications, architecture, engineering, and transportation, among others. Although all of these innovations are certainly driven by monetary gain, and some will in time undoubtedly be proved to be of dubious worth (perhaps genetically-modified foods among them), there are many astounding and potentially life-altering advancements with the potential to do great good for humankind. Sophisticated weather-tracking technologies, "smart" drugs that target disease without injury to patients, and computerized safety equipment on vehicles are just a few innovations generated through American entrepreneurial efforts that address real human needs and concerns.

One could spend the whole day compiling lists of such advancements and not see the end in sight. But despite their obvious usefulness and potential to improve lives, one must always evaluate the ultimate worth of any innovation and the entrepreneurial efforts that produced it by a single criterion: does it actually further our ability to love God and one another? If not, for all the wonder modern advancements may engender, they are *not integral* to the business of God's kingdom. That assessment may sound prudish and harsh, but in terms of the ultimate worth of our lives and the efforts we put forth in our lifetimes, it is the gospel truth. Still, within God's economy, redemption is always at work such that even the most wasteful plastic trinket can be designed, produced, bought and given to the glory of God. Thus, in the midst of apparently despairing circumstances involving money-hungry consumerism and the effort to produce more of it, hope springs eternal—blooming in the form of God's redemptive presence shining "like a lily among thistles" (Song 2:2, NLT). More on that theme in part IV.

TECHNOLOGICALLY INFATUATED

In a secularizing society infatuated with material possessions, innovation, and entertainment, it is not difficult to see why Americans are so enraptured with technology. Technology is, in essence, just another means of controlling our environments and furthering our progressive, goal-oriented interests—no different in principle from the axes and muskets donned by our Pilgrim forbearers. But technology has taken a life of its own and we can't seem to resist the latest versions of wireless devices that keep us remotely in touch, informed, and in-tune with everyone and everything we deem important. Nor can we resist spending billions to send the latest space probe into the far corners of the universe, ostensibly to probe our origins and better understand ourselves and our place in the universe (somehow improving life on earth). Driven by entrepreneurialism, free-market capitalism, and seemingly continuous breakthroughs in the fields of science and technology, Americans are surfing a massive and growing wave of technological innovation—and loving it! Those who aren't savvy about "the complex dynamics of this new world infrastructure, especially the transformative electronic, digital, and mobile environment," warns futuristic technology guru Thomas Freidman, will fail to succeed in "today's new world order" that over the last decade has become "hyperconnected . . . [and] interdependent . . . [thereby] changing every job, every workplace, every industry."[14]

The downside of our technological infatuation, however, is a separation of important person-to-person interaction, the kind that builds and sustains individuals and communities. Things tend to get in the way of people. Our exchanges with people still exist, but when done via machines they become more distant, less affirming and, ultimately, less effective and satisfying. Human touch and eye-to-eye contact—the two most effective and emotive means of social intercourse and the means of communication

---

14. Freidman, "New World," http://www.nytfriedmanforum.com/index.php, accessed July 28, 2013.

around which our psychophysiology is built—are quickly being replaced by images and electronic representations that are only faint reflections of real people. One need not respond to e-communications in the same way one is expected to reply to a real person in one's presence. Behavioral norms for digital communications are much more impersonal. We're becoming accustomed to a virtual reality that insidiously replaces the real thing, inculcating distance between self and the world—people, nature, and, arguably, even God. As such, technology can become an idol, or at least a serious distraction from the most important dimensions of life. One can visualize this in the scenario of a mother surfing the web while her child vies for her attention: "Mommy, mommy!" "Not now dear. Mommy's busy." Technology does keep us busy, but not always with the things that matter.

In his 1992 book *Technopoly: The Surrender of Culture to Technology*, Neil Postman warns that America has become a nation in which technology is deified.[15] No longer merely tools employed for human needs within the framework of cultural traditions that include religious belief, Postman describes America's "technopoly" as a state where every dimension of culture is sublimated within the confines of "technique and technology," leaving humans to seek meaning and purpose in machines and the techniques that produce them. It is a dehumanizing world that not only idolizes technology, but one that sucks the life out of traditional human institutions, morality, and meaningful interactions between individuals.

A dehumanized world permits us to more easily launch drone strikes on suspected terrorists in Yemen (American citizens, no less) and still get to sleep at night, because the scores of women and children who die along with the targets are unavoidable "collateral damage." In a "technopoly," people become numbers and statistics rule. Reams of information, non-directional and without context, become the primary product and currency. A technology-savvy elite is now emerging, wielding a technology-based cultural monopoly over other ways of being and knowing ("knowledge equals power"). That's why it can be so humorous when grandma asks how in the world "texting" works, or what the devil "IMing" means.

Infatuation with technology can easily become an addiction—part of the complex that includes over-consumption mentioned above. They are both means by which we can take our eye off the ball and completely miss what life is all about. Like the gun it has produced in ever more frightful forms, technology is in itself not inherently wrong or evil. To think otherwise is to entertain an unbiblical form of utopianism—to espouse a contemporary, escapist ideology. But Christians are compelled by our

---

15. Postman, *Technopoly*.

faith to subject technology and our fascination with its latest manifestations to a higher calling and a more noble purpose than is inherent in the things themselves and the sophisticated methods used to produce them. Secular American culture cannot offer that higher purpose, for it is bereft of any ultimate meaning beyond the temporal satisfaction of human desire in its myriad forms.

Yet for the person who has "eyes to see and ears to hear," even secular culture and the awesome technologies that derive from our feverish techno-machinations point us to something higher, something beyond mere existence and the satisfying of an endless cascade of desires. The emptiness that attends a life devoted to material effects, however stupefyingly impressive those gadgets may be, can itself be the catapult to thrust one toward that which is ultimately meaningful. The nihilism inherent in modernity can funnel the seeking heart right into the arms of the eternal God. Desperation is sometimes a good thing. But it is the church's job to point the way and faithfully model the love and grace inherent in that arms-wide-open divine embrace, and not itself become mired in the *culture d'jour* with its plethora of distracting material entrapments and the questionable behaviors that tend to accompany them.

LITIGIOUS AND POLITICIZED

In his well-researched and insightful book, *To Change the World*, sociologist James Hunter describes the emergence in contemporary America of a "politicization of nearly everything."[16] It is a phenomenon he attributes to a sharp increase in litigation over the last several decades in response to decreases in our overall consensus on issues and how to address them. Hunter argues that the more diverse we have become as a people, the more special interest groups have tried to wrestle power away from competing groups and institutions that oppose the culture and values they espouse. In the battle, politics and the legal arena have become the instruments of choice through which groups of every size and ideology seek to forward their own self-aggrandizing agendas in an increasingly pluralistic society.

Drawing on the work of earlier social theorists—Jacques Ellul in particular—Hunter details the way in which each differing division of American society seeks to utilize the state and its laws to promulgate its particular ideology vis-à-vis competing groups and ideologies. The rhetoric and tension has built in intensity over the years even as it has spread throughout every sector of culture and society, encompassing areas previously considered

16. Hunter, *Change the World*, 102.

neutral, such as science, technology, education, and the media. For Hunter, the resulting "culture wars" have inundated civic life with sectarian squabbling among ideologically opposing factions that employ a distinctively negative political psychology he terms *ressentiment*—an aggrieved point of view that takes the decided position of victim, viciously demonizing competing groups in an attempt to gain political power and ascendancy. The resulting politicized culture contains within itself a strong motivation for groups to lash out vengefully to right the wrongs that have supposedly been done against them, casting all who oppose their particular ideological position as abusive and even immoral. *Ressentiment*-inflamed behaviors litter the social and political landscape and are not hard to miss.

According to Hunter, the church has fallen right into the mix—a topic to be picked up in part III.

NIHILISTIC AND CYNICAL

The negativity and vilification informing our society's culture wars is part of a deeper collective discontent rooted in the emptiness of secular, consumer culture. Life looses meaning if and when it is reduced to simple existence, no matter how extravagant the lifestyles fashioned around it. An empty house is still empty, no matter how magnificent its façade. It is what Hunter refers to as "dissolution"—the state of contemporary life wherein there are no fixed reference points by which to judge right from wrong, good from evil, and the ultimate meaning of life in a world where everything has become relative. Only "a will to power" remains, according to Hunter, and that is "rooted in desires and judgments that have no justification but are their own measure of moral worth and significance."[17]

Thus, despite the outward optimism that drives commerce, politics, the media, and so many other dimensions of life in America, an undercurrent of despair threatens individuals and the society as a whole. It manifests in norms that reflect the negativity and nihilism mentioned in the sections above. One can see it bubbling to the surface through a collective cynicism that can go largely unnoticed by those in its grip. It is a "Murphy's Law" way of looking at life, a focus on what's wrong rather than what's right, a Rodney Dangerfield perspective that insidiously inhabits one's inner world and poisons interactions with others.

Cynicism is verbalized through a habit of complaining. And most Americans complain loudly whenever things don't go just right: the coffee isn't hot enough, the mail is late, the traffic heavy, and so on. Cynicism and

17. Ibid., 206.

complaining are related to the sense of privilege and superiority mentioned in chapter 6. "Scratch a cynic," the saying goes, "and you'll find a romantic underneath." Our romanticized American ideals (see "myths" in next chapter) lead many to believe that we are entitled to fun-filled days and a cushy lifestyle. When it doesn't happen—that is, when "reality" gets in the way—the blaming and moaning start, tapping into deep reservoirs of subsurface negativity. Some have called it "going into victim mode."

The blaming is directed at whomever or whatever fails to live up to the cultural ideals set for ourselves and others: punctuality, efficiency, productivity, among others. Sporting such ideals, many Americans plow through their day on a hair-trigger, ready to take offense at the slightest hint of "impropriety"—over-caffeinated and *always* in a hurry. Thus, the girl who is a bit slow at delivering a fast food order is just as likely to get blasted as the government agency that mishandles an important business application; the garbage guys who leave the trash bins askew become equal-opportunity recipients of the wrath reserved for those incompetent, "do-nothing" members of Congress. Many people behave as though any mistake or inefficiency deserves condemnation, contaminated by a collective cynicism that seems to expect things to go wrong. This occurs because much of American idealism is rooted in values that are simply *not* practical and human-oriented. Rather, they are geared to the dictates of the marketplace and the progress-oriented values and norms it generates. We should not really be surprised at widespread cynicism, given our constant bombardment with advertising that promises what can never be delivered through mere goods and services—the joy, acceptance, and meaning in life that is not its to give.

The norms and values of commerce have, unfortunately, come to dominate most interactions we Americans have between ourselves and the rest of the world, toward which many cast a distaining glare whenever American standards are not met. We are as a whole, quite frankly, cultural imperialists and, thus, too often deserving the "ugly American" moniker that regularly gets applied to us abroad. Obviously there are plenty of exceptions to this characterization, plenty of good folks doing good things in all walks of life, both at home and beyond our shores. But if one is tempted to think the "ugly American" designation is itself only a "cynical" assessment, why do we take notice whenever someone we encounter is kind, patient, or especially attentive? It can only be because that person stands out from the crowd and culture from which we have come to expect so much less.

The negative behaviors described above are, of course, far from Christian. They represent fallen human nature cloaked in contemporary cultural forms. But the church and all of us who call it home must endeavor to take a conscious and vigilant stand against absorbing such behaviors that will otherwise suck us into their powerfully negative vortices. The means to do so, once again, rests in the alternative values and worldview represented by the kingdom of God—values that almost exclusively must be inculcated from sources outside the dominant culture that defines America today.

PRIVACY HOARDING

The core values of individualism, materialism, and privilege/superiority work in tandem with competitive and consumerist cultural norms to produce a distinctly American sense of privacy. Privacy can easily be considered a cultural value but our focus will be on the behaviors it generates, for that is where we best recognize its power. No other country in the world is so self-consciously private in its behavioral norms, driven by its attendant conceptions of individual rights. As George Clooney so cleverly put it, "I don't like to share my personal life . . . it wouldn't be personal if I shared it."[18] Celebrities, of course, are legitimately starved of privacy because, as a well-known Christian writer put it, "Since I've become fairly well-known, it seems that everybody wants a piece of me."[19] The George Clooneys of the world are constantly being commodified as cultural icons paid for and owned by their adoring public—or so the public assumes. Celebrities profit handsomely at the expense of their private lives, which they must then pay handsomely to protect.

Most Americans are attentive to a related identity problem. We tend to worry about adequately hiding our identity and our assets from those who would exploit them. Because we live in a world of haves and have-nots, we are taught to believe that the have-nots are hell-bent on having what the haves have. It's the downside of affluence no one warned us about. The funny thing is that those who have nothing to lose need not worry about issues like identity theft. As the incomparable Janice Joplin once sang, "Freedom's just another word for nothing left to lose."[20] Of course, having nothing is no fun either.

Yet privacy in America goes well beyond concerns over protecting one's wealth, possessions, and identity. It engages that age-old dimension of human nature that seeks to control one's immediate environment, so forcefully expressed throughout America's culture history and the subjugation

---

18. Clooney, BrainyQuote, hwww.brainyquote.com/quotes/authors/g/georgeclooney .html, accessed September 10, 2013.

19. Out of respect for this author and the intention behind the quote, he shall remain anonymous.

20. Joplin, "Bobby Mcgee."

of nature and outsiders to the cause at hand. Privacy necessitates a way of looking at the world in which the individual or group must fend off threatening others from a self-determined sense of ownership of identity, time, space, and resources. It involves a defensive, protective orientation against a world of would-be intruders, real and perceived. Privacy says, in essence, "My life is my own, and it's my right to share it how, when, and with whom I want—or not to share it at all."

Our needed sense of privacy is inversely related to our sense of vulnerability in an increasingly interconnected world. We set our Facebook privacy settings according to an estimated sense of exposure to the presence of diabolical forces "out there." We demand the right to determine who can come into "our world"—in essence, who has permission to cross the threshold from impersonal to personal. We insist on guarding our personal borders in a microcosmic analogy to the country's right to fence off its geographical frontiers with concrete, razor wire and armed patrols. We perceive danger beyond our door and it is up to us to keep it at bay.

No one would argue that there are no serious dangers in our world. Foreign and domestic terrorists who plot to attack U.S. interests and do ill to our citizens are a dime-a-dozen, just as countless rapists and murders roam our towns and cities in search of innocent victims to draw into their malevolent clutches. The police and military, for all the misuse of power they can't seem to avoid, are a God-given means of curtailing evil (Rom 13:1-3), and we can be more than a little grateful for the evil they thwart. But the frame of mind that attends the need to protect oneself from the harmful elements of our world, whether actual or imagined, is a far cry from the faith-based perspective the Bible invites us as Christians to make the centerpiece of our worldview.

Not to sound like a broken record, but the marketplace has taken our concern over privacy and ballooned it through fear-generating sales of contrivances vast and varied, all meant to preserve a sense of privacy and the supposed peace of mind it brings. Car alarms—which go off so frequently no one pays attention anymore—home and business alarm systems, computer software protection, gated communities, and a national defense system that puts everyone on edge, all contribute to a generalized fear that seeps into our collective soul. Americans seem to have become enculturated to a life of fear.

Another result of all our defensiveness is that somewhere along the line we buy into a dodgy notion that ripples outward through our kids and colleagues alike. It's the belief that our time, possessions, and our very selves are rightfully of primary concern. When our behaviors are all self-protective in nature, it cultivates the value that self should come first, that comfort is more important than sacrifice, that giving is limited to convenience, that security of every sort is self-determined, and that we can draw a line between ourselves and others that fully justifies acting impersonally and in our own self-interest. The way Americans practice privacy encourages an unengaged isolationism that promotes ethnocentrism and self-centeredness. It finds its justification in the oft-heard assertion among American youth, "Whatever! . . . *I'm* having fun." Such values are absolutely appropriate to the age and quite useful for those who wish to adapt to it. But they are alien to the kingdom that Jesus bids his followers to inhabit and propagate.

MOBILE AND DISPLACED

We revel in our mobility and why not? Jobs often require extensive travel to and from home; plus, there is a wonderful world to see out there. But for all the time we spend moving about, we are mostly in our cars and don't go very far from home, by-and-large traveling the same routes over and over. The percentage of Americans who travel abroad is very low for the level of affluence in our country. Only 30 percent of Americans hold a valid passport. Apparently Americans with free time (not always a given in our work-fixated culture) prefer to stay in the U.S., or not go further than Canada, Mexico, or the Caribbean. Skepticism and ignorance are involved, according to international travel blogger Matthew Kepnes.[21] He believes media reports of bad things happening in foreign countries—as opposed to the many good things regularly happening there—make most Americans apprehensive that their health and safety are at risk should they travel far beyond our shores. Kepnes points to a basic unawareness about foreign lands and cultures that tends to generate fear about travel to them, justifying a host of reasons to stay in or close to the U.S.

Americans' need to feel in control of their circumstances (related to the "Humans Over Nature" value from chapter 5) means most of us just aren't comfortable in too many places that don't look like home. We like to know ahead of time the food we'll eat, condition of the beds we'll sleep in, and all the variables that will allow us to keep discomfort at arms length. A little adventure is fine, so long as it doesn't make one late for dinner. This orientation helps produce a monolithic cultural landscape that anthropologist Marc Augé refers to as "non-place."[22] When every airport, fast-food restaurant, gas station, interstate highway, and motel room look the same, we've

---

21. Kepnes, "Americans Don't Travel," http://www.huffingtonpost.com/matt-kepnes/why-americans-dont-travel_b_790827.html, posted December 2, 2011.

22. Augé, *Non-Places.* 79

entered Augé's "non-place," and become isolated from local environments and people through built environments that offer the exact same surroundings wherever we go. It is a process that depersonalizes space; and by doing so helps foster a one-dimensional world where the richness and variety of cultural traditions are fast disappearing in the face of an artificial sameness that is at once boring and sad.

America's continual movement toward "non-place" culture leaves many of us feeling displaced from the personable, interactive communities we need and desire. Too many residences are filled with people who don't know their neighbors and don't feel any significant connection to their local natural environments. (But that's life in the real world, right? Get over it!) The real way for Christians to get over it is to counter the trend with a biblically-based approach to the people and places we encounter each day. And that means personalizing our world, engaging others in genuine relationships, and living in sustainable ways within our communities and ecosystems. Also, should we have the wonderful opportunity to travel abroad, there are options to engage in ecotourism that benefit poor local communities—some of them Christian— in many developing countries (see chapter 11 under "Personalizing the World").

CASUAL AND INFORMAL

Like . . . dude. What's your problem? Just chill!

That's good advice at times, but perhaps it leaves a little to be desired as a philosophy of life. The sentiment does underscore a deep orientation in America toward the informal and casual, whether in speech, behavior, dress, or attitude. Jeans, a T-shirt, and a pair of old sneakers symbolize the state most of us want to be in most of the time. The impulse to "chill" and its millions of manifestations in our country is partly rooted in a collective sense of identity that involves both a reaction to the formalities of a more solemn British-European heritage and the practicalities mandated by our New World environment. Top hats, laced corsets, and deferential speech were associated with a world our ancestors rebelled against and, besides, such things put one at a disadvantage in a "howling wilderness" where chopping wood, planting corn, fending off wild beasts, and surviving harsh winters were the order of the day.

The endless list of cultural norms reflective of our informal approach to life—from consonant-dropping dialects of English to eating microwaved dinners in front of Jeopardy—are also linked to the core values of individualism, egalitarianism (the classless ideal), and our penchant for fun and relaxation. In addition, because we work so diligently, we need our downtime to keep life in some kind of balance. The youth-heavy Silicon Valley tech companies with their flex-hours, dress-down styles, skateboard-friendly offices, and on-sight recreation areas are an appealing means of expressing those values in an informal way that actually seems to increase productivity.

The marketplace appears to be responding favorably to these more informal—and thus culturally relevant—workplace environments. Numerous companies are following Microsoft's lead by instituting similar, if somewhat less indulgent, changes to their employees work environments. Some have incorporated employee perks such as workout gyms, lactation rooms, childcare facilities, and nap "pods" or "quiet rooms."[23] Thus, informality—which is really a contemporary cultural value in itself—is now making normative behaviors that a few decades ago would have been horribly maladaptive in the workplace. The key to changing any cultural norm is always the perceived advantage it provides toward achieving collectively approved goals. So if relaxing more at work is thought to engender more productivity, the gods of American culture are all on board.

HIGHLY SEXUALIZED

"In America sex is an obsession, in other parts of the world it is a fact," said the German-born American actress Marlene Dietrich,[24] whose films spanned the pre and post-WWII era. If that was true half a century ago, it has only become more so since. Of course, pornography has always been around to sexualize culture wherever there are societies with red-blooded men, unbridled impulses, excess money, and access to media. America is no different in that regard, but we are now seeing a worldwide explosion in pornography because of access to the internet where the anonymity of consumers meets the inability of traditional societal strictures to monitor, and thus "shame" to some degree, both purveyors and consumers. It used to be that one had to publicly purchase pornography in the form of magazines or movies; and that had some dampening effect on its proliferation. But with the internet and mail-order DVDs, there is no longer a need to "expose" oneself, resulting in a booming pornographic industry and a large contribution to further sexualizing American culture.

23. *Bloomberg Businessweek*, http://www.businessweek.com/magazine/content/10_36/b4193084949626.htm, created August 26, 2010.

24. Dietrich, BrainyQuotes. http://ww.brainyquote.com/quotes/authors/ m/ marlene_dietrich.html, accessed July 28, 2013.

Pornography, of course, is just one manifestation of a sexualized culture. The whole of American popular culture is becoming sexually saturated with forms both overt and implied. Language reflects this norm, now captive to sexual innuendo as never before. Religious people have blamed the trend on any number of factors relating to an overall moral decline in America, and certainly some of their concerns have merit. But the simple fact is that *sex sells*, and in a market-based economy that reality means the profit motive is the main driving force behind the phenomenon.

The saddest side of the equation, however, is that adults are no longer the only target for marketing sex. "The sexualization of 'tween girls, girls between the ages of 8 and 12, is a growing problem fueled by marketers' efforts to create cradle-to-grave consumers," according to journalism professor Dr. Gigi Durham of the University of Iowa. "A lot of very sexual products are being marketed to very young kids," she said while criticizing "the unhealthy and damaging representations of girls' sexuality, and how the media present girls' sexuality in a way that's tied to their profit motives."[25] It is a classic example of conflicting cultural values in America, where a deep rooted moral and religious heritage has become uneasy bedfellows with consumer culture and its flirtatious obsession with profitability. The arrangement creates moral conflict within most Americans, who are at a loss to define the exact parameters of the problem and find anything approaching a practical solution.

One value related to the sexualization of American culture is the emphasis modernity places on the physical as being of primary importance. Humans have always judged one another by outward appearances (1 Sam 16:7), but the values of scientific-materialism, with its reductionist view of human beings as little more than gene-driven machines, has helped foster the view that humans are mere collections of biological parts rather than whole persons. And this objectification of persons plays right into marketing *images* (see below) rather than real people.

Sexual intercourse has itself become objectified and removed from the context of love and relationship, taking on consumptive or mere clinical associations. What not so long ago was called "making love" has degenerated into "having sex," as one might have an ice cream or a medical exam. The wonder and beauty of sexual intercourse has been despoiled and taken from the position of an integral but sublimated part of life to become the primary focus. Meant as a sacred, yet pleasurable means of strengthening the life-long bonds between a couple that will then produce a loving, supportive environment for their children, the sexual act has been wrenched

---

25. U of I, "Profit," http://www.news-releases.uiowa.edu/2008/april/042508lolita_effect.html, created April 25, 2008.

from its God-given role and thrust into the limelight as one of modernity's premiere idols. The tragedy, as G.K. Chesterton put it, is that "the moment sex ceases to be a servant it becomes a tyrant."[26] America is now under the tyrannical control of a highly sexualized culture of our own making. We've willingly given up an enriching, life-giving liberty for a form of mediocrity and bondage. It seems that as long as it benefits the economy, it is a bondage to which many are more than willing to submit.

IMAGE CONTROLLING

Part of the attempt to control our environment in order that we might better adapt to it involves the attempt to control the image we project as individuals within society. Because we have become so image conscious in America, that means a large amount of energy is expended attempting to groom that image—as one would a pet. As previously mentioned, manipulating images is central to marketing sex in America, as any fashion magazine cover will attest. But we are also enculturated to constantly manipulate our physical appearances for reasons beyond sexual attraction. Jobs, social acceptance, and even self-acceptance are too often tied to the appearances we cultivate in hopes of conforming to idolized images of "successful" people. Of course, the media is at the center of the fray, generating images of those we are supposed to admire and emulate. Getting the image just right has become a big industry, involving a revolving cache of clothes, expensive accoutrements, ever-changing hairstyles, and even facelifts and breast enhancement surgeries. The ads shamelessly tell us that we will feel better and perform better if only we look better. And lacking a source of real self-esteem and acceptance, too many people buy into the farce.

Image-making, however, is a universally observable human trait. Adornment with facial tattoos, lip plates, and even penis-gourds are just some of the ways it is done in traditional, small-scale cultures across the continents. One could even argue that image control is found throughout nature, where male birds in particular grow fantastically colored feathers and engage in dive-bombing, moon-walk style dancing, and elaborate songs reserved just for spring to project an irresistible image for the wooed mate. But unlike the avian world, Americans have consciously chosen to become fixated with controlling and manipulating our images for virtually every endeavor we undertake.

---

26. Chesterton, http://gutenberg.net.au/ebooks09/0900611.txt., last updated August 2009.

One of the more entertaining ways we manipulate image is through today's carefully coiffed "disheveled look." One's hair, a well-known universal symbol for virility and sexual prowess, must be meticulously combed in supposedly random directions, presenting the "Oh, I couldn't be bothered to mess with my hair" look. Interestingly, it not only is meant to identify wearers as "cool" and "hip," but also signals that one's outlook on life in general is relaxed and unaffected. Dread locks are an extreme variation on the look, bearing the additional message that wearers have a mystical dimension reminiscent of wandering *sadhus* whose focus lies beyond the mundane affairs of the ordinary. One can hardly wait to see what future styles await us.

In a sense, the disheveled look is refreshing because it represents a reaction to the other side of the image-control spectrum in America, and that is our pretensions toward professionalism. The guys who pick up the trash have become "sanitary control technicians," and every phone salesperson is now an "associate" or "consultant" of some stripe. We all seem to want to be "professionals" in our fields, too often substituting image and pretense for diligence and integrity in a world where economic priorities generate constant posturing. For the most part, the "professional" designation is ultimately a form of packaging no different than the glossy plastic wrap that encloses most items these days. We may complain about the cheap products that come from China and India which *look like sturdy, well-made goods*—too often proving to be otherwise—but then we unwittingly participate in the same sort of rouse whenever we put on airs to present ourselves as something more than who we really are. I think we are all a bit relieved to come across someone, in any field of life, who isn't playing that silly game.

GENDER BENDING

In the latter half of the twentieth century the feminist movement stirred up the pot of American and Western culture through a major push to redefine the rights and roles of women in society. Their inspiration was rooted in the women's suffrage movement of the late nineteenth century which, in America, focused on discriminatory voting laws, forced prostitution, and child welfare issues, among others. Today women activists continue the struggle through focusing on issues such as the seemingly insurmountable disparity in pay scales between genders, along with other "glass ceiling" barriers. More women are gaining political office than ever before, leading the charge toward equality under the law, all the while putting more and more distance between America and traditional, non-Western countries and cultures, which seem to lag far behind our values in that regard (though many think we are the ones to be pitied, thank you very much).

American men with traditional concepts of male and female roles have had a rather hard time of it over the years, watching our patriarchal advantages erode under an onslaught of legislation many aren't sure about supporting. Equality is, of course, *theoretically* ok, but then who willingly gives up power and advantage? And doesn't the Bible say women are to be subject to men—or does it? Still, the culture as a whole has now taken sides and men are forced to jump on the bandwagon or be caught "on the wrong side of history," as they say. The women's movement forces both men and women to constantly renegotiate who they are and what their legitimate roles should be in society, and all the while our children are watching, taking their cues and trying to figure out the parameters that will define them and their emerging world.

And if that weren't enough for us guys, now gay, lesbian, bisexual, and transgender movements are bending the issue of gender even further. Gay marriage rights and the legal protections it allows seem to fall under the equality under the law value we Americans consider pivotal, yet it all feels somewhat threatening to most men (and women) with traditional views on gender. Many Americans are left wondering how to define male and female . . . and "other." Is "Pat" a he or a she? Some young people are now advocating an essentially genderless ideology, where a person can define which gender he/she is on any given day according to how he/she feels that day; or, eschew gender categories altogether as archaic and oppressive categorizations.[27]

Americans are now desperately seeking to know what role genetics and hormones play in any given individual's person and personality. Many are wondering if God created us male and female, then who are these other people and how do they fit in? What is important for the purposes of this book is simply to recognize the volatile nature of the issue, the cultural momentum that is building behind it, and the way each of us reacts personally to it; for these are all cultural issues that influence our sense of self and our relationship to the world around us. These are the issues shaping the expression of our behavioral norms which, unless we are cognizant of their formative influence, will invariably end up being reactive in nature. A biblical perspective—and there is always one to be had for even the thorniest of issues—will need to wait until later. However, it can be said that it will definitely *not* be reactive in nature, nor will it justify hatred and the exclusionary agendas of the self-righteous.

---

27. Adler, "Young People," www.npr.org/templates/ story/story.php?storyId=202729367, created July 16, 2013.

POWER STRUGGLES

Gender is just one of numerous ongoing struggles for power in America. Much of that struggle takes place in the political and legal spheres, as previously discussed, where the focus is on the power to define the tenets of accepted culture and the essence of what America should look like in the future. It was also mentioned that this struggle pertains to the fields of education and science, where many proponents, but by no means all, have a determined agenda to wipe religious belief from the minds of educated Americans—constitutional language and provisions be damned. For them, religious belief is antithetical to the goals of progressive thought and behavior, not only for America, but for the whole civilized world. The "religion-free world" proponents are convinced that any allowance for a religious/metaphysical dimension will only keep humanity in a backward state and produce more war and superstitious nonsense. And by equal measure, religious folk—fervent Christians at the fore—are wrestling for the power to shape (reshape?) our culture and its institutions into "God-fearing" forms that match their personal worldviews. But these two factions are not alone.

Environmentalists are struggling for the power to define human-nature relations in ways that are more sustainable toward the ecosystems that support us all, and Christians are also right in the midst of those important efforts. Both liberal and conservative groups struggling for the power to define and represent the kind of America they prefer, do so according to their respective visions of what America was always *meant* to be. Racial, ethnic, and religious minorities are struggling for the power to overturn majority attitudes and opinions that persistently reflect some form of superiority and preference. Meanwhile, others try to put their stamp on America's role in the world and what obligations and involvements we should have toward countries like Sudan and Congo that offer no obvious and immediate benefits to America. Many of the pitched battles in these struggles take place not in the courts or Congress (although many end up there), but in the media and other venues where public opinion is shaped and promulgated among most Americans.

For all of these groups and factions, the issue is power—that supposedly necessary but corrupting entity without which it appears that no one has any chance of getting their way. Power is the commodity by which we change and control culture, or so *our* culture teaches. That power traditionally rests in the hands of those with money, status, racial and ethnic dominance, and social connections among other power brokers—such that networks and mutually beneficial alliances can be formed to beat out the competition. All our power grabs feel like normal behavior because our culture has taught us that approach is the only right one.

We are given few alternatives to power as a means of furthering whatever cause we feel to be justified. The system seems to require it. But we easily forget that the Civil Rights movement in America eschewed power, at least in the traditional sense that entailed force and violence. Their voice was one of justice, faith, and determination, which generated its own source of power—though it was of a very different order—appealing to the conscience and that deep-down knowledge that we are *all* shaped in one wonderful Image. Yet the most effective power available to any of us comes in the form of love, and only One person in history has adequately demonstrated the life-altering force it can generate when given the chance. To experience that love is to realize we can cease the struggle to obtain all lesser powers and the often self-serving agendas promoted through them. But I'm getting ahead of myself again.

SEGMENTED PLURALISM

The world is becoming exceedingly diverse . . . or at least we are finally noticing it is. Add mobility to the mix and America, which has long welcomed the world to our shores (if only in quota-like fashion), has now become defined by the breadth of its diversity. Our country's diversity of human races, ethnic groups, and representative nationalities is one of the true hallmarks of greatness in this country. It represents a bit of the marvelous diversity of humankind that will characterize the coming kingdom (Rev 7:9). I feel proudest to be an American when I see us as a country celebrating the diversity in our midst. It is a truly inspiring sentiment that I know many others share.

The vast array of peoples and cultures that now comprises our country has found ever-broadening support in our constitutional rights to free speech, religious freedom, and a legal basis for the noble conviction that all people *really are* created equal. These rights have spilled out into public life, creating a pluralism that is now normative in the world of business, education, the arts, the military, and many other social and institutional areas of life. America may not quite be the utopia immigrants to this country dream of—just ask the "Lost Boys of Sudan" about their before and after impressions—but few differences raise eyebrows quite so high as they once did. In fact, those of us exposed to a healthy dose of diversity are a little shocked to see areas of the country where it is still scarce, precisely because diversity has come to represent who we Americans are in so many metropolitan areas from coast to coast. Something seems wrong, or at least culturally and ethnically deficient, when we find ourselves in all white communities—which are quickly becoming bastions of the past.

But America's pluralism is by and large segmented into ethnic and racial geographic pockets within the cities where it exists. In urban areas around the world, birds of a feather flock together, and America is little different in that regard. Chinatowns, Little Italys, Hispanic enclaves, and black-populated low-income neighborhoods mark virtually every American metropolis. Middle Eastern communities in Chicago and Cuban neighborhoods in Miami create a disparity between the school and workplace—where pluralism reigns—and living spaces where as yet it does not. Thus, pubic and private life differs markedly in America, creating an ethnically-layered effect to our pluralism.

In addition, many suburbs reveal another type of segmentation based on economic factors and purchasing power, which have a large say in determining who ends up living where. Sociologist Steven Klineberg calls it a "class divide" based on income ". . . where the gulf between rich and poor is widest."[28] Houston, the city with the most parity in terms of ethnic makeup, displays the largest income-based segregation of any city in America. Klineberg points to a Pew Research Center study which found that the widening divide fell between skilled, college-educated young immigrants to Houston (a large number of Asian-Americans among them) and low-skilled, low-educated blue collar workers, most of whom are Latino.[29]

We can therefore surmise that income and ethnicity combine to produce a segmented quality to pluralism in America. We behave accordingly, living part of our lives in a pluralistic society in which diversity is celebrated as a strength, and part of it segmented into ethnic and economic enclaves where pluralism is not normative or necessarily appreciated. The dualistic character of our society—where we see but don't encounter or even speak the language of those who do our menial tasks—mirrors the larger world, where both rich and poor groups within nations, and rich and poor nations around the globe, live separated lives with ever widening distances between them. America's pluralistic society is certainly more integrated than most developing countries, thanks in large part to mandatory public schooling, but we lag behind many European countries that have done a far better job of lessening the ethnic and economic gaps that keep groups separated, thereby lessening tensions between them.

28. Perrottet, "Big Heart," 62–71.
29. PRC, "Houston Tops," http://www.pewresearch.org/daily-number/houston-tops-the-list-of-major-metro-areas-in-economic-segregation-by-income/, accessed October 20, 2014.

Pluralism is inherently life-giving to any society within which it is encouraged to flourish, and the sooner America fully embraces the richness of its pluralistic citizenry, the sooner we will benefit from the social, economic, and even spiritual wealth it creates. It is helpful to realize that no one came to America outside of God's will and purposes for us all. None of us is here by accident or mere human will (Acts 17:26).

DEMOCRATIZED SPIRITUALITY

The impressive diversity of peoples and cultures in the U.S. has combined with the democratizing influence of our political and legal systems to produce a curious effect on our collective religious life. Adherents of foreign-based faiths have intermingled with traditional Christians, non-Trinitarians, Muslims, Buddhists, quasi-religious groups, and New Age spirituality practitioners to create a pluralism of faith that gets expressed culturally through a cognitive and behavioral norm I call "democratized spirituality." Although individual religious groups may feel their brand of faith to be superior (in fact, all do whether they confess it or not), the public and collective expression of our beliefs involve egalitarian and democratic principles that tend to generate social sanctioning or "shaming" for those who refuse to publicly confess a position of absolute parity.

The media happily complies with this taboo-laden arrangement out of fear that promoting one religious system or belief over another will create protest that leads to advertising losses and even law suites. Government, of course, must avoid religious favoritism like the plague because political careers and litigation are at stake. Thus, fear hovers over the topic like a heavy fog over San Francisco Bay. The irony is that all religious groups espouse an explicit or implicit position of moral superiority by the very tenants of their faith—but they cannot show it here. Even belief systems that adhere to the underlying unity of all religions, such as the Baha'i faith or certain New Age constructs, implicitly claim to be morally superior by virtue of their supposedly all-embracing, best-of-all-traditions posture. Those with exclusive religious claims are thought to be more primitive and ethnocentric by comparison—at their best when deconstructed and reformulated into something more inclusive and less "offensive." Thus, non-converters are often interested in "converting" converters to their "con-converting" position.

Democratized spirituality in America has nothing to do with religious tolerance, which is a good and necessary moral stance and a constitutional right. Rather, it is an unspoken cultural norm that guides behavior through culture-generated collective adherence. It also has a denigrating effect on religious belief in general by implicitly positing that if no one religion is "the Truth," then none are ultimately worth more than mere opinion. One can pick whatever seems to fit one's needs, or mix-and-match to customize a spirituality that brings the most personal happiness for the least investment of time and energy. Traditional Christianity with its social and cultural moorings in this country is, as one might guess, more than a bit compromised by this phenomenon. Some of us think that may not be a bad thing, for Christianity has always tended to flounder when it is too closely associated with any one state or culture. In chapter 9 we will look at this issue again and consider the importance of the reaction Christians have to it.

Although democratized spirituality exists as an unspoken orientation that generates behavioral norms for both public and private life, it would be inaccurate to infer that a truly egalitarian ethic regarding religion prevails in America. Spiritual egalitarianism is an ideal that Americans hold, but it is far from realized. Alongside the ideal there is a hierarchical view of religious belief, depending on which subculture one is polling. For most Anglo and African-Americans, as well as those with conservative political leanings, Christianity is near the top and Islam toward the bottom. By virtue of its past association with black-power groups in America and its current association with terrorist groups that openly threaten the U.S., opinions toward Islam are conflicted and steadily losing support among the general public.[30] Other lesser known religious traditions, such as Hinduism and Buddhism, along with New Age spirituality and non-Trinitarian faiths reside somewhere in between the two, depending on whom you ask.

The point of emphasis here, however, is that the topic must be privately conceived and surreptitiously expressed because cultural norms dictate that public life must embrace a non-sectarian approach to religious belief. Favoritism is no longer considered appropriate to the ideals of the country; and from any number of perspectives, that position seems justified. But we are a long way from integrating our public and private views on religion, which seem to operate in almost completely separate realms, eliciting conflicting behavioral norms. As the Apostle James reminds us, a double-minded man is unstable in all his ways (Jas 1:8).

COMPLEXLY INEFFECTIVE

One final contemporary American cultural norm must be mentioned because of its rising influence in political, legal, and economic circles. It is the

---

30. PRC, "Public Remains," http://ww.pewforum.org/Muslim/ Public-Remains-Conflicted-Over-Islam.aspx, accessed July 2, 2013.

immensely complex nature of all those spheres combined, which produces a megalithic institutional beast of such massive proportions as to render the whole thing essentially unmanageable. The formal spheres that comprise our society have developed an integrated life of their own under the direction of no one person (e.g., the President), entity (the Congress or military and secret services), or institution (the Courts or Wall Street). Individual interest groups can rarely influence its direction. And the effect of the institutional behemoth that has become America is its necessary inefficiency and/or ineffectiveness. The larger a system grows, the more unwieldy it becomes; and our country's unwieldiness has grown to such proportions that few people understand how it all works, and even fewer have any real control over its functioning. America as an integrated structure is a steamroller on the move to God knows where, embedded in a world system that displays the same trait.

There are two important repercussions stemming from contemporary life being so complex and ineffective. The first is its tendency to become ever more impersonal. Life and death decisions regarding drone military targets, corporate mergers that engulf small businesses, and governmental decisions to raise or lower interest rates are all done on a macro level far beyond the interests of any single individual or group. Large systems simply cannot be personal to function well, struggling by their very nature to function at all with their inherent and unavoidable inefficiencies. But the less personal they become, the potential increases to also become less humane and further from the biblical ideals of treating people as human beings created in the divine image.

The second effect of a massively complicated socio-economic-legal-political system is the general sense of unease it creates in the psyche of its citizens. When government fails to serve as protector but rather engages in surveillance of its own citizens; when the Supreme Court appointees are overtly political pawns; when the media and entertainment industry continue to devalue truth and moral values in pursuit of ratings and profits; when our economy is characterized by uncertainty, sustaining shock waves throughout Wall Street with every international incident or each new Federal Reserve Board announcement; when jobs get scarce and young people with higher education degrees cannot find employment to pay rent and educational loans, it all helps create a vague insecurity in the hearts and minds of the masses of Americans, especially those with young children. Worry runs rampant among those yet to start families, those who have, and those who have prepared all their lives for a secure retirement that appears to be disappearing like a Death Valley mirage.

Many people naively believe that if we can just get the right candidates from the right political parties into the right positions, then all will be fine. We'll regain control over the runaway system and reinstitute a better world. But modernity's problems are so very much larger than that. Many young people sense a deeper problem, especially since realizing that their aspirations for a new world order after the election of President Obama floundered upon the rocky shores of American political realities—congressional gridlock ended that fantasy—and, indeed, life's hard edges. Ironically, today many of our youth are drawn together by their perceived plight as victims of a broken country and damaged world they inherited but would never create. They personally experience the worry inherent in contemporary American life, yet still imagine a more humane and sustainable country and planet, driven by youthful energy, enthusiasm and the pressing need to find solutions with which they and their children-to-be can live. But today's youth are like sailors upon their own sinking ship, themselves needing rescue. We shall see in part IV just how the Christian faith can be the means to address this disheartening scenario and remove the anxiety that accompanies it. Although that faith may not be the means to revive our nation and eradicate all its mounting ills, it does provide an understanding that in the larger scope of things all is just as it should be—a redemptive story unfolding under the indisputable auspices of a benevolent and unequivocally omnipotent Author. There's great comfort in simply knowing and acknowledging that fact.

8

Enduring American Myths

God created war so that Americans would learn geography.
—MARK TWAIN

NOW THAT WE'VE TRACED the expression of human nature into specific cultural values and norms reflective of the culture history of Americans, we are in a position to identify some of the major myths that drive, reflect, and promulgate the dominant culture. As stated in chapter 2, myths are stories or narratives that serve to shape a people's perceptions, behaviors, and collective sense of identity and destiny. They may be true, partly true, or completely false. Yet they are active within culture to create a prevailing sense of purpose, directing and shaping social and cultural expression on every level, from the individual to the nation as a whole. Their powerful sway is self-reinforcing as it pulsates through the lifeblood of a culture. To fully understand the ideational, psychological, and behavioral characteristics of our society, it is essential to identify and unpack the most prominent of these myths.

The list below was chosen because I consider them the most influential in terms of the purposes of this book. These myths inform American life and culture in countless ways, which include a significant impact upon the American church and its sense of identity and purpose in the larger world (further detailed in chapter 9). Each myth reflects certain previously identified characteristics of human nature in combination with particular American values and norms. I will not draw attention to all the linkages, expecting the reader to be more than capable of doing so on his or her own.

But I will occasionally point out important associations in order to better elaborate the basis of the myth and its multiple roles in contemporary American culture.

THE GREATEST NATION ON EARTH

We hear it said often, especially by politicians who routinely use the phrase in associative ways to bolster themselves and their agendas in the eyes of a scrutinizing public. Yet many of us have actually come to believe that we are indeed the uncontested "greatest nation on earth." Of course, we must ask by what criteria the judgment is made, at which point things get . . . well, a bit subjective. There are, of course, no agreed upon criteria and so it boils down to the way one *feels* about her country—no different than any citizen in any country in the world, most of whom would voice a similarly patriotic opinion.

But if we aren't the greatest, why does everyone want to come here? The short answer is: they don't. Most people are perfectly content with their native countries and many of those who do immigrate to the U.S. have plans to return and retire in their home lands. They are waiting for their kids to be educated and perhaps naturalized, and for their savings to accrue to the point where they can live comfortably in their countries of origin (especially with the support of a child who may end up staying in the U.S. with a well-paid job!). For many immigrants, America is more of a marketplace than a beloved home. It's a good place to make a handsome sum that can be hauled back to enjoy in their slower paced, more socially-interactive native land. This may be the greatest country for someone to begin from scratch and earn his way into a fortune, but that is such a grossly over-generalized statement as to be essentially meaningless. Such a transition can happen anywhere, from Algeria to Zambia. And not every immigrant experiences upward mobility. Many of the cabs in American cities are piloted by immigrants who've gone in the other direction—finding their only employment to be below the skills, training and experience they brought to this country. (I know of one doctor from El Salvador who settled for a cleaning job because he couldn't practice medicine in this country.)

America vies for number one in some rather dubious categories: CO_2 emissions, national debt, teen pregnancy rates, and prisoners held.[1] But, of course, that is the underbelly of a country that really does have a lot of positives that are missing in many other parts of the world, including my abil-

---

1. See, for example, ICPS, http://www.prisonstudies.org/highest-to-lowest/prison-population-total?field_region_taxonomy_tid=All, accessed October, 28, 2014.

ity to honestly say what I think without fear of retribution (although those expressing unpopular opinions can expect a bit of social "shaming" to come their way). I readily admit that, like most Americans, I take for granted the freedoms and opportunities I have in this country, knowing that if they were taken away I would more fully recognize their true worth. But does any of that make us the greatest?

For people of faith, there is the associated mini-myth that God favors America. He "blesses" us in ways he does not bless other countries because . . . well, we are special. We have a special role—to be "leader of the free world" and the primary purveyor of democracy (our "International Manifest Destiny"). Some believe the material wealth of our nation is proof that God's favor rests upon us. I'll return to the issue of God's favoritism in chapter 10, but it must be stated here that there can be no biblical basis for such a belief. The Bible, in fact, states just the opposite (Deut 10:17; Job 34:19; Rom 2:11). As for leader of the free world, that is a self-appointed position that finds little support outside of this country. We may act as though we are the leader, but that does not make it so. And true leaders, whether individuals or nations, lead through humility and service (Matt 20:26). It doesn't appear that the U.S. is currently fulfilling that proviso in quite the way some may imagine (see "America Is Generous" below).

If one were to define her criteria, then talk of America's ranking in the world could proceed in a less emotional manner. The criterion I most like, offered by Pope John Paul II in a 1995 appeal directed at U.S. lawmakers considering abortion rights legislation, is that the greatness of a country has to do with how it treats the *most vulnerable and powerless* in its midst. Although the Pope was specifically referring to the unborn, the poor are also powerless and poverty in America is widespread and growing as income inequality increases. It is well known that wealth is rapidly becoming more and more concentrated at the top, where today 1 percent of the population owns 40 percent of the wealth in this country, while the bottom 80 percent of Americans own just 7 percent.[2] Indices that avoid traditional GNP (Gross National Product) and GDP (Gross Domestic Product) measures and focus on income inequality as it relates to living standards, place the U.S. at number 16 out of 18 developed countries surveyed.[3] These figures are not what one would expect from the greatest nation on earth.

America has certainly shown greatness over the years in other areas, such as its massive commitment to AIDS research and treatment in Africa

2. Jilani, "Unequal," http://thinkprogress.org/economy/ 2011/10/03/334156/top-five-wealthiest-one-percent/?mobile =nc, accessed September 10, 2013.

3. Babones, "Income Distribution," http://inequality.org/unequal-americas-income-distribution/; accessed September 10, 2013.

under the Bush Administration, large-scale responses to natural disasters in Haiti, Indonesia, and Ethiopia over the last few decades, and the long-running establishment of our national parks system (inspiring other countries to do the same). One can argue that the ability to do such things hinges on wealth creation by the richest Americans who should be allowed to do their thing unimpeded. But the wealthiest 10 percent of Americans, who earned 45 percent of all income in 2010, paid roughly the same tax rate as did the middle class, with some 4,000 households earning over 1 million dollars and paying nothing at all because of the way tax codes are stacked in their favor. In other words, the wealthy are not paying their fair share, leaving a strained middle class to bear a higher burden than would otherwise be necessary. Given this arrangement, it then follows that the middle class disproportionately fuels U.S. humanitarian endeavors.

But the larger issue—the proverbial "elephant in the room"—is not whether America is the greatest nation, whatever the criteria, but *why we feel the need* to be the greatest. What insecurity drives us in that direction? Can it be rooted anywhere other than in uninspiring motives—competition and egotism—which are just one more manifestation of the same old sentiment that childishly proclaims, "I'm better than you!" Such impulses should not be foundational to any Christian's ethical framework; and if they are, they are in need of a bit of creative transformation. More than likely God is already at work doing just that, using life and all its vagaries to shape hearts into more loving and magnanimous proportions—true measures of greatness.

THE LAND OF EQUAL OPPORTUNITY

Perhaps we can say that America's greatness lies in the equal opportunity we offer any and all our citizens. Many people believe that to be true, illustrated by the assertion that *anyone* born in this country can become President. Although *theoretically* so, the last non-millionaire president was Harry Truman (1945–53), and Calvin Coolidge before him (1923–29). Opportunity in America, as in most countries, is directly related not only to one's assets, but to educational level, race and class, and other forms of privilege and "social capital" discussed in chapter 5 under "Egalitarianism." There is no need here to reiterate matters of social capital and its importance to succeeding in the U.S. today, but it is important to remember that it is *key* to opportunities in America, reaffirmed by a recent study of regional factors associated with upward mobility.[4]

4. Chetty et al., "Economic Impacts," http://obs.rc.fas.harvard.edu/chetty/

There is no doubt that innumerably more economic, educational, and even political opportunities are available for someone born poor in America than for someone born into poverty in a country like Nepal. The differences in opportunities are enormous—a fact I have sadly witnessed—as wide as the disparity in GDP per capita incomes between the two countries (US $694 to US $53, 143 in 2013, according to World Bank data).[5] But that discrepancy is a different matter than *believing* there really is equal opportunity in America, which simply does not exist. Any Anglo can can prove it by divesting himself of all his assets and access to credit, then cosmetically altering his appearance to that of a minority (which has been done to shocking effect), and then attempting to get a job outside of his training and experience. That is the starting point for many, and it just ain't a level playing field. Every effort we make as a society to truly level that field will increase our greatness as a country and, dare I say, our favor in God's eyes.

The power of the misleading myth of equal opportunity, however, is its effect on behavior. As long as we believe equal opportunity exists in America, we will not find the motivation to confront discrimination and change laws or behaviors to further alleviate it. Perception either promotes or negates action, and if we think things are as they should be, it will surely engender only lethargy toward any effort to establish justice and make things right.

THE INVISIBLE HAND STILL GUIDES US

If we all pursue economic self interest, the "invisible hand" of Adam Smith will guide the market toward the unequivocal benefit of all, or so goes the argument undergirding much of contemporary America's economic behavior. It stems from the notion that an unimpeded marketplace can generate jobs and wealth for the entire country through a process of "trickle-down" economics. Likewise, a world economy unfettered by tariffs and trade barriers will generate wealthy nations that will ultimately benefit poorer ones. Also known as "laissez-faire" economics (leaving the marketplace alone to self-adjust in favor of all), in the U.S. it is now famously associated with Ronald Reagan and the Republican Party. Although I admittedly lack any sophistication in my understanding of economic theory, I cannot help but take note that those who tend to support free market capitalism unleashed from significant government oversight tend *not* to be those who must rely

---

tax_expenditure_soi_whitepaper.pdf, accessed October, 21, 2014.

5. World Bank, "GDP per capita," http://data.worldbank.org/indicator/NY.GDP.PCAP.CD?order=wbapi_data_value_2012+wbapi_data_value&sort=asc, accessed October, 21, 2014.

upon what "trickles down" to survive! Rather, they tend to be those at the top of the system most likely to benefit from a free-reign approach, profiting disproportionably from the social capital at their disposal.

The "invisible hand" has theological implications as well, although most economists are happy enough to understand the concept as pure metaphor. Many Christians who espouse an unregulated market economic ideology, however, tend to believe that it is divinely instituted and even biblically mandated. Although I have no great interest in disabusing anyone of that belief, there are a plethora of biblical references regarding economic justice and lifting up the poor through direct giving that simply don't support such thinking. In chapter 10 we shall have a closer at the biblical text and what it has to say about caring for the poor as part of living in and promoting God's kingdom.

If we believe in the inherently progressive nature of free-market capitalism, it not only affects domestic policy and a large percentage of Americans who fall below the poverty line (nearly 47 million according to 2013 figures), it very much affects our country's stance toward the many nations and peoples for whom poverty is a daily struggle. According to the Harvard economist and senior U.N. advisor Jeffery Sachs, some 75 of the world's poorest nations lack the domestic resources to end the cycle of extreme poverty *on their own*. And not successfully ending it generally leads to other serious problems such as internal armed conflicts, rampant diseases, and serious environmental degradation. Sachs maintains that such countries require direct assistance from bi-lateral and unilateral sources in order to have any hope of breaking free of the "vicious spiral of deepening poverty."[6] He, along with many other informed voices, warn that the fate of the poorest countries will be the fate of us all, for we are inextricably bound together into one global economy, and if we ignore the poorest, we will all eventually be pulled down with them. "Trickle down" approaches, though perhaps well-intentioned, ultimately amount to a form of apathy because they simply don't work well enough for those who need help most. Whether we are speaking of international or domestic policies, "people of the Book" would be hard pressed to justify any form of apathy toward their fellow human beings; and apathy toward those in need is a form of favoritism toward the wealthy—not the type of attitude meant to characterize believers (Jas 2:15–17).

---

6. Sachs, "Economic Development," http://jeffsachs.org/2013/05/qa-integrated-development-for-global-impact/, accessed October 29, 2014.

NATURE IS STABLE AND BOUNTIFUL

This myth has predominated since Americans first set foot on the continent, but it is now undergoing rapid change. Hurricanes Katrina and Sandy and other recent "intense weather events," from killer tornados and floods in the mid-section of the country to record heat and wildfires out West, are quickly shifting the paradigm. The long-held notion that nature has the capacity to almost effortlessly sustain the impacts of modern civilization due to its sheer mass and inherent powers of rejuvenation has been dealt an apparently fatal blow by the events of the past few years. Fading along with this view of the invincibility of nature is the idea that man-made chemicals are innocuous to human life, and talk of ice sheets melting and holes in the atmosphere are little more than left-wing conspiracies.

The most interesting thing about the myth, however, is what lies behind it. It is what I call the "image of unlimited good," a pun-laced reference to the "image of limited good" first described by anthropologist George Foster in his ethnographic fieldwork among peasant farmers in Michoachán, Mexico.[7] Foster found a certain cognitive orientation among the Michoacháni farmers that turned out to characterize poor rural peasants elsewhere. It was the belief that there was only so much good to go around in life—good health, good luck, enough money, and so on—and whoever increased their amount of good did so at the expense of others, for good was *always* in short supply. To take more than your share would short-change someone else. One can understand how a culture of poverty can create such an outlook on life; and for the very same reason a culture of affluence can create the opposite cognitive orientation—an "image of unlimited good."

Contemporary American affluence has fostered the dominant cultural ideology that no limit exists to the good things available to us in life. By pursuing as many of those good things as we can, in as large a quantity as our hearts desire, we are "living the American Dream" and no harm can come of it. In fact, as explained above, the myth relates to the invisible hand which is thought to magically insure that the more we consume the better for us all—whether non-durable goods, investments, or simply pleasure.

Nature, which has heretofore been seen as part of that limitless universe, is beginning to change the equation by calling the whole ideology into question. Its unruliness over the past few years has altered the position of some of the most stalwart representatives of the "unlimited good" camp. American farmers, whose knowledge of the natural world and dependency upon its proper function is unparalleled, have recognized that there is

---

7. Foster, "Peasant Society," 293–315.

trouble on the horizon and joined in sounding the alarm about man-made climate change and its hazards to us all. No rain means no crops and no "good life."

Cohorts of resistors to the changing ideology still abound, especially among the most conservative elements of society. Those Americans with worldviews yet to change on the issue of modern civilization's deleterious impacts on the environment draw inspiration from a statistically tiny number (3 percent) of scientists who insist that there is nothing to worry about. They fall into three camps: 1) those who think the data is incorrect and no climate change is occurring, 2) those who say there is change but it is nothing more than a natural cycle and not worthy of concern, and, 3) those who believe the changes we do see are so minimal that they will have no significant impact on us. But 97 percent of the world's scientists and every major American government-run agency with responsibilities pertaining to the environment now acknowledge that humans are altering our environment in harmful ways that will sooner or later pose *major* problems. This mass of "officialdom" is definitively shifting public opinion on the issue, with a majority of Americans (54 percent) now convinced that man-made climate change is taking place (another 34 percent believe it probably is), and a larger number (64 percent) now favor additional government regulations to curb greenhouse emissions.[8]

It remains to be seen how much this shift in public perception on the state of the environment will lead to changes in the rest of America's paradigm of "unlimited good." As for now, the myth seems alive and well if one considers our massive levels of food consumption and waste as a guide—which both indicate that, as a country, we think there to be a never-ending supply at hand. This is not, as we will see in chapter 11, a biblically sound way to live and think, however much one feels God is pouring out his blessings.

THE NOBLE SAVAGE LIVES ON

Alongside the myth of a limitless environment is another curious set of beliefs regarding the natural world and its inhabitants prior to the advent of modern civilization. Many Americans (and Europeans) have long adhered to a romanticized, Rousseauian view that prior to European contact the American continent was inhabited by "noble savages" who lived in a pristine wilderness. Western civilization came in and spoiled it all, according to

---

8. Mayer et al., "Americans Think," http://nicholasinstitute.duke.edu/sites/default/files/publications/ni_pb_13-01_0.pdf, accessed June 10, 2013.

this line of thinking. "Primitivists," the name given by historian Roderick Nash to those who hold such beliefs, "believed that man's happiness and well-being decreased in direct proportion to his degree of civilization."[9]

But the truth is that there was little, if any, "pure" wilderness when Europeans first arrived, and native peoples were certainly not living in harmony with one another and their environments.[10] Intertribal warfare that included enslavement of captives was commonplace, and the landscape in all of the Americas had long been altered by Aboriginal hunting, cropping, and burning that created what has been called an "anthropogenic" landscape seen the world over. Anthropologist Michael Dove, who studied the matter in rural Pakistan, has described man's historic interaction with his environment as an unavoidable "co-evolution between nature and culture."[11]

There is no doubt that the coming of Europeans had a devastating impact on Native Americans and the ecosystems of North America, but the lives of native peoples were far from idyllic prior to contact. Indians did flourish here from the Pacific Northwest to Florida, and New England to California, but the reason was primarily due to scale and not to ecological quality of life. The small impact of their pre-industrial lifestyles, though imposing enough to permanently alter the naturally occurring flora and fauna in their inhabited ecosystems, was the result of the small-scale societies in which they lived.[12] Even then, on occasion native peoples overwhelmed their local environments, leading to degradation and the need to move elsewhere. "Slash-and-burn" horticulture, which has been practiced throughout the Americas for millennia, can only work if there is a large land base to accommodate new areas for planting to replace the degraded areas the technique necessitates.

The importance of calling out the "noble savage in pristine nature" myth is that it continues to impact American concepts of identity, our history, and our view of the future. Looking wistfully back to a "paradise lost" characterizes some subgroups in America today who view industrial civilization as essentially evil. Thus, pre-contact people and their environments function as an *idealized* past by which they tend to judge and evaluate all that is considered dysfunctional in contemporary America. The myth itself has roots in the Judaeo-Christian myth of Eden, which provides the cognitive backdrop upon which romanticized native cultures and their relationship to their environments are then superimposed. (Importantly, the

9. Nash, *Wilderness*, 47.
10. Denevan, "Pristine Myth," 369–87; Kay, "Aboriginal Overkill," 359–98.
11. Dove, "Dialectical History," 231–53.
12. Bodley, *Cultural Anthropology*, chap. 1.

Christian idea of a new heaven and earth that reinstates Eden's paradisiacal qualities can help direct our notions of steering modern civilization toward harmonious, sustainable lifestyles in the future.)

But it doesn't stop with a few discontented subcultural groups of young people. The same tendency to idealize the past is apparent in older Americans who view our agrarian past with a very similar type of romanticized longing. The "life-was-better-back-when" notion carries up through the 1950s for many people who feel that America was really great back then, but things have only gone downhill since. Men were men, gas was cheap, and America was strong and respected on the world stage. The longing to return to "the good old days" now orients how many Americans face not only the present but the future—not attending to the world as it is but trying to shape the world into what it was (or what they think it was). This type of nostalgia seems to inform a number of different segments of American society that feel a sense of disaffection with the present, and look somewhere in the past for a model that can be applied now and in the future. Again, it is not a biblical orientation but a highly culturalized, wistful one.

CULTURAL EVOLUTION

The idea that cultures develop from simple to complex forms dates back to the European Age of Exploration and the influence of the seventeenth century philosopher Thomas Hobbes. Early anthropologists incorporated the idea as part of a theory that so-called "primitive" peoples developed in progressive stages toward modern civilization—the apex of human development. Darwinian biological theory provided an analogical format employed by anthropologists to discuss the stages of cultural development, with some positing a universal, unilineal direction from band level societies to complex civilizations.[13] Although the unilineal model has long since been abandoned by social scientists for reasons, not least of which, is its inherent racism, the notion is still embedded in many contemporary worldviews from various "civilized" societies around the world—America among them. We consider our civilization—its laws, customs, level of economic development, system of ethics, and political philosophy—to lie at one end of a continuum toward which we think other nations and cultures ought to progress.

Civilizations throughout history have thought of themselves as both the center of the civilized world and the forefront of progressive advances toward higher and higher forms of human development. Thus could China's Shang Dynasty (ca. 1600–1100 BCE) refer to itself as "All Under Heaven"

---

13. Tylor, *Primitive Culture*; Morgan, *Ancient Society*.

and "at the center of the world,"[14] while the Inca called themselves *Inty* ("Children of the Sun") and named their capital "Navel of the world" (*Cuzco* in Quechua). Babylonian, Egyptian, Roman, Greek, Byzantium and the British Empire all shared a sense of cultural advancement and superiority over those they ruled. For many, God or the gods had privileged them to dominate their worlds, although many ancient rulers thought *themselves* to be that divinity. Of course, one must make a distinction between rulers and their subjects in terms of their view of, and concern about, the status of their empire. The point here is that America and the Western world follow a long line of civilizations that felt themselves to be advanced and further advancing beyond their contemporaries.

One may wonder how seemingly opposing myths—the "noble savage" and "cultural evolution"—could both have a part in a modern American worldview. On the one hand they act as counterpoints in the same way we noted that opposing cultural values co-exist side by side. Myths need not be logically consistent with one another, and for the most part they are not. But inconsistency does not keep them from seeming real and exerting their inherent power. Myths come to us as either an inheritance of our shared culture history, or they form as part of society's collective attempt to adapt to and flourish within changing circumstances. Opposing myths within the same culture can also occur because there is no uniform culture in complex societies like our own. There is only an amalgamation of subcultures with overlapping norms and values shaped by diverse culture histories that become sublimated within a dominating cultural complex. Thus, different subcultures adhere to the myths with which they most closely identify, influenced by their particular brand of nostalgia. A unified cultural complex is then formed from a multiplicity of disparate cultural elements. Culture, like personality, is not always harmonious in its components.

The American value of hard work and progress helps generate and sustain the myth of cultural evolution, just as the myth supports the values themselves. That is the way myths work. They powerfully shape, inspire, and motivate behavior in a collective manner. For those Americans who believe we truly are progressing toward a better life and world, the myth motivates them in their work because they strongly feel that work contributes toward onward social progress.

Finally, perhaps the most important aspect to the myth of cultural evolution is not the existence of the myth itself, but the idea it generates that we *are and should be* progressing toward higher levels of civilization and consciousness. Such a stance contributes to the belief that the economy

14. Strayer, *Ways of the World*.

must be growing steadily to be healthy—a frightening prospect if one looks at countries like China and India espousing similar views, and the deleterious impact of their current levels of industrialization on the global environment. As for "consciousness," there is the distinctly humanistic concept among intellectuals and New Agers alike that knowledge and general human awareness are lifting humanity into ever more advanced states of being. One still hears talk of the "Age of Aquarius" and a new age dawning.[15] All of it smacks of misplaced hope. Perhaps it is the misdirected hope that rightfully emerges from the divinely-placed longing for God's kingdom, which we all intuit and long for, though many know not the source of the impetus. Christians know, or should know, that God's kingdom is the only real hope for humanity, whose vaunted civilizations and consciousness can, on their own, never lead beyond the confines imposed by unredeemed human nature.

AMERICA IS GENEROUS

As discussed in chapter 6, benevolent giving is a deeply held core value among Americans. Although it is certainly rooted in the centuries-old Judaeo-Christian tradition of tithing and caring for the poor and disenfranchised, charity has been embraced in modern times as a way to be a "good" American: viz., caring for neighbors, giving to charities, and volunteering for local causes. As stated before, charitable giving serves as a necessary cultural counterweight to the stark materialism and individualism that has ensnared the heart of many an American, leaving anyone with a modicum of conscience feeling so soul-sick he needs to find solace and fulfillment through participating in caring, non-material causes.

Never mind that some of the reasons behind our charity are tainted by a certain degree of self-interest (e.g., tax deductions, publicity), we Americans wrongly associate our giving with unabated generosity. I suppose we just assume we are generous if we give at all, because in comparison to giving nothing (the norm in some cultures) anything looks generous. There is no doubt that some people are extremely generous in giving their time and resources to causes close to their hearts, such as those who have publicly pledged to give a third or even a half of their gross incomes to charity.[16] In fact, Americans give more to the causes that matter to them through

---

15. I've repeatedly encountered this recycled idea in private conversations in northern New Mexico among individuals with a spiritual orientation that can best be characterized as New Age—imprecise and loaded with preconceptions as that designation may be.

16. Singer, *The Life*.

private sources than through public ones—more than Europeans who proportionally give more through government channels than private ones.

But the myth persists that, as a nation, America gives generously to the rest of the needy world. Yet the facts tell a different story. In 2012 the United States was nineteenth among twenty-two industrialized nations in terms of development assistance as a percentage of our Gross National Income (GNI). It amounted to the largest dollar figure of all nations (30.5 billion), but represented only 0.19 percent of our GNI—a figure more than five times lower than Luxemburg, the top giver.[17] In addition, and perhaps most important, the lion's share of our assistance does not go toward poverty alleviation in desperately poor countries, but toward politically-based military support for countries like Egypt and Israel. The actual percentage of American aid that goes where it is most needed—especially to the poorest nations in sub-Saharan Africa—is quite meager by comparison. "It's the crumbs off our tables we offer these countries," said U2 singer and Christian humanitarian activist Bono.[18]

For our purposes, the important point is not how Americans actually compare to other countries or to an abstract concept of generosity, but that we *think* we are much more generous than we are. It's important because if we think of ourselves in this way, we are less likely to feel motivated to give more of our time and resources, even if we are more than able to do so. That applies to individual giving and to giving as a nation. The humanitarian Peter Singer maintains that if all affluent persons in high-income countries gave only 1 percent of their income as assistance to the poor, extreme poverty could be completely eliminated throughout the world.[19]

It is sobering to realize that there was another dimension to the sin of Sodom than what immediately comes to mind for those familiar with the biblical account. In Ezekiel we are told that the people of Sodom were "arrogant, gluttonous, and lazy. [They] never gave help to the poor and needy" (16:49, TV). Stinginess goes hand-in-hand with other immoral behavior, while generosity always accompanies justice and righteousness.

---

17. OECD, www.oecd.org/dac/ stats/aidtopoorcountriesslipsfurtheras governments tightenbudgets.htm, accessed September 10, 2013.

18. Stossel and Binkley, "Are Americans Cheap?" http://abcnews.go.com/2020/ story?id=2682100&page=1, posted August 21, 2007.

19. Singer, *The Life*.

AMERICANS KNOW ENOUGH ABOUT THE WORLD

Except for math and science, where we admit to being behind the rest of the developed world, most Americans feel pretty good about our general knowledge of life and the world we live in. That is, we don't feel ourselves to be an ignorant people, out of touch with what is important. After all, we have a system of universal compulsory education through age 16–18, depending on the state, which is better than most of the world. Uganda, for example, sees less than one-quarter of its schoolchildren move beyond Primary school level.[20] The U.S., by contrast, can now boast that fully one-third of its young people (ages 25–29) have completed a college education.[21] Most of us access some level of news source during the day, going on-line, watching TV, listening to the radio, or reading the local newspaper when we have time. If there is something *really* important going on in the world, we *assume* we will hear about it through one of these ubiquitous outlets.

The problem is that American media is focused on America, and rarely reports on international concerns except as they pertain to our country and its economy. The disservice this does is enormous, not only leaving the general pubic virtually ignorant of the goings-on in foreign countries, but also leaving us thinking that we are fairly well-informed. Except for the Public Broadcasting Stations (PBS) and journals specifically devoted to international affairs (and who wants to read such things on their lunch break?), the American public is simply not exposed to the world beyond our borders. We are as isolated in terms of knowledge of the world as we are geographically separated from it; and therein lies the likely basis for the deficit. Americans simply don't see the need to become informed about people and places that don't appear to have an immediate impact on their daily lives. Things are complicated enough as it is, aren't they?

There are, of course, many highly-educated Americans, a growing number of whom are experts in various matters pertaining to issues beyond our national borders and concerns. As well, there are many Americans resident overseas—excluding the military, 6.3 million in 160 countries in 2011[22]—and they are certainly aware of cultural, economic and political issues pertaining to their countries and regions of habitation. But foreign-based Americans are the exception to the rule. Many of the rest are woefully

---

20. Education Encyclopedia, http://education.stateuniversity.com/pages/1585/Uganda-EDUCATIONAL-SYSTEM-OVERVIEW.html, accessed April 8, 2014.

21. NCES, http://nces.ed.gov/fastfacts/display.asp?id=27, accessed October 29, 2014.

22. AARO, http://www.aaro.org/about-aaro/6m-americans-abroad, accessed October 29, 2014.

ignorant of the geography, social and political life, and economic plight of the world's nations. Polls show this lack again and again, and it is disturbing to those who recognize its consequences. Former National Security Advisor Zbigniew Brzezinski opined about the matter in a televised interview: "We are a democracy. We can only have as good a foreign policy as the public's understanding of world affairs. And the tragedy is that the public's understanding of world affairs in America today is abysmal ... It is probably the least-informed public about the world among the developed countries in the world."[23]

"Ignorance is bliss," the saying goes. Who needs the added worry about the state of our world today? The truth is that ignorance about the world and its people is our loss, not our gain. We are poorer for not knowing what lies beyond our little sphere of existence. Lack of understanding about the world we inhabit leaves us like the subterranean blind society in H.G. Well's classic short-story, *The Country of the Blind*, who simply could not believe their sighted visitor's report of a beautiful world existing above ground—a world they had never seen and, being blind, couldn't comprehend.[24] Christians especially need to be knowledgeable if we expect our faith to be more than a comforting security blanket. How can we expect to impact a world we know little about? As Nelson Mandela put it, "Education is the most powerful weapon which you can use to change the world."[25] It begins by first changing us.

AMERICANS ARE NOT RACIST

This is a touchy area but an important one. The heading would probably be more accurately stated "Racism May Exist in America, But *I* Am Not Racist." We may perceive racism in America, but we will never admit to it personally. Behind this façade is an ideal of equality in America, highly esteemed but still largely unattained, that haunts us as individuals and as a nation. We have more or less accomplished equality in terms of legal strictures; but laws don't govern the hearts of men and women. Rather, laws reflect the need for the human heart to change; for laws exist because left to their own free will, humans are highly prone to do wrong. (If you doubt this, read about what

---

23. Brzezinski, NewsHour, http:// www.pbs.org/newshour/bb/business/jan-june12/ brzezinski_02-08/, posted February 8, 2012.

24. Wells, *Country of the Blind.* http://www.gutenberg.org/ebooks/11870, accessed October 21, 2014.

25. Mandella, ThinkExist, http://thinkexist.com/quotation/education_is_the_most_ powerful_weapon_which_you/144638.html, accessed November 12, 2013.

happens in cities during blackouts.) So it is with racism, which persists in the human heart and oozes its ugliness out into society through the expression of attitudes and behaviors not readily subject to laws. Racism is alive and well, as any "minority" will tell you, because the fallen side of human nature that gives it birth continues unabated—involving the self-centered, prideful, focus on physical, belligerent, and scapegoating traits. Until the heart is transformed, the fallen side of human nature and the racism it spawns will remain.

Racism will remain because race is the easiest means for one human being to exclude another from her rightful position as an indisputable child of God—absolutely equal to all others in his sight—who we are told is no respecter of persons (Acts 10:24). It is the "natural" line at which to draw the self-other divide, given our penchant for judging things based primarily on outward appearances. Of course, all such lines are culturally delineated; meaning children are taught to be racist. Yet given their propensity to sin like any human being, children don't need much encouragement to adopt negative and hurtful attitudes based on racial profiling. They only need to see it in others and learn to associate it with their own particular group of identification—which can stem from family, friends, church/mosque, and/or ethnic group. Yet children are also the best hope for eradicating racism in America, in as much as that is humanly possible. Just as they are the most vulnerable to adopt racist values—absorbing the culture around them like sponges—so are they the most open to new and transcendent values. But those values must first be adopted, lived, and taught by their elders, and we are quite a far distance from attaining that as a nation.

But what exactly is racism? We *think* we know and will vehemently deny being racist ourselves (whatever our racial makeup), yet any American would be hard pressed to actually define what the essence of racism is because race is not a fixed entity. In different societies it is defined differently, especially in countries like Brazil where mixing of Latin, African, Indian, and European (mainly Portuguese) populations has gone on for centuries, obscuring normal physical associations with race. None-the-less, unlike in the U.S., a Brazilian with light skin but other features representative of a "non-white" heritage (e.g., hair texture, nose and lip shape), is considered "white."[26] "Whiteness" is often erroneously associated with race, as in India where lighter-skinned peoples are found among the higher castes, particularly the Brahmans who traditionally consider themselves racially superior to typically darker-skinned lower castes. In America today Latinos are often miscategorized as a different "race" because they are "people of color." It is a

---

26. Davis, *Who Is Black?* 101.

highly subjective matter. Anthropologists have argued the issue for decades, with the vast majority appealing to the idea of race as essentially fluid and culturally constructed. The better part of wisdom seems to avoid intransigent positions on the topic.

An accusation of racism in America today is tantamount to a kind of secular heresy. Along with sexism (another slippery category), racism is now what atheism and communism once were in decades past—*personae non gratae*. Moral indignation accompanies ongoing public accusations of racism, which the media is all too happy to publicize. Yet so powerful is the stigma attached to the label that everyone denies it in knee-jerk fashion. Yet I believe few Americans, indeed few people anywhere, are truly and completely free of racist inclinations; for those inclinations and their manifestations are rooted in the exclusivity that comes so easily to us all via shared fallen human nature. Racism is rooted in the same bias toward self that gives rise to other biases: sexism, ageism, classism, and all types of discrimination toward the disabled and disadvantaged. The self-other divide casts a very wide shadow indeed.

There is only one cure for racism and all forms of discrimination, and it extends beyond the law. It requires that we to learn to view one another as individuals, not categories. In other words, we are to learn to see one another as God sees us—unique persons formed in his ineffable image. We can do this by "personalizing the world" (see chapter 11). But it requires refocusing our vision from the outward to the inward person that we may learn to see anew, judging as Jesus did by standards that have *nothing* to do with the physical presentation (Isa 11:3–4). Unless and until we can obtain some version of that transcendent vision, racism will never be laid to rest in America. It will simply smolder under the surface of cultural sanctions, erupting from time to time to wreak destruction before proceeding to morph into ever changing disguises.

IT'S OUR JOB TO MAKE THE WORLD DEMOCRATIC

In his famous speech before Congress on April 2, 1917, President Woodrow Wilson sought a Declaration of War on Germany, which Congress would pass four days later, thrusting the U.S. into Europe's long-standing and bloody conflagration. As part of his justification for the bold move, Wilson forthrightly asserted, "The world must be made safe for democracy." His view, and the prevailing but by no means unanimous view of the Congress and the country, was that "America is privileged to spend her blood and her might for the principles that gave her birth and happiness and the peace which she has treasured. God helping her, she can do no other."[27]

Thus was launched a new myth in American culture: The now deeply held belief that America is obligated by virtue of her form of governance and way of life to extend our democratic ideals beyond our shores to the far reaches of the globe—by any and all available means. Opposition to non-democratic forms of government and support for countries espousing democratic principles has become our new "Manifest Destiny" and our national calling. We have rarely looked back since Wilson's pivotal speech, revisiting the same European theatre to oppose the same tyrannical foe in WWII, then proceeding later to confront non-democratic governments and forces in Korea, Vietnam, Dominican Republic, Panama, Haiti, Granada, Iraq, and Afghanistan, among other countries.

Before Wilson, we were more or less content to defend our democratic way of life domestically, or at least regionally, with an isolationist bent that persisted into the mid-1940s among a vocal faction that opposed entering the Second World War. Yet the focus to expand our concerns to Europe and well beyond, eventually leading to our self-appointed position as monitor and "leader of the free world," had its official beginning with Wilson's famous line about making the world safe for democracy.

The names of some of our country's post-Vietnam military initiatives are instructive of the ideology that lay behind them: "Operation Uphold Democracy" (Haiti), "Operation Just Cause" (Panama), "Operation Infinite Reach" (1998 bombings in Afghanistan and Sudan), and "Operation Enduring Freedom" (Afghanistan 2001–present). Since WWII the U.S. has been the premiere military force in the world—a position which, coupled with the nation's economic ascendancy, has greatly strengthened the "democracy-upholder" myth that now has thoroughly incorporated an insistence upon free-market capitalism. In essence, it is a myth that purports to export the entire American way of life, inclusive of political, economic, and even sociocultural spheres that are inseparably linked in America.

The purpose here is not to condemn the myth, which would not be that difficult from a biblical point of view, but to recognize its existence and powerful influence on our national culture and the collective behaviors it spawns. For example, astronomically high military budgets that keep our national debt rising and devalue the worth of the dollar are none-the-less considered essential because our ubiquitous military presence in the world is questioned by very few politicians and their electorate. Our "interests" are

---

27. Wilson, "Declaration of War," http:// www.firstworldwar.com/source /usa war-declaration.htm, accessed March 31, 2013.

now worldwide because our economic system is globally interlinked. Thus, any interference with either the sources from which our country's goods and materials are derived (e.g., labor markets in Pakistan and China, oil from the Middle East, or coffee beans and sugar from the Caribbean and South America), or the markets to which they are sold around the world is *now a domestic issue*. Our economy, like all developed economies, reaches tentacle-like into every region of the globe. We therefore are extremely protective of those "interests" and will defend them accordingly.

Protecting our way of life now requires the United States to monitor the world in order that resources and markets remain freely accessed. Although we do believe in the superiority of our democratic structures and their relevance to the rest of the world, we also need a justification by which our military might can be deployed and utilized to protect our economic interests, and thus the entire structure upon which our society—and Western society in general—is built. Democracy is that justification and "human rights" are its supportive principles. Again, I am not here attempting to condone or condemn that orientation but only point out that it powerfully influences American culture. It has been associated with a "savior complex" among Americans, influencing our foreign policy precisely because we feel so strongly that we are meant to guide the rest of the world—a perspective that makes it all but impossible to remain uninvolved when a conflict breaks out in a heretofore unengaged country like Syria.

The myth has numerous ramifications for American Christians, which I can only list but not detail here. First is the issue of conjoining militarism with faith, and the dilemmas that poses for Christians who are sincerely attempting to follow the example of Jesus. Should the church legitimately support the actions of a military that often leaves resentment and ill-will behind in places like Iraq and Afghanistan because so many innocent victims get caught in the cross-fire? Second is the fact that believers can and do easily confuse our calling to share the gospel with the myth that we are meant to spread our American way of life. Democracy is not Christianity and promoting it is not promoting the kingdom of God, which the Bible teaches is decidedly *not* of this world (John 18:36). Third is the impact of our economic reach on local peoples, who are often exploited in order to produce cheap goods and services for our consumptive lifestyles. Christians have an obligation to insure that our economic influence is consistent with our faith, which is at least partly possible to do through purchasing "fair trade" and environmentally sustainable items. And finally, Christians should wrestle with the errant notion that democracy is a necessary precursor to the gospel. In some cases the institution of democracy will mean that anti-Christian religious majorities will rule countries through legitimately elected officials. When that happens, which it does, it sometimes follows that the Christian minority in those countries are worse off than if a dictatorial leader had not been replaced (as in Iraq where persecution of Christians followed the American invasion and toppling of Saddam Hussein, and in Egypt where the Muslim Brotherhood apparently condoned persecution of Christians after winning democratically-held elections to oust Hosni Mubarak). Solutions are not always straightforward and often the lesser of two evils seems the only course of action. Yet our faith demands that we at least become aware of the cultural forces driving the larger society and the reasons behind social pressures for us to conform to and support national policies. Elucidating our national myths is one important step in that direction.

OUR ADVERSARIES ARE THWARTING OUR PROGRESS

As pointed out in chapter 5, one of the foundational core values in America involves an orientation toward progress. We are a goal-driven, results-oriented people because our human nature-derived bent toward purposefulness has been aligned with a broad set of values and norms that rewards us for moving in that direction. As individuals and as a nation we set lofty goals and then resolutely set out to attain them. Whether the goals are achieving a secure job and nice home with all the requisite accruements or a healthy economy and conflict-free world, Americans are determined to fulfill progressive visions both large and small. It is what makes us who we are and there is nothing inherently good or bad about it. But what happens when we fail? How do we deal with coming up short, and what or whom do we blame for not achieving what we set out to do?

As mentioned in chapter 3, fallen human nature leads us to want to scapegoat someone or some group when things go wrong. We could blame God or fate but that never gets one very far. We need something more tangible and an unredeemed nature will vilify whoever seems to stand in opposition to goals that one feels worthwhile and even sacred. This inability to adequately cope with the distance between one's goals and achievements is the breeding ground for the myth that inevitably one or more adversaries are the cause when things go awry, goals aren't met, and progress halted. The myth entails a sense of victimization, and that self-categorization in turn seems to justify some form of retribution toward the supposed source(s) of the problem—the "adversary."

On an international level we blame other countries and their oppositional stance toward our national goals. George Bush famously identified the "Axis of Evil"—Iran, Iraq, and North Korea—for stirring up trouble for America and the rest of the world with their nuclear ambitions (real and imagined). The "evil" countries were posing problems for the goals and aspirations of the "good ones." Islamist countries are often placed in this category in modern times, replacing the old communist adversaries of a few decades ago and the totalitarian regimes before them. (More recently, radical Islamist movements such as the renegade Islamic State of Iraq and the Levant (ISIL) are replacing national governments as notorious objects of focus). On a national level, political parties and special interest groups cast one another into adversarial roles, sometimes accompanied by vicious name-calling and spirited campaigns to denounce the opposition through all manner of media outlets. On a more personal level, various individuals and narrow sectarian groups accost one another as the despised enemy that is blocking progress and achievement. Those who practice traditional medicine are often set against alternative practitioners, humanists against religionists, pro-lifers against right-to-lifers, gays versus straights, and so on. One's identity gets shaped in relation to what one is against.

Obviously real opposition exists for every cause. But the myth maintains that the opposition is the *primary* reason for goals not being met and progress attained. If only the adversary weren't so dim-witted, short-sighted, godless, self-centered, backwards, or downright mean-spirited, then all would be well and we could move forward—or so the thinking goes. Through all the angst and hand-wringing, one thing becomes apparent: Our belief is that the problem lies "out there." Rarely, if ever, do any of us ask if there is a problem or misperception or irrational thinking *within ourselves* that needs to be addressed. Many Americans never evaluate their own motives or question their intentions to see if perhaps they are projecting their own dark side onto those who see the world differently—turning those who are simply different into villains. The worst adversary, at least on a personal level, always lies within—the unredeemed nature projected onto those we don't tolerate well because we don't really understand ourselves.

The notion that our adversaries are preventing progress and causing things to go amuck is found, not surprisingly, in every culture. Every faction within every society entertains the idea that some oppositional force is "out there" threatening their well-being and must be dealt with in an efficacious manner. In traditional cultures adversarial thinking is most often directed toward neighboring groups who, like the Surma peoples described in chapter 1, tend to be competitors for scarce natural resources. By vilifying the other group, which in the case presented was an unacknowledged kin group, aggressive and destructive behaviors can be justified, theoretically making access to resources more readily available. Many conflicts within and between nations involve factors relating to scarce resources—land and water heading the list. The bloodbath in Rwanda and Burundi, ostensibly a tribal conflict between Hutus and Tutsis with a long history of animosity, took place in an area where farmland had been repeatedly subdivided over generations until only tiny, relatively unproductive plots remained, and they were overused by owners who could not afford the necessary inputs (e.g., fertilizers). Some say the Gulf Wars were fought because of America's need for oil.

Shamans are often employed to deal with adversarial forces both seen and unseen among individuals and groups in traditional cultures. It's not as strange as it may seem to us "enlightened" Westerners who employ our own "experts" in the form of political strategists, lobbyists, and lawyers to do our "juju" against our perceived adversaries. Shamans, however, most often act as mediators between the spirit world and the society to which they belong. The pattern is an interesting one, usually involving either a spirit entity causing trouble or illness (such as a deceased ancestor being ritually ignored) or a malevolent power representing the evil opposition to life's benevolent powers. Historically, religious cosmologies almost always entail such an oppositional spiritual realm with dueling powers—and our Judaeo-Christian faith is no exception. The devil, our "adversary" as Peter calls him (1 Pet 5:8, NASB), is prowling around in search of someone to devour. We deal with the devil by staying alert and exercising our faith in God's superior power, or by directly resisting the evil one (Jas 4:7).

Thus, a good-evil cognitive prototype exists in our religious worldview, however theologically metaphorical we modern Christians may have rendered the devil. The prototype also lies within the cognitive schema of nearly everyone; for a good-evil dimension is inherent to virtually all religious systems. Even those individuals who consider themselves non-religious exhibit oppositional conceptions along the same lines. What this means is that essentially every human being, Americans of course included, has a worldview in which "the good" (with which the subject is of course aligned) stands in opposition to "the bad" (represented by all that opposes one's group and its "noble" goals). It therefore becomes quite natural to cast our perceived opponents into the adversarial category, vilifying and blaming them when things appear to go wrong for us and the progress we are attempting to achieve for ourselves and our group, people, or nation. Once again, it behooves Christians to become aware of this tendency and seek ways to subject it to a higher ethical standard that can rightly direct behavior.

LIFE SHOULD BE FUN AND MAKE US HAPPY

The Rapper Snoop Dog put it well: "It ain't no fun (if the homies can't have none)."[28] That sentiment fairly well sums up many Americans view of what life is all about—which boils down to making sure that we entertain ourselves and have a good time, whatever else is going on. Having fun is considered something of a right we have as Americans—a sacred privilege embedded in the Declaration of Independence in its assertion that we have an "inalienable right" to "life, liberty, and the *pursuit of happiness*." Scholars have argued the origins of the phrase, which many feel was taken from an essay by the seventeenth century English philosopher John Locke, who surmised that political society exists primarily to protect a person's private property—his "life, liberty, and estate."[29] However, Jefferson switched the word "estate" for "happiness," purportedly out of his concern that government shouldn't meddle with the private property of American citizens. Most early associations with the "pursuit of happiness" phrase seem to focus on that particular issue of property rights, or else associate "happiness" with the individual's right to pursue higher goals in life—goals that benefit society as a whole.

But the phrase has been usurped by modern sensibilities and recast as part of a more self-indulgent narrative which includes our "right" as Americans to have a good time. It is part of an ongoing shift in America toward individualistic concerns reflective of the so-called "Me generation." One author in *Psychology Today* called the trend in America a "happiness frenzy" and evidenced the huge upswing in recent years in books on happiness, happiness workshops, seminars, life coaches, and college courses devoted to the topic—even as indicators show us becoming ever more unhappy as a nation.[30] Our inability to find happiness was explored in chapter 6 under the headings "Materialism" and "Fun and Entertainment," where it was suggested that happiness as an independent goal is nothing more than a chimera.

For the Christian, our goal must be redefined away from the notion of a fun-filled, happy life toward the idea of joy, meaningful work and interaction, and peace (shalom) based on fulfillment through personal faith, active love, and service. No one is saying it is easy to counter the puissant pull of the dominant culture. Yet if we get sucked into believing the myth that life is supposed to be fun and full of happiness, it sets us up to be unhappy when it

---

28. Snoop Dogg, "Aint No Fun."

29. Locke, *Two Treatises*, § 87.

30. Flora, "Pursuit of Happiness," http://www.psychologytoday.com/articles/200812/the-pursuit-happiness, accessed October 21, 2014.

doesn't come about despite valiant efforts to facilitate it. And when a whole culture is built around and directed by such a myth, it makes it all the more difficult to avoid the rip-tide of pressure and orient one's life differently. An awareness of the myth and its spurious origins in our consumer culture is a promising start.

ARE WE THERE YET, MOM?

Interestingly, most of the myths listed in this chapter fall into one of two categories. Either they entail the belief that we Americans have already "arrived" somewhere desirable (viz., the greatest nation on earth, land of equal opportunity, America is generous.), or they imply that we ought to get somewhere else that is decidedly more desirable (viz., a more progressive society, a democratic world, a happy place). The first category of myth tends to create complacency in the very areas where circumspection and change is needed, while the second tends to set us on various quests that contain an intrinsic element of futility. If we let them, our myths will yo-yo us into cultural conformity, which is decidedly outside the orbit of biblical faith.

In order to avoid mindless conformity, we need to recognize the inherent power of myths to drive culture, inform worldviews, and determine behavior, and then we must identify and evaluate those myths according to criteria that lie outside the society and culture that generates them. Otherwise we cannot gain perspective on the validity of any given myth, and we make ourselves vulnerable to being driven in unwarranted directions by the assumptions inherent in them. Thus, as with the cultural values and norms in America, our national myths must also be subjected to scriptural analysis to adequately evaluate their legitimate place, if any, in our lives.

Some of these myths contain warped notions that reflect more noble and biblically justified beliefs and perspectives. These "look-alikes" are perhaps the most dangerous, for they can appear biblically justifiable without actually being so. For example, the myth that America has a calling to democratize the world fits the exact pattern of the biblical injunction to take the gospel into all the world. In part IV we will take up the tools to evaluate American myths from a biblical point of view—the same tools that will prove effective in appraising the myths that currently influence the American church. It is to the church we now turn to apply a cultural understanding that will hopefully shed new light on an otherwise all-too-familiar topic.

PART III

Who Are We American Christians?

PART II

Who Are We? Critical Questions

9

Christianity in America

Going to church doesn't make you a Christian any more than going to a garage makes you an automobile.

—Billy Sunday

WHAT IS CHRISTIANITY?

Christians espouse a faith that comes in thousands of different forms spread among the most disparate of peoples, places and cultures. From Rio's dilapidated *favelas* to the opulent mansions dominating Hollywood Hills; from mud-caked Australian Aborigines to coifed, urbane citizens of Seoul, Korea; from despised and exploited Pakistani brickyard slave laborers to European royalty with all their attendant glitz and glamour, the church universal encompasses an incredulous array of humanity's races, classes and cultures. In its full scope, it is the most universal of all human groupings, bar none. No other social, political, religious, or cultural categorization even comes close.

It is believed that those who profess faith in Jesus Christ currently number some 2.1 billion, or nearly one in every three people on the planet. And the numbers are apparently growing exponentially. According to those who research such things,[1] worldwide "born-again" Christians are growing at an annual rate of 8 percent. If that trend continues, it means that

---

1. Welton, *Normal Christianity*, 155–56. The author sources the 8 percent figure from Rutz, *Mega Shift*, 25–27.

by 2032 there will be no non-Christians left on earth! Yet the universal church as we know it today is fractured by countless divisions, branches, and denominations reflective of the incredibly disparate array of peoples, cultures, and subcultures that compose it. The unity within all this diversity is a central focus of this book; for it is important to identify the core that ties together all who profess Jesus as the incarnate and resurrected Son of God. But in order to do that, we need to start by asking just what a Christian is—or is not.

Defining Christianity may seem a rather simple or even silly endeavor to some. But that is only because we who call ourselves "followers of Christ" are so familiar with our faith—or so we think—that we imagine we know precisely what we believe without giving it a second thought. Of course, that's the power of culture imposing itself yet again upon our unsuspecting, culturally-patterned way of thinking—our particular worldview. Christianity is so deeply embedded in Western culture that, quite frankly, if one were to try and remove it the result would be something so strange and alien as to be virtually unrecognizable. If it were somehow possible to wrench Christianity from Western culture, the result would be a "giant sucking sound" (a la Ross Perot) as the familiar form and function of Euro-American culture deflated into a limp, unrecognizable blob—like a popped balloon. Faith and culture are always so tightly interwoven that they form two virtually indistinguishable sides of a single tapestry of life. Western culture is inextricably linked to the Christian faith, and it shall always be so, no matter how far the citizens of various Euro-American nation-states veer from actually following Jesus, the faith's founder and enduring center.

For that reason it is extremely difficult to actually explain what the Christian faith consists of without drawing upon the cultural associations we use to define it. For instance, we may say, "Christianity entails the belief that Jesus is the Son of God." And that would be true. But just what is a "Son of God"? What exactly does that designation mean? Is there a precedent? Muslims have a terrible time accepting such a categorization because to them the term entails the blasphemous idea that God had some form of sexual relations—another cultural imputation. And the idea of a virgin birth—which doesn't sound too terribly strange to those of us brought up with the Christmas story—only complicates the matter further for Muslims and other religious devotees because it defies all logic regarding human reproduction. No wonder so many Muslims believe that the Trinity (an impossibly difficult concept to wrap one's brain around anyway) is none other than God the Father, Jesus the Son, and Mary—one happy, holy family. *Oy!*

A missionary friend to the Ambo Tibetan people of China has run into this problem of explaining just who Jesus is in her own ministry. "Son of God" is meaningless to those Buddhist/animists with whom she interacts because there is no culture history to infuse meaning into the term. So she and her colleagues use terms like "Deliverer Jesus" and "Savior Jesus" because they best denote/connote a meaningful equivalent in Ambo culture (delivering and saving from oppressive political circumstances is virtually pancultural knowledge). It has always been thus, as Jesus reminds us in Mark 10:42 (NLT), "You know that the rulers in this world lord it over their people, and officials flaunt their authority over those under them."

Over the centuries, many missionaries have had quite a time trying to explain the concept of the Christian God to people who have a totally different understanding of who or what God is, and just what that would make his Son to be. Throw in a completely unique language along with pre-existing notions of the spirit world and you can get an idea of what missionaries are up against in this regard, and why Bible translation is as much art and anthropology as it is linguistic acumen.

Ironically, the same situation is now becoming commonplace within America where a "BYOG" (bring your own god) culture has spawned. Mention God in public these days and no one can be certain to whom or what you are referring. During his campaign speeches, the Texas-implant comedian and one-time gubernatorial candidate Kinky Freidman regularly supplanted the perfunctory benediction "May God Bless America" with the oh-so-politically-correct alternative "May the god of your choice bless you." His humor was both endearing and irritating to his listeners, depending on their given view of things and that day's reading on their "don't-offend-me" meter. Kinky lost the election. Yet reactions to his theatrical campaign are, in fact, how we know we are dealing with things cultural, in that culture is so deeply ingrained in us that it directly engages emotions hard-wired to its beck and call.

If one steps back a bit and tries to understand the tenants of the Christian faith from some imagined neutral point (an impossibility, but still a worthwhile exercise), it would become apparent just how odd the whole affair can seem to those from non-Western, non-Christian backgrounds—not to mention those from our own culture who possess an inquisitive disposition. From a rationalistic point of view, it is in fact nothing less than an absolutely bazaar set of beliefs that Christians promote with a perfectly straight face. We claim to worship the spirit of a deceased rural laborer who lived over two millennia ago half way around the world in an inconsequential backwater of a long-fallen ancient, pre-European empire. We think we can talk to this person's spirit and that spirit actually lives somewhere inside us! Furthermore, bad things we do today are made right because this deceased person died a propitiatory death two millennia ago—the blood from his hideous torture and death mystically appropriated to amend for our unsavory thoughts and actions today. Talk about time travel! We also believe this deceased person morphed into a spirit-body that passed through walls, eventually rising into the upper atmosphere, one day to make an airborne return in order to judge humankind and assume his rightful rule over the entire universe.

And that's just the tip of the iceberg. Christians also believe the broken up molecules of dead people will, in a uniquely transformative process, somehow be reassembled in the form of the person to whom they once belonged, no matter how geographically scattered the parts and how distant the time of their passing. In other words, the very structure of nature's elements will, contrary to everything we've ever learned about chemistry, physics and biology, reconfigure into some new dimension that is no longer subject to entropy or any other of the laws that currently govern matter (hello quantum physics!). And beyond that, we think nothing of communicating with a transcendent, invisible Being who can simultaneously hear in 8,000 plus unique languages every word of over 6 billion people, not only remembering and responding personally to each individual, but discerning their every thought and intention in the process! *Oy vey*!

No wonder atheists like Richard Dawkins (himself now deceased yet without claims of post-mortem stirrings) and others of his persuasion have had such a field day with Christianity. It all sounds like one big fairytale—a fantastical myth of such enormous proportions that even the most creative sci-fi writers couldn't devise a more esoteric arrangement. The whole thing is so wild sounding that if one were to go into the office of a psychiatrist who had never heard of religious faith and mention these beliefs, a grave look of concern would overcome his or her face, followed by a diagnosis of psychosis and the hurried prescribing of numerous pharmaceuticals. And yet, "It's so crazy it just might work" as the saying goes. Men and women of Einsteinian intelligence believe it. Why? Why would any intelligent person believe something so utterly contrary to scientific rationalism—the linchpin of modern Western paradigms? Although it turns out that reason and logic firmly undergird a Christian worldview,[2] whose historicity is by far more well-founded than any other ancient person or event known to humankind, the key tool for grasping Christianity's "logic" is simple faith—that inexplicable way of "seeing" and "knowing" that provides a knowledge base beyond the limits of reason and sensory perception.

This chapter thus far is all pretext to say to say that we must acquire a better understanding of what exactly what our Christian faith is; and in

---

2. Groothius, *Christian Apologetics*, 419.

order to do so we need a way to examine it outside the perspectives we normally employ. Centuries of cultural accumulation, like barnacled layers on a ship, have encrusted the jewel of the simple gospel of Jesus—the "good news" that so enlivened the early church that they went out and transformed the world of their day. Unless we chip away at the encrusted deposits, we will find ourselves in the same cognitive ruts that have historically constrained us to the well-worn, hackneyed views we inherited through two millennia of enculturation—interpreted through the limits of our own particular life experiences. And so we must begin to chisel away at what typically passes for Christianity in contemporary America—a thankless task that will certainly rub some the wrong way.

Each of the headings given below is deeply rooted in the soil of the American cultural values and norms elaborated in part II. Furthermore, each extends yet deeper into the subsoil of human nature elaborated in part I. It is simply not possible to trace all the linkages due to space. Therefore my focus will be on just a few key links in order to establish the process by which one can evaluate the intersection of faith and culture in America, leaving it to the astute reader to then fill in the blanks that remain. Again, it is helpful to remember the formula that drives the logic behind this analysis: human nature plus culture history plus the contemporary environment (social, cultural, political, economic, and natural) equals contemporary cultural expression (beliefs, values, and behavioral norms).

CHRISTIANITY AS RELIGION

As the prolific Franciscan writer Richard Rohr points out, Christian faith must be anchored in tradition lest it be cast astray by every wind of modern culture. Borrowing a quote from Greek mythology—"Give me a place to stand and with a lever I will move the whole world" (Archimedes), Rohr outlines an apt analogy for the Christian faith. Our faith has the power to "move the whole world," Rohr maintains, so long as it has a firm and necessary fulcrum point (historic and orthodox Christian faith) to provide the essential point of leverage. Modern expressions of faith, from house fellowships to formalized Christian denominations, lack the necessary purchase from which to express substantive, life-altering faith unless they are solidly rooted in historic biblical Christianity. Without that anchor they tend toward ecclesiastical reflections of shifting cultural trends in a youth-oriented modernity that, as youth have done from time immemorial, think history begins with themselves. The same is true outside the church, where Rohr points out that post-modern liberalism, for all its openness and experiential orientation, has no substantative mooring, and thus can't avoid being fickle and ultimately self-oriented[3]—a precise reflection of the culture that spawned it. One can see this orientation in the oft-used admonition to "believe in your dreams"—a sanitized, culturally-acceptable way to pursue self-indulgence under the guise of a higher calling.

Yet we must also question the culturally-inherited roots of all traditional expressions of Christianity, whether Catholic, Orthodox, or Reformed, ever measuring their legitimacy and appropriateness against a more culturally unbiased historical and biblical template. It is a two-way street, because the church always influences the shape of the culture within which it flourishes even as it is influenced by that culture—exhibiting a dynamic exchange between the two. The process is apparent in language, which is itself reflective of culture even as it shapes it. The traditional parting, "God be with you" has been transformed over time into the emasculated conjunction "goodbye." Likewise, "God bless you" has in modern times morphed into a secularized form which is less offensive to modern sensibilities. The ubiquitous bastardized expression, "Bless you," reveals the contours of an ongoing, dynamic exchange between faith and culture. The process has incorporated the contemporary desire to meticulously avoid allowing God into public venues while benefiting from the inherently positive associations that religious morals have traditionally provided the culture-at-large.

While tradition has an important—even critical—place, the church needs to reorient toward an openness to God's Spirit moving in new and unique ways. Tradition tends to mitigate against such openness by locking the present into forms and expressions venerated from the past. Thus, a deft balance between tradition-based understanding and in-the-present openness and engagement seems the best approach. Without that balance, Christianity can slide right into fossilized religion. And Christianity is at its most dangerous as mere religion, which, in the words of one contemporary Christian author, "exchanges[d] the Good News for a 'do it yourself' morality program."[4]

A healthy equilibrium between tradition and modernity isn't always easy to attain, and inevitably people get upset when either one or the other seems to be winning the tug-of-war. The use of gender-neutral language in reference to God is a prime example. Many younger believers feel it important to eliminate all male associations with God, who is clearly beyond gender according to scripture (John 4:21). Their reasons are often personal (bad associations with men and/or father figures) and no one should denounce

---

3. Rohr, *Jesus' Plan*, 67.
4. Crowder, *Mystical Union*, 24.

the practice if it serves the higher purpose of helping to personalize God for them. It is, however, a cultural norm adopted from secular society and linked to other agendas (some positive, some not), and has a tendency to be foisted upon those who are not comfortable with it (yet). When that happens, gender neutrality becomes its own religious norm, and just as easily becomes a formal religious expression no different, in essence, than the use of the masculine pronoun for God. In this book, I have chosen to stick with the traditional reference that designates God as "he" because I feel it paramount that the personal aspect of God's nature be emphasized (it cannot be overemphasized!), and in English there is no way to adequately do that with gender-neutral language. Without the use of a personal pronoun for God (and "she" comes with its own untenable baggage), the use of God as a pronoun in English sounds stiff, formal, and far from the deeply personal nature "he" has revealed to us in Christ. As previously mentioned, Christ always comes to us through culture.

Christianity, by its very design, is a relationship between God and each person. Whenever the focus becomes creeds and doctrines, or prescribed behaviors (e.g., good Christians don't drink and dance), it moves from a vital relationship to mere religion, and begins to reflect the culture or subculture of those who define the tenets of their particular brand of Christianity. As stated above, Christian doctrines and traditions are necessary and important, but they are far from central to a faith that *must* find its core in an ongoing exchange between the in-dwelling and ever-present God of love and mercy, and those who through Christ continually receive, share and return his love, grace, and goodness. And though the core of the faith remains unchanged and unchangeable, shifting cultural trends require new and effective means to facilitate connections between that historic faith and the contemporary lifestyles and sensibilities it seeks to address.

If we fail and Christianity is diluted into mere religious forms, it becomes little more than one more cultural expression among many rather than a life-generating template for all peoples and all cultures everywhere. Christianity as mere culture can be a serious distraction from the genuine gospel because of its distinctly religious cloak. The devil could do no better. Through the ages, too many Christians have settled for being good religious people, and substituted viable faith for a culturally-determined "morality program." Christianity as religion takes the teeth out of historic, biblical faith, because prescribed religious culture is anathema to the gospel.

In discussing the faith-generating power behind a Christianity replete with the miraculous, Bill Johnson states that simple doctrine-based faith is usually a cover-up "to justify weaknesses" and make the church feel better about its pathetic impotence, especially in the area of signs and wonders.[5] Rather than model the "true revolutionaries" that Jesus intended, Johnson says the church has become populated with those who have settled for the ineffectual role of "nice people."[6] He believes that religious culture leads to "a Christian lifestyle [that] can be accomplished by people who don't even know God."[7] In full agreement with this assessment, Jonathan Welton declares that "The Average Christian [sic] has grown quite accustomed to living in awareness of a list of rules, rather than living in awareness of the heart of God."[8] If true, Christianity as religion differs not a lick from every other worldview, religious or secular, that inevitably expresses the norms and values of the cultural influences that inform and guide them. Christians alone have the means to express beliefs and behaviors that go beyond the culturally-sanctioned dictates of society. If we don't employ that option, our Christianity becomes more culture than substance, more learned behavior than living faith.

COUNTRY CLUB CHRISTIANITY

The American church, like churches the world over, is always and forever struggling with the paradox of being both inclusive and exclusive. Denominational affiliations make little difference in this regard, because each ecclesiastical grouping has its members and attendees who represent the "inner circle" of the church body, while everyone else necessarily lies outside that designation. Inclusion always comes through ritualized initiations of some sort (confessions of faith, membership commitments, regular tithing and/or attendance), and those at the center of decision-making and influence (generally pastors and elders) necessarily encourage others, both inside and outside the church body, to move more and more toward the center of the church's life and distinct ecclesiastical identity.

At the same time, the Christian faith admonishes all believers to focus outward in order to share the gospel through word and deed with a lost and hurting world. Yet those who refuse that faith, or accept it according to the dictates of theological and/or cultural faith communities that are very different from one's own, are too often categorized and shunned as reprobates or renegades (even branded "unsaved"). The inbuilt conflict between the "brethren" within one's own congregation and those outside of it can easily

---

5. Johnson, *Heaven Invades Earth*, 215.
6. Ibid., 119.
7. Ibid.
8. Welton, *Normal Christianity*, 75.

become fodder for exclusionary and condemning attitudes and behaviors. The tendency to judge and exclude arises from the "self-other" divide within fallen human nature, and is reinforced through a number of American cultural values and norms such as individualism, patriotism, privilege and superiority, competition, and segmented pluralism.

When these natural and cultural propensities are put ahead of biblical Christianity and its emphasis on the all-encompassing kingdom of God, "Country Club Christianity" is the result. It is a culturally-sanctioned expression of faith wherein *our* faith community is *the* true body of Christ, and every one else represents varying degrees of wrongness. Though rarely expressed in such terms, the "we've got it right and you don't" attitude has infected virtually the whole church in America. Mainline Protestants, Evangelicals, Fundamentalists, Anabaptists, Catholics, and Orthodox all struggle with this identity issue, mostly unaware.

The struggle has helped create an American Christianity that is extremely fragmented—an incredible patchwork of faith expressions that cater to the uniqueness of America's diversity. Yet those outside the faith find the schisms baffling and not a little humorous. There is, of course, a method to the madness. A legitimate purpose lies behind the fragmentation. America's wide diversity in class and culture naturally leads to subdivisions within the church that can best address the unique sociocultural and psychospiritual needs and preferences of different faith communities. "Birds of a feather flock together," and individuals are obviously drawn toward church groups that most closely align with their own particular cultural backgrounds. High Episcopalian parishioners naturally find it difficult to express their version of Christianity in a "full-gospel" church with dancing in the isles and folks getting "slain in the spirit"—and vise versa! Yet the extreme diversity is ultimately a sign of failure—an overemphasis on social and cultural preferences that create a landscape littered with Christian groups that have little to do with one another. To our shame, Sunday morning is the time when America is the most segregated.

The segregation, whether along racial, sociocultural, or theological lines, is crippling to the life and ministry of the church as a whole, which is called to be a reflection of God's glorious kingdom on earth—a kingdom without exclusionary borders. Yet exclusionary cultural forms have been unknowingly absorbed into church life. For instance, from where do we get the ubiquitous necessity for church membership? It is certainly not found in the biblical record. By all counts, membership is a cultural add-on that draws upon the "self-other divide" and numerous other American cultural traits that are indicative of a country-club mentality. Church membership seems innocuous at first glance, but it can help foster an exclusionary outlook that leads to other exclusionary and privileged cultural practices that thoroughly mix up faith with specific cultural norms and values. In the case of church membership, one can only surmise that economic viability (via membership vows of commitment) and pastoral control over the flock are heavily involved, similar to any secular organization in America. As a reaction to this situation, some have begun to question the need for church buildings, as well as salaried and ordained pastors, none of which is essential to the local expression of the Body of Christ.[9]

Every faith community is equally vulnerable to ethnocentrism toward other faith communities, just as America as a nation is toward other countries. It is a panhuman trait that must be vigilantly guarded against lest we end up sacralizing forms of religious bias, eventuating in a depressingly culturalized Christianity. When that happens, we end up revering everything with which we are associated (e.g., our theology, way of life, country, and race), which to some degree necessarily demonizes those with whom we differ. One can't simultaneously adhere to a country-club mindset and a kingdom consciousness, any more than one can simultaneously love God and despise his neighbor. Membership must be firmly established in one realm or the other.

FORMULAIC FAITH

The dominance of form over substance characterizes all expressions of culturalized Christianity in America. As noted in chapters 1 and 3, unredeemed human nature prods us to prioritize forms and the physical over the essence of a person or thing. Unless we purposefully learn to see deeper than the surface, the surface is all we will see. As discussed in chapter 7, cultivating image has become a highly prized endeavor in America, prompting us to primarily define ourselves, our communities, and our enterprises by the images they project (or we think they do). In this way the culture builds upon fallen human nature, leading us to believe that the superficial is indeed what's important and real. Through enculturation we are made to believe that what we see on the surface is what we really get. It is a form of self-deception.

Mix in the high value Americans place on rationalistic ways of knowing, and a strong orientation toward progress and predictable outcomes in life, and it stands to reason (hello left brain!) that we have become a "formulaic" people. We've perfected the art of creating formulas that supposedly give us the power to direct our endeavors toward the outcomes we desire.

9. See Rutz, *Mega Shift*.

Our formulations, whether in business, industry, politics, or personal endeavors, give us a false sense of control over the environments we encounter, as when well-designed marketing strategies attempt to steer consumer spending toward a particular product. We have come to heavily rely on developing and utilizing various formulas as an essential cultural tool by which we attempt to shape and control virtually every facet of life within a constantly changing modernity.

Not surprisingly, the formulaic obsession has sprouted up in the American church as an unquestioned mode of operation. It causes faith to become more a recitation of religious jargon than a heartfelt response to God. In religious cultures around the world, formulaic faith relies on ritualized words, behaviors, and objects to elicit a desired standing before or response from the deity/universal order. For example, strictly prescribed religious behaviors motivate Tibetan Buddhists to create incredibly elaborate and time-consuming sand paintings (*mandalas*) that, when purposefully destroyed by the monks who created them, ingrain the belief that the whole material realm is illusory and transitory (which it is). Similarly, animistic shamans around the globe recite secretive incantations to control and appease the spiritual realm they rightly perceive. Yet does any of it differ from the way we Christians insist on the use of certain predetermined words and phrases to effect repentance and salvation, or expect that a viable faith must entail specific conduct (e.g., church membership, regular "quiet time," speaking in tongues)? Is agreement with and regular recitation of the Nicene Creed essentially any different than reciting the Vedic mantra "Om Shanti Om"?—or the national anthem for that matter? We are all seemingly wired to substitute forms for the real thing—the "substance" of faith.

Perhaps Protestants are most apt to do this with our view of scripture. "Sola Scriptura" is the requisite Reformation battle cry, one that is reminiscent of my fellow Texans impassioned declaration, "Remember the Alamo!" Have post-Reformation believers divinized the scriptures in a manner that merely replicates the formalities of a Catholicism against which they originally reacted? Richard Rohr points out that "it's impossible" to embrace a position of "scripture only." He rightly recognizes that "You necessarily come from a culture, from a temperament, from an economic worldview, a social worldview. Luther did too."[10] We would do well to ask if the Bible—or any aspect of religious belief and behavior—has any sacredness outside of the Spirit who must enliven it (see John 6:60–63). We are prone to unquestioningly idolize objects and practices, especially things religious. (In Pakistan, believers do not allow their feet to touch the Bible, fervently convinced

---

10. Rohr, *Jesus' Plan*, 49.

that this custom adopted from their Muslim neighbors—for whom it is one of the very worst offenses due to cultural associations with dirty, sandaled feet—is inherently sacrosanct.)

Are Christian believers who think there to be errors, additions, and mistranslations in the scriptures, or who think there are seventy-three rather than sixty-six books therein, any less loved and accepted by God on account of such things? What of those who believe that faith and evolution are not contradictory? What I am asking is how much faith, and of what sort, is necessary to be among "the elect"? None, according to John Crowder—at least none that we can generate. Rituals, formulas, and even sacred cow theology all fall under the rubric of "religion" for Crowder, who offers the grand insight that it (they) "always throws you back upon yourself for salvation."[11] The church and every believer on the face of God's green planet would do well to extricate himself from the belief that anything other than the unequivocal love and grace of God is the basis of our faith. There is no need to be anything other than grateful and gracious recipients of God's undeserved favor in Christ Jesus. Our culture, and especially our religious culture, will tell us differently; but such perspectives and the formulations they entail only lead into forms of legalism that eventually separate us from both God and one another. The only real borders to the gospel are those we have constructed out of the fear and insecurity we bring to it.

CHRISTIANITY AS POWER AND INFLUENCE

Our culture is virtually defined by the mantra of majority rule. We are rightly proud of this democratic tradition, yet beneath it lies the unspoken understanding that a majority can only rule by flexing its muscles. "Might makes right," and only those who collectively push their shared agenda find themselves in the position to exercise that right. Admittedly, it's simply "the way of the world," though it is deeply rooted in fallen human nature (chapter 3) and the particulars of American culture ("Privilege and Superiority" and "Power Struggles" in chapter 6). The cultural values that give birth to the idea that the strong and powerful—by virtue of money, numbers, and inherited power and privilege—have the right to impose their agendas on others has seeped into the church and the way it views its role in the world.

There are innumerable examples of how the church has adopted and legitimized the use of power and influence, but for the sake of space I will focus on one area that is well documented by sociologist James Hunter (introduced in chapter 7). Hunter makes a compelling case that Christians in

---

11. Crowder, *Cosmos Reborn*, 247.

America have followed the general culture toward politicizing every aspect of life, leading to three main positions in what he calls "political theologies."[12] They represent the conservative, progressive, and neo-Anabaptist segments of American Christianity, cutting across every denomination and confessional tradition. Each has accommodated matters of faith to fit the political culture of the day, which is to say that each adopts a victimized self-image that helps justify their confrontational position vis-à-vis other groups and the culture-at-large.

Hunter contends that the conservative Christian Right shares with the progressive Christian Left the desire to "change the world" by way of gaining the political power that will enable them to establish their differing visions for America—the former based on winning back the Christian values and way of life that has been lost to secularization, and the latter redirecting a self-absorbed, materialistic society toward issues of community, equality and justice for the poor and disenfranchised. The third segment, the neo-Anabaptist tradition, is framed as highly suspicious of government and political engagement, viewing it as evil and antithetical to the Christian life and witness. According to Hunter, the neo-Anabaptists operate under the myth that the unrestrained market economy in America has set the country and culture in opposition to the church, which can never coexist with the power-based structures of the state and the economic system it legitimizes. Thus, neo-Anabaptists have determined to bear witness to and influence the larger culture indirectly through their own parallel ecclesiastical society that is oriented toward the things they consider paramount—peace, justice, moderation and community.

Hunter's thesis is that all three factions of American Christianity are wrongly motivated because their orientation is toward that which they oppose (see "Reactionary Christianity" below). They possess an identity formed in opposition to perceived threats, rather than an identity based on affirming what each group supports, freed from a sense of victimization and vengeful, vilifying ideology. In addition, Hunter argues that all three groups fail to understand both the nature of culture and the means by which cultures change. Thus, their desired impact on the larger culture is not realized, nor can it ever be.

Operating on the periphery of the network of elites that Hunter believes are those with the real power to change culture, each faction of American Christians remains largely on the outside of contemporary culture and culture change networks, thus having little or no impact on its formation and direction. For Hunter, the only viable alternative to the misdirected and

---

12. Hunter, *Change The World*, 109.

ineffective positions of the contemporary American church is to reestablish a historic position of "faithful presence." His suggestion is that the church should penetrate, participate in, and engage all segments of society (thereby going "into all the world") to bear a positive witness in both word and deed without falling prey to the futile desire to control and micro-direct our evermore pluralizing post-Christian culture. The American church's best hope, in Hunter's learned estimation, is to live one's faith "in the world" without being "of the world" through the pursuit of excellence and faithfulness to one's given calling in life, actively engaged in all areas that promote "human flourishing." The results we are to be left in God's able hands, free from the anger and angst that currently epitomizes too much of the church's public presence. (It is interesting to note that Jesus was able to effectively and permanently alter the power structure of his day without using or being a part of that structure to do it.)

There's a hard lesson for all believers to learn here; one that came with great difficulty to the Apostle Paul, the early church's mover-and-shaker who summed up his struggles with God's sometimes inscrutable ways with the well-known verse from 2 Corinthians 12:9: "My power is made perfect in weakness." Whatever the "thorn in the flesh" Paul asked God to remove, he eventually realized that the way the rational mind goes about getting things done was not God's way. Every believer has need to learn this same lesson to the degree that he or she struggles to trust God with the things that seem worth achieving but lie beyond human ability to facilitate.

REACTIONARY FAITH

Hunter's declaration that the church has sold out to the culture through its reliance on power politics and litigious endeavors extends to other areas of life as well. What they have in common is the tendency to be reactionary in nature—to define ourselves by what we are not. Nowhere is this seen more acutely than in our theological declarations, which typically seek to delineate what a particular denomination believes vis-à-vis other groups of believers. Our statements of faith are very often statements of what our group does *not* believe and *does not* want to be associated with, such as speaking in tongues. When this happens, we descend to the level of defining ourselves as a reaction to that which we disapprove of in others. It is an essentially negative orientation that derives directly from fallen human nature and all the self-interest that accompanies the "self-other" designations outlined in chapter 1.

Once again, this is the way of the world. Individuals, groups, and institutions generally carve out an identity that is precisely what they *don't want to be*. It's a form of identity by proxy—a way of being that contains within it the seeds of condemnation and exclusion. The church is full of such efforts to stand apart from whatever it shuns. We seem quick to accord ourselves the elevated status of being beyond reproach (liberally applying to ourselves the verse from Romans 8:1 [ESV], "There is therefore now no condemnation for those who are in Christ Jesus"), but slow to extend the same to those outside our well-defined group. But the way of Jesus was and is different. He identified himself and the church in exclusively constructive terms that were without negating references to the identity and position of others. Both his words and actions displayed an unequivocally inclusionary stance. He opposed only those who attempted to use their power and position to exclude others from the kingdom (Matt 23:13; Luke 11:52).

A simple way to know if we are subject to the rampant cultural attitude that identifies and elevates self at the expense of others is to ask if we are loving God in those other persons. Can we see Jesus in our adversaries, or at least feel God's love for them? Would our attitude and sense of self-identity shift if we were to pray for the welfare of those we oppose? St. Augustine put the matter this way: "Whoever, then, thinks that he understands the Holy Scriptures, or any part of them, but puts such an interpretation upon them as does not tend to build up this two-fold love of God and our neighbor, does not yet understand them as he ought."[13] We should never cease asking God if we understand the scriptures as we ought, for their depths are plumbless.

RESPECTABLE CHRISTIANITY

Not many Christians arise each morning with a prayer for the day that includes a request to be made a "fool for Christ" (1 Cor 4:11). In fact, we long for just the opposite—to be understood, appreciated, and respected for who we are and what we do. It is, of course, only natural to want it that way. But Jesus warned that authentic discipleship comes at a cost in terms of our standing in the world (John 16:33).

And there is a vast difference between being considered foolish because of our faith and making fools of ourselves because we've concocted and propagated a Christianity that is laden with ludicrous cultural trappings (e.g., Does empowerment by the Holy Spirit necessitate red-faced shouting

---

13. Augustine, *Christian Doctrine*, chap. 36.40, http://www.ccel.org/ccel/augustine/doctrine.xxxvi.html, accessed October 21, 2014.

from the pulpit?). None-the-less, *most* Christians in America are seemingly desperate to appear respectable to those outside the church, often guided by the mistaken notion that by appearing sensible and practical people our faith will gain a hearing among those who have thus far rejected it.

There are many ways in which Christians regularly attempt the futile task of projecting an air of respectability. The problem is that what is respectable to some is foolishness to others, and Christians lie all along the continuum of what defines respectability in our diverse society. Working hard and supporting civic causes (especially our troops) is for some portions of the population much less important than promoting civil rights and protecting the environment. Likewise, issues such as abortion, gay marriage, and universal health care divide American Christians and their church denominations in ways identical to non-Christians. Education levels, social standing, and geographical location have much to do with the values we espouse. Thus, ultimately respectability is only in the eye of the beholder, and whenever the church orients itself to garner the approval of others, it betrays its true purpose and identity as representative of Jesus and citizens of the kingdom of God. That's the goal we must keep our eyes on.

The desire to be relevant is a disoriented cousin of the desire to be respected. As the Jesuit writer Henri Nouwen noted, the devil's first attack on Jesus was the temptation to be relevant—to turn stones into bread and thereby place practicality, productivity, and worldly success ahead of the will of God.[14] Human efforts outside of God's leading will ultimately be in vain, no matter how apparently worthy the cause (Ps 127:1). Nouwen gave up a Harvard professorship and tons of respectability in order to live among and serve the mentally handicapped, who cared not a wit for his credentials; and in his "downward mobility," the erudite and highly-acclaimed academic discovered a joy and sense of meaning that previously escaped him.

There is absolutely nothing wrong with Christians excelling at their vocations as academics, politicians, scientists, and even soldiers (though some argue the morality of military involvement), but any accolades that come their way should be the by-product of their devotedness to Christ and not the result of currying favor among the powerbrokers and agenda-setters of this world. Likewise, Christian institutions can only truly reflect the principles of the kingdom (see next chapter) by a willingness to side with the poor, powerless, and disenfranchised in their lonely plight—the very people who are generally shunned by "respectable" segments of society. In fact, many of those respectable segments have laid the groundwork to

---

14. Nouwen, *Name of Jesus*, 31.

create the conditions that lead to poverty and lack of opportunity for the poor in the first place.

The church can only really obtain respectability by being fully itself, and not what it thinks the world wants it to be. The same applies to individual Christians, who cannot follow Christ without the "offense of the cross" (Gal 5:11) posing an inevitable affront to some whose paths they cross. In the final analysis, believers are not called to give an account to their colleagues, employers, political parties, or nation-states, but to the One able to offer the only authoritative commendation (Matt 25:23). By seeking his approval first and foremost, we will occasionally also gain the approval of society-at-large and its power brokers; but it is neither a motivation nor a goal that should hold any attraction for those who hearts are aligned with the kingdom of God and its distinctive purposes on earth.

COMPETITIVE CHRISTIANITY

It's not very hard to see how our highly competitive culture has seeped into the church and its agenda. Much of American Christianity has taken on a glossy finish meant to attract souls from competing versions of faith, similar to the way companies create fancy packaging to attract consumers to their products. And like the packaged food products that too often lack adequate nutritional value, sometimes the content of worship and the quality of fellowship is lessened by an emphasis on ostentatious buildings, exquisite choirs, and other superficialities. In some respects, America has become barren ground for lost souls, as the same soil gets tilled over and over by those sowing the gospel (or some version of it). Competition can get fierce, leading in some cases to reliance on baubles and gimmicks to attract unbelievers—"faith lures," as it were. Christian radio, for example, has assumed a pop-culture format that closely mimics successful secular stations, while Christian television programs tend to sensationalize their content in order to survive in what has become a top-heavy industry. The Christian publishing industry has followed a secular lead by focusing on name recognition and popularity as guides for choosing what to publish. (Admittedly, all print media is in sink-or-swim mode from the proliferation of and increasing preference for wireless versions of books, journals, and newspapers).

Regrettably, soul saving has become the measure of success for most congregations, ministries, and missions. Conversions get counted up the way corporations count profits, with success measured in strictly numeric terms. Missions are especially prone to this type of distorted faith, reporting souls saved to supporting churches the way corporations offer profitability reports to stockholders. Often the motivation is concern over sufficient operational funds to keep ministries afloat in a belt-tightening economy. The staggering overhead for mega-churches, outreach ministries with paid staff, and mission/aid organizations working overseas (the latter of which I have had direct experience) drives churches and parachurch organizations to constantly appeal for funds and seek new donors. Give a single gift and watch the plethora of mailer appeals from the receiving ministry and others with whom your personal information somehow got shared! Many American Christians give their hard-won dollars to see tangible results in the form of increasing numbers of converts, which fits right into the goal and progress-oriented set of cultural values we have inherited as Americans.

"Sharing the gospel" sometimes gets isolated into one activity among others that constitute "Christian ministry"—a formalized and essentially artificial expression of faith. It is like a UPS-delivered package. We tend to forget that *every aspect of our lives is our gospel*, and isolating some parts of the Christian life from the rest of living is contrary to the all-encompassing nature of biblical faith. In our desire to "witness" to others, we would do well to recall the words attributed to St. Francis: "Preach the gospel at all times and use words when necessary."

Another facet of American culture that has stamped its dubious image on the church is the notion that our faith is something to be consumed. In an effort to be relevant and attractive, a lot of churches strive to entertain parishioners through the use of rocking-it-out bands, multimedia shows, and hippified sermons with their requisite "late-night" style jokes and youth-speak. Although Paul did say he became all things to all people so that he might win some for Christ (1 Cor 9:19–22), one could argue that segments of the church have given in to American demands that church gatherings should, like other endeavors worth leaving home for, be unquestionably entertaining. Of course, one would hope a church service might be engaging as opposed to boring, but it is very easy for believers to become acculturated to values that measure Christian venues by secular standards that rely heavily on superficial attractiveness and entertainment value.

Another trend in the church that is reflective of American culture is the so-called "Health and Wealth Gospel." Personally, I do feel there to be plenty of biblical and experiential justification for supernatural healing today, and it's difficult to argue for a biblical definition of *sozo* that does not include material prosperity.[15] But the idea that God means us all to be wealthy by today's extravagant standards is a far cry from the biblical model found in

---

15. See, for example, books by some of the writers quoted in this manuscript: John Crowder, Heidi Baker, Jonathan Welton, Mel Bond, and Bill Johnson.

1 Timothy 6:8, ". . . if we have food and clothing, we will be content with that." Paul goes on to say, "Those who want to get rich fall into temptation and a trap and into many foolish and harmful desires that plunge people into ruin and destruction. For the love of money is a root of all kinds of evil. Some people, eager for money, have wandered from the faith and pierced themselves with many griefs" (Tim 6:9–10).

Jesus did say that he came that we might have life in abundance (John 10:10), yet the abundance of which he spoke was primarily related to the fruits of the Holy Spirit in our lives—love, joy, peace, patience, kindness, goodness, faithfulness, gentleness, and self-control (Gal 5:22–23)—and not the excessive trappings of our materialistically-obsessed culture. There's a huge difference between abundance and excess. If we accept the kind of abundance God freely provides, we are more than content with just our basic needs met. Excess has no attraction when we recognized that abundance is very much an attitude of the heart.

CEREBRAL CHRISTIANITY

Since the Renaissance, Western culture history has moved decisively toward favoring the mind over other ways of knowing and experiencing the world, self, and others. It was our Greek heritage, of course, that got the ball rolling in the first place. As noted in chapter 6 under "Logic and Reason," this orientation has been primary within Euro-American culture since the advent of the Industrial Revolution, which helped foster the economics-driven view that humans can be reduced to machines. In American culture, rationalistic constructs have become normative through our reliance on science-based systems of knowledge, technological innovations, constitutional legalism and litigation, and formulaic approaches to education, medicine, commerce, and politics—in fact, virtually every dimension of life.

The church, so much a reflection of the culture in which we live, expresses the primacy of the rational mind in numerous ways: creedal-based faith, theological legalism, sectarian denominational apologetics, and a defensive stance against integrative and novel ways of encountering and understanding the world (e.g., ecotheology). Perhaps the most crippling of these is the tendency for American Christians to view the faith as a rationalistic system of beliefs that separates God from man, heaven from earth, and other theological dualisms. Although Christianity is not irrational and, as has already been argued, makes more sense logically than any other system of philosophical or religious belief known to mankind, it is best to see faith as a-rational or supra-rational; that is, beyond or more than logical to the human mind.

The problem with a Christianity that is primarily apprehended through rational thought processes is that it leads directly into a works-oriented faith that encourages adherents to earn their salvation through self-generated faith and will-based efforts to be upright and moral. The mysterious, intuitive, and often paradoxical *knowing and experiencing* God that is innate to the Christian faith gets pushed aside by the rationally-bound mind that is forever relying upon its own resources to explain what is, in essence, the inexplicable—the eternal triune God become man, whose presence sacralizes the whole material world, including mortal flesh.

John Crowder, among others, has addressed this shortcoming within much of North American Christianity in his writing.[16] The gospel, he maintains, "is an utterly supernatural message . . . [that] is otherworldly" and not human.[17] It speaks of our "union with God . . . [who] Christians experience . . . directly through our belief in Jesus Christ, enabling us to apprehend spiritual truths that are inaccessible through intellectual means."[18] Crowder goes to great lengths to show that historic Christian faith has until fairly recent times been viewed from this "mystical" perspective, especially within the Catholic tradition.[19] Contemporary Anglo-American Christians have shied away from this aspect of the gospel for fear that it will not jive with scientific rationalism—which it cannot because biblical faith goes so far beyond the confines of human thought and understanding (Isa 55:8–9).

Unless the gospel is understood in a super-rational, pan-cultural fashion—one that incorporates all aspects of historic faith across cultures—it will be severely limited by the dominant culture within which it is found. In America, that means a heavy coating of logic-based and works-oriented faith that has some practical application or goal orientation acknowledged by the culture-at-large. Our "Protestant work ethic" has bequeathed us a Christianity in which we generate works-based religious conviction rather than joyfully live out the freely-given faith generated in us since our conversion (Gal 3). Likewise, the practical, goal-oriented bent of our culture leads us to believe that the kingdom of heaven is a place "out there" which we will inherent if we maintain enough faith in this life, rather than a realm of which we currently partake through pure and unadulterated grace and

---

16. See, in particular, *Miracle Workers*, *Reformers*, and *The New Mystics* and *Mystical Union*.

17. *Mystical Union*, 13.

18. Ibid., 12.

19. *Cosmos Reborn*, 101–12.

Presence (Luke 17:20–21; Romans 14:17). Resting in God and his utterly wonder gift is seemingly antithetical to American culture; a pity because all our striving only throws up barriers to those non-believers who would otherwise find a great attraction to a faith that relieves them of the stressful burdens of contemporary life, while providing all the benefits they seek in complete futility in all the wrong places.

CHRISTIANITY AS PUBLIC SERVICE

It may seem that I have focused almost exclusively on what is wrong with the church in America today, so it's important to provide some balance because much is also right—that is, in accordance with biblical and historic Christianity and the principles of the kingdom. One could, in fact, construct a rather impressive list that would include faith-based education at every level of society, ecumenism, emphasis upon civil rights and environmental stewardship, and well-funded outreach efforts that stretch from local neighborhoods to remote regions around the world. Although not representative of the whole church, such things widely exist and need to be duly acknowledged.

The best of what is right with the church in America may be subsumed under the heading of "love and service" which, after all, has been the defining characteristic of the church since its inception (John 13:35; Heb 13:1–3; James 1:22–27). One can go to almost any town or neighborhood around the country and find Christians hard at work serving their communities. It is very heartening to find believers lending a hand or spearheading local efforts to address human need and seek justice for those who lack it. Soup kitchens, homeless shelters, medical clinics, and youth mentoring programs are just a few examples of Christian ministries that serve God through the often dire local needs. If fact, if some progressive volunteer program is impacting a local community almost anywhere in the U.S., chances are quite good that Christians will be involved in it at some level.

These efforts are not just "good works," but an indication that faith is alive and well because love and service naturally flow from it. They are a true barometer of what is right about the faith American believers have in Jesus, who scripture tells us went around his world healing and doing good to *all those in need* (Matt 9:35, Acts 10:38). As stated previously, love is intrinsically active. The love of the Father found active expression through the incarnation of Jesus into our world of woe. It can be no other way. No "good works" can ever earn, deserve, or lead to *agape* love. That love must always precede and engender those good works; otherwise, religious values will flip the script as fallen human nature seeks to justify itself and find fulfillment primarily through human effort. The tipping point between faith-generated good works and works-based religiosity is a subtle one that easily becomes sublimated in the values many Americans hold dear.

Although American Christianity is noted for its activism, there is so much more that viable faith could and should generate—though not through any modicum of guilt, shame, or favor-gaining religiosity. Those means are the *modi operandi* of fallen human nature, apparent in various and sundry cultural expressions of ecclesiastical "do-goodism" in our country. But if we Christians open ourselves up to the fullness of God's transforming love, there *will* follow an explosion of good that can utterly transform every dimension of society. Such an outpouring would make it difficult to find the poor, disenfranchised, and wounded souls who now wander our streets and fill our inner cities. God's explosive love is the only true source of "renewable energy" that can legitimately generate *every good work* (Titus 3:1, ESV); yet like an unknown deposit of precious stones, it lies largely undiscovered and untapped by the contemporary church in America.

POST-CHRISTIAN CHRISTIANITY

The church in America is going through an identity crisis unlike any it has ever known before. Having for so long been part-and-parcel of the dominant culture, yet now rejected by that culture in favor of materialistic and narcissistic self-determinism, the church is now in the process of reinventing itself (or, better yet, rediscovering what it really is). Not all dimensions of the church are on board, privy to this understanding that the old forms of institutionalized Christianity have become passé, especially for the largest branches and denominations that constitute the ecclesiastical establishment. Modernity has stripped away the foundations of traditional Christianity, exposing a church that is often out of touch with and largely irrelevant to contemporary life.

The identity crisis has led to a diverse effort to reinvent or reinterpret not only what the church is and should be, but to redefine what it supposedly was in the first place—during its formative years in the first few centuries. Segments of the church have taken the rejection of the dominant culture to heart and set off on what Crowder terms a "new Reformation,"[20] (the first, he maintains, did not go nearly far enough). Yet in the U.S., the "re-formation" movement is by no means limited to Protestantism. Catholics are well represented and in many respects leading the charge. Pope John Paul, who

---

20. *Mystical Union*, 17.

most Catholics consider a big-time reformer within the Roman Church, is very well received in the U.S. precisely because he represents a leader more in step with change and the need to be relevant on the modern world stage.

Various names have been associated with one stream of this re-formation—though there is a strong effort to refuse names and categories—among them the Emerging Church, the Seeker Church, Trinitarianism, and the New Monasticism movement. The primary characteristics of the resurgence are an emphasis on ecumenicalism both within and outside the faith, mysticism that links the modern church with broader Christian expression over the past two millennia, more inclusive and non-dualistic ways of thinking and knowing, informal small-group fellowships that better reflect early Christianity, a personalized and experiential faith centered on the person of Jesus, and a degree of scholarship that seeks to honestly understand the place of faith and the scriptures within the context of modernity (especially in relation to science-based knowledge)—all of which constitutes an effort to be relevant in a positive way rather than essentially reactive in a negative one.

Related to the mystical dimension of the re-formation is a vibrant revival of the supernatural in the form of divine healing and "signs and wonders." These manifestations of the supernatural push beyond the theological, philosophical, and ethical issues that are central to the focus of the aforementioned stream of the re-formation movement, which seem more keen to make Christianity relevant to the hot-button issues of contemporary culture (peace, justice, sexual orientation, ecology, etc.). According to those who "move in the supernatural," the church will only be relevant to the degree that it separates itself not only from traditional culturalized forms of Christianity, but also from the ways of the world in general—both being heavily dependent on materialistic (i.e., naturalistic) and humanistic modalities.

According to the proponents of a supernaturally-endowed church, as believers step into their intrinsic calling to go beyond expressing a gospel of God's love and forgiveness (which they feel is necessary but incomplete) to demonstrating the supernatural power of the Holy Spirit, then and only then will the church become relevant. To offer a witness without also manifesting God's supernatural power is "a major shortcoming," according to Bill Johnson, who says, "It is impossible to give an adequate witness of God without demonstrating His supernatural power."[21] The reason, he offers, is that demonstrations of power in the form of healings and the miraculous have the express purpose of changing hearts as nothing else can. "Power exposes," Johnson declares. "It draws a line in the sand and forces people to a decision.

---

21. Johnson, *Heaven Invades Earth*, 134.

... [It] removes the middle ground ... [and] forces the issue because of its inherent ability to humble mankind."[22] God is glorified, the true and complete identity of Jesus established, and non-believers are able to "break ... loose from the rationale that this material world is the ultimate reality"[23]—a feat that is much less likely to occur through "powerless" Christianity. Johnson and others have called such faith "normal Christianity." They argue that it was practiced by the early church and at various times throughout history, but has been lost to the bulk of Western believers over time. However, the supernaturalists (non-cessationalists) believe the rightful place of "power and love"[24] as a tandem force authenticating the church and its gospel message is rapidly gaining ground in the U.S. and around the world.

The supernatural brand of "normal Christianity" that ministers such as Crowder and Johnson advocate (referring to it as a modern-day revival or renewal movement) will, in their opinions, eventually become normative for the whole church, as "the present and coming revival will surpass all the accomplishments of the Church in all history combined. Over 1 billion souls will be saved. Stadiums will be filled with people 24 hours a day, for days on end, with miracles beyond number: healings, conversions, resurrections, and deliverances too many to count. No special speaker, no well-known miracle worker, just the Church being what God has called her to be."[25]

The Bethel School of Supernatural Ministry, which Johnson founded in association with his non-denominational, charismatic church in Redding, California, is but one of a number of such schools in the U.S. Another prominent one is The Global School of Supernatural Ministry, founded by Randy Clark through his Global Awakening ministry based in Mechanicsburg, Pennsylvania. Within these schools, young people in their twenties constitute the bulk of those who receive communally-focused training in supernaturally-endowed Christian faith and practice. A large percentage of their student body is international, coming mainly from developed countries in Europe and Asia. The schools are not accredited by the US Department of Education but do charge tuition.

---

22. Ibid., 135.

23. Ibid., 143.

24. "Power and love" is both a proclaimed ministerial emphasis and the name of a particular ministry that conducts "schools" (seminars) around the U.S. to train Christians in "power evangelism"—that is, techniques to "demonstrate the gifts of prophecy, word of knowledge, and healing in the world." http://powerandlove.org, accessed February 15, 2013.

25. *Heaven Invades Earth*, 210.

The Global School offers that it "place[s] an emphasis on impartation and equipping students for a life spent walking in the supernatural."[26] The Bethel School posts this motto on its website: "We Owe the World an Encounter with God," alongside a quote from one of one its pastor-teachers: "We're equipping a company of revivalists to transform the world."[27] In Redding, I met a bright young man in his thirties who was in the second year of a three-year program, having quit his job as an engineer in Los Angeles and used his savings to pursue the deep conviction that God had called him to a ministry that included the supernatural. His passion and dedication, along with that of other students I met, was nothing less than palpable.

One can thus conclude that the American church is currently characterized by two seemingly opposing positions. On one side is the traditional church that melds into the culture and generally reflects the dominant cultural values in its members' worldviews and lifestyles. Stability rather than change is prized. Yet the other part of the church actively seeks to foster distinction and to set itself apart from the old structures in order to be relevant in the modern world through more biblically and historically accurate representations of Christian faith. In this respect the church-at-large continues to follow the culture, which itself is characterized by traditional versus modern lifestyles and worldviews (e.g., consider the divisiveness within the general population of issues like gay marriage, environmentalism, and legalization of recreational marijuana).

But it's fair to say that in at least two areas *the church is shaping the culture*. One is through the church's holistic effort to engender a form of spirituality applicable to all of life and society, as the Emerging Church and similar movements are attempting to do. The other is an out-and-out assault on the naturalistic and hedonistic dimensions of American culture through a vibrant alternative spirituality that incorporates the supernatural into daily living. Hollywood—a sure-fire way to gauge the cultural trends within America—is following the church's lead by creating TV and movie offerings that reflect this indigenous cultural shift toward holistic spirituality and the supernatural. No doubt Hollywood will manipulate and misrepresent those church-engendered perspectives, but in the process it will perhaps unintentionally move the culture toward a more spiritual orientation, and an open mindedness to possibilities that lie beyond the boredom and nihilism of scientific and materialistic thinking.

---

26. Global Awakening, para. 1. http://globalawakening.com/schools/gssm, accessed October 29, 2014.

27. Vallotton, BSSM, http://bssm.net, accessed October 21, 2014.

We have said that the church at once shapes and is shaped by the dominant culture in America (through the process of memes discussed in chapter 3). This symbiotic interplay is perhaps best seen in the wide diversity of beliefs and behaviors that now exist within the church—as broad as the variety of worldviews, lifestyles, and ethnicities represented in the wider culture and society. The church's delicate calling to be "in the world but not of the world" (John 17:14–16) is thus a massive challenge. There seem to be plenty of indicators that it is firmly *in the world*, but fewer that it is not *of the world*. Perhaps accepting and even celebrating the wide diversity that exists both within the church and within American society as a whole is one concrete step toward fulfilling the in-the-world-but-not-of-it challenge, and a tangible expression of the kingdom of God in our midst. Certainly the embrace of Christian mysticism and the missing ingredient of the supernatural dimension of the gospel is, for the church, a huge leap away from the bondage of its centuries-old role as the lap dog of cultures defined by post-Renaissance materialistic worldviews. Both streams are at once refreshing and cause for great hope.

BACK TO THE FUTURE

In Colossians 2:8 (TV) the Apostle Paul spoke of "misleading philosophies and empty deceptions that are based on traditions fabricated by mere mortals." His words are as applicable to the church and American culture today as they were to the Colossian church of the first-century Greco-Roman world. The philosophies and deceptions of which he spoke lie behind all of the less than encouraging characterizations of the American church listed above. Those characterizations are sourced from the elementary principles (read: fallen human nature) originating in a world that has never recognized its need for the God of the Bible. The world has always been either too self-preoccupied or too reliant on purely humanistic agendas that represent a modern-day Tower of Babel. And the church throughout its long history has by and large complied with the stipulated program and lost its identity in the larger dominant culture.

By allowing itself to be culturalized into submission, the church became virtually indistinguishable from the secularized fabric into which it was woven—and almost always for the worse. Like a colored thread in a patterned quilt, faith got lost in the overall pattern and shape of worldly goals with all their garish appeal. Rather than shaping its native cultures through its God-imbued presence, too often Christianity has become a domesticated product of those cultures—bred into impotence and unable to offer an alternative to the status quo. In the case of the U.S., that has long meant a nominal church that blends in and legitimizes a host of social, political, and religious agendas that are decidedly alien to the gospel and the kingdom it announces.

Exceptions abound in individual lives and novel congregations as mentioned above, but the church-at-large will never be confused with the glorious kingdom of God precisely because it tends to reflect so well the kingdoms of this world. By choosing religion over faith and respectability over truth, the American church has long aligned itself with a culture that has herded it into almost total disregard and a pathetic irrelevance—the very end it desperately meant to avoid. Church and culture have long been homogenized in an America that has blended morality with materialism and biblical faith with rationalized formulations for success. The Founding Father's separation of church and state was meant to protect the church. Yet no less dangerous has been the wedding of church and culture, which we now recognize was already present from the start of our highly-vaunted history. In fact, the liaison between church and culture has been the norm for Western Christianity since the early fourth century when Constantine first declared it the official state religion—in the process, sounding something of its death knell. Despite our longing to make them so, the Founding Fathers were not heroes of the faith so much as well-intentioned men firmly ensconced in the culture of their day. Faith has survived, but history teaches that it is most viable when not aligned with the state.

Yet we can take heart that change is in the air; and only time will tell where the church-culture divide ends up. The solution to falling prey to cultural assimilation, as much as one can venture to speak of a viable alternative to culturalized Christianity, lies in recognizing the distinctiveness of the kingdom of God and the largely unsung gospel of Jesus Christ—which should form the backbone of the church, but has unfortunately long been peripheral to it. Chapter 10 will seek to elucidate the distinctives of the gospel and consider how utterly unique they actually are from the *culture du jour* that characterizes modern America. For the most part, the American church is yet to glimpse that its true inheritance is far more magnificent than anything our forbearers or modern charismatic leaders could ever imagine. The church is nothing less than God's incomparable presence and ever-expanding kingdom upon earth—the reflection of a vision so grand and glorious that, should we dare to take our lamp from underneath the lampstand, the whole world could not help but be drawn to its irresistible light. In whatever measure we grasp the essential understanding of that gospel and the glorious kingdom it proclaims, to that degree we will find them far more elevating and transformative than the most inspired of human endeavors, past or present.

PART IV

Who Are We Meant to Be?

10

The Kingdom of God

The Bible is not man's theology but God's anthropology.
—Abraham Joshua Heschel

How does one begin to describe a reality that is so far beyond words, concepts, and the limits of the human imagination (1 Cor 2:9)? The answer: with humility and as many caveats as possible. The kingdom of God is such a reality—one that cannot possibly be represented through thoughts and script, yet one that cannot be ignored because of its centrality not only to the Christian faith but to all of life. Though far beyond our abilities to adequately comprehend, we Christian believers are none-the-less called to make God's kingdom the focal point of our lives, livelihoods, goals, and way of thinking (Matt 6:33; 13:44–46). One can only assume that making it so is therefore possible on a practical level.

Given the purposes of this book—to elaborate the distinctions between Christian faith and American culture—this chapter attempts to detail some of the major characteristics of the kingdom of God as reflected in scripture, with particular emphasis on the life and teachings of Jesus. The application of those characteristics will find fuller expression in the chapter to follow, "Living in the Kingdom in America." It will set about to transcribe kingdom characteristics into applied norms and values that directly relate to American culture and the American church. First, however, it will be instructive to point out a few things the kingdom is not.

MISCONCEPTIONS ABOUT THE KINGDOM

Over the centuries, popular culture in the Western world has left us with many biblically questionable notions about the realm of God's kingdom. A few of the more egregious ones should be dispatched before attempting to outline the scripturally-sound dimensions of the kingdom and the values inherent in them. Perhaps the most prevalent misconception is that the kingdom of God is equivalent to heaven—the place the Bible says believers go to be with the Lord after death. In Revelation 21 it is figuratively represented as the New Jerusalem.

Various biblical passages attest that the kingdom of God is more than a realm to be entered in the future, clearly describing a reality that penetrates into the present (Luke 11:20; 17:20–21; Col 1:13). It is, to be more precise, an eternal realm that, from the human historical perspective, is "always now-and-not-yet."[1] More importantly, it is a realm that exists only through the presence of God—the kingdom's king. Imagination, lived experience, and paradox are some of the tools we must employ to even approach any degree of understanding kingdom realities, which span both this world and the next. Jesus employed all these modalities in his parables, but never attempted the futile task of attempting to directly describe that indescribable reality. Without unitive (non-dualistic) thinking, which doesn't come easily to minds crafted to the practical and worldly enterprises that generally engage America and the West, we are destined to miss the fact that God's kingdom is present in the now, whenever and wherever God's rule extends into human hearts and the affairs of mankind. What tends to obscure the kingdom's presence among us are the foibles of unredeemed human nature: viz., pride, arrogance, willfulness, self-dependence, and self-interest. They often combine to elevate human reason and logic above other ways of knowing. Thus, the kingdom is rightly thought of as far more encompassing than the traditional understanding of a spiritual realm beyond this life and material world.

The second fallacy regarding the kingdom is the misplaced notion that we must somehow attain it through spiritual effort. Simply put, this fallacy posits that we earn our way into God's kingdom through our own efforts to live a dedicated and sanctimonious life. Though some may realize the kingdom is here and now, as well as beyond the grave, it is still widely thought to be something earned through moral acumen and religious dedication. The biblical emphasis is that the kingdom is present if and when we cease our moral struggles and simply allow God's Spirit to manifest within

---

1. Rohr, *Jesus' Plan*, 110.

our thoughts and actions, because he is already fully present at all times in every believer (Matt 28:20; 1 John 3:24). Simply resting in his presence is an invitation for the kingdom to become manifest. Jesus called it "abiding" in him (John 15:4).

A third related misconception is the idea that God's kingdom will in some way emerge out of human agency and an earthly structure. To some adherents of this position, the earthly structure (kingdom) is the United States of America—God's "special" nation. Such folk naively view their efforts to better our nation, especially as it relates to conservative politics, as helping to create the conditions under which the kingdom will emerge. Thus, they believe it necessary to get Christians into influential positions in government in order to "take America back for God"—an endeavor which, though largely unacknowledged, links a morally and spiritually viable United States of America to the biblical kingdom of God. In this instance, God's kingdom becomes dependent upon ours.

Behind this heavily culturalized misconception is what Gregory Boyd called *The Myth of a Christian Nation*,[2] in a book by that title. Boyd details the false association between the U.S. and biblical Christianity, maintaining that America is in essence but one of the "kingdoms of this world" (nation-states in modern parlance) referenced in the Bible—all of which stand in *basic opposition* to the kingdom of Christ, which is decidedly "not of this world" (John 18:36). The second and third misconceptions both fail to recognize that God's kingdom and the fullness of its coming on earth is in no way contingent upon human efforts or agendas (and we praise him for that!).

The fallacy of human agency at times takes on subtle yet pious forms, such as missionary endeavors that employ the Great Commission of Matthew 28 to propose that unless Christians get off their duffs and make sacrificial efforts to ensure that the gospel is preached among every people group in the world, the Second Coming and the establishment of Christ's kingdom on earth simply won't happen. This erroneous conviction posits that God is at our mercy, so to speak, and fails to recognize that in his sovereign grace he allows us to be highly privileged participants in his otherwise unimpedible plans. Given the American cultural values that have become part-and-parcel of the church, the God-is-dependent-on-us position is exactly what one might expect; for we Americans are acculturated to think of ourselves as indispensable, in charge, and masters of our own fate—whether it be politics, religion, or any other endeavor.

---

2. Boyd, *Myth*.

WHAT IS THE KINGDOM OF GOD?

It is little more than a "fool's errand" to attempt to put into words the ineffable nature of God's glorious kingdom, so finite is the human mind and so limited the language we must employ to stimulate self-transcendent thought and imagination. In a real sense the kingdom can only be experienced first-hand, similar to love and life itself. Jesus used allegory and metaphor to teach about the kingdom, methods that employed knowledge and experiences common to daily life, as a means of offering hints and allusions into spiritual realities. He also demonstrated the kingdom through his person and actions. From those sources certain kingdom characteristics can be deduced, although, once again, they can only be interpreted by reference to our own world and experience. Note that the term "kingdom" itself is a borrowed reference to human governance and thus highly fraught with inadequate and often misleading inferences. For that reason, some prefer the phrase the "reign of God" or the "rule of God."

In an admittedly brief and overly clinical description, I offer the following: The kingdom of God is the place (realm, situation, consciousness) in which God's rule is absolute (due to the nature of his holy, loving, and omnipotent presence) and uncontested (by human, angelic, or demonic will). Yet in time, no creature's will can resist the kingdom's full expression on earth—the time when Christ returns bodily and God becomes all in all (1 Cor 15:28). Although the kingdom is so much more than a place or realm—heaven, as it were—Jesus sometimes spoke of the "kingdom of heaven" in reference to it.[3] Thus the kingdom of God can be thought of as a reality—*the ultimate reality*—that infuses all of eternity, space, and every metaphysical dimension both known and unknown. Perhaps it is most easily conceived as simply the "atmosphere" of God's presence. No physical or spiritual realm or inhabitant therein can exist as part of God's kingdom without the indispensable element of his radiant presence.

The fact that scripture allows for realms and creatures that evidently exist in opposition to or unaware of God's presence and rule does not negate the all-encompassing nature of it. They merely allow for a phase in which God's kingdom, by virtue of his will and omnipotent purposes, is in the process of becoming fully manifest in our temporal/spacial/will-linked

---

3. The Gospel of Matthew uses the term "kingdom of heaven" some thirty-three times, yet it is found no where else in scripture. It uses the phrase "kingdom of God" only four times. Although some maintain the "kingdom of God" and the "kingdom of heaven" refer to two different realities, the vast majority of scholars recognize that since Matthew was written primarily for Jews for whom there was a "reverential reluctance to use the name of God," the two designations are best considered synonymous. See Barker et al., *NIV*, 1489.

realm. When from the cross Jesus cried, "It is finished!" the kingdom of God and its all-encompassing parameters were established once and for all time. What appears to be another reality operating beyond or alongside God's rule (i.e., the world, the flesh, and the devil) is but a chimera—the fading image of things forever altered two millennia ago when the resurrection became the immutable "hinge of history."[4] All that went before and all that came later would find its bearing and sole purpose in that singular divine, sacrificial act of unadulterated love.

Thus, history is not properly conceived in a linear fashion, beginning with past human origins and stretching onward toward our future destiny, but as a divinely-directed *Christocentric* endeavor in which past and future fold ever inward toward the cross—the nexus of time and eternity (Rev 13:8c). All notions of human progress only have validity as they relate back to the cross, the origin and only real measure of all that is truly progressive. Outside the cross, there can be no progress . . . only the illusion of it. Unless that truth is grasped—a matter requiring divine revelation and a bit of human mental gymnastics—no adequate understanding of the kingdom can ever be reached.

Although futilely awaits all who attempt to directly describe God's glorious kingdom, it is possible to consider its characteristics as indicated in scripture, particularly those attributed to the incarnate Son who best knew and represented that eternal realm. One can surmise from his words, and the authors of scripture who experienced God's kingdom through visions and transportations, something of the true nature of it. My goal is to render these descriptions into characteristics and/or principles, which can then be applied as "kingdom norms and values" for the stated purposes of this book.

Once again, I readily admit to the limitations of this approach, which is necessarily hampered by the inability of the human mind to get beyond itself and adequately comprehend the realities governing the subject at hand. We humans are like moles blurrily peering out of our burrows at the far reaches of the cosmos. God's kingdom is its own reality, yet we have no way of approaching that reality outside of the one we experience "through a glass dimly" (1 Cor 13:12) in this transitory life upon our entropy-plagued planet. The only language we posses to speak of God's kingdom is that which relates to our own world and our bounded human experience. In anthropological terms, we are forced to approach kingdom realities anthropocentrically (human centered) and ethnocentrically, necessarily invoking the deficiencies of human-generated and culturally-derived perceptions. Yet as long as we keep in mind the many constraints that accompany these perspectives (i.e., their

---

4. Crouch, *Culture Making*, 145.

unavoidable inadequacies and biases), there is still utility in doing so; for no honest inquiry into the nature of God's kingdom goes unrewarded, and God bids us to seek his kingdom specifically because he endowed humans with the capacity to find and experience it (and him in the process) in a substantive way (Matt 6:33; 2 Chr 15:2).

THE LAW OF LOVE

If God is love (1 John 4:8) and his kingdom is the realm of his absolute rule, then that kingdom will know no other order than that of divine (*agape*) love. Of course, divine love cannot be described in terms of a literal law (a reference we project from our world) because laws presume the propensity to break them. There is no such propensity in the kingdom of God, only the desire for an unrestrained love that supersedes all law. For that reason, Jesus could claim that love of God and neighbor was the fulfillment of all the divinely-instituted laws deriving from the Hebrew scriptures (Matt 22:37–40), which otherwise required the impossible—that is, human perfection. Paul elaborated the same principle under the auspices of his New Covenant teachings when he stated that those who are led of the Spirit are not under the law, for the manifestation of the Spirit in the believer's life produces fruit that no law condemns or even addresses: viz., love, joy, peace, patience, kindness, goodness, faithfulness, gentleness and self-control (Gal 5:18). Laws are only meant to curtail human behaviors based on opposing sentiments (1 Tim 1:9–11); thus, the law of love is of a completely different order.

These scripture references reveal a number of interesting things about the realm of God's kingdom. They tell us that it extends into or infuses our known world, involves God himself in the person and actions of both Jesus and the Holy Spirit, and fulfills or even supplants all other moral and ethical systems by which humankind governs itself. The kingdom of God is thus wholly other even as it is simultaneously omnipresent and applicable through the Spirit's influence in human hearts and culture. That is why two people can see the very same thing quite differently, poetically expressed by both Jesus and William Blake who saw heaven in a wildflower,[5] while some only perceive molecular structures and genetic processes. For those without the spiritual eyes to see it, the kingdom right before them often remains completely unobserved and unencountered (2 Cor 4:3).

Pure and unimpeded relationship is another kingdom characteristic made plain by scripture. Jesus continually referred to his perfect union with

---

5. Matthew 6:28-29; Blake, "Auguries of Innocence," http://www.poetryfoundation.org/poem/172906, accessed October 22, 2014.

the Father (John 5:19–21; 10:30; 17:21) and the Holy Spirit (John 15:26)—a relationship based on mutual love (John 3:35; 15:9). It has been said that God is more of a verb based on relationship than a noun based on being, for love is by its very nature relational and, apart from that key orientation, love has no basis or meaning. Divine love can never be an abstraction. It can never be put in the objective realm; it is only subject.

The gospel is the incredibly good news that through the death and resurrection of Jesus Christ, God has woven humanity into this glorious relationship of pure reciprocal love (John 17:21; Gal 4:6). In the process, not only did God restore the original relationship he had with the first humans, he vastly improved upon it by upgrading that relationship from one where he walked beside Adam and Eve to one where he now lives in us and we in him (Rom 8:10–11; 1 John 4:12–13, 15).[6] The Kingdom of God is thus the realm of an enhanced restoration of God's original creation (including mankind), which was itself nothing less than wonderfully good (Gen 1:31). So what does that say about the quality of his creation and his relationship to it now?

Because God's inherently relational nature is imprinted within humankind (and the whole of the created order, as we now acknowledge through ecotheology), we only become fully human through entering into loving relationship with both God and the rest of creation (humanity at the fore)—without exceptions. We cannot fully become who we are designed to be as human beings and remain outside of a vibrant, loving relationship with both God and man; while to participate in that relationship, which finds its complete embodiment in the kingdom of God, is to be whole in every sense of the word. To be separated from either God or man is to be fragmented at a basic level, not only from our Creator and fellow human beings, but from our very selves. We are simply not ourselves when we are at odds with God or others. That separation leaves us like murderous Cain, stranded in the inhospitable lands east of Eden, where he spent his toilsome days "a restless wanderer" (Gen 4:12), forever stuck between the glories of Eden lost and the never-to-be-seen joys of the New Jerusalem to come. That separation was, in his own words, "more than I can bear" (Gen 4:13). In that tragic rift he represented not only himself, but the whole of humankind longing for redemption and restoration.

---

6. See Crowder, *Mystical Union*, 104.

GOD'S WORD IS TRUTH

In the kingdom of God, which we have seen encompasses this world, God's Word constitutes ultimate reality. This means that every utterance that issues from God is, by definition, more real than anything else in the created realm, the spiritual realm, or the realm of human will, thoughts, emotions, and imagination. That is why Jesus, the Word (*logos*) of God incarnate, could say "I am the way, *the truth*, and the life." Because he spoke only what he heard from the Father (John 12:49–50), every word he spoke was not only true, but Truth itself.

The implications of this understanding are "earth-shattering" indeed. It means that every realm of the mind and senses that appears contrary to the declared word of God is false; it is unreality or, at best, partial reality. Furthermore, it means that another faculty inclusive of but well beyond human reason must be employed to "comprehend" or experience the kingdom of God, for reason alone cannot possibly attain such depths of understanding (1 Cor 1:23; 2:13–14). That faculty, which is generated through the work of the Holy Spirit, is faith—the currency of the kingdom in this life.

Human reason, when rightly constituted, points in the same direction as faith, yet culture and fallen human nature contort human reason so that without faith it inevitably fails in its potential. It is faith that grants us the otherwise unattainable capability to be fully engaged citizens of the kingdom even as we inhabit this material world of cause and effect. Faith, which is a relationship-based radical trust in the person of God, allows us to live *in* the world and not be *of* it. And faith, we are told, comes through hearing the Word of God (Rom 10:17), which is Truth itself. Thus, we are designed so that God's Word of Truth generates in us the faith we need to guide and supplement our other given faculties (particularly human reason), allowing us to understand and live in the wider reality of God's kingdom. Yet the Bible makes it crystal clear that faith is a divinely-bestowed gift (Eph 2:8–9; 1 Cor 12:9), and no amount of human willpower can manufacture it. American culture and its "can-do" mentality predictably produces an egocentric and works-oriented religiosity ("ugly morality" to borrow one writer's terminology)[7] whenever faith is presented as something to be drummed up by the flesh.

Yet when we "rest" in the gift of God and absorb the faith he alone can produce in us, we find emerging a kingdom perspective that determines the borders of our worldview. It is that divinely-inspired perspective that not only opens doors of understanding into the very nature of reality and

---

7. Rohr, *Spiral of Violence*.

the physical realm we inhabit, but also allows for kingdom realities such as miracles to become manifest in our lives and world. That is why many speak of faith as generating a new awareness or awakening (a mental "turning around") that constitutes "salvation," rather than something akin to moral redirection centered on emotion-based convictions.[8] Yet any awareness of kingdom realities is a gift and not an elevated perception generated through human agency. This distinction is a watershed divergence between Christianity and all other religious systems that promote "enlightenment" based upon human efforts to attain higher states of consciousness. The kingdom, as well as our understanding and perception of it, is pure revelatory gift (Mark 4:11; Luke 12:32; 2 Cor 4:6; Col 1:13).

It is God who "quickens" in us the faith necessary to perceive his kingdom through *exposure* to his Word (hearing per se is not required, as every deaf person will attest). We respond to his Word of Truth by way of his Spirit acknowledging that Truth within us, creating the awareness of kingdom realities and the faith necessary to trust God's declared Word over any and all conflicting information.[9] That information may come in the form of intuitions, sensory perceptions, or knowledge derived from and limited to logic-based processes. The mind and physical senses together drive all worldviews based on naturalism, as well as all religious worldviews based on culture-specific perceptions of the spiritual world. Christianity alone sets a different standard by offering a unique perspective that includes, yet supersedes, the mind and all perceptions

Certainly the rational mind and its perceptions are true in a literal but limited sense (no one doubts that apples fall to the earth due to gravitational pull), but even the elements and our understanding of them are ultimately subject to a deeper Truth embodied in Christ, who created "all things" and in whom "all things hold together" (Col 1:16–17). When he walked on the

---

8. Rohr describes conversion as "a complete turnaround of worldviews" that is "not a learning as much as it is an unlearning," in *Jesus' Plan*, 7; Johnson says that repentance is "to change our way of thinking until the presence of His Kingdom fills our consciousness," in *Heaven Invades Earth*, 38; and Torrance speaks of conversion as "what happens in the regeneration of the human mind," in *Mediation of Christ*, 85–86.

9. It is important to acknowledge that the scriptures are, in one manner of speaking, mere cultural forms. As such, they reflect the values and worldviews of representative cultural groups, both ancient and modern, associated with specific translations, biblical narratives, and word associations. The distinction between *logos* (Jesus Christ as the cosmic, revealed Word of God) and *rhema* (voiced, personalized Word) is noteworthy because it highlights the work of the Holy Spirit, who takes the written and spoken Word as cultural form, animating and personalizing it for the reader/hearer. A constant theme in this book is that without the Holy Spirit's enlivening, any and all cultural forms (especially those within religious culture), remain devoid of the divine, life-giving substance foundational to Christian faith and the life of the church.

water and raised the dead, his Truth found expression beyond the smaller truths we now call the "hard" sciences. Nothing has changed. Truth is "the same yesterday, today, and forever" (Heb 13:8). And that is why it is important for Christians to own the Truth and separate it from the cultural factors (which in the case of Americans includes naturalism, patriotism, and other cultural "truths") that have been unwittingly fused onto the simple but profound Truth of the gospel, who is a person and not a cultural or theological construct.

HOLINESS, POWER, GOODNESS, AND GRACE

This heading list of features of the kingdom clearly reflects the person and character of God as manifest in his person and presence. To be more precise, the presence of God as Father, Son, and Spirit *is* the kingdom, for the kingdom can have no reality outside of God's triune person and presence. The kingdom is not a place, realm, or reality that exists *on its own*, just as a personality cannot exist outside of the person from whom it emanates. In addition, these four characteristics of God and the kingdom, as well as other scripturally-based attributes that could be added (e.g., omniscience, immutability, infinitude), are merely abstract concepts outside of their embodiment in the person of God. It is he who gives them substance and meaning, each integrated with the others through the binding thread of infinite love that constitutes the foundation of the kingdom and the defining essence of the Trinity itself.

It would be inappropriate to list these kingdom attributes without qualifying their scope, which lies as far beyond our conceptions as the dawn of time lies distant from the present moment. We cannot understand the holiness, power, grace and goodness of God except in a restricted and culturally-conditioned way, which is woefully inadequate when compared to the reality. Even though we have the historic Jesus with whom to associate these kingdom attributes, our conceptions necessarily fall infinitesimally short of who he actually was as the one and only God-man; for we simply have no other reference point to adequately comprehend that categorization.

God's goodness and grace expressed as his kingdom are so boundless that we cannot in this life fathom anything close to their true depths, a realization echoed by Paul in 1 Corinthians 2:9. Our tendency, like the Israelites whose fear-filled image of God reflected their relationship with their harsh Egyptian taskmasters, we impute to God so much of our faulty and culturalized conceptions of what grace, goodness, power, and holiness constitute in our world of human relations. The only way around this shortcoming is to look ever more steadily beyond our cultural definitions into the face of Jesus, allowing the Spirit to continually transform our hearts and minds (Rom 12:2) into his likeness and image. As we do so, we will find our conceptions of divine goodness and grace exponentially expand toward the reality of who our God of love actually is. Of course we will never actually get there in this life, but we will progress steadily in the right direction. In that regard, our conceptions (and the experiences to which they refer) are a bit like one of NASA's exploratory spacecraft sent out years ago to probe the "deep space" beyond our solar system, launched on one-way missions toward the edges of an endless universe. We will forever be exploring and contemplating the plumbless depths of divine love, mercy, and goodness in both this life and the next.

THE KINGDOM IS EMERGING

If the kingdom is the place where God's loving, healing presence and his reign of truth and justice are freely and fully manifest, then every obvious expression of those conditions is one in which "heaven invades earth." As Johnson puts it, ". . . the realm of the Spirit is the realm of the Kingdom."[10] Thus, whenever the gifts or power of the Holy Spirit are evident, it represents an expression of the kingdom that accompanies his presence—not the full and final expression that Jesus promised will one day mark his return to earth, but an unambiguous bubbling up of kingdom realities in the here and now. Johnson identifies the Holy Spirit as "the invading agent of heaven"[11] and quotes Jesus' declaration that "The Kingdom of Heaven is at hand" (Matt 3:2) to mean that it is "a present reality . . . within arm's reach."[12]

Those who insist that God's kingdom is only in the future do so under Gnostic influences that employ dualistic thinking that relegates the physical world to something less than sacred. They are generally worried about "liberal" theology polluting the pure gospel of which they are self-appointed protectors. Although their intentions may be noble and their theology well-crafted, in the end the kingdom of God has nothing to do with either. As Paul tells us in his epistles, "the kingdom of God is not just a lot of talk, it is living by God's power" (1 Cor 4:20, NLT), and "the kingdom of God is . . . righteousness, peace and joy in the Holy Spirit" (Rom 14:17). Fear, in all its manifestations, including fear of the spread of unorthodox theology, is not from God. Fear always divides and vilifies, defining itself by way of what

10. Johnson, *Heaven Invades Earth*, 75.
11. Ibid., 86.
12. Ibid., 88.

is perceived to be threatening. The kingdoms of this world (even our little ego kingdoms within which we are always right) vie with one another for control and the right to define truth and reality, while the kingdom of God unifies through the peace and joy the Spirit engenders.

The irrepressibly good news of the gospel is that God's goodness and grace overshadow all differences among us, and those under its influence are more interested in what binds us together in our faith than what separates us through left-brained theological constructs. This realization is also a sign of the kingdom's emergence, for it represents the work of the Holy Spirit to unify all believers in our singular faith (Eph. 4:2-6). If one looks for kingdom expressions, they are everywhere to be found—from peace and justice ministries to supernatural healings and resurrections. According to Paul, our minds are to be directed toward such elevated concerns (Col 3:2), opening our eyes to see kingdom realities wherever they manifest. In a very real sense, we only see what we are looking for, and nearly always miss what we are not. Surely that is an important part of what Jesus meant when he said that the kingdom of God is within us (Luke 17:21).

Christ's proclamation unveils perhaps the greatest of insights into the present dimensions of his kingdom—that its emergence prior to his return is fundamentally in and through the lives of believers. Although kingdom realities are clearly seen through the fruit of ministries of healing, deliverance, and service, it all begins in the inward transformation that God initiates in those he calls from darkness to light. His presence in the innermost part of every believer is the epicenter of the kingdom's emergence in this world. This theme will be revisited in the next chapter, but for now it is enough to recognize that the human heart is the launching pad for all kingdom manifestations, for it is the place where faith, hope, trust, and love are generated by the Spirit, issuing forth in redemptive acts that evidence God's loving presence and benevolent rule among us.

THE DEVIL WREAKS HAVOC

The Bible makes the unequivocal pronouncement that whatever is not part of God's kingdom is under the influence of the prince of this world and the kingdom of darkness (Col 1:13; Acts 26:18; 2 Cor 4:4). It's a laughable proposition to those constrained by modern sensibilities, and a source of great embarrassment for many Christians who desperately want their faith to appear "reasonable" in terms of those modern sensibilities. Yet Jesus and all the epistle writers are unified in their presentation of a worldview in which believers are locked in a raging spiritual battle between two diametrically opposing kingdoms. The Bible presents the kingdom of God as set in fundamental opposition to both the kingdom of Satan and the kingdoms of this world, both of which are linked by way of what they are not—the realm of God's uncontested rule. This understanding makes sense of Jesus' words, "Whoever is not with me is against me" (Matt 12:30), but it leaves somewhat vague the exact nature of the relationship between earthly kingdoms and Satan, whose sway always involves human compliance.

Many ministers of the gospel focus their attentions on direct confrontation with Satan and the demonic, identifying early death, disease, poverty, and all manner of human distress and destruction with the evil one and his destructive work on earth.[13] There is plenty of biblical justification for their direct confrontational efforts to take on and reverse the "works of the devil" (1 John 3:8) in the lives of believers and nonbelievers alike. Theirs is a battle fought in the invisible spirit realm where some claim the gifting to actually "see" the demonic as one would see the material world.[14] Again, this is all nonsense to most Westerners, for whom there is nothing beyond the elemental world but our overly active imaginations. All manner of social shaming keeps at bay any who dare to publicly disagree, a situation with which the devil himself is quite delighted.

Yet the reality of a nefarious realm that imposes its deleterious nature onto humanity has never been in question by virtually the entire non-Western world, in which there are innumerable culturally-sanctioned means to deal with it (e.g., ritual, the shamanic, incantations). Many "non-religious" Americans actually acknowledge the reality of evil through belief in the tenants of astrology and/or karma, neither of which represents a coherent epistemology because they require a conscious but unacknowledged Presence to direct. Neither can they explain the origin and existence of evil (nor can any other religious, philosophical, or naturalistic system). Only a Judaeo-Christian apologetic can adequately explain the origin and nature of evil,

---

13. Johnson puts it this way in *Heaven Invades Earth*: ". . . what happens when the sick are healed or the demonized are set free . . . [is that] His world collides with the world of darkness, and His world always wins. Our battle is always a battle for dominion—a conflict of kingdoms" (p. 71).

14. Mel Bond, a Native American Pentecostal pastor, has written a book titled *How to See in the Spirit World* in which he describes his own ability to visually perceive spiritual creatures inhabiting the natural world—both angels and demons—and offers instructions for all believers to do the same. In another of his books, *God's Last Day's People*, he offers the fascinating perspective that Native Americans are more naturally and culturally endowed with an ability to perceive the supernatural realm. "The Indian mind," Bond writes, "thinks and sees in the supernatural so deeply that the average person would think it is foolish" (p. 13).

which it does through the Fall and subsequent corruption of original good, both in humans and the rest of creation.[15]

Yet many Christians who acknowledge the devil and his influence in the world often fail to also recognize that much evil comes in the form of good in disguise. The devil, Paul tells us, is known to "masquerade[s] as an angel of light" (1 Cor 11:14), which may well be the most effective way to operate. And this is where culture comes in, hiding and legitimizing that which is malevolent through subtle and obscure means. Apathy (through busyness, the supposed integrity of upholding the sovereignty of nation-states, etc.) can be one of the most destructive of cultural norms. History attests that culturally-justified apathy has produced a sad legacy in which hundreds of millions of innocent citizens have been murdered through campaigns of ethnic cleansing. Jews, Rwandans, Armenians, Syrians, and so many other groups have fallen prey to genocide in recent times while the world looked away, absorbed in its own parochial interests. The same holds true for millions who have starved or died from preventable diseases (and continue to do so) while the larger world apathetically goes about "business as usual."

Whenever culture legitimizes behaviors that harm people, it provides the justification for evil to persist in spite of tugs from a divinely-implanted human conscience to do otherwise. Religion is perhaps *the* most common cultural venue by which evil gains a footing among any group or nation-state, precisely because it purports to be and do that which is considered good. In the guise of good, religion can provide the authorization for those in power to remain that way and to abuse their power at will. Although Americans will think immediately of Muslim extremists as a perfect example of those who appeal to religious beliefs to justify their own selfish and occasionally murderous agendas, the problem has been around throughout human history and across every manner of country and culture, including our own.

In America, perhaps the most subtle way that religion promotes the diabolical is not through murderous campaigns (though we have seen that too), but through forms of culturalized faith that divorce professing Christians from a vibrant relationship with the living God. It has many differing manifestations, from myopic views on denominational affiliation to politicized faith and misplaced patriotism. But one of the most destructive is by way of over-intellectualizing the gospel—that is, confining the Bible and God to the realm of ideas. As Johnson states, "Any time the people of God become preoccupied with concepts and ideologies instead of a Christ-like

---

15. Groothius, *Christian Apologetics*, 624–27.

expression of life and power, they are set up to fail no matter how good those ideas are. Christianity is not a philosophy; it is a relationship."[16] For Johnson and others, much of Christianity in America has become "dead religion" because its adherents have settled for "a cerebral Gospel."[17] Rohr sounds the same theme, stating that "religion is one of the surest ways to avoid faith and to avoid God."[18]

Certainly religion is one of Satan's favorite means to distract, preoccupy, and provide a false sense of security not only to those outside of the church but also those within it. Keeping the gospel of Jesus in the realm of mental and theological constructs is a brilliant and effectual way of removing the heart of the gospel, which is centered upon a vibrant relationship between God and humankind. While appearing good and proper on the outside, religious formalism devoid of personal relationship leads people into nominal faith that provides empty spirituality and false assurance. The gospel must move from the head to the heart in order to engage both. Unless it does, the kingdom of God remains abstract and thus distant—isolating pseudo-religious persons in a kingdom without a legitimate King. Rohr describes the way in which denial plays a part: "In our cerebral theology we're not sure that there is a devil. But we go out and build the atom bombs. . . . Personally I've witnessed too much evil to simply deny the existence of such a presence in the world."[19]

Yet it is also demonic whenever believers remain trapped in the "lesser" evils of this world, which include loneliness, despair, disease, and poverty. In fact, anything that is not of the kingdom Jesus came to offer—a realm of joy, peace, love, health, and abundance—is ultimately a manifestation of the kingdom of darkness. If intellectualizing the gospel to the point of leaving it culturalized and devoid of life is the best way for the devil to rob believers of the inheritance that is theirs in Christ, then why would he bother using any other approach? In other countries and cultures he employs other culturally-appropriate tactics to accomplish his diabolical agenda to "kill, steal, and destroy" because, as previously stated, he is a crack anthropologist. In America and the West, that seems best done through norms and values that fragment the inherent integrity of the person while giving priority to the mind and intellect. The result is the same: culturalized faith that poses little threat to the powers of darkness. Social shaming is the devil's means of reinforcing the ruse of religious formalism by convincing many

---

16. *Heaven Invades Earth*, 102.
17. Roth, *Normal Christianity*, 10.
18. *Simplicity*, 33.
19. Ibid., 34.

believing Americans that the cost of a besmirched public image is too high a price to pay for professing unflinching faith within contemporary society.

REDEMPTION IS AT HAND

Whenever and wherever the kingdom of God interfaces with the kingdoms of this world, redemptive acts erupt. It is simply the nature of God and the goal of his kingdom to redeem every single effect of the Fall upon mankind and the natural world, both of which are resolutely slated for total liberation at the end of the age (Rom 8:18–23). Yet here's the irrepressively good news: "The time is [already] fulfilled and the kingdom of God is at hand" (Mark 1:15, KJV). Believers are commissioned to proclaim its arrival in the person and presence of Jesus (Matt 10:7). We need not wait for a future emancipation from sin and its deleterious effects on ourselves and our world, for the glories of the kingdom have already sprung forth in those in whom the Spirit of Jesus resides. The King's domain is reflected in the eyes of his subjects. In his inimitable style, John Crowder puts the matter this way: "You are a suit He [Jesus] wears in the Earth."[20] Jesus—*the Redeemer* and the king of the kingdom—is present and active in this world through each and every believer. How could there then not be ongoing redemptive consequences? "Everywhere you go," Crowder exclaims, "the Kingdom is released, expanded and confirmed because you are a born-again son of God."[21]

Certainly there will be plenty of tasty "pie in the sky" awaiting believers, but the party got started when Jesus rose from the dead to reclaim his kingdom, beginning in the hearts of humankind. Convincing the church that this life is all about hardship and suffering that can only be made right in the life to come is another page straight out of Satan's playbook. It keeps believers passive and defeatist, defensively reacting to a topsy-turvy world in which our lives are in fact meant to effect redemptive acts on a grand scale. The obvious disconnect between the lives and proclamation of most believers doesn't escape the non-believing world, which wants and needs a gospel that pertains to their deepest concerns here and now.

That lack of present relevance led the likes of Karl Marx and Vladimir Lenin to reject Christianity and scoff at the doctrine of a futuristic heaven that seemed to them to ignore the need for escape from the perils and injustices of their day.[22] Many a vain social and political movement has followed

---

20. Crowder, *Mystical Union*, 188.
21. Ibid., 124.
22. Marx famously wrote, "Religion is the sigh of the oppressed creature, the heart of a heartless world, and the soul of soulless conditions. It is the opium of the people."

suite, leaving peoples and societies around the world littered with destructive human alternatives to the kingdom. The comprehensively redemptive message of the gospel must be fully applicable to human needs today or it will hold little attraction to those whose needs are immediate and pressing. Marxism-Leninism and the Communist ideologies it spawned promised bread and justice for those who were hungry and oppressed (a promise they could never seem to deliver[23]), while the church was seen to offer only an imagined future that was easily manipulated to maintain an intolerable status quo, with which it was inescapably linked. Bill Johnson summed up the basic problem this way: "Any gospel that doesn't work in the marketplace, doesn't work."[24] The gospel is better designed for the streets than the pews.

There is a tendency to either project the kingdom into a distant and irrelevant future or to construct a present one that mirrors the shortcomings of its human architects, whose best designs always entail oppressive agendas, the abuse of power, and idol worship in the form of deified leaders. The real kingdom of God can be neither shaped by human hands nor suppressed by human will and/or ignorance. God has set about bringing it into the world and none can stop it. The emerging kingdom is more predictable than the spring that follows winter's harsh rule. Though sometimes unseen, life eternal is inexorably emerging with an innate vibrancy and brilliance that mirrors its ever-present Author.

Yet the promise of the kingdom has never been what was expected among human beings. Its fullness at Christ's coming will unquestionably surpass what human minds and imaginations can presently conjure up (1 Cor 2:9). Its glories cannot be overstated. However, its present emergence is also different than we might have guessed, so given are we to looking for that which reflects our image and furthers our own agendas. Like the Jews who wanted a Messiah to fit their religious and political hopes and aspirations, we are often blind to the presence and purposes of God in our own times and circumstances. Yet the more attuned we become in our personal lives to the presence of the reigning King, the better we will be able to recognize and live in alignment with the kingdom he is establishing all around us in every nook and cranny of our wayward world.

A *Contribution*, Introduction.

23. I witnessed the failures of Marxist-Leninist-inspired Communism in Ethiopia. During the 1970s, rural farmers had been forcefully resettled onto communal farming cooperatives that proved remarkably unproductive. The cooperatives were slowly abandoned by farmers who surreptitiously escaped by night to return to their inherited properties and private farms. Rusted, broken-down tractors and farming equipment were all that remained of the defunct and abandoned rural cooperative I visited in 1990.

24. *Heaven Invades Earth*, 198.

GOD'S ECONOMY OF INVERSION

Jesus described the dimensions of a realm that both thrilled and shocked his listeners, depending on their station in life. In was unlike anything they had ever seen or heard before. In fact, the highly unconventional realm he called the kingdom of God stood in stark contrast to everything they associated with the social, political, and religious orders of their day—a distinction that still holds true. What Jesus offered amounted to an inverted vision of life, an image that reversed the basics of how things were and "should" be done. It was an about-face that simultaneously presented the outline of a new and better world while it condemned the injustices of the present order and those who profited by and maintained it. The one thing the kingdom did not do was to allow anyone to remain unchanged or unchallenged, for it addressed the heart of things that matter to everyone.

In the new kingdom that was dawning through the words and life of Jesus, there was a definitive proclamation that the rules of the game were changing. In Christ, God was rewriting the manuscript to provide a happy and just conclusion. He was providing the means to "flip the script" by breaking the bonds that linked the kingdoms of this world to the kingdom of darkness itself. Henceforth, there would be a new kid on the block—the Holy Spirit—who would insure God's plan among humankind by changing the venue from an external set of legalistic codes to an internal, heart-centered knowledge centered in divine presence. Kingdom knowledge would flow from a Spirit-written script of the heart, and it would guide its bearers onto a stage where the liberating truth they shared often jeopardized their own lives. Those who had the most to lose from the old system based on the rotted fruits of fallen human nature would most resist the new order. Such persons would end Jesus' life, yet, in the sovereignly redemptive power of God, Christ's death instituted the very kingdom his killers resisted. "It was not because he walked around saying 'I am God,'" that Jesus was crucified, writes Rohr. But because his teaching, healing, and miracles "were a rearranging of social relationships and therefore of social order."[25]

Among the most threatening elements of social reordering that would accompany Jesus' kingdom proclamation was a reversal in which those on the bottom would be elevated to the top, and vise versa (Matt 19:30; 20:16). The scheme held out the hope of remediation for all the wrongs that power, greed, and hatred had created in the lives of the needy and powerless victims of the systems of this world. But it would come at the cost of the privileges of those who benefited most from the status quo of those systems. Like the rich

---

25. *Jesus' Plan*, 20.

ruler who could not part with his wealth to follow Jesus (Luke 18:18–25), the gospel of the kingdom did not sound like "good news" to everyone—although it was, in fact, just that because it had the power to liberate everyone from the very things that personally oppressed them, though few realized it.

The kingdom challenges everything in this world that restricts true freedom, whatever form it takes from one individual to another or one culture to the next. The gospel of the kingdom is not only the good news that God is for the poor and oppressed, it is the pronouncement that, in the words of Andre Crouch, ". . . he is *for* humanity in our collective poverty, our ultimate powerlessness in the face of sin and death."[26] Thus, for many it is good news in disguise, though none can recognize it as such without the enlightenment God alone provides.

Given the limits of human understanding, the most marvelous of kingdom inversions will seem odd and even menacing without the spiritual discernment to recognize their inherent goodness. This is especially true for the changeover from exclusion to inclusion which lies at the heart of the kingdom. Fear and fallen human nature make it seem advantageous to retain exclusionary borders based on culture, politics, race, and other categories reflective of self-interest. But the exclusionary fences humans construct around themselves and their domains are actually prisons that isolate and dehumanize the builders. The gospel of the kingdom breaks down every barrier that separates us from one another, which turns out to be the same barriers that separate us from God and our true selves. We find liberation in inclusion.

Along with the announcement that the kingdom would restructure the social, cultural, and natural order was the declaration that God's moral order was very different than previously thought. In Christ, God was clearly revealing what had to date only been vaguely understood: that his ways were far above the ways of men (Job 11:7-9; Isa 55:9; Matt 13:7). In God's economy, we learn that victory comes through failure, as befits a redeemer king. The cross, mankind's ultimate implement of cruelty, oppression, and disgrace became God's instrument of love, grace, and redemption. A ruthless symbol of inhumanity conceived of fallen human nature, the cross was transformed into a symbol of God's loving restoration of his divine image in the whole created order.

The kingdom of God and its transformational ability was rooted in the cross and the resurrection power that emanated through it. The new order God was instituting through the death and resurrection of Jesus meant everything had changed. *Everything.* Grace replaced works and legalistic

---

26. *Culture Making*, 209.

striving. Humility and faith had power over arrogance and self-reliance. Acceptance and forgiveness displaced rejection and resentment. Joy emerged from heartache and loss. Even cooperation took precedence over competition. Differences could now be seen for what they were—strengths and not threats. The reactionary, confrontational, and condemning spirit that defined the old world order was forever displaced by God's life-affirming, joy-enhancing, all-embracing kingdom reality. The source of enmity, our broken and dysfunctional human nature, had been fully repaired. What looked like a kingdom inversion of the social and moral universe was in fact only the righting of what had gone askew from God's original plan for humankind. Yet the kingdom not only represented a reemergence of the original plan, it represented a vastly improved version of it. Henceforth God would not simply walk in our midst in the cool of the day, he would live within us and we in him in a wondrous world without end.

ALL THE WORLD IS SACRED

When God rent the temple veil from top to bottom as Jesus expired upon the cross, it served to reinforce a seismic shift that originally took place at the Incarnation, when God came to dwell in human flesh, and in the process sanctified the whole material realm. The divide between spirit and matter, holy and common, sacred and secular had been completely bridged, forever canceling the misperception that an inherent dualism separates the visible from the invisible realm.

A holistic view of God, humankind, and the world of nature was actually central to the Hebraic worldview, but by the time of Jesus it had become warped by notions that fused Greek dualism with Jewish legalism, resulting in holiness codes and priestly arrogance toward the commonplace—peasants and everything associated with their lifestyles. In ancient Israel, as elsewhere, the mind of fallen human nature had misunderstood the loving and relational nature of God and his purposes, leading to a misinterpretation of who he was and thus what his creation (including humankind) represented. God was cast in the image of man, who put God on the side of the powerful and their oppressive agendas toward their fellow man and, sometimes, toward nature itself. In doing so, the Israelites merely copied the rest of humanity and human history, from Greek philosophers to Eastern mystics to Mesoamerican priests and rulers, who created a separation where none existed and thereby justified cruelty and exploitation.

In the person of Jesus all false separations were erased. Saint and sinner, holy and profane, temporal and eternal were fused into one. His resurrection marked the first step toward God redeeming the whole cosmos from the vile effects of the Fall, which included the darkened thinking of and preeminent position given to the human mind and will. In Christ, God had taken charge of his sacred ship and would steer it safely to port through the turmoil fallen humanity had created. He would do so by extending his kingdom throughout the earth, incorporating the last stronghold of earthly resistance—the human heart—from which he would then shed abroad his loving presence and redemptive purposes.

Through Christ and his sacred presence in human flesh, God re-enlisted his creation in his plan to reestablish the all-embracing nature of his glorious kingdom. Jesus re-sanctified the world he came to inhabit by way of association with his own divine nature. There was no longer any justification for a spiritual-natural divide, nor was there reason to cast any human being as evil, thereby justifying oppression and abuse of any sort. Jesus broke the back of the old moral order. There were no more *bad* people, only unredeemed people created in God's holy image—people who were acting *badly* through believing the lies of the counterfeit order, and living accordingly.

In the light of Jesus, humanity could be rightly seen as "deposed royalty . . . questing after a lost throne beyond [their] mortal grasp."[27] Jesus reestablished our divinely instituted royal heritage. There were no more grounds upon which to consider anyone a true enemy; no more excuses to use ethnicity or nationality to ostracize; no more false conceptions that fetuses were mere collections of tissue—for all enemies, all foreigners and strangers, all the poor and outcast, every womb and all the unborn showed themselves to be the holy temple of God. Emmanuel ("God with us") was henceforth to be seen in every living person, no matter how vulnerable, incomplete, or impaired their physical or mental state might appear by old world order standards.

Nature too was included in God's scheme of redemption. Along with the prophets of old, the whole created order had long awaited the coming of the Redeemer—the One by whom it all was fashioned (Col. 1:16). Because of who he was, all he made participated in his sacred status. The presence of God in Jesus corrected the two primary fallacies that had long plagued the perceptions of humankind: that God was either distant and disconnected from the world of nature and matter, or that he was embedded within a deified cosmos. Those two designations made him either an unconcerned deity (Aristotle's "unmoved Mover"[28]) or an idolatrous one (pantheism and

---

27. *Christian Apologetics*, 435.

28. In *Metaphysics*, 12.1072a, Aristotle describes God as "that which moves without

animism). Jesus proved that God is both lovingly present with and in his creation, yet wholly Other.

In correcting not only our hearts but our misconceptions, Jesus offered a better way forward—one in which we could worship God in truth while still honoring him through our treatment of every facet of his sanctified creation. Jesus not only taught but embodied the truth that the entire world is sacred because its Creator is so.[29] In the words of Wendell Berry, "There is no sacred and unsacred; there is only sacred and desecrated."[30] Our worship, along with our thoughts, words, and actions, is one interwoven and utterly inseparable whole. Thus, we honor God when we love his children and his world, and dishonor him (and ourselves) when we desecrate either.

WHENCE THE KINGDOM?

So why is God's kingdom not yet fully manifest? Why does the world and its occupants seem to overwhelmingly operate according to the system Jesus' death and resurrection rendered defunct? As Yeats so eloquently put it, "Things reveal themselves passing away."[31] It is in the dying of the old world order that the kingdom comes to light, just as the death of Christ illuminated the wondrous nature and purposes of God. The illusion that the kingdoms of this world and the kingdom of darkness are still in charge is a fading chimera, a lie temporarily kept alive by everyone who lives according to it. We are called to reveal the utter barrenness of the dying world order by living according to the dictates of the kingdom that has been established to replace it.

Scripture tells us that only God has the power and authority to finally and forever institute his kingdom on earth in a manner that conforms to human dimensions of time and space. Yet we are given the opportunity and privilege to participate in that kingdom reality by declaring and living in the present according to its preeminence upon the earth here and now. Each

---

being moved," while elaborating the philosophical concept of a primary cause behind all things. A. J. Heschel took the phrase and reversed it, describing God as the "most moved Mover" in *The Prophets*, 224.

29. The creation was, of course, sacred before the Incarnation. Yet by becoming fully human as a descendant of Adam, who was formed from and forever linked to the "dust of the earth" (Gen 2:7), Jesus represented divinity and holiness clothed in humanity—God embedded within the material world—and thus symbolized a physical and conceptual reference for sacred matter.

30. Berry, "Wendell Berry."

31. Yeats, *Yeats*, 306, http://www.scribd.com/doc/79247890/Autobiographies, accessed March 7, 2014.

time we proclaim the Lord's Prayer, "Thy kingdom come, thy will be done on earth as it is in heaven," we agree to its emergent nature and inevitable final establishment and triumph. And each time we declare kingdom realities through thought, word, or deed, we align ourselves with the uncontested truth of the kingdom over the exposed falsehood that appears on the surface to now have sway.

Thus, we can live according to the truth of the emerging kingdom or according to the fallacies of the defeated and fading old world order. And though we humans cannot ourselves establish the kingdom on earth in its finality, we can choose to add to the false perception that it has no power, authority, or inevitable conclusion. Yet each time we rightly declare kingdom realities, we realign ourselves with eternal truth and the loving Presence that will one day completely fill every crevice of creation, from human hearts to distant galaxies. In the chapter to follow we will consider some of the ways available to us to live in the reality of God's kingdom in America today.

11

Living in the Kingdom in America

We love the stars too much to fear the night.

—Jeffrey Burton Russell

Perhaps the greatest challenge facing the church in America today is learning how to live *in* the world yet not be *of* it.[1] By "the world" I mean the values, norms, and legally-established and enforced systems (economic, political, and even religious) that constitute American cultural expressions derived from human nature—particularly fallen human nature with all its unsavory bits. The kingdom of God, which represents the manifest presence of God in our midst, stands as both a counterpoint to "the world" and a measuring stick by which to assess all of the components that comprise any and all cultures. With that in mind, the attributes or characteristics of the kingdom from the previous chapter will help guide the effort in this chapter to identify "kingdom culture" values that promote believers' ability to live in "the world" of America while firmly rooted in the kingdom, within which we are citizens with permanent resident status.

One way to know that we are participating in the kingdom even as we live in the world is that kingdom-promoting acts of redemption will be evident in and through our lives. Redemptive fruit is always the outcome

---

1. Two classic works addressing the topic of Christian engagement with society and culture are H. Richard Niebuhr's *Christ and Culture*, and Francis Schaeffer's *How Should We Then Live?* In addition, there is a less well-known but very insightful book on the topic by Albert Nolan titled *Jesus Before Christianity*.

wherever the kingdom of God intersects with or overlaps the affairs of this world, no matter the venue or circumstance. However dire or disheartening the situation, it is the nature of God's Spirit to bring life out of death, evil, suffering, and apparent futility. The more dire and disheartening the circumstances, the more one can expect a redemptive upside whenever God is involved, as is indisputably evident in the work of the cross. It is our job to learn to look for each and every perceptible redemptive expression of God in and around us, for each evidences the presence of the kingdom and it's breaking forth into our lives in a way that is expressly purposeful. Otherwise there is a tendency to remain blind to the marvels occurring all about us every moment of each and every day.

Yet manifestations of the kingdom are not always overt and extraordinary. They often come in subtle and easily overlooked forms, as when simple acts of human empathy and kindness follow tragedies like Sandy Hook. Yet all apparently trivial acts can have a redemptive and transformational side and serve to represent God's express purposes in and through human affairs. The sum total of those kingdom purposes reflect, in the words of Richard Rohr, "God's dream for the world."[2] It is a dream echoed in the Sermon on the Mount, which is a vision of the world as God would have it, and will have it. The Sermon represents a divine engagement with humankind and a firm commitment to right the wrongs that, due to the Fall, now appear as "normal life" to most of us.

God's kingdom always stands apart from the kingdoms and cultures of this world; and yet it can be expressed in and through this world's kingdoms and cultures despite their fundamentally antithetical natures. In fact, that is its primary mode of expression. The capacity of the kingdom to surface through human culture is due exclusively to the transformational presence of God's Spirit, who penetrates and utterly transforms even the most egregious circumstances and expressions of fallen human nature. Christians are tasked with the job of helping to facilitate God's redemptive work in our particular cultural settings and the larger world (2 Cor 5:18, 2 Pet 3:11). Among other things, we participate in that endeavor each time we offer the Lord's Prayer. "When we pray for his kingdom to come," Bill Johnson explains, "we are asking Him to superimpose the rules, order, and benefits of His world over this one until this one looks like his."[3] Kingdom transformation occurs to the degree that we are willing to be the answer to our own

---

2. *Jesus' Plan*, 29. The full quote is "The Kingdom is Jesus' way of describing God's dream for the world."

3. *Heaven Invades Earth*, 71.

prayers, or at least an active participant in the answer God is only too happy to provide. "You are God's dream, with skin on it," as Heidi Baker put it.[4]

What follows are generalized expressions of "kingdom culture" within the context of American life and society. I purposely avoid any attempt to elaborate those expressions, knowing that to prescribe specific behaviors would result in the sort of religious legalism I have previously criticized and now wish to scrupulously avoid. It is my hope, however, that from these generalizations individual believers will discover a kingdom-based guide by which to evaluate the expressions of their beliefs and behaviors within their own selective niche of contemporary American life.

INWARD-OUTWARD

What is the key to living in the kingdom while living in this world? In fact, the kingdom lives in us and articulates through our lives as we allow it to. Kingdom culture entails a kingdom-consciousness that emanates from the Spirit of God dwelling in and altering our innermost being. His presence within results in a way of thinking, living, and being that signifies God's kingdom in our midst. The indwelling Christ expresses in and through us his kingdom on earth, until the day he comes again to establish it in its final glorious and all-encompassing form. It is worth restating that human efforts cannot generate his kingdom, which is what fallen human nature and the cultural/institutional values that proceed from them vainly attempt to do. Form follows substance in the sense that expressions of kingdom-generating faith proceed from an indispensable personal relationship with the living God before they manifest outwardly as cultural expressions.

In Jesus there was no separation between the inward and outward person, between word and deed. His spoken word and his every act perfectly mirrored his interior life, where the Spirit dwelled in fullness. His gospel was writ in flesh. And so it should be with us. Our inward and outward lives should harmonize. People should be able to see, hear, and experience a unity between our person, our speech, and our behavior. Otherwise disingenuousness surfaces and can be sensed by others. Whenever our outward behaviors become misaligned with the inward person we are in Christ, both God and the gospel are dishonored and the kingdom remains distant.

American culture mitigates against cultivating inward spirituality because of the intense focus our culture places on outward appearance and personal productivity as indicators of identity and individual worth. The believer has to find a way to counter these overwhelming pressures in order

4. *Compelled*, DVD.

to establish a viable inward spiritual life, or be consumed by a world that is more than happy to dictate one's inner life as a reflection of the *culture du jour*. I will offer no detailed prescriptions for how to achieve a healthy spiritually-centered lifestyle, which has to be an individualized issue (plenty of others seem willing to have a go at it though!). I do know, however, that many Americans think it impossible to find the time in their busy lifestyles to facilitate a "quiet time," which itself can add to the pressures and become something of a legalistic spiritual exercise. However, I believe most Americans can and do find the time and opportunities to do what they consider most important in life. In fact, our use of time indicates exactly what we do feel is most important. And it seems reasonable to assume that God will provide us with enough time to do what he considers important for our lives. Meting it out appropriately is our call.

Yet true inward spirituality is not *something we do* but *something we are*. Learning to cultivate it is all about resting in the finished work of the indwelling Christ. All our spiritual exercises are only to get us to a place of simple faith and radical trust. American culture, and American religious culture in particular, presses us to define things externally. We must keep it straight: We *do r*eligion; we *are* Christians. To lose focus and attempt to *do* Christianity is a mistake that culturalizes the faith and removes the source of its power and vitality, namely the Holy Spirit whose presence we apparently have the power to quench (1 Thes 5:19).

Elizabeth Elliot addressed the inward-outward life of faith with the following statement: "Questions of how to conduct oneself . . . must be answered by life itself—the life of the individual in his direct responsible relationship to God. *This is a dynamic, never a static thing* [emphasis added]. And how can we speak at all of the true meaning of conduct and service if we do not speak first and last of love? For it is love which sums up all the other commands. The one who loves knows better than anyone else how to conduct himself, how to serve the one he loves. Love prescribes an answer in a given situation as no mere rule can do."[5]

There is one thing that be can said about cultivating a vibrant spiritual life that spills out into loving conduct: you'll know when you get there. It's not about guilt, or compulsion, or any impulse or method based in negative impulses. Letting go of such self-imposed religious impediments is an absolute prerequisite to true spirituality. Rather, it is about delighting in the presence and goodness of God in such a way that we are left longing for more, just as a lover delights in the company of the beloved. For some people that may mean spending the first two hours of each day in "centering

---

5. Eliot, *Liberty of Obedience*, 93–94.

prayer,"[6] while for others the focus will be on relaxing and rejoicing in spontaneous union with God at all times of the day.[7] God meets us at the point of our individual personalities, experiences, and life circumstances, and is always thrilled to engage the object of his endless affections. And as we know from scripture, God is never really absent from us no matter how deep our distractions or how we are feeling about him, others, or ourselves. He is closer to each of us than the very air we breathe. Faith rooted in love knows this truth in a way that transcends all cognition and every sentiment that arises from the capricious reaches of the human heart and mind.

IN GOD WE TRUST

So reads the inscription on every form of currency minted in the United States over the last half a century—a tradition that originated in the Civil War period. There is more than a little irony in the fact that the phrase is placed on what is, for all intends and purposes, the preeminent representation of *all that is not* the kingdom of God (recall Jesus' remark about "rendering unto Caesar" in Mark 12:17). Yet for that very reason it is probably *the very best place* to put the inscription, reminding us Americans of exactly where our real trust should lie, and challenging us to put it there and there alone.

Trust is the operative side of faith. We employ our faith when we have full confidence in God, when we trust him utterly. Yet we trust him, not out of "blind faith," but from knowing him for who he actually is: viz., loving, faithful, merciful, and absolutely good all of the time. It is precisely *because* we love this benevolent God that we trust him. Trust based in love is a perfectly natural response built into our human constitution specifically because God made humans to respond to his exact person—the embodiment of love itself. Although stated previously, it bears repeating that neither faith nor trust can be generated from human will. All is pure gift. And when we come to realize that crucial truth, it serves to generate even more faith, trust, hope and love in the One who is the Alpha and Omega of all goodness (Jas 1:17).

---

6. Centering prayer is practiced by widely varying Christian groups, but I am most familiar with it through the DaySpring Church community in Germantown, Maryland. For its members, daily centering prayer is a crucial though time-consuming part of the "Inward-Outward" journey that precedes daily life and ministry. The interplay between the two is famously described in Elizabeth O'Conner's books, *Call to Commitment* and *Journey Inward, Journey Outward*.

7. In their book, *Practicing God's Presence 24/7*, Dennis and Jen Clark offer a specific method to experience God's constant presence in one's life. In his book *Mystical Union*, Crowder offers another method to accomplish the same goal.

In America there is one prominent cultural pitfall into which most Americans and too many Christians tumble headlong. It involves our apparent inability to trust anything that lies beyond our control. For Christians, that culturally-imbued value makes it difficult to trust God unequivocally in every dimension of our lives. The origins of this nearly ubiquitous cultural trait are rooted in a system of values that elevates self-interest, self-reliance, materialism, and a number of other well-established norms and values. In essence, we have trouble believing and thus acting as though *God is always enough*, fearing that unless we instigate, facilitate, implement, or at least supplement his provision for our lives, there will be a distressing shortfall.

Although we live in one of the most affluent countries in the world—one where we can afford to throw away 40 percent of our food and still get fat—many Americans suffer from a poverty of spirit. That is, they constantly *feel* deprived because the dominant culture tells us through advertising both overt and sublimated that we are missing out on something needful, and to be whole we need to buy it, own it, or consume it. That perpetual sense of lack or need has now permeated every facet of American life, perpetrated by a consumer mentality that never allows us to be satisfied with anything less than everything; and that includes youthful looks, excessive possessions, retirement security, and even sexual virility into old age. This is the *kingdom of America*, the "land of opportunity"—or at least that is the contorted shape it has taken under the gale force winds of unbridled capitalism and a surfeit of humanistic worldviews.

Sadly, the church has by-and-large succumbed to the charade, often recasting Christian faith as a self-fulfilling, possessions-accruing, competition-based spirituality that does more to promote American culture than the kingdom of which we are, first and foremost, citizens and ambassadors. Many believers have no idea they have adopted a "mentality of lack" because it is so prevalent in the larger culture. Yet it is recognizable through the subtle sense of dissatisfaction many believers have with their lives, and even themselves.

In their book, *Always Enough*,[8] Rolland and Heidi Baker detail the incredible life and ministry God called them to pursue in Mozambique, working among the poorest and most destitute children in what for many years was the world's poorest country. There they set out to care for any and all children who were abused, abandoned, or destitute, most of whom were orphans from war, famine, AIDS, and grinding poverty of an order that few Americans can fathom. The Baker's never asked for money to support their ministry, trusting God to provide for *his* work. The ways he always did

---

8. Baker and Baker, *Always Enough*.

so are amazing and quite inspiring, but the Bakers always emphasized that God's provision went well beyond money and material needs.

Heidi had one period where a health setback required months of bed rest, and on another occasion she was so overpowered by the presence of God that she was rendered totally incapacitated for a full week. Both times she learned to depend on God for *everything*, including her basic health and strength, her growing family's well-being, and every aspect of the ministry and its evolution. That total trust and dependence ran counter to Heidi's personality and the culture of "can-do" Americans from which she and Rolland hailed. Yet God taught them to live in total and radical trust in him alone, arriving at a place that most American Christians never reach—the place of *God's always enough*. Ironically, it was the children who helped with the Baker's divine instruction through constant encouragement and their own wildly abandoned faith in God in the midst of their own destitution. The results impacted the entire nation of Mozambique for God, and have since spread into many nations around the globe.

Whether in Mozambique or elsewhere in their multi-country ministry, the Baker's embodied what it means to live in the kingdom. For the rest of us, living in and reflecting God's kingdom should arise out of the same place of counter-cultural radical trust in our loving God. Only that kind of full abandonment to faith in the goodness of God can free us from the dual threat of poverty of spirit and a sense of entitlement that currently afflicts both rich and poor Americans alike. Our dependence cannot rest upon a wonderful but flawed constitution or any external religious structure but on God alone, in whom we are called to put the utmost confidence, regardless the circumstances.

Rather than believe the culture-generated position that we are trapped in a "bad economy" or that the opposing political party is ruining our country and our faith, we can exercise the biblical response of complete trust in the One who has promised never to leave or forsake us, and to meet every need no matter the circumstance (Deut 31:6, Heb 13:5, Phil 4:19). It is a "glass half-full" way of thinking that elicits praise and thanksgiving not only for what God has provided and done in our lives, but for the knowledge that he will always be there for us because of his unfailing love and goodness. When we live in the kingdom, God always provides enough of everything we need and so much more. Even during difficulties and suffering, which everyone experiences to some degree at some point in their lives, trusting God fully launches the kingdom into the situation. And *in the kingdom there is no lack*. No matter the personal prison in which we find ourselves, shackled by circumstances beyond our control, the minute God shows up everything turns into a palace of blessings in the light of his transforming presence.[9]

When we dwell in a place of trust in and thanksgiving to God, we open the door to the kingdom not only in our own lives but in the lives of those around us. It is our agreement with the reality that the kingdom exists in our midst—a reality based on the abiding presence of God both within and without—that we are freed from every natural and cultural constraint that tries to pretend otherwise. By the same token, Satan is empowered in our lives, communities, nation and world through our continued agreement with him and his seedy agenda.[10] Whenever that agenda manifests, it always entails a complaining spirit and lack of faith that God has not only the capacity but also the desire to provide every good thing to make his children's lives flourish and fruitful. There is no end to the riches of Christ, and he has given us full access to them all. Repentance—turning away from those aspects of culture and fallen human nature that insist we live lives of spiritual and physical poverty contrary to our faith—unlocks the vault where all the goodies are kept, and allows them to spill forth unabated into our lives and world.

THE LANGUAGE OF THE KINGDOM

Our words reveal what we really think and believe. If we live in the kingdom where there is never any lack, we speak the language of abundance and blessing—not only in our own lives but into the lives of those we encounter each day. As Solomon wisely declared, our words have great power to bring life and healing or to promote death and destruction (Pr 18:21). To a large degree, we speak reality into existence through our words, though it is probably more accurate to say that, for Christians, we have the power to affirm the reality that is the kingdom of God or else perpetrate the illusion of a lesser reality. Either way, we have the God-given capacity to effect what we speak, a fact not lost on medical science and the counseling professions.

Americans are known as generally optimistic people, at least when compared to other countries and cultures where hardship and oppression have left a mark of hopelessness on the souls of many. But still, it is commonplace to hear a great deal of complaining and worrying in the everyday conversations of Americans, even among believers who are instructed in the Bible to avoid such negative proclamations (Eph 4:29, Col 4:6). Much of it comes back to an attitude of entitlement and the belief that something

9. I am grateful to Gordon Hugenburger for this insightful descriptive image.
10. *Heaven Invades Earth*, 31.

essential is lacking in one's life—and someone else is to blame for it. The language of "rights" is regularly employed to insist on getting what is perceived to be lacking by way of demands that appeal to many of the unquestioned cultural values covered in previous chapters (e.g., privilege and superiority).

Yet, at the same time, it has become somewhat trendy in America to promote and project a more positive and hopeful outlook, prompted in part by the bitter complaining that can be heard just about anywhere one goes. "Have a good day" (a good indicator that Americans feel they should be in control of their own destiny) is part of the language of optimism to be heard just about everywhere now, especially among the young. It is welcome relief from the pall of pessimism that hangs over many public venues, despite the fact that the phrase is often uttered perfunctorily.

By contrast, the language of the kingdom is in a completely different dimension than mere optimistic affirmations or contemporary models of positive thinking, which can and do change like the weather. The language of the kingdom is based on truth and not sentiment or simple good will. It is not caffeine-enhanced hopefulness, but rather ultimate reality that forms the language believers have learned from the likes of Jesus, the apostles, and the prophets. "Kingdom talk" is the language of love and trust in a Person whose presiding reality overrides any and every circumstance that threatens to oppress, consume, or rule us. When we speak the truth of the kingdom, our words align with life as God has designed and maintains it for his purposes and our benefit.

One of the most needful areas for truthful proclamation among believers in America is our standing in Christ. We are told in 2 Peter 1:3 that, "In him we have all things," including a personal righteousness that nothing can take away. We are beloved in his sight. The self-critical, negative spirit that creeps about our culture, affecting many through an impossible standard of perfectionism, lies at the opposite end of the spectrum of reality that we inhabit as believers. There is no condemnation for those in Christ Jesus (Rom 8:1)—*None*! God's total love and acceptance of each one of us has absolutely nothing to do with our looks, talents, competence, or any other cultural or ethical standard by which we tend to judge one another's worth in America.

To speak of ourselves and one another from a kingdom perspective is to declare the reality of the kingdom in our midst. It is to liberate one another from the lies and constraints of the world, along with the destructive demonic forces that entrap humanity into assorted forms of earthly anguish. Yet it doesn't end with believers. We have the opportunity to speak the realities of the kingdom into the lives of all people, whoever and wherever they may be. To speak the truth of the kingdom to unbelievers in a manner relevant to their lives and cultural background is to draw them out of the shadows of untruth and into the liberating luminescence of the living God.

The heart of the gospel—God loves every human being and made a way through Christ for each of us to live in his lovingly abundant presence—can be shared in countless ways through both word and deed. There is no need for compulsion or sense of religious obligation, just a joyful desire to share from an overflow of living waters that heal and liberate as they stream into a parched and pain-filled world grown accustomed to exploitation and offense. Voice your faith in whatever way the Spirit moves, and the life-giving music of the kingdom will be heard over the dissonant shrieks of a culture ensnared in the gloomy domination of self-defeating materialism.

PERSONALIZING THE WORLD

One of the defining pillars of the kingdom is the centrality of loving relationship. Each believer has been incorporated into the Trinity's vortex of all-consuming love[11]—a far cry from the loss of personhood characteristic of many Eastern religions which, as best as I understand them, advocate the dissolution of self into an impersonal void. By stark contrast, the God of the Bible is deeply personal and has engineered that distinctive characteristic into the hearts of humanity, a fact clearly reflected in the relationship-oriented behaviors that issue from our human nature. God is a lover obsessed with his beloved. In Christ he went to the most extreme of measures to make that love known and accessible to all.

If, then, the Creator's image is embedded within every person, we know there is absolutely no one who lacks the ability to respond to his intensely engaging love.[12] And that is precisely how we are to see others, no matter how exotic the labels they bear, if we want to participate in the life of the kingdom. Kingdom love knows no boundaries. It proclaims a gospel

---

11. In *Cosmos Reborn*, Crowder describes the believer's mystical connection with the three persons of the Trinity: "Christ wove mankind into the Trinitarian life—there is forever a resurrected human being sitting in the middle of the Godhead. And there we sit in Him, fully united to God in heavenly places" (p. 18).

12. The New Testament obviously presents the concept of "election" or "predestination" (Eph 1:4; Romans 8:29–30; Romans 9, John 6:37–45). But the point here is that because all humans are created in the image of a personal and relational God, that image includes the intrinsic ability of *every human being* to be responsive to God's engaging love. Logically speaking, personal choices and/or cultural influences can and do negate this innate human responsiveness. Yet because it is innate, no cultural, physical or psychological trauma or pathology can ever completely erase the human capacity to be responsive at some deep and efficacious level—whether it be atheism, autism, abuse, or a coma. See, for example, Alexander, *Proof of Heaven* and Pistorius, *Ghost Boy*.

without borders that floods over categories and labels of exclusion that inevitably dehumanize those wrongly confined to them. Pentecost was the coming out party of the kingdom, when the Holy Spirit broke down long-standing divisions and animosities between immensely differing peoples. The partitioning of humanity that took place at Babel, birthed of human pride and godless self-will, was fully reversed at Pentecost when shared understanding once again brought unity and joy through the collectively-experienced goodness of God.

The same Spirit who moved at Pentecost now dwells in every believer, and he has not altered his intent to break down the barriers that cause separation. To live in his kingdom in America is to participate in a borderless embrace, not only of other believers, but of all those who bear the image of our passionately engaging God. When we see his likeness in those beyond our socially-constructed perimeters, particularly foreigners and supposed enemies to our given causes, the kingdom emerges in our midst and its gates swing wide open for all to enter. From a kingdom perspective, everyone bears the image of God and thus deserves a personalized encounter on our part. In doing so, scripture says we represent nothing less than the divine presence (2 Cor 5:20). No longer are there any true strangers or adversaries, for kingdom culture views each person through the lovingly redemptive eyes of a God who determined that *every such person* was worth the cost of his only Son. Christ died so our enemies could be saved. Shall we negate his intentions?

We believers can cultivate the ability to perceive others with the personalized perspective of the kingdom simply by allowing the Spirit to have his way in our lives. He will gladly disarm our prejudices and replace them with the love of Christ for every living soul. He will replace the errant notion that someone else has to be disparaged to give us value, or someone else has to be torn down to build us up. Our only real task is to get out of the way and allow him to shine through us, which means letting go of whatever impedes our walk with Christ—comprising a different laundry list of issues for different people.

Yet the transformation for those who will let go is amazing. It provides us the capacity to love our neighbors because we've learned to see in them a reflection of the One we already love without reservation. As the Spirit helps us to perceive God's divinely-embedded image in others, we enter a realm of freedom that constitutes the basis for the only truly healthy love of self. Thus, we simultaneously learn to properly love ourselves and others through the Spirit's abiding presence in our lives, which prompts us to recognize God's ineffable image both within and without. As Rohr put it, "We eventually love others, quite simply, as we have allowed God to love us..."[13]

This point of seeing God's image in others was driven home to me by the story of Katheryn Deprill, the so-called "Burger King Baby" who was abandoned by her mother on the bathroom floor of a Burger King in Allentown, Pennsylvania only hours after her birth in 1977. Kathryn was adopted into a loving family and grew up to marry and start a family of her own, when she began the search for her birth mother. As an Emergency Medical Technician, Kathryn often went into the homes of older people in and around Allentown, and on every occasion she looked around at the residents and the pictures in their homes to see if perchance someone resembled her; for Kathryn hoped to identify the mother she desperately wanted to meet and draw into the circle of her own loving family. Kathyrn employed a perspective that scrutinized the faces of every older woman she encountered because she possessed an innate love for her mother that longed for expression. In every face Kathryn entertained the possibility that it was that of the mother she so very much wanted to find and embrace.[14]

Christians are encouraged to look for the face of Jesus in others, particularly the needy (Matt 25:31-46). It is absolutely transformational to look for the face of a loved one in whomever we meet, which simply cannot be done if we entertain categories of exclusion or denigration. We personalize the world of humanity and manifest kingdom culture whenever we allow God to show us how people look to him, which is just what he longs to do. He deeply desires to show us the world through his loving, benevolent eyes, which beam forth full of mercy and acceptance, not animosity and condemnation. A kingdom perspective always puts people ahead of things, and lives in unstinting forgiveness toward others, holding nothing against anyone no matter the offense. That is a freedom the world does not know. It is a purposeful stance that personalizes the entire human race, extending to others the level of acceptance and understanding we inwardly long for others to extend toward us.

Kingdom culture opens us up to look for God in unexpected places. If, after all, he could speak through Balaam's ass, then he might be lurking in

---

13. Rohr, *Daily Meditation*, http://myemail.constantcontact.com/Richard-Rohr-s-Meditation—The-Mirroring-Gaze.html?soid=1103098668616&aid=WQVEgAw8Cgg, posted February 18, 2014.

14. Kathryn Deprill's mother eventually came forward, allowing the two to meet and subsequently develop an ongoing relationship. Kathryn had this to say after the initial meeting: "She is better than anything I could've ever imagined. She is so sweet and amazing. I'm so happy." Fox News, http://www.foxnews.com/us/2014/03/26/burger-king-baby-katheryn-deprill-reunites-with-mom-after-27-years/?intcmp=latestnews, posted March 25, 2014.

the words or faces of those we consider the least likely candidates to house his divine presence. But when we allow ourselves to be consumed with insidious doubt and distrust, always asking "Is that person really a believer?" or "Is what they are saying orthodox?" then we relinquish the opportunity to be sensitive to God's Spirit, and end up defending borders of fear, distrust, and insecurity that we have constructed around ourselves and our theological certitudes. In a sense, emptiness allows for openness. If we empty ourselves of wrongful preconceptions and judgmental attitudes, we allow space for God to manifest in both ourselves and others. His Spirit is great at taking the trash out of our lives.

PARTNERS IN TRANSFORMATION

The immensity of God's passionate, engaging love extends beyond humankind to the whole of the created order, none of which lies outside the bounds of his personal care and attention (Ps 145:15–16; Matt 10:29). We share in that personalized view of the natural world through a kingdom perspective that recognizes the shimmer of its Maker's Shekinah glory evident in every facet of it.[15] Through personalizing the natural world, we align our perspective with that of God, who looked upon his creation and declared it all good (How could it be otherwise as his reflected glory?). We see him and his goodness in all that he has made, which by association bears the stamp of his sacred nature. As the philosopher Holmes Rolston, III put it, "There is in every seed and root a promise."[16] It is the promise of life and redemption that mirrors God's plans for the world, and flows through all he creates and does. Without a personalizing perspective of the natural world, we invite the dark side of human nature to manifest through various forms of exploitation and abuse—just as it does in the world of peoples and cultures—now disturbingly apparent through significant degradation of our lands, seas, and atmosphere.[17]

---

15. Within Judaism, the Shekinah was thought of as God's tangible, manifest presence among his people or within his temple. It was the perceptible "settling" or "dwelling" of the "glory of the Lord." Christian theology refers to the Shekinah as a "theophany" or action of God, visible in the created world but not fully representing his essence or being. See Russell, *History of Heaven*, 33. I apply the term to the luminous dimensions of creation that humans rightly perceive as gloriously reflective of God's existence and presence throughout the material world he has lovingly fashioned (see Ps 19:1–4a; Rom 1:20).

16. Rolston, "Nature Need," 209.

17. The personalized perspective I am suggesting is analogous to what I understand of the Jewish religious philosopher Martin Buber's "I-Thou" relationship, which

Most of us learned to personalize the places where we grew up, especially our little corner of nature where, were we so lucky, we played and become intimately familiar with all manner of living things. In the process, what was mere *space* to others became transformed into a highly personalized sense of *place* to us. Growing up in St. Paul, Minnesota, Garrison Keillor described the vicinity as a "personal geography" that was "imprinted in my brain." Over the years, St. Paul became for him a repository of emotions related to family, faith, and other valued dimensions of his life. "When a man has lived in one place for most of his life," Keillor muses, "he walks around hip-deep in history."[18] That is the way American Indians viewed their natural environments prior to the dissolution of their pre-contact cultures through thoughtless campaigns that wrenched away natal lands, causing irreparable damage to their societies and cultures. It is also the way St. Francis viewed the created order, the different constituents of which he personalized as "brother" and "sister" of a common, loving Creator. To wit, personalizing the world of nature entails caring for it as part of the sacred web of life within which we are all intertwining participants under the benevolent care of a holy God.

Furthermore, the Bible tells us that we are partners with the creation in a redemptive process that will culminate in the mutual transformation of both parties (Rom 8:19–23). Paul declares that the natural world suffers from human sin and longs for the outworking of God's redemption of humanity that it too might participate in a transformation that will lead to a new heavens and new earth. A kingdom perspective provides the understanding that there is an unbreakable and sacred interdependence of the human and natural worlds. To abuse nature is to harm humanity as well as to flout our common Maker. As T.S. Eliot put it, "A wrong attitude toward nature implies, somewhere, a wrong attitude toward God."[19] "How we treat the earth and all of creation," declared Patriarch Bartholomew, "defines the relationship that each of us has with God."[20] We can assume that the opposite is also true, for we can love and serve God through fulfilling our calling to be stewards of the earth by lovingly caring for it.

So interwoven are the worlds of nature and humanity that one cannot be affected without directly affecting the other. Abuse of nature always entails abuse toward other human beings, especially the poor whose

---

he contrasts sharply with the "I-It" objectification of another person or object. See Buber, *I and Thou*.

18. Keillor, "No Place like Home," 58–83.
19. Eliot, *The Idea*, 62.
20. Bartholomew, *Green Bible*, 114.

livelihoods are often directly tied to subsistence lifestyles that suffer disproportionately from environmental degradation. C.S. Lewis rightly noted that, "What we call Man's power over Nature turns out to be a power exercised by some men over other men with Nature as an instrument."[21] The linkage between human beings and treatment of the environment is not only true in America, where we have seen ecological changes impact food-producing industries through droughts and other weather events, but deeply impacts the developing world where man-made degradation of local environments have caused famines and other crises. Such events not only create local and regional political, economic, and social instability, but reverberate throughout the whole world, affecting Americans right along with everyone else. We now live in a global village where everyone and everything is interconnected.

To care for our environment and all the teeming species that throng throughout its countless niches is to love and serve the poor. As Gordon Aeschliman pointed out, "Loving the earth is loving the poor."[22] One way to assist the poor at home and abroad is through strategies that enhance the natural environment and thereby minimize the abuse and neglect that generally follows poverty-driven practices that derive from the desperation many face to survive at all costs.[23] In the process, everyone is benefited and strengthened for the long run, and God is honored through those efforts.

Kingdom culture generates a long term view of things, especially as it relates to ecological issues. Our lifestyles today define the inheritance of future generations, in both the world of nature and the world of human relations. If we leave our children and grandchildren with a degraded environment and a quarter of the world's population living in poverty which, despite noble intentions is just what we seem to have done, then we have bequeathed to them virtually intractable problems that will make them and their world poorer in every respect. No loving parent would wish that upon his or her child. Furthermore, no Christian would willfully wish to dishonor God in such a way, yet that is what the Bible says comes from abusing the poor through any sort of neglect. We cannot love God and ignore the poor whom he loves. "Its 'personal' against God to harm the poor,"

---

21. Lewis, *Abolition of Man*, 54.
22. Aeschliman, "Loving the Earth," 91–97.
23. I witnessed this phenomenon numerous times in Nepal and Ethiopia, where the immediate need of firewood, water, and other daily necessities made it all but impossible for poor people to properly plan for the future in ways that protected their local environments: viz., trees, water sources, and even seeds for the coming year's crop. Thus, poverty drove the environmental degradation that, in turn, kept people poor.

declares Aeschliman, who backs up his statement with a memorable verse from Proverbs 14:31: "Those who oppress the poor insult their Maker."[24]

Christians living in contemporary America can easily hid behind the imposing cultural curtain that separates us from thinking deeply about such things. There once was a time when American Christians chose to live moderate lifestyles (think of the Amish and Mennonites who still purposely live that way) so we could share our resources with the needy and thereby obey the scriptures and honor God (Isa 58:7–10; Luke 12:23; Eph 4:28). Aeschliman points out that cultural factors have worked to separate us from our legitimate religious inherence. "In our romantic bond to the modern lifestyle and the promise of pleasure that comes through wealth and technology, we have lost our mooring as people of faith. . . . The cultural preoccupation with wealth and its temporal benefits is not founded in the faith tradition. Indeed, that preoccupation is as dangerous to our spirituality as it is to the bodies of the poor."[25]

Thankfully, there are a significant and growing number of believers who are conscientiously bucking that trend in America. Many are drawing us back to a biblically-based faith that better reflects a kingdom perspective and God's own love for the whole of humanity as well as the natural world he has lovingly and purposefully created. They can be found in every sector of American society promoting Christ-centered, effective ministries among the poor, disadvantaged, and hopeless who, as a category are always more responsive to the redemptive message and impact of the gospel than the wealthy and self-satisfied of this world. Many Christian ministries are focused specifically on the environment, education, mental health, or social justice. The variety and thrust of non-traditional Christian outreach across the country and around the globe is truly inspiring, and represents kingdom interests that run contrary to the general culture and the myopic self-interest that pervades so much of it.

Of note are efforts to alleviate poverty in the U.S. and countries of the developing world by hundreds of outstanding non-profit organizations, from the mind-boggling size and scope of world-wide programs run by World Vision to tiny NGOs (non-governmental agencies) such as the Mpambara-Cox Foundation that operates with a miniscule but highly-leveraged budget. The latter effectively links American and African elementary kids with programs that include environmental education and revolving micro-loans to rural women in Uganda who make a community-monitored commitment to keep their children in school through Primary level (grade 7).

24. Aeschliman, 94.
25. Ibid., 95.

Then there is the remarkable work of Mercy Ships, which offers incredibly inspiring medical assistance to the poor and disfigured in ports along West Africa. Another innovative ministry, The Ecotourism Project run out of Eastern University, addresses developing world poverty and environmental degradation through programs that engage the two-thirds world church in business ventures that preserve local culture while protecting vulnerable habitat through sustainable eco-tourism. The Evangelical Environmental Network and Earth Ministry are two non-profit organizations actively engaging the church in the urgent matter of environmental stewardship.

All of the ministries that address human need and promote human flourishing in the name of Christ are ultimately interlinked. The poor, the environment, the world economy, democracy, America's welfare, and Christian faith are all inseparably interrelated parts of a singular whole (see "One World" below). All of these ministries together, offered in the name and love of Jesus, represent an outpouring of the kingdom in our midst. They are evidence that the indwelling Spirit of God will gush forth in effervescent fashion toward a needy, hurting, and spiritually-parched world whenever believers allow God to personalize his concerns for the whole of creation through his church. That is the point at which we become partners with God, shedding abroad the unreserved love of Christ, whose munificent purposes include his plans of full redemption for the entire cosmos.

THE FREEDOM OF INCLUSION

The kingdom is the land of unobstructed grace. Divine grace affords an ever-widening circle of inclusion that leads to a wide open, ever-expanding outlook marked by freedom from every cultural constraint that militates against the gospel and its liberating essence. Although the gospel is adept at functioning in and through culture, it is not limited by or subject to any particular cultural framework. Kingdom culture supplies the capacity to fully love what is good and familiar within culture, yet to expand that capacity of love and concern to include all that lies outside it as well—a process that grows exponentially until all becomes personal and thereby significant. One can love Malawi as she does America, and empathize across every border. The plight of suffering children in war-torn Syria is, in essence, no different than a tragedy occurring in one's own neighborhood, among friends and family. Kingdom culture sees past all culturally-loaded categories, such as "Muslim," "enemy," or "not-my-people," to unreservedly embrace all who are dear to God—which includes everyone everywhere.

In America, rather than perceiving virtually everything as a political or economic issue couched in predetermined categories consisting of conservative or liberal ideology, a kingdom perspective views things in their larger context as human issues within the larger global context. For example, the ethics surrounding genetic engineering of crops in the U.S. cannot be limited to its potential economic benefits for a few American entrepreneurs and stockholders. A kingdom perspective expands our understanding to include potential impacts on developing world farmers who will be affected in ways that appear likely to threaten their long-term health and livelihoods. In the same way, kingdom culture provides the understanding that efforts to recycle and lower carbon-emissions in America are not some left-wing, fear-mongering political ruse, but represent an act of loving concern and service toward our fellow citizens, populations around the globe, and future generations. The gospel of the kingdom loudly proclaims that we are our brothers' keepers—every last one of them.

Yet kingdom culture is not wed to a worrisome, mettlesome attitude that cultivates fear, animosity, and even hatred—negative emotions often apparent among activists who lack a faith perspective. Rather, it promotes an informed and engaged stance toward the *present* world and *all* its citizens even as it looks with confidence toward the coming of a new and better one. Joy, peace, and a well-founded optimism are hallmarks of kingdom culture. They are fruits of the Spirit, whose love and compassion toward humanity never manifests as a burdensome set of chores and obligations, but as a confident enthusiasm that God is working his redemptive wonders wherever believers focus their faith-infused attentions. The very existence of heartfelt compassion toward anyone in need is itself a sign of the Holy Spirit's presence in believers' lives as they engage the world around them.[26]

Manifestations of the kingdom always begin with an internal cognizance of the person and love of Jesus, and then expand outward into wider and wider circles of concern for the world he made and came to redeem. By contrast, the kingdoms of this world, including churchy kingdoms, often begin with egos and human personalities, and grow ever narrower and more exclusive as they expand outward. One can recognize them by their agendas, which inevitably set borders and boundaries at the extent of pre-determined personal interests and concerns, thereby most benefiting those associated with the center while excluding those who lie outside a prescribed sphere of self-identification.[27]

---

26. *Heaven Invades Earth*, 86.

27. The issue of expanding circles of self-interest is evident in the fact that two-thirds of American philanthropic giving is done in a manner that promotes the lifestyles and special interests of the wealthy, whose giving targets museums, orchestras,

Although kingdom culture is universal and all-embracing in its vision, it is not a form of Universalism.[28] Christians are called to be welcoming and loving toward all, offering love, service, the gospel, and practical assistance to any and all who will accept it.[29] Yet the faith we proclaim needs no defense by way of human prohibitions against non-Christians. Many believers become overly-concerned with trying to remain distinct from the efforts and agendas of non-Christians whose own programs provide all manner of commendable assistance within the U.S. and around the world. But such concern is unfounded, because we know that *every* good thing originates in God (Jas 1:17), and kingdom culture grants believers the freedom to love and work alongside any who help provide God's good gifts for humankind.

God can take care of himself without our "protection," and, besides, believers have been given the opportunity to live free from all worry, including worries about the nature of our witness (Phil 4:6; 1 John 4:18). Whatever emotions are based in anxiety and fear—regarding false doctrine, syncretism, humanistic agendas, and our image as Christians—is simply not from

---

and other elitist-linked causes. See Crouch, *Culture Making*, 209.

28. In *Cosmos Reborn*, Crowder draws a distinction between Christian and non-Christian universalism, noting that there is a scriptural necessity for believers to acknowledge hell and the need for salvation in this life. Following the lead of other Trinitarians, most notably Robert Capon, Crowder offers that "Everyone is objectively included [in the salvific work of Christ on the cross], but everyone hasn't subjectively realized it" (p. 138). Crowder allows for mystery and paradox to be present regarding the issue of universal salvation, reminding us that "The sectarian, pharisaical mind is always attempting to put up walls of separation and lines of demarcation between the believer and the unbeliever. But the Gospel is the very wrecking ball sent to tear those barriers down" (p. 138). Perhaps Crowder's position can best be summed up in his two statements, "The Trinitarian view sees everything through a lens of God's inclusive love" (p. 138) and "Every question is summed up in the basic revealed truth that God is love—the height and depth of which we will ever explore" (p. 139).

29. My model for this kind of selfless service is the missionary surgeon couple Drs. Tom and Cynthia Hale, whom I had the privilege of meeting in Nepal during their twenty-five years of work there. In the Preface of his book, *Don't Let The Goats Eat The Loquat Tree*, Hale describes their calling to serve the Nepali people this way: ". . . God has called us . . . to communicate the love of God to the Nepali people through our service and through our lives . . . Out of that love has grown a desire to introduce others to the person who has meant more to us than any other: Jesus Christ . . . To withhold from [the Nepalis] this greatest gift would be no longer to love them . . . There is no pressure, no enticement, no ulterior motive, no effort to undermine the many wonderful aspects of their own culture, which we not only admire but from which we have learned and profited. Rather we seek to work among the Nepalis as friends and equals, contributing our professional skills where needed and involving ourselves as much as possible in their national aspirations. During the course of all of this, it is perfectly natural for us to share with them, as occasions arise, our hearts' deepest feelings. They can take Christ or leave him: we shall serve them regardless," (p. 12).

God, who has imparted to us his Spirit of love, joy, and unshakable assurance (John 1:16; Rom 5:5; Col 2:9–10). Such worrying concerns stem from religious culture, not faith-based Christianity; for "... where the Spirit of the Lord is present, there is freedom" (2 Cor 3:17b, NET).

Christian cults and secular-humanistic organizations, however similar in appearance to the church and its ministries, are always self-excluding from the kingdom. Believers need not be exclusionary toward non-believers and their ministries because those very people will exclude themselves through denying the person and centrality of Christ in their ministries, and refusing to be associated with those who do. Although Jesus never turned anyone away, in scripture many turned away from him on their own accord because they knew he represented a direct threat to something they idolized in their lives (e.g., their religious culture, social standing, wealth, or personal/organizational agendas). The offer to join the King's wedding feast is rejected by many because of the priority they give to pre-determined interests and concerns (Matt 22). Kingdom matters don't jive with such things. Because the cross and all it entails conflicts with worldly concerns, agendas, and worldviews, it inevitably appears as either offensive or foolish to those who oppose it (1 Cor 1:23). People and organizations will separate themselves no matter how inclusive and embracing believers' are toward them. We are to fear nothing and no one, but to unreservedly love and serve all we encounter. The freedom to love others is freeing to us.

It is the despised and destitute who, through the mystery inherent in God's economy of inversion, seem to most clearly hear the sweet voice of Jesus calling them to himself through the words and deeds of his church. From a logical point of view, those on the bottom of society have less self-imposed junk in their lives that obstructs the call to join the wedding festivities—obstructions such as social standing, wealth, and all the other temporal distractions that tend to generate soulless pride and fleeting self-satisfaction. In her work among the desperately poor in Mozambique, Heidi Baker describes many occasions in which the poverty-stricken Mozambicans she encountered had "no resistance to the Gospel."[30] "What is it about the poor," she pondered, "that literally brings the Kingdom of God, that allows them to experience the Kingdom of God in a way that the well-fed don't? It has to do with hunger. It has to do with their need. They know they need God."[31]

---

30. Roland and Heidi Baker, *Always Enough*, 141, 157.

31. Ibid., 165. See also *Walking with the Poor* by Bryant Myers and *Rich Christians* by Ronald Sider.

In America, there are so many who fit into that same category of conscious need—not only among the poor, but among minorities, unwed mothers, the gay community, and the mentally and physically challenged. These "outsiders" in America, as elsewhere around the world,[32] are the very people the gospel is custom-designed to include. Just read the Sermon on the Mount and then have a look at Jesus' own genealogy, which foretold the wildly-inclusive nature of the kingdom he came to establish. Among those within his direct line of descent were two non-Jews, a harlot, and an adulterer. And he hailed from a minority tribe within Israel. Jesus announced through his own ancestry that he had no interest whatsoever in man-made categories of racial or ethnic purity, or any of the other exclusionary categorizations we use to justify the position that our group is superior to another person or group. "All that My Father gives to Me comes to Me," declared Jesus. "I will receive everyone; I will not send away anyone who comes to Me" (John 6:37, TV).

Is this not the same God who has sovereignly brought to the U.S. so many recent immigrants who represent an enormous variety of ethnic, religious, and cultural backgrounds? Is there not a message here for American Christians that he intends his kingdom to be filled with people who are very different from the rest of us? There is always more to learn regarding the expansive nature of his kingdom, which is inherently expandable beyond every limit that makes us comfortable with our culturally-derived identities.

Diversity is strength, a concept well known in biology and genetics. By the same token, monoculture entails weakness and vulnerability, whether one is talking about biodiversity in nature or cultural, ethnic, and genetic diversity among human populations. The wide diversity of peoples and cultures apparent today in virtually every American demographic is perhaps the country's most valued asset, well ahead of technological, medical, and political advancements. In fact, it is our diversity that greatly strengthens our democratic way of life—a diversity that many Americans are now learning to celebrate rather than fret over. Henry Louis Gates, when asked what he wanted his legacy to be, said the following: "I want to be remembered as someone who celebrated the diversity of humanity. The triumph of American democracy is diversity."[33] The American church has yet to fully embrace

---

32. In India there are a disproportionately high number of Christians among low caste groups, especially the "untouchables" that have historically responded the most favorably to the gospel; whereas high caste groups have been much less responsive. The same trend is apparent in other countries with strict social stratification that leaves certain groups ostracized at the bottom of the social ladder, with strictures in place that offer them little to no hope of upward mobility.

33. Gates, "A Conversation."

this understanding, and by failing to do so we are overlooking a key component of the kingdom to which we belong, and the liberating influence it can exert in our lives, ministries, and world.

ONE WORLD

Kingdom culture-generated inclusion is only perceptible through a Christocentric lens. It all starts and ends with Jesus, who the Apostle John aptly described as the Alpha and Omega (Rev 1:8; 21:6). In Christ all things are unified, and apart from him all remains fragmented from the otherwise irreparable effects of the Fall. In Jesus, who is the heart expression of God, we see all of life and history come together into a singular purposeful whole (2 Cor 5:19). To catch a vision of that whole and to grasp something of its significance to our faith requires unitive thinking. It necessitates an all-encompassing worldview that accords with a pancultural gospel.

Kingdom culture is antithetical to a mind ensnared within the limitations of dualistic thinking. Yet perceiving the world in dualistic terms comes quite naturally to all humans, as discussed in an earlier chapter where it was mentioned that healthy mental and social development begin with learning to differentiate between self and non-self. Upon this early framework, culture then casts its numerous other dualisms that juxtapose good and evil, "appropriate" and "inappropriate behavior," "our people" from "not our people," and so forth. In America, we have yet another layer of dualism inherited from our Greek cognitive ancestry, which separates the physical from the metaphysical or, if you prefer, the natural from the supernatural. All cultures have their dualisms, especially some form of separation between the worlds of culture and nature. Such separations are necessary on a practical-functional level for individuals and societies. Yet, in America we are especially ensconced in worldviews that impose oppositional categories onto everybody and everything, including nature, identity, religious beliefs, and body-mind conceptions.

Unfortunately, many American Christians have transposed these dualisms onto our faith, especially in our understanding of the kingdom of God as it pertains to contemporary life and the physical world. Many have delegated the material world to a Greek-derived lesser, unspiritual realm that stands in opposition to the higher, spiritual sphere of a distant God. The Bible does present dualisms, yet they all are subsumed under the broad oppositional category of the sacred and the profane. Contrary to popular opinion, God is not set in opposition to Satan or evil—the first of which is but one of many of his fallen creatures, and the second of no association whatsoever, since sin and Satan are the biblical progenitors of death and evil. Rather, the Bible presents God and his kingdom as contradistinct from all that is fallen from the original goodness that issued from his person at creation. The goodness and holiness of God are juxtaposed with the fallen (profaned) worlds of men, angelic beings, and nature (currently operating under a "survival of the fittest" model). God is not "against" anyone or anything, as we might be. One needn't oppose what one has complete authority and full control over. We anthropomorphize God when we think that way. His creation turned against him, but all was formed out of his goodness; and out of his goodness he has laid the groundwork for a total redemption of the entire cosmos (Isa 65:17; 2. Cor 5:19; Rev 21:1).

Through the work of Christ on the cross the sacred-profane rift has been permanently repaired, though its manifestation in time and space is still unfolding.[34] The kingdom Jesus came to establish is anchored in the reality that redemption was effective for all that was fallen; that which was profaned has been permanently reconsecrated through his blood. The temple was extended into the marketplace; the secular subsumed within the sacred; Jesus supped with sinners. As Pierre Teilhard de Chardin expressed it, " . . . by virtue of the Creation and, still more, of the Incarnation, nothing here below is profane for those who know how to see."[35] Thus, there is no purely natural realm.[36] All is sacralized; that is, every molecule is encompassed within God's sacred order. To view the world otherwise, "becomes a sacrilege before God, and a catastrophe for humanity."[37]

We are now therefore privy to a divinely-begotten holism centered in Christ and manifest in the kingdom of God—something that did not exist between the Fall and the Resurrection. It is a holism for which we

---

34. In their annunciation creed, the Byzantine Church acknowledges an understanding of the unifying effect of redemption. The creed states, "The Byzantine Christian worships God with his whole person, and recognizes the presence of God in all of his senses, bearing witness to the fact that, in Christ, there is no distinction between 'sacred' and 'profane,' but that in the Kingdom of God, which is manifested in this world by the Church, all things are fulfilled in Christ to be what they were created to be—namely, a means of communion with Him." Annunciation, para. 3. http://www.annunciationbyzantine.org/our_faith.html, accessed March 31, 2014.

35. Teilhard de Chardin, *Divine Milieu*, 112.

36. Quantum physics has provided the understanding that reality extends well beyond the material realm into a multidimensional "multiverse . . . with our universe being relegated to one among many." The fledgling science's relatively new "inflationary paradigm" accords well with a religious worldview, although few of its proponents acknowledge it as such. See Greene, "Listening," 19–26.

37. Gunness, Teilhard de Chardin, §4. http://www.explorefaith.org/faces/saints_prophets_and_spiritual_guides/pierre_teilhard_de_chardin.php, accessed October 30, 2014.

were designed as God's image bearers. As the philosopher Holmes Rolston, III put it, "We are made for fellowship at multiple levels: with God, with persons, with the Earth."[38] Importantly, kingdom wholeness also means we have become whole within ourselves—body, mind, and spirit. And that is important, for accepting and loving others is contingent on accepting and loving self; and an inability to accept others always stems from some form of self-rejection. We are purposely made that way (Matt 7:1–2).

A kingdom perspective allows us to see ourselves as whole and part of a larger reality that includes everyone and everything. We are in Christ, and in Christ all things hold together (Col 1:17). Everything will, in *chronos* (chronological, quantitative, sequential) time, be incorporated into the redemption Jesus secured upon the cross; and indeed, the redemptive finality of all life has already occurred in *kairos* (epic-making, qualitative, iconically-eternal) time. A kingdom perspective is based in *kairos*, the divinely present now that transforms and transcends all time and space. That is why from the cross Jesus could declare, "It is finished," (John 19:30) and bear the sins of all humanity past, present, and future. It is also why the scriptures offer that Christ was the Lamb who was slain before the foundation of the world (Rev 13:8). In *kairos*, the kingdom is a present actuality in which every event or issue is not confined to what appears as the linear present. The present always represents a redemptive opportunity for believers to impose *kairos* onto *chronos* and thereby infuse kingdom realities into temporal matters.[39]

The sports announcer Robin Williams, who fought a public battle with cancer and won, said, "Make your mess your message."[40] It is that redemptive approach which makes possible kingdom realities where otherwise there is only human effort based on capitulation to a cause-and-effect world. God's miraculous intervention breaks into the material world at the point of faith and his eternal kingdom's preeminence over all of life. Neither time, space, or human limitations can stop the kingdom's emergence into this world when faith is properly exercised. Faith thrives on the seemingly impossible because it is based on the faithfulness of God and not the boundaries of human resources. "Unbelief," in the words of Bill Johnson, "is

---

38. Rolston, "Nature Need," 226.

39. See Reardon, Chronos and Kairos, http://www.orthodoxytoday.org/articles5/ReardonChronos.php, posted October 14, 2005.

40. Williams, in accepting the Arthur Ashe Courage Award at the 2013 ESPYs, shared this phrase she had learned from her mother and now applies to all of life. Strauss, *USA Today Sports*, July 18, 2013, http://ftw.usatoday.com/2013/07/robin-roberts-espys-classy-moment/, accessed October 23, 2014.

anchored in what is visible or reasonable apart from God."[41] Yet faith boldly declares, "With God all things are possible" (Matt 19:26).

The American church has in large part settled for what is possible or reasonable apart from God because that is the *modus operandi* of the dominant culture in our country. Because our culture is firmly planted in a specific culture history that includes Western dualistic thinking that has greatly influenced contemporary church theology, many believers find themselves bereft of the faith needed to negotiate their way through all but humanly solvable problems and issues. The transformative power of the kingdom lies distant to much of what the church does today; but God has plans afoot to change all that.

GOD'S DREAM FOR AMERICA

There are two interrelated parts to God's "dream" for the United States of America. The first is that his church, which includes every believer of every theological preference, would forego his or her various forms of abstract and theoretical Christianity for a living faith based, not merely on ethical or theological constructs, but on a vibrant love-relationship with him through Jesus Christ. The second is that from the resulting genuine and energizing faith of that relationship, there would flow a compulsion-free, uninhibited generosity toward all of those within the country and beyond who lack the seemingly endless opportunities and resources with which he has endowed his church. Those opportunities and resources go far beyond money and possessions to include our time, social capital, career choices, spiritual gifts, and even our future plans for ourselves and our children. The two parts of the dream are inseparable. The reason, as Heidi Baker observed, is that "All fruitfulness flows from intimacy . . . To the degree that we are united with the heart of Jesus, God will bring fruit in our lives. To the degree that you are in love with Him, you will be fruitful."[42]

God's dream is actually an invitation for us to participate in an ongoing upsurge of the kingdom in our midst—a celebration of faith so wild and wonderful that all the petty concerns that normally occupy our conscious attention will be forgotten and abandoned in the sheer joy of experiencing God's presence and blessings in our midst. He has firmly established a new order comprised of a new vision for humanity; one that is devoid of the stereotypes that derive from the old tribal thinking. God is on the look-out for any who are willing to participate in his new world order. The alternative

41. *Heaven Invades Earth*, 48.
42. Ibid., 176.

is culture-driven tribalism that keeps us stuck in a worldly arrangement not of his making—actually positioning ourselves in opposition to him and his purposes.

In America that other arrangement invariably means ingesting and propagating what amounts to "an adolescent culture,"[43] where Christianity has been domesticated to serve the narrow goals and interests of the larger society and culture. Yet we can make a choice to live in America as citizens of the kingdom, freed from the cultural restrictions that always fall short of God's intentions for the whole of humanity and the rest of creation. Although the kingdom is subversive to every guiding principle of this world, it is not ultimately anarchist or antithetical in nature because it offers a viable alternative that works to renew all things to God's original plan.

His original plan was for his *shalom* to extend into the farthest reaches of the creation. If God has blessed America, it is not for its own sake. Rather it is for the sake of the entire world, which is equally dear to him. Ancient Israel apparently missed the boat in that regard, believing that God's blessings were primarily for them (of course, scripture does reserve a special place and calling for the Jewish people). Yet throughout the whole of biblical history, God's plans were always inclusive of every people, tongue, and nation. If we ask God to bless America today, it should be so that we can share his abundant blessings—including material, educational, technological, and spiritual—to lift up the needy in our midst and far beyond our borders. In the same way, scripture instructs individual believers that their personal prosperity is not an end in itself, but a God-given means to practice benevolence toward others (Rom 12:8; 2 Cor 9:11; 1 Tim. 6:17–19). It is un-Christian and anti-kingdom to get caught up in the culture-generated trap which declares "God bless America," without also desiring that blessing for non-Americans too. That message of inclusion is loud and clear in scripture.

The Sermon on the Mount represents an outline of the kingdom of God applied to human affairs. As well, the New Jerusalem depicts the ideals of redeemed human nature expressed in a cultural form that includes not only a vibrant natural world but also the involvement of the "nations," whose abundance derives from the River of Life that flows from within the City of God (Rev 21–22). It is an image of "unlimited good" that stands in stark contrast to the human-derived "image of limited good" discussed in chapter 8. The kingdom's unlimited good includes much more than overflowing material abundance; it is replete with love, healing, and true community under God's gracious rule. The coming of this idyllic kingdom was the primary

---

43. That is, a culture that fosters and perpetuates the desires, habits, and behaviors of an adolescent stage in life. See Plotkin, *Nature*, http://www.natureandthehumansoul.com/newbook/chapter1_naths.htm, accessed October, 30, 2014.

message Jesus proclaimed as "good news" (Luke 8:1), and not the secondary message of personal salvation which many American Christians have made the sole focus of the biblical message.[44] Personal salvation has no meaning or purpose outside of the kingdom and its centrality to God's purposes. Apart from the kingdom, personal salvation is nothing more than spiritualized individualism. Who wants to be alone in heaven?

At the end of the day, we must never let theology or religious culture become a substitute for an encounter with Jesus, as the disciples tried to do to the woman at the well, and the early Jewish Christians attempted to do to uncircumcised Gentiles who came to faith. The world doesn't need any more polarization, so disfigured is it now from every form of fragmentation that humans can possibly impose. God's kingdom stands as the only true unifying hope of a grossly splintered world, and the King is calling *everyone* into the light. Every act of love, healing, hope, and service announces the kingdom's luminous presence in the darkness that unavoidably pervades the affairs of men.

The church in America has the opportunity to promote God's glorious kingdom or promote some lesser form of humanism or humanistic religion. And that is exactly what happens, according to Richard Rohr, "when we piously say 'Thy Kingdom come,' but don't immediately add, 'My kingdom go.'"[45] Rohr also cautions that "we become like the God we adore."[46] Our adoration can either be toward the true and living God whose glorious and expansive kingdom has no end or limitation, or toward the temporal gods we have fashioned in the form of self-serving group identities that, unfortunately, include religious culture and country. The key to getting things right is discovering, fully embracing, and totally resting in our true identity in Christ—the topic of the final chapter.

---

44. The strict emphasis on individual salvation in the West, and especially in America, is directly related to the high value we place on individualism. There are numerous instances of entire families, tribes, and communities converting to Christianity *en mass* in non-Western cultures where the individual's identity is largely subsumed within the culture group of which he or she is a member. In addition, the Koine Greek term for salvation (*sozo*) has a much broader meaning than simply "saving the soul," including "to keep safe and sound, to rescue from danger or destruction; to save one (from injury or peril); to save a suffering one (from perishing) from disease; to make well, heal, restore to health." See NAS, http://www.biblestudytools.com/lexicons/greek/nas/sozo.html, accessed October 30, 2014.

45. Rohr, *Simplicity*, 59.

46. Ibid., 82.

12

Conclusion: It's All About Image

If I find in myself desires which nothing in this world can satisfy, the only logical explanation is that I was made for another world.
— C.S. Lewis

THE NEW NATURE

It seems so obvious, yet so easily gets forgotten or overlooked: The starting point determines the outcome.[1] If we start with a culturalized version of Christian faith, a version intertwined with the norms and values intrinsic to American culture, then we never progress to faith that aligns with the kingdom of God, God's overarching purposes, or the abundant life available to each believer. "Churchianity" is what happens when culture shapes faith, rather than faith determining the contours and relevance of culture. Churchified Christians often look like spiritually-enhanced versions of typical Americans, which means they are all-around good citizens, faithful patriots, savvy consumers, proud and vocal representatives of specific ethnic and political interests, and rationally thinking biochemical machines—but still not fully human.

Historic and biblical Christianity starts us in a different place, and thus takes us to a different outcome. It tells us we are beloved children of God, refashioned in the image of Christ Jesus (Rom 8:29). That is our true and

---

1. This principle, along with the idea of an "upgrade" mentioned later in the chapter, comes from Graham Cooke. See "Building the Right Mindset," http://www.youtube.com/watch?v=sYlpHy3Pvlo, accessed November 2, 2013.

abiding identity—who we really are prior to the accumulation of any and all cultural residue. It's an identity that goes beyond reflecting God's image simply because, like all of humanity, we were created in his likeness within our human nature, to one in which God's *divine nature* dwells in and enlivens us from the very core of our being (2 Pet 1:4; John 14:23). Christ within is the transforming divine presence that creates all things new so that we are no longer subject to the domination of fallen human nature and its cultural bi-products (2 Cor 5:17). Our natures are transformed through his presence, so that the core of who we are as persons is merged with Christ in God (Eph 2:6). Our divinely-imprinted birth nature has been enhanced, and we have been incorporated into the very heart of God.

This elevated starting point puts believers on a completely different trajectory through life. We are no longer prisoners to the fallen human nature that was our unwanted inheritance as Adam's progeny, for now the Second Adam has negated the effects of the first and made us partakers of his divine nature (1 Cor. 15; 2 Peter 1:4; Rom. 8:29). "You are," as Crowder writes, "clothed fully in divinity. In robes of His righteousness."[2]

Thus clothed, we can wear our culture lightly. Our citizenship as Christians has been transferred from an earthly, human-focused dimension to a heavenly, Christ-centered realm that is at once transcendent yet ever-present (Phil 3:20; Eph1:21–23). Not only have our natures been transformed, our allegiances have been transferred in the process. Now we are full citizens of the kingdom of God, and all our goals and endeavors stem from that eminent position.

The Christ nature within includes countless "upgrades." Scripture tells us we have been retrofitted with the mind of Christ (1 Cor 2:16), which transforms our thinking through his indwelling Spirit so that we come into alignment with God's purposes and perspectives, guided by his divine wisdom. The Spirit of Jesus within means we now operate out of the love (Rom 5:5) and humility of Christ (Phil 2:5–8), which are two inseparable divine characteristics, because love necessarily concerns itself with the good of others in relation to self. In addition, all the fruits of the Spirit are now operative within believers as a benefit of the indwelling divine nature (Gal 5:22–23). And the gifts of the Spirit as described in 1 Corinthians 12–14 are conferred as an additional benefit to facilitate the transformative impact of the Christian life, witness, and ministry which the Spirit directs in accordance with the will and purposes of God. In short, we are totally different now because of the indwelling Spirit, and our lives have been reoriented onto a completely new trajectory.

---

2. Crowder, *Mystical Union*, 204.

CONCLUSION: IT'S ALL ABOUT IMAGE

One could say this is grounds for a massive superiority complex, because all of this talk of divine union surely means believers think themselves better than others. Yet the truth is that the transformation God effects in those who place their faith in Jesus is not the attainment of some silly notion of superhumanity, but the *divinely wrought means by which we become truly and fully human*. The Spirit of Christ living within the human heart makes us for the very first time whole human beings, as we were originally designed to be. It completes us. We are transformed from a state of disfigurement and deficiency—spiritual residue of the Fall—into wholeness, fullness, and completeness. In Christ we become who we really are as human beings and children of the living God.

In a sense, our completion in Christ makes us more human than those who do not believe. That is because believers are freed from the control of the evil one, whose diabolical involvement in human affairs is always destructive toward God's original design and intent (Mark 4:15). The devil lays waste to human life and potential, unhinging humanity from its divinely-crafted, fundamentally-good nature and true vocation as righteous children of a loving God (1 Pet 5:8). Inviting the world to believe in Jesus is inviting them to embrace their own full and glorious humanity. It is an invitation to reverse the state of "deposed royalty," and regain humanity's conferred status given by God at Creation, but subsequently despoiled and stolen away by Satan through the Fall. It is not an invitation to escape the world but to be fully in it for the very first time, engaging humanity and the rest of creation through the inherent goodness, love, and power that God's inward presence provides. It is the only means to properly do what humans are meant to do: fashion culture so that life flourishes all around to the benefit of all, therein celebrating and promulgating the essence and glory of the Author of all things good (Jas 1:17; 1 John 1:5).

EPIGENETICS

In that science provides a window into the composition and workings of creation, it also helps us to better comprehend our new nature. Biology and genetics have opened our understanding into the building blocks of all living things. The human genome project has mapped out some 30,000 genes in our DNA, and one day scientists hope to identify those genes complex roles in determining the shape and function of human life. Our genes are basically coded instructions inherent within the double-helix structure of our DNA. Yet we've learned that the inbuilt instructions do not always manifest, or manifest improperly or only under certain conditions, because of another intrinsic feature known as the epigenome ("beyond the gene")—the chemical markers and switches that exist outside the genes to turn them on and off. The environment (stress, nutrition, radiation) drives epigenetic expression, switching on or turning off functions like disease processes that otherwise lie latent in the gene sequences.

What does this mean for us? It quite possibly reveals one way human beings not only inherit the fallen dimension of human nature, but a mechanism by which the indwelling Spirit can reconfigure that nature so it again falls into alignment with God's original intent. Some think that epigenetics may well have identified one or more of the very biochemical process by which the "iniquity of the fathers [is visited] on the children, even to the fourth generation" (Ex 20:5, KJV).[3] If so, then epigenetics has also identified a process by which the offspring of those whom God blesses continue in that blessing (Ex 20:6), for the process would be the same in reverse.

The science of epigenetics has now verified links between the lifestyle and environmental choices individuals make today and their effect several generations later on in one's offspring—for better or worse.[4] This means that the human behaviors we maintain as contemporary cultural norms and values will affect the physical and mental health and well-being, not only of ourselves, but the generations we engender. One can see in this process a means by which fallen human behaviors and the cultural forms that perpetrate them lock humanity and its various cultural expressions into a continually fallen state. The affected DNA that perpetrates sin among humankind is very much like a cancer-causing genetic mutation that continues to replicate itself from one generation to the next, reinforced by the additional process of memetic cultural replication.

Yet the same design feature inherent within the epigenome should allow for transformation in the direction of the original pre-fallen nature of humankind. The Holy Spirit within can be the positive environmental influence to switch off the chemical messages that cause ongoing disease, death, and destruction through contaminated gene expression—the "wages of sin"—and switch on the chemical messengers that promote the divine image still inherent in humanity's genetic makeup. Through epigenetics, it is possible to imagine how Christ within activates good gene expression that might otherwise lie latent, and switches off genes that have become

---

3. See Brooks, "Original Sin,"§8a, http://www.inplainsite.org/html/original_sin_or_epigenetics.html, accessed April 26, 2014.

4. Skinner, et al., "Ancestral Exposure," http://www.biomedcentral.com/1741-7015/11/228, posted October 23, 2013; Manikkam et al., "Transgenerational Actions," http://www.plosone.org/article/info%3Adoi%2F10.1371%2Fjournal.pone.0031901, accessed, posted February 28, 2012.

defective and destructive through the effects of the Fall. By this reasoning, the indwelling Spirit provides the catalyst needed to literally transform us into new creatures (Rom 8:1–2; 2 Cor 5:17), and in the process make us more fully human because we come more fully in line with the pattern of God's original design.

This is, of course, full of conjecture and undoubtedly things are far more complex. Yet it is fascinating to ponder the ways science can provide a better understanding into the realities of God's presence in the world and his tangible effect upon the lives of his children and the rest of creation. I am certain that much more startling insights into the workings of the divinely-crafted cell and its genetic components are yet to come, and if properly interpreted they will further confirm and support the biblical view of humanity and the manifest presence of God within his creation. That has been the legitimate role of science all along,[5] until it was wrongly usurped by those who felt a need to use it as a basis for their hegemonic materialist worldviews. But regardless the outcome of the study of epigenetics and its application to faith and the Bible, the fact is that by some process(es)—currently understood or not—God *is* actively changing us into the image of his Son, which is our true identity and celebrated calling (Rom 8:29; 2 Cor 3:18).

OUR TRUE IDENTITY

In Colossians 3:3 it states that we died to the old self and our lives are now hidden with Christ in God. Whatever self-image we previously had, based as it inevitably was upon numerous false cultural images we assumed for ourselves, must be let go to make room for the new identity in Christ—the true identity, the true self. As Rohr puts it, "God sees the divine image in you as you see your image in your children."[6] There simply is no more elevated image we can have of ourselves than the way God sees us as his sons and daughters in Christ. Nothing compares in this world; all alternatives are but pathetically-deficient substitutes.

To fail to receive the inheritance we've been given as Christians is to live a fractured, incongruent life behind masks that distort the treasure of our real identity. It is to live in the shadows, identifying with the Fall

---

5. In his thought-provoking book, *The Wonder of the World*, Roy Abraham Varghese details the history of modern science as the outcome of those who held firm religious convictions—men and women who integrated faith and science to the mutual benefit of both. He posits that science is in fact dependent upon a theistic religious worldview, because only such a worldview provides the necessary certainty in the law and order of nature that lies behind all scientific inquiry (p. 79).

6. Rohr, *Everything Belongs*, 163.

rather than the Resurrection. In Christ, Crowder says, "You are no longer an Adamite. You are now sons of God. Just as Christ was a man, yet more than a man, so are you in this world (1 John 4:17)." After declaring that in Christ we have for the first time become "truly human," Crowder goes on to explain that "As a result of the fall of Adam, mankind become 'less than human,' in that we had fallen away from the original image that God had created. Now you have been restored to the original design of humanity. But it goes further still. Your relationship with God is now better than Eden."[7]

To embrace who we really are in Christ is not only to embrace reality, it is to avail ourselves of the abundant life Jesus came to offer (John 10:10). "Its simple," as Mel Bond put it during a healing service, "God is good and has given us all things in Christ."[8] There is no lack of any sort when we live out our true identity as believers (2 Pet 1:3). We become whole in every way when we live in the One who makes us more fully human than was ever possible before. In him, we are free to *thrive*; whereas according to the "old man" and the ways of the world, our orientation was always just to *survive*. The one speaks of the abundance of life Christ came to give, and the other of life's harsh necessities that entail contending with others to get our share.

Thriving means flourishing—"growing luxuriantly"—in the fullest sense of the word. It means celebrating who we are as children of God *and* bearers of the divine nature. We were made to be royalty in the divine court. It is imprinted in our genes and revealed in our physical constitution, as evidenced, for example, in the structure of the human ear. Its design speaks of the fact that we are made to rejoice and celebrate the goodness and glory of God through unbridled song and celebration. Researchers tell us that some two-thirds of the cilia that cover the inner ear only resonate at 3,000 to 20,000 hertz, levels that comprise the higher musical frequencies.[9] Those cilia lie dormant in "normal life" but engage during higher-pitched musical activities. Who put them there and for what reason? In short, they are there for song and celebration—the hallmarks of joyful worship. It is what we are made to do, engaging the "whole" person in a total expression of celebratory praise and thanksgiving.

Even the sounds of worship confirm our calling. The "Ah" in "Alleluia" are said to cleanse the emotions and "vibrate[s]s the heart [as] the sound of praise and wonder," while "Ou" stimulates the gut region where we experience emotions evoked from the ear through the neural channel of the vagus

---

7. Crowder, *Mystical Union*, 104.

8. Bond, sermon, "Breaking Free" healing service, Albuquerque, New Mexico, November 14, 2013.

9. Campbell, *Mozart Effect*, 134.

nerve.[10] Like David before the Ark of the Covenant (2 Sam 6:14), we are created to rejoice and celebrate with profound emotions that set our feet to dancing at God's awe-inspiring presence in our midst. As John Piper writes, "God is most glorified in us when we are most satisfied in Him."[11]

Put simply, we are made for the kingdom, which is exactly what God's manifest presence effects. His presence is the abode for which our identity in Christ is tailor-made. And that is why Jesus warned his disciples, "In the world you will have trouble" (John 16:33). Because Christ and his kingdom were not of this world (John 8:23, 18:36), his followers would also not be comfortably at home here (John 15:19). They were to remain in the world as full participants (John 17:15), but like the forefathers of their faith, their hearts would belong to another, better realm still to come (Gen 23:4; Ps 119:19, Heb 11:13; 1 Pet 2:11).

That realm, of course, is God's emerging kingdom—the only place where heart, mind, and spirit can truly feel at home. The world, including America and its familiar cultural formulations, is too confining for those destined for the riches of the kingdom. Worldly culture, including religious culture, inevitably binds and constricts like an ill-fitting suit. Only the kingdom gives us the "relaxed fit" for which we are fashioned in Christ. Our calling is to wear our "comfort-fit" Christ nature happily and fruitfully within the cultural constraints of America, mindful that, though we are called to be fully engaged and committed to the present, our "clothing" will never be fully appropriate wear in this world. If it feels that way, then we have yet to fully "clothe [ourselves] with the Lord Jesus Christ" (Rom 13:14, NIV).

THE HIGH CALLING

Just as humans are designed to find their completion in union with God, this world (*kosmos*) is destined to find its completion in the kingdom of God. Every facet of life on earth, from nature's fragile but elegant ecosystems to human governance and culture, is destined to be brought into conformity to God's emerging kingdom. All will be transformed through Christ (Acts 3:21; Eph 1:9–10; Col 1:15–20). Through him God will rescue everything from the deleterious effects of the Fall (Isa 65:15–25; Dan 7:14; Rev 21:3).

Our job, as citizens of the kingdom and those who embody the divine nature, is to humbly but whole-heartedly help facilitate the kingdom's coming on earth (Matt 6:33; 2 Cor 5:18–20), though its full manifestation must

10. Hale, *Sacred Space*, 5, 18.

11. Piper, "Christian Hedonism," para.1, http://www.desiringgod.org/articles/christian-hedonism, posted January 1, 1995.

await the Second Coming and God's establishment of his unrivaled *shalom*. Meanwhile, the church exists to point toward and facilitate his kingdom, and at every opportunity to pull its next-world realities into this world through embodying Christ in word and deed. In the person of Jesus rests the epicenter of all kingdom realities; so by living fully in him, and he in us, we make manifest his kingdom whatever our station or circumstances in life (John 15:5–6).

In this present age, Christ does not exist in a cultural vacuum. The church is constrained to employ cultural/religious forms, many of questionable worth, to present him and his kingdom to those unaware of the wonderful gift that is relevant to and freely available for all. Yet those same forms constantly threaten to disarm the gospel message and its transformative power by usurping the centrality of its message and stealing away the primary focus of attention—the living God. The early church faced the very same issue, which forms a major theme running through many of the epistles. False teachers were everywhere, offering compromise with the accepted cultural practices of the day, especially certain forms of early Gnosticism that embraced the hedonistic indulgences of the day.[12] The heresy the early church faced was a gospel message indistinguishable from the surrounding culture—a situation no different than today.

All cultural forms, and especially forms relating to religious culture, must be judged relative to their ability to reflect and facilitate the simple but powerful gospel of the kingdom. Many norms and values will prove useful—those that honor marriage, family, and human flourishing—yet none is irrevocably sacred, for every last one of them can be misappropriated when linked with fallen human behaviors (e.g., co-dependent marriages, dysfunctional families, and unbridled materialism). It is the presence of the Holy Spirit in the lives of the individuals who live out their cultural norms and values that makes the norms and values useful conduits for the kingdom. It bears repeating: no cultural expression is sacred in and of itself, and Christians are not called to be guardians (or repairmen) of even the most honored of cultural expressions. We are called to abide in Christ, so that regardless the cultural format of our lives, our attitudes and behaviors will, by association, reflect him and his kingdom.

---

12. The Gnostic belief that only the spiritual realm was real actually led away from asceticism for some adherents, who reasoned that since the body did not ultimately matter, one could indulge it however one pleased. Gnostic hedonism was addressed in various New Testament letters, including 2 Peter 2 and Jude 1. See Grabbe, "Whatever Happened," para. 12, http:// www.bibletools.org/index.cfm/fuseaction/ Library.sr/CT/ ARTB/k/1193/Whatever-Happened-Gnosticism-Part-Two-Defining-Gnosticism.htm, posted December, 2006.

Our high calling as representatives of Christ is to unveil something utterly new and transformative—the pure gospel—in and through our given cultures. The more we stay on track and keep the focus on the person and presence of God, the more we embody the kingdom and facilitate its emergence in America and the world. It will not look like any law or institution this world has to offer. Rather, it will appear in the form of redemptive and transformational acts among humankind—acts that call forth the divine nature lying dormant in the sacred genetic imprint God engineered into all human flesh at the dawn of creation.

There is no Christian culture, only Christians with culture. Faith is dynamic, whereas cultural forms are flexible but limited. They progressively drift over time into different formulations, but do not change their essence as group-sanctioned behaviors which are inevitably influenced by self-interest born of unredeemed human nature. Faith *irrupts* in and through culture yet is not limited to or by it—at one minute present in particular cultural forms and missing the next, rendering the forms themselves secondary and often superfluous. There is only innate legitimacy in "kingdom culture," which is the momentary embodiment of God's Spirit moving through humanly-derived cultural configurations. It constitutes a life-giving essence that cannot be formalized or institutionalized because its dynamic nature always offers only a fresh and direct encounter with the transcendent presence of God.

The best way to facilitate kingdom culture and thus enhance the cultural forms that represent the church and our American way of life is to start within oneself. It is to consciously center upon God's abiding presence within, inviting and allowing his transformative Spirit to then emanate outwardly through one's chosen cultural and religious/theological forms. As Heidi Baker succinctly put the matter, "Jesus is perfect theology."[13] His presence is what counts, not formalized or abstract concepts about his form and nature—though each of those endeavors has its time and place.

In the same way, Jesus makes for perfect (kingdom) culture. It is his presence in and through the practitioners of culture which provides the only notable distinction for any cultural form, including religious forms. Just as the Spirit's presence infuses human nature and all its fickleness with the steadfast strength and holiness of divine nature, so does his presence transform the cultures of humankind into kingdom culture—moment by moment, gesture by gesture. Without his transformative presence in us as both a people and a society, we remain like Ezekiel's valley of dry bones awaiting God's breath to give us the means to rise up from among the dead and truly live (Ezek 37:1–14).

---

13. Baker, *Compelled by Love*, DVD.

AMERICA THE BEAUTIFUL

To the degree that the church in America can represent kingdom culture in and through the superficial forms and formalities of institutional and religious culture, America will become truly beautiful. All the noble ideals for which America stands—equality, fraternity, justice under the law, human rights, and opportunities to flourish—are but faint reflections of the defining characteristics of the kingdom of God, the realm of his perfect *shalom*. The kingdom's beauty is unmatched, for within it dwells the splendors of divine love, inscrutable peace, perfect relationship, and idyllic community—not just between human beings, but between God and all of his creation. All earthly kingdoms must be judged according to the standard of the kingdom of God, and each nation becomes more beautiful the more closely it can replicate that kingdom.

America's beauty is more than its landscape, diverse peoples, and novel way of life—its highly vaunted natural, human, and cultural configurations. In a sense, America has come to play a special role over the centuries as an earthly symbol of the kingdom, not because of any intrinsic worth or nobility of its citizens and/or culture, but because it has in modern times come to *symbolically represent* for many the inspired hopes of a better world. America has come to symbolize what many other countries have expressly failed to be—just, accommodating, humane, and tolerant of difference. Of course, the U.S. will always fail to effectively deliver the promise projected by many onto it because, after all, it is only a nation comprised of mortal men and women subject to the Fall like every other grouping of human beings.

Within America, however, dwells its church, which has an opportunity and a mandate to redirect the ubiquitous human longing for paradise toward its only fitting goal. The American church's *raison d'être* is to offer its citizens and the larger world the only genuine hope available to humankind—Jesus and his glorious kingdom. Yet it must do it by way of the imperfect cultural and institutional structures that so easily misrepresent the true hope of the gospel with counterfeit hopes invested in the nation and our American way of life.

The church can't perform its function to be a prophetic guide if it unswervingly identifies with any singular faction within American culture, be it political, economic, social, or religious. It can only fulfill its high calling to represent the kingdom of God and the redemptive hope of Christ through a dogged determination to adhere to kingdom culture as its only legitimate option. And it can only do that when individual believers first grasp and then maintain a firm focus upon their true identity as ambassadors of Christ and representatives of his simple but powerfully transformative gospel.

Just as immigrants throughout its history have come to America through a combination of the "push-pull" forces mentioned in chapter 4, so is there an analogous process affecting the church today and the gospel it is called to proclaim. The failures of America to live up to the idealized hopes and dreams of its citizens and those drawn to its shores represent the "push" of unrealized human hopes for paradise embedded deep within the human soul. No one can find that hoped for paradise in any human-designed government or institution, and many end up with bitter disappointment because of the country's inability to deliver it as expected. As long as fallen human nature is around, America will never eradicate racism, the lack of equal access to economic opportunities, and the overbearing stresses and at times pointless nature of much of modern American life. Meanwhile, the love of Jesus and the kingdom he came to proclaim represents the "pull" that tugs every human heart toward it's yet to be fulfilled desire for the *shalom* of God. Projection rules the day, as generations continue to misplace their deepest longings onto that which cannot satisfy. It's a clarion call for the church to respond and correct the misplaced longings of humankind.

The church is in a position to identify the "push" of every false hope placed in culture, institutions, human beings and their impressive achievements, while simultaneously representing and illuminating *for all* the rightful "pull" of Jesus and his kingdom. He said, ". . . if I am lifted up from the earth, I will draw *all people* to myself (John 12:32, HCSB). As Charles Spurgeon noted, the Greek word for "lifted up" (*hupsoō*) signifies more than Christ's manner of death on the cross; it speaks of "exaltation," of exalting Christ in every venue.[14] The church is thus called to exalt him within the varied secular and religious cultures of America. It cannot settle for what Spurgeon called "mere morality," "mere doctrine," and mere "learning." The emphasis must be on the person of Jesus and not religious culture, social structures, or the culture-at-large as a substitute for the real thing. Such forms and formulations have a place and a purpose, but it is not the one rightfully reserved for the deepest hopes of humankind.

READY THE BRIDE

The American church is in no position to properly exalt Christ if it is sublimated within either the dominant culture or one of its many distinct and

---

14. Spurgeon, "Christ Lifted Up," §3. http://www.spurgeon.org/sermons/0139.htm, accessed April 23, 2014.

exclusive subcultures. It must own its one true identity as the salt and light of a singular vision for humanity, the one revelation that can decisively fulfill the longings of mankind along with the latent potential of our God-imaged nature. It is a vision of the church as engaged sojourners—representatives of the kingdom who are also fully occupied with the minutiae of everyday life in a nuts-and-bolts, scuffle-to-work world. It is characterized by a simultaneously other-worldly yet all-in-the-present orientation.

Paradoxically, the more our hearts are given to living as pilgrims and sojourners with gazes firmly fixed upon the kingdom, the better citizens we become in this world and in our given vocations. When the American church is fully itself—a tangible manifestation of Christ within society and culture—then those within it become the very best of Americans. It is not because they mimic the culture-at-large, as some may think. Rather, it is because believers are so engrossed in the kingdom and its transcendent calling that they are freed of the trivial distractions of sectarianism, materialism, and every other "ism" that parades as truth as it vies for human allegiance.

The church must grasp and embrace its real identity as the embodiment of the divine presence in the world so we can, first and foremost, liberate *ourselves* from the partial truths that entangle us in culture and culturalized Christianity. Those partial truths are as dangerous a vehicle for the powers of darkness as any overt form of Satan worship, if not more so; for they masquerade as truth and light while serving to obfuscate the same (2 Cor 7:14).[15] When Jesus came down hard on the Jewish leaders of his day, it was because they misrepresented the true loving, forgiving, and inclusive nature of God toward those he adored—the poor, disenfranchised, and humble folk who thirsted for him and his unrivaled rule of righteous (Matt 23). By failing in that sacred calling, the religious elite were denying God's people the opportunity to embrace their true humanity—their nature wrought in his ineffable image—and the fullness of life he wanted for them all.

Sometimes Christians act a bit spiritually elitist themselves, as though they own God, with Jesus and the Holy Spirit corresponding to religious mascots. Yet God belongs to the whole of humanity, and Jesus died and rose again for *all* (Heb 2:9; 1 John 2:2). Every human heart senses him through the elevated dimensions of life—the beauty of nature, the wonder of children

---

15. It is interesting that the symbol of the beast in Revelation 13 is 666, a number that is one digit shy of the symbolically perfect number 7, which the Bible consistently associates with God. In Revelation, the beast as antichrist performs miracles and engenders worship among men because of his imitatively divine-like powers. There is a parallel between this idea of evil as near-but-skewed divinity with the suggestion that partial truths are often the most misleading, and thus the most dangerous in terms of their effect.

and unrestrained laughter, the faithful love of friend and spouse—though many are yet to know the source of their inspiration in *personal terms*. Still, we are all fashioned to be drawn toward God, and every person deserves the opportunity to meet their lifelong Love without frivolous add-ons and misleading distractions.

Every religion and system of philosophical thought, including atheism, contains some elements of truth—if only the acknowledgement that there exists an overarching patterned reality that accounts for life and the structure of human belief and behavior. In most religious thought there is at least the fundamental biblical truth that life is transitory and full of illusions, as Proverbs and Ecclesiastes also attest. But half-truths are also half-lies, and most of the world inherits a patchwork of customs and beliefs that, despite some obvious elements of truth and good in each, inevitably lead away from the truth and goodness of God's incomparable kingdom. We "owe" this world of half-truths "an encounter with God," to borrow the words of Bill Johnson.[16] Yet how can the church do that if it consistently degrades the gospel message into its own half-truths by dressing it up in cultural forms unrelated to its simple essence, thereby depreciating the gospel into so much *less* than it really is.

FLOURISHING EAST OF EDEN

In the Garden after the Fall, God compassionately clothed Adam and Eve for their departure into a fallen world where they would have to struggle mightily to survive. Their clothing was a gift from God that represented culture—a "tool" they would thereafter need to successfully meet their impending struggles. The possession of culture allowed the first couple's descendants to better control and adapt to their environments and the unpredictable circumstances that life posed outside of Eden. Yet culture also represented a heart-rending separation from the Garden and the *shalom* that reigned there under God's benevolent presence and provision. It symbolized a dismal *substitute* for the glories of Eden lost—animal skins and walking sticks were a poor replacement for the tree of life and carefree strolls in the company of their loving Creator.

In Christ the process was set in reverse. In the one called Emmanuel, God again came to dwell among humankind, and the kingdom began to

---

16. The full idea expressed by Bill Johnson is as follows: "Bill teaches that we [the church] owe the world an encounter with God, and that a Gospel without power is not the Gospel that Jesus preached." iBethel.org, para. 3, http://www.ibethel.org/users/billandbenijohnson, accessed October 30, 2014.

break forth from his very person and presence. Reliance on culture as a necessary substitute for the abundance of God's direct rule became superfluous to a large degree, leaving a residue of human coping mechanisms that fit the lands east of Eden but not the New Jerusalem toward which God's kingdom resolutely pointed. The *shalom* of God was resident in Christ, who put Eden's goodness back into human hearts through his indwelling presence. In Christ, Eden became internalized. Jesus reconfigured and changed the quality of culture that had served humans prior to his advent through the introduction of a kingdom culture inseparable from his person.

Through the redemptive work of Christ, God began a process of weaning mankind from what was now an unnecessary overdependence on *culture as a survival mechanism*—appropriate to a fallen world but not the one he brought with him. Among his followers (the church that would, in time, become his presence in the world) he began the process of replacing blighted human culture with kingdom culture, the necessary accoutrement for the new digs ahead—the New Jerusalem. Jesus had come with a "new covenant" sprinkled in his blood, one that spoke "a better word than the blood of Abel" (Heb 12:24). The culture Adam's descendants had developed to survive outside of Eden was stained with Abel's blood—full of self-interest, fear and isolation, and calls for retribution. The transformation Christ wrought through *his* blood made such things obsolete, as mutuality, peace, forgiveness, inclusion, and grace exemplified the new culture of the kingdom. In Christ came a new mandate that required a new adaptation to the emerging kingdom and the new order God initiated through the cross.

WELCOME HOME

God forever altered the course of human history when he spoke to a descendant of Adam named Abram in a land somewhere east of Eden's wilted gardens. He called Abram to leave his people and culture because God had plans to build a new people with a unique culture that would better suit the new world he envisioned and was bringing into being. Through Israel, a new and unique revelation was given: There is no God but Jehovah, the one who is intimately engaged with humankind and the whole of the created order he made to reflect his goodness. Through his incarnate Son, God divulged yet another revelation: He is pure love and grace and has provided a way for humanity to dwell once again in his glorious presence, through the surprising miracle of his dwelling within those he created. In time, the memory of Eden lost would be completely erased by the transfixing hope of a new and better realm of unending love and celebration that attends his life-giving presence within.

The church has been tasked with the mission of proclaiming this compounded revelation and the glories of the kingdom, both present and future, through a gospel to be spread by word and deed to the entire habitable world. To do the job correctly, the church must fully adapt to its new identity as the primary abode of God on earth, and the new kingdom environment that accompanies his presence among us. It means swapping out the old cultural tools appropriate to surviving east of Eden for kingdom culture tools appropriate to the reconfigured circumstances and the end-goal purposes of God. Struggle, self-interest, and keeping the dangerous inhabitants Cain feared at arms length has been replaced by a culture of resting in God, unleashing his healing power, loving one's neighbors, and inclusion of even the most distant descendants of Adam.

The changed circumstances require a new adaptation to the impending alteration of all life on earth. The changes have already been anticipated and written upon mankind's original blueprint, which manifests whenever God's Spirit is allowed to displace the old and useless forms with those fitting his emerging kingdom. That kingdom steadily moves forward like a glacier inching toward the sea of God's eternal love and purposes for his creation, transforming the entire landscape of human life and culture along the way. The church and every living person has a choice to align his or her life with the inexorable flow of God's powerfully transformative kingdom. Such an affirmation begins within one's own heart and mind, from which it then extends outward to the farthest reaches of the cosmos. Or, each person has the God-given choice to ignore the inevitable coming of the kingdom and pay the consequences for not being a part of it.

The gospel is God's open invitation to everyone to "go with the flow" and join the great procession through submitting to and resting in his irresistible goodness and benevolent plans for every human being and all of Creation. The alternative is to be crushed by the sheer force of God's transforming power as his kingdom completely alters everything within its all-consuming path. Every human endeavor devoid of kingdom concerns will be completely transformed or left for the "wood, hay, and stubble" (1 Cor 3:12) that it is. Yet the expansive beauty of the King and his kingdom is precisely what every human heart and endeavor unconsciously desires, but so often seeks in all the wrong places.

The gospel the church has been privileged to offer is a message of the wonders of God's incomparable love made available to all as pure gift. His most profound desire is to bring the whole of humanity back home into his doting presence (John 3:16), for he longs to reestablish the intimacy he knew with his beloved children in the Garden. He longs so deeply that he personally came in Christ to fetch us back so he might live with us and forever rejoice over the depths of his plumbless love. The prophet Zephaniah saw his kingdom coming and beautifully prophesied the day God would joyfully rejoin the errant human race that he went forth to rescue from the desolate lands east of Eden. "For the Lord your God is [now] living among you. He is a mighty savior. He will take delight in you with gladness. With his love, he will calm all your fears. He will rejoice over you with joyful songs" (3:17, NLT). Our Creator God sings songs of joy over us!

Yet those lands of desolation east of Eden still extend into America today. The church is privy to participate in the rescue effort through a gospel that proclaims the old tools of survival are no longer necessary. The Master has brought a new set of tools appropriate to the kingdom that attends his presence among us. The culture of the kingdom is now our new way of life, and it will remain so throughout eternity. Its transformative power is available *now* to everyone tired of the fundamental emptiness of a fallen and passing world and all the tattered forms used to temporarily prop it up. To all who are ready to enter the wide open gates of God's lush gardens of grace, his arms of compassion are already extended in effusive welcome. He does so through the wide open arms of Jesus splayed upon the cross, whose bloodied hands and feet resolutely bore the dust of Adam heavenward—reconsecrating a world gone terribly astray. We now have the opportunity to remove the soiled animal skins that served as a pitiable means of survival in a realm that has forever passed. They are no longer needed. We've been graciously clothed in robes of righteousness (Isa 61:10; Rom 3:22), and there is more than enough room for all of God's children to thrive in the abundance of his eternally loving embrace.

Darkness cannot drive out darkness; only light can do that.
Hate cannot drive out hate; only love can do that.

—Martin Luther King Jr.

Don't copy the behavior and customs of this world, but let God transform you into a new person by changing the way you think. Then you will learn to know God's will for you, which is good and pleasing and perfect.

—Romans 12:2, NLT

Bibliography

Abbey, Edward. *The Journey Home: Some Words in Defense of the American West*. New York: E.P. Dutton, 1977.
Achieve and Johnson, Grossnickle and Associates. The Millennial Impact Report, 2012. http://www.themillennialimpact.com/research-2012.
Adler, Margot. "Young People Push Back Against Gender Categories." *National Public Radio*. Transcript from *All Things Considered*, July 16, 2013, hosted by Melissa Block and Audie Cornish. http://www.npr.org/templates/story/story.php?storyId=202729367.
Aeschliman, Gordon. "Loving the Earth Is Loving the Poor," In *The Green Bible*, edited by Michael G. Maudlin et al., Introduction 91–97. New Revised Standard Version. New York: HarperOne, 1989.
Alexander, Eben. *Proof of Heaven: A Neurosurgeon's Journey into the Afterlife*. New York: Simon & Schuster, 2012.
Amsden, L. T. "Bear Hear Williams." *New Mexico Magazine* (August 2005) 24.
Animal Welfare Institute, "Do Animal's Have a Sense of Humor?" *AWI Quarterly* 63, 2011. https://awionline.org/awi-quarterly/2011-winter/do-animals-have-sense-humor.
Annunciation Byzantine Catholic Church. "Byzantine Christian Worship: God is With Us," http://www.annunciationbyzantine.org/our_faith.htm.
Antrosio, Jason. "Human Nature and Anthropology." *Living Anthropologically*. http://www.livinganthropologically.com/anthropology/human-nature.
Aristotle. *Metaphysics*. In *Aristotle, vols. 17 & 18*. Translated by Hugh Tredennick, 1933. Cambridge, MA: Harvard University Press. London: William Heinemann Ltd., 1989. http://www.perseus.tufts.edu/hopper/text?doc=Perseus:text:1999.01.0052:book=12:section=1072b.
Association of Americans Resident Overseas. New Government Estimate of Overseas Americans. http://www.aaro.org/about-aaro/6m-americans-abroad.
Augé, Marc. *Non-Places: Introduction to an Anthropology of Supermodernity*. Translated by John Howe. London: Verso, 1995.
Augustine of Hippo. *On Christian Doctrine, Book 1* [397]. Christian Classics Ethereal Library. http://www.ccel.org/ccel/augustine/doctrine.xxxvi.html.
Babones, Salvatore. "U.S. Income Distribution: Just How Unequal?" *Inequality.org*, 2012. http://inequality.org/unequal-americas-income-distribution/.
Baker, Dennis and Heidi Baker. *Always Enough*. Grand Rapids: Chosen, 2003.
Baker, Heidi. *Compelled by Love*. Lake Mary, FL: Charisma, 2008.

———.*Compelled By Love*, DVD. Global Films, Inc., 2013.
Bankhead, Tallulah. Goodreads. Tallulah Bankhead Quotes. http://www.goodreads.com/author/quotes/373651.%20Tallulah_Bankhead
Barker, Kenneth, et al, eds. *The NIV Study Bible: New International Version*. Philippians 2:12 footnotes. Grand Rapids, MI: Zondervan, 1985.
Bartholomew, Ecumenical Patriarch. In *The Green Bible*, edited by Michael G. Maudlin et al., Introduction, 97. New Revised Standard Version. New York: HarperOne, 1989.
Beecher, Henry Ward. IZ Quotes. Henry Ward Beecher Quotes. http://izquotes.com/quote/14539.
Berry, Wendell. "Wendell Berry: Poet and Prophet." *Public Broadcasting Service*. Moyers and Company. Televised interview with Bill Moyers, December 2, 2013.
Bible Presbyterian Church Online. Westminster Shorter Catechism Project. Question 1, Westminster Shorter Catechism.BPC.org. http://www.shortercatechism.com/resources/wsc/wsc_001.html.
Bird-David, Nurit. "Tribal Metaphorization of Human-Nature Relatedness: A Comparative Analysis." In *Environmentalism: The View from Anthropology*, edited by Kay Milton, 112–25. London and New York: Routledge, 1993.
Blake, William. "Auguries of Innocence," Poetry Foundation. Poems and Poets. http://www.poetryfoundation.org/poem/172906.
Bloch, Maurice. *Essays on Cultural Transmission*. London School of Economics Monographs on Social Anthropology 75. Oxford: Berg, 2005.
Bloomberg Businessweek. "Napping Gets a Nod at the Workplace." Behavior, August 26, 2010. http://www.businessweek.com/magazine/content/10_36/b4193084949626.htm.
Blow, Charles. "Radical Life Extension," *New York Times*, Opinions, August 7, 2013, http://www.nytimes.com/2013/08/08/opinion/blow-radical-life-extension.html?_r=0.
Bodley, John H. *Cultural Anthropology: Tribes, States, and the Global System*, 5th ed. Walnut Creek, CA: AltaMira, 2011.
Bonaparte, Napoleon. Goodreads. Napoleon Quotes. http://www.goodreads.com/quotes/47684-history-is-the-version-of-past-events-that-people-have.
Bond, Mel. *God's Last Day's People* (publisher not listed) ISBN 9782-1-82318-06-4, 2007.
———. *How to See in the Spirit World* (no publisher or ISBN listed), 2013.
Boyd, Gregory. *The Myth of a Christian Nation: How the Quest for Political Power is Destroying the* Church. Grand Rapids: Zondervan, 2007.
Broca, Paul. ThinkExist. http://thinkexist.com/quotation/the_least_questioned_assumptions_are_often_the/184203.html.
Brooks, Carol. "Original Sin and Epigenetics," *InPlainSite.org*, Section 8A . . . A Question of Salvation/Original Sin. http://www.inplainsite.org/html/original_sin_or_epigenetics.html.
Brown, Donald E. "Human Universals, Human Nature, and Human Culture." *Daedalus* 133 (2004) 47–54.
Brzezinski, Zbigniew. "Brzezinski: U.S. Should Work with Russia, Turkey to Solve Global Problems." *PBS News Hour*, February 8, 2012. Interview with Judy Woodruff. http://www.pbs.org/newshour/bb/business-jan-june12-brzezinski_02-08/.

Buber, Martin. *I and Thou*. Translated by Walter Kaufmann. New York: Touchstone, 1971.
Campbell, Don. *The Mozart Effect: Tapping the Power of Music to Heal the Body, Strengthen the Mind, and Unlock the Spirit*. New York: Avon, 1997.
Campbell, Joseph. *The Flight of the Wild Gander: Explorations in the Mythological Dimension: Select Essays, 1944–1968*. San Francisco: New World Library, 2002.
Casals, Pablo. Goodreads. Pablo Casals Quotes. http://www.goodreads.com/author/quotes/198277.
Center for Human Rights and Global Justice. "Every Thirty Minutes: Farmer Suicides, Human Rights, and the Agrarian Crisis in India." New York University School of Law, 2011. http://www.chrgj.org/publications/docs/every30min.pdf.
Centre for Bhutan Studies and GNH Research. Gross National Happiness. http://www.grossnationalhappiness.com/.
Chesterton, C.K. *St. Francis of Assisi* [1923]. Project Gutenberg Australia eBook, 2009. http://gutenberg.net.au/ebooks09/0900611.txt.
Chetty, Raj, et al. "The Economic Impacts of Tax Expenditures: Evidence from Spatial Variation Across the U.S." Harvard University and University of California Berkeley, July 2013. http://obs.rc.fas.harvard.edu/chetty/tax_expenditure_soi_whitepaper.pdf.
Christian Freedom International. http://christianfreedom.org.
Clark, Dennis and Jan Clark. *Practicing God's Presence 24/7*. Maitland, FL: Xulon, 2012.
Clark, Randy. *There is More: The Secret to Experiencing God's Power to Change Your Life*. Grand Rapids: Chosen, 2013.
Clinton, Bill. *Giving: How Each of Us Can Change the World*. New York: Knopf, 2007.
Clooney, George. BrainyQuote, George Clooney Quotes. http://www.brainyquote.com/quotes/authors/g/georgeclooney.html.
Conniff, Richard. "The Body Eclectic." *Smithsonian* 44 (2013) 40–47.
Cooke, Graham. "Building the Right Mindset." Presentation at Art of Thinking Brilliantly Conference in Vacaville, California, March 3, 2011. http://www.youtube.com/watch?v=sYlpHy3Pvlo.
Crouch, Andy. *Culture Making: Recovering Our Creative Calling*. Westmont, IL: Intervarsity, 2011.
Crowder, John. *Cosmos Reborn*. Portland, OR: Sons of Thunder Ministries and Publications, 2013.
———. *Miracle Workers, Reformers, and the New Mystics*. Shippensburg, PA: Destiny Image, 2006.
———. *Mystical Union*. Portland, OR: Sons of Thunder Ministries and Publications, 2010.
Curry, Andrew. "The Secret Life of Dirt." *Smithsonian* 44 (2013) 40–45.
Damick, Andrew Stephen. "[He] didn't see any God there." *Roads from Emmaus (blog)*, October 4, 2009. http://blogs.ancientfaith.com/roadsfromemmaus/2009/10/04/he-didnt-see-any-god-there/.
Davis, James F. *Who Is Black? One Nation's Definition*. University Park, PA: Penn State University Press, 1991.
Dawkins, Richard. *The Selfish Gene*. Oxford: Oxford University Press, 2006.
Denevan, William. "The Pristine Myth: The Landscape of the Americas in 1492." *Annals of the Association of American Geographers*, edited by Karl Butzer, 82 (1992) 369–87.

de Tocqueville, Alexis. *Democracy in America*, vols. 1, 2. London: Saunders and Otley, 1835, 1840.

———. "Social Condition of the Anglo-Americans," *Democracy in America, vol 1*. University of Virginia. http://xroads.virginia.edu/~Hyper/detoc/1_ch03.htm.

Dietrich, Marlene. BrainyQuote. Marlene Dietrich Quotes. http://www.brainyquote.com/quotes/authors/ m/ marlene_dietrich.html.

Dodson, Helen. "Melanoma Survivors Still Forego Sunscreen and Use Tanning Beds," *YaleNews*, April 10, 2013. http://news.yale.edu/2013/04/08/melanoma-survivors-still-forego-sunscreen-and-use-tanning-beds.

Douglas, Preston. "The 9-ooo-year-old Man Speaks." *Smithsonian* 45 (2014) 52–63.

Dove, Michael. "The Dialectical History of 'Jungle' in Pakistan: An Examination of the Relationship between Nature and Culture." *Journal of Anthropological Research* 48 (1992) 231–53.

Duina, Francesco. *Winning: Reflections on an American Obsession*. Princeton, NJ: Princeton University Press, 2010.

Durham, Gigi. *The Lolita Effect: The Media Sexualization of Young Girls and What We Can Do About It*. New York: Overlook, 2008.

Education Encyclopedia–State University.com. "Uganda-Educational System-Overview." http://education.stateuniversity.com/pages/1585/Uganda-EDUCATIONAL-SYSTEM-OVERVIEW.html/.

The Elie Wiesel Foundation for Humanity. Equality. http://www.eliewieselfoundation.org.

Eliot, T.S. *The Idea of a Christian Society*. London: Faber & Faber, 1939.

Elliot, Elizabeth. *The Liberty of Obedience*. Ann Arbor: Servant Ministries, 1987.

Fisher, Suzanne Woods. *Amish Proverbs: Words of Wisdom From the Simple Life*. Grand Rapids, MI: Revell, 2010.

Flora, Carlin. "The Pursuit of Happiness." *Psychology Today*, January 1, 2009. http://www.psychologytoday.com/articles/200812/the-pursuit-happiness.

Foster, George M. "Peasant Society and the Image of Limited Good." *American Anthropologist New Series* 67 (1965) 293–315.

Fox News. "'Burger King baby' Kathryn Deprill's Search for Mom Draws Facebook Frenzy." Northeast, May 28, 2014. http://www.foxnews.com/us/2014/03/10/burger-king-baby-katheryn-deprill-search-for-mom-draws-facebook-frenzy/.

Franklin, Benjamin. BrainyQuote. Benjamin Franklin Quotes. http://www.brainyquote.com/quotes/quotes/ b/benjaminfr151622.html.

Freidman, Thomas L. "The Next New World," Presentation at the The New York Times Global Forum, San Francisco, California, June 20, 2013. http://www.nytfriedmanforum.com/index.php.

Gardner, Howard. *Intelligence Reframed: Multiple Intelligences for the 21st Century*. New York: Basic Books, 2000.

Gates, Henry Louis. "A Conversation with Henry Louis Gates, Jr." *Public Broadcasting Service* televised interview with Suzanne Malueque, September 1, 2010.

Gelfand, Michele J., et al., "Differences Between Tight and Loose Cultures: A 33-Nation Study." *Science* 332 (2011) 1100–1104.

Girard, René. *The Scapegoat*. Baltimore: Johns Hopkins University Press, 1989.

Glacken, Clarence J. *Traces On The Rhodian Shore*. Berkeley and Los Angeles: University of California Press, 1967.

Global Awakening. Global School of Supernatural Ministry. Onsite. http://globalawakening.com/schools/gssm.

Goldman, Jonathan. *Healing Sounds: The Power of Harmonics*. Rochester, VT: Inner Traditions, 2002.

Gow, Peter. "Land, People, and Paper in Western Amazonia." In *The Anthropology of Landscape: Perspectives on Place and Space*, edited by Eric Hirsch and Michael O'Hanlon, 43–62. Oxford: Clarendon, 1995.

Grabbe, David C. "Whatever Happened to Gnosticism? Part Two: Defining Gnosticism." *Bibletools*.org, December, 2006. http://www.bibletools.org/index.cfm/fuseaction/Library.sr/CT/ARTB/k/1193/Whatever-Happened-Gnosticism-Part-Two-Defining-Gnosticism.htm.

Greene, Brian. "Listening to the Big Bang." *Smithsonian* 45 (2014) 19–26.

Greenwald, Robert. *Wal-mart: The High Cost of Low Price*. Brave New Films, Culver City, CA, 2005.

Groothius, Douglas. "Deposed Royalty: Pascal's Anthropological Argument." The Journal of the Evangelical Theological Society 41 (1998) 297–313.

———. *Christian Apologetics: A Comprehensive Case for Biblical Faith*. Downers Grove, IL: IVP Academic, 2011.

Gunness, Margaret. Pierre Teilhard de Chardin. *Explorefaith.org*, 2007. http://www.explorefaith.org/faces/saints_prophets_and_spiritual_guides/pierre_teilhard_de_chardin.php.

Gutierrez, Ramon "Pueblos and Spanish in the Southwest." In *Major Problems in American Environmental History*, edited by Carolyn Merchant, 45–53. Lexington, MA: D.C. Health and Company, 1993.

Hale, Susan Elizabeth. *Sacred Space, Sacred Sound*. Wheaton, IL: Quest, 2007.

Hale, Thomas. *Don't Let the Goats Eat the Loquat Tree*. Grand Rapids, MI: Zondervan, 1986.

Hallowell, Billy. "Did You Know a Socialist Baptist Preacher Wrote the U.S. Pledge? Here's the Odd Story." *The Blaze*, July 4, 2013. http://www.theblaze.com/stories/2013/07/04/one-nation-under-god-the-odd-complex-and-socialist-history-behind-the-pledge-of-allegiance.

Harrison, K. David. "When Languages Die." In *Book of Peoples of the World: A Guide to Culture*, edited by Wade Davis and K. David Harrison, 58–61. Washington, D.C.: National Geographic Society, 2007.

Helbawy, Kamal. "The Muslim Brotherhood in Egypt: Historical Evolution and Future Prospects." In *Political Islam: Context versus Ideology*, edited by Khaled Hroub, 61–85. London: Middle East Institute at School of Oriental and African Studies, 2010.

Heschel, Abraham Joshua. *The Prophets*, vols. 1 & 2. New York: Harper and Row, 1969.

Holmes, Oliver Wendell. *BrainyQuote*. Authors. http://www.brainyquote.com/quotes/quotes/o/oliverwend152697.html.

Hunter, James D. *To Change the World: The Irony, Tragedy, and Possibility of Christianity in the Late Modern World*. New York: Oxford University Press, 2010.

———. *Culture Wars: The Struggle to Control the Family, Art, Education, Law, and Politics in America*. New York: Basic Books, 1992.

iBethel.org. Bethel. About. http://www.ibethel.org/users/billandbenijohnson.

International Centre for Prison Studies. Prison Population Total. http://www.prisonstudies.org/highest-to-lowest/prison-population-total?field_region_taxonomy_tid=All.

Jilani, Zaid. "How Unequal We Are: The Top Ten Facts You Should Know About the Wealthiest One Percent of Americans." *ThinkProgress.org*, October 5, 2013. http://thinkprogress.org/economy/2011/10/03/334156/top-five-wealthiest-one-percent/?mobile =nc.

Jerryson, Michael K., and Mark Juergensmeyer, eds. *Buddhist Fury: Religion and Violence in Southern Thailand*. Oxford: Oxford University Press, 2011.

———. *Buddhist Warfare*. Oxford: Oxford University Press, 2010.

Johnson, Bill. *When Heaven Invades Earth: A Practical Guide to a Life of Miracles, Expanded Edition*. Shippensburg, PA: Destiny Image, 2013.

Joplin, Janice. "Me And Bobby Mcgee." *Janice Joplin's Greatest Hits*. Columbia Records, 1973. Lyrics by Kris Kristofferson and Fred L Foster.

Kay, Charles. "Aboriginal Overkill: The Role of Native Americans in Structuring Native Ecosystems." *Human Nature* 5 (1994) 359–98.

Keiller, Garrison. "There's No Place Like Home." *National Geographic* 225 (2014) 58–83.

Keith, Thomas. *Man and the Natural World: A History of the Modern Sensibility*. New York: Pantheon, 1983.

Keller, Tim. "The Grand Demythologizer: The Gospel and Idolatry—Acts 19:23–41." Presentation at The Gospel Coalition National Conference in Rosemont, Illinois, April 21, 2009. http://resources.thegospelcoalition.org/library/.

Kepnes, Matt. "Why Americans Don't Travel Abroad." *Huffington Post*. Travel, December 2, 2010. http://www.huffingtonpost.com/matt-kepnes/why-americans-dont-travel_b_790827.html.

Kockalumchuvattil, Thomas. "The Crisis of Identity in Africa: A Call for Subjectivity." In *Kierkegaardian Subjectivity and African Philosophy: A Cross Cultural Approach*. Saarbrücken, Germany: Lambert Academic (June 2010) 108-22. http://www.kritike.org/journal/issue_7/kochalumchuvattil_june2010.pdf.

Kohn, Alfie. *No Contest: The Case Against Competition, 2nd edition*. Boston: Houghton-Mifflin, 1992.

Kurtz, Stanley. "I and My Brother Against My Cousin." Ethics and Public Policy Center book review of *Culture and Conflict in the Middle East*, Philip Carl Salzman, Amherst, NY: Humanity, 2008. http://eppc.org/publications/i-and-my-brother-against-my-cousin/.

Lambardi, Vince. ThinkExist. Vince Lambardi quotes. http://thinkexist.com/quotation/dictionary_is_the_only_place_that_success_comes/15116.html.

Leaf, Carolyn. *Who Switched Off My Brain? Controlling Toxic Thoughts and Emotions*. New York: Thomas Nelson, 2009.

Lewis, C.S. *The Abolition of Man*. New York: HarperOne, 2009.

———. *The Joyful Christian*. Nashville: Broadman & Holman, 2000.

———. *Mere Christianity*. New York: HarperOne, 2001.

Lincoln, Bruce. *Theorizing Myth: Narrative, Ideology, and Scholarship*. Chicago: University of Chicago Press, 2000.

Locke, John. *Locke: Two Treatises of Government, 3rd edition* [1689], edited by Peter Laslett, Cambridge, NY: Cambridge University Press, 1988.

Loren, Sophia. *BrainyQuote*, Sophia Loren Quotes. http://www.brainyquote.com/quotes/authors/s/sophia_loren.html.

Luna, Emilia. "Secular Europe and Religious America? Tufts Scholars Debate Religious Differences Across the Atlantic," Features, 5. *The Tufts Daily*, February 16, 2011. Tufts University. http://issuu.com/tuftsdaily/docs/ 2011-2-16.

Lutz, Ashley. "These 6 Corporations Control 90% of the Media in America," *Business Insider*, July 14, 2012. http://www.businessinsider:com/these-6-corporations-control-90-of-the-media-in-america-2012-6.

Mac, Toby. "Made To Love," *Made to Love*. Portable Sounds, 2006.

Mandela, Nelson. ThinkExist. Nelson Mandela Quotes. http://thinkexist.com/quotes/nelson_mandela/2.html.

Manikkam, Mohan, et al., "Transgenerational Actions of Environmental Compounds on Reproductive Disease and Identification of Epigenetic Biomarkers of Ancestral Exposures." *PLoS One* 7 (2012) e31901. http://www.plosone.org/article/info%3Adoi%2F10.1371%2Fjournal.pone.0031901.

Marks, Jonathan. "The Biological Myth of Human Evolution." *Contemporary Social Science* 7 (2012) 139–65.

Marx, Karl. "A Contribution to the Critique of Hegel's Philosophy of Right, Introduction [1843]." *Deutsch-Französische Jahrbücher*, February 7 & 10, 1944, Paris. Works of Karl Marx 1843. https://www.marxists.org/archive/marx/works/1843/critique-hpr/intro.htm.

Mayer, Frederick, et al. "Americans Think the Climate is Changing and Support some Actions." The Nicholas Institute for Environmental Policy Solutions, Duke University, February, 2013. http://nicholasinstitute.duke.edu/sites/default/files/publications /ni_pb_13-01_0.pdf.

Meadors, Gary T. *Baker's Evangelical Dictionary of Biblical Theology Online*, edited by Walter A. Elwell, 1996. Conscience. BibleStudyTools.com. http://m.biblestudytools.com/dictionaries/bakers-evangelical-dictionary/conscience.html.

Merchant, Carolyn, ed. *Major Problems in American Environmental History*. Lexington, MA: D.C. Health and Company, 1993.

Merriman, David and Joseph Persky. "The Impact of an Urban Wal-mart Store on Area Businesses." *Economic Development Quarterly* 26 (2012) 321–33.

Mohabat News. "Trend towards Christianity." Iranian Christian News Agency, April 24, 2012. http://mohabatnews.com/index.php?option=com_ content&view=article&id=4439:trend-towards-christianity-among-iranian-armed-forces-on-rise&catid=36:iranian-christians&Itemid=279.

Molle, Andrea. "Spiritual Life in Modern Japan: Understanding Religion in Everyday Life." In *Religion: Spirituality and Everyday Practice*, edited by Guiseppe Gioran and William H. Swatos Jr., 131–39. The Netherlands: Springer, 2012.

Morgan, Lewis H. *Ancient Society*. New York: Henry Holt, 1877.

Morley, Patrick. "How America became Entangled by Materialism." New Man. *CharismaMagazine*, January 31, 2013. http://www.charismamag.com/life/men/16655-materialism-comes-with-a-dark-side.

Morris, Henry. "The Mathematical Impossibility of Evolution." Articles. The Institution for Creation Research. http://www.icr.org/article/mathematical-impossibility-evolution/.

Myers, Bryant. *Walking with the Poor: Principles and Practices of Transformational Development*. Maryknoll, NY: Orbis, 2011.

Nash, Roderick F. *Wilderness and the American Mind*, 3rd edition. New Haven and London: Yale University Press, 1982.

National Center for Charitable Statistics. Urban Institute. Data and Statistics. http://nccs.urban.org/.

National Center for Education Statistics. Fast Facts. Institute for Education Sciences. http://nces.ed.gov/fastfacts/display.asp?id=27.

Neimark, Jill. "Allergic to Life." *Discover* (November 2013) 44–51.

The New American Standard New Testament Greek Lexicon. Sozo, Biblestudytools.com. http://www.biblestudytools.com/lexicons/greek/nas/sozo.html.

Niebuhr, H. Richard. *Christ and Culture*. New York: Harper and Row, 2001.

Nolan, Albert. *Jesus Before Christianity*. Ossining, NY: Orbis, 2001.

Nouwen, Henri. *In The Name of Jesus: Reflections on Christian Leadership*. New York: Crossroads, 1989.

O'Conner, Elizabeth. *Call to Commitment*. New York: Harper and Row, 1975.

———. *Journey Inward, Journey Outward*. New York: HarperCollins, 1975.

O'Conner, Flannery. "The Displaced Person." In *A Good Man Is Hard To Find And Other Stories*. New York: Harvest/HBJ, 1983.

Open Doors. About Christian Persecution. https://www.opendoorsusa.org.

Organization for Economic Co-Operation and Development. "Aid to Poor Countries Slips Further as Governments Tighten Budgets," 2012. http://www.oecd.org/dac/stats/aidtopoorcountriesslipsfurtheras governments tightenbudgets.htm.

Parker, William, and Jeff Ollerton. "Evolutionary Biology and Anthropology Suggest Biome Reconstitution as a Necessary Approach toward Dealing with Immune Disorders." *Evolution, Medicine, and Public Health* (May 17, 2013) 89–103.

Pascal, Blasé. *Pensées*. New York: Penguin, 1966.

Perrottet, Tony. "The Big Heart." *Smithsonian* 44 (2013) 62–71.

Pew Research Center. "The American-Western European Values Gap." Global Attitudes Project," February 2011. http://www.pewglobal.org/2011/11/17/the-american-western-european-values-gap/.

———. "Houston Tops the List of Major Metro Areas in Economic Segregation by Income." Daily Number, August 14, 2012. http://www.pewresearch.org/daily-number/houston-tops-the-list-of-major-metro-areas-in-economic-segregation-by-income/.

———. "Public Remains Conflicted Over Islam." Pew Forum on Religion and Pubic Life, August 24, 2010. http://www.pewforum.org/Muslim/ Public-Remains-Conflicted-Over-Islam.aspx.

Pinker, Stephen. *The Blank Slate: The Modern Denial of Human Nature*. New York: Penguin, 2002.

———. "The Moral Instinct." *The New York Times Magazine,* January 13, 2008.

Piper, John. "Christian Hedonism." *Desiring God Blog*, January 1, 1995. http://www.desiringgod.org/articles/christian-hedonism.

Pistorius, Martin. *Ghost Boy: The Miraculous Escape of a Misdiagnosed Boy Trapped Inside His Own Body*. Nashville: Thomas Nelson, 2013.

Pitney, Jr., John J. "The Tocqueville Fraud," *The Weekly Standard,* November 13, 1995. http://www.tocqueville.org/pitney.htm.

Plotkin, Bill. *Nature and the Human Soul: Cultivating Wholeness and Community in a Fragmented World*. Chapter 1. Animas Valley Institute. http://www.natureandthehumansoul.com/newbook/chapter1_naths.

Porterfield, Amanda. "North America." In *The Wiley-Blackwell Companion to World Christianity*, edited by Lamin Sanneh and Michael McClymond, New York: Wiley and Sons, (in press). Currently accessible as "Christianity in North America," Amanda Porterfield Recent Essays. https://religion.fsu.edu/faculty_amanda_porterfield.html.

Postman, Neil. *Technopoly: The Surrender of Culture to Technology.* New York: Vintage, 1993.

Power and Love Ministries. http://www.powerandlove.org.

Protagoras. Plato's *Theaetetus* [360 BCE]. Translated by Benjamin Jowett. Classics, MIT. edu. http://classics.mit.edu/Plato/theatu.html.

Qu'rān. Surat An-Nisā'(The Women). http://quran.com/4.

Reardon, Patrick. "Chronos and Kairos." Commentary on Social and Moral Issues of the Day. *OrthodoxyToday.org*, October 14, 2005. http://www.orthodoxytoday.org/articles5/ReardonChronos.php.

Rohr, Richard. *Jesus' Plan for a New World: The Sermon on the Mount.* Cincinnati: St. Anthony Messenger, 1991.

———. *Everything Belongs: The Gift of Contemplative Prayer.* Crossroad, 2003.

———. *Simplicity: The Freedom of Letting Go.* New York: Crossroad, 2003.

———. "The Spiral of Violence: The World, the Flesh, and the Devil." Audio CD. Center for Action and Contemplation, Albuquerque, NM.

———. "The True Self," Richard Rohr's Daily Meditation, Center for Action and Contemplation, February 18, 2014. http://myemail.constantcontact.com/Richard-Rohr-s-Meditation—The-Mirroring-Gaze.html?soid=1103098668616&aid=WQVEgAw8Cgg.

———."The World, the Flesh, and the Devil," Richard Rohr's Daily Meditation. Meditation 21. Center for Action and Contemplation, June 25, 2013. http://myemail. constantcontact.com /Richard-Rohr-s-Daily-Meditations—The-World—The-Flesh—and-The-Devil——Ecumenism——June-25—2013. html?soid =1103098668616&aid=8TQcogt_nuU.

Rolston, Holmes, III. "Does Nature Need to be Redeemed?" *Zygon: Journal of Religion and Science* 29 (1994) 209.

Roosevelt, Eleanor. GoodReads. Eleanor Roosevelt Quotes. http://www.goodreads.com/quotes/45956-remember-always-that-you-have-not-only-the-right-to.

Rosenbaum, Ron "First Blood." *Smithsonian* 43 (2013) 27–34.

Roth, Sid. Forward to *Normal Christianity*, Jonathan Welton. Shippensburg, PA: Destiny Image, 2011.

Rotholz, James M. *Chronic Fatigue Syndrome, Christianity, and Culture: Between God and an Illness.* Binghamton, NY: Haworth, 2003.

———. "What Makes Obama Black?" *Scholars & Rogues,* November 2, 2008. http://scholars androgues.com/2008/11/02/what-makes-obama-black/.

Ruskoff, Douglas. *Life, Inc: How Corporatism has Conquered the World, and How We Can Take It Back.* New York: Random House, 2011.

Russell, Bertrand. "Dreams and Facts" [1919]. The Bertrand Russell Society, Drew University. http:/./www.users.drew.edu/~jlenz/br-dreams.html.

Russell, Jeffrey Burton. *A History of Heaven: The Singing Silence.* Princeton: Princeton University Press, 1997.

Rutz, James. *Mega Shift: Igniting Spiritual* Power. Colorado Springs, CO: Empowerment, 2005.

BIBLIOGRAPHY

Sachs, Jeffery. "Q & A: Economic Development for Global Impact." *Sustainable Development*, May 14, 2013. http://jeffsachs.org/2013/05/qa-integrated-development-for-global-impact/.

Sahlins, Marshall. "The Segmentary Lineage: An Organization of Predatory Expansion." *American Anthropologist* 63 (1961) 322–45.

Sayings Around The World. Traditional Amish Proverb. http://www.listofsayings.com/sayings/sayings-around-the-world/amish-sayings/.

Schaeffer, Francis. *How Should We Then Live?* New York: Crossway, 2005

Shaw, Charles. "Are You Unhappy? Is it Because of Consumer Addiction?" *Personal Health, AlterNet*, April 10, 2008. http://www.alternet.org/story/82013/are_you_unhappy_is_it_because _of_ consumeraddiction.

Shaw, George Bernard. ThinkExist. http://thinkexist.com/quotation/no_man_ever_believes_ that_the_bible_means_what_it/169760.html.

Shiva, Vandana, "The Seeds of Suicide: How Monsanto Destroys Farming." Global Research Centre for Research on Globalization, March 13, 2014. http://www.globalresearch.ca/the-seeds-of-suicide-how-monsanto-destroys-farming/5329947.

Sider, Ronald. *Rich Christians in an Age of Hunger: Moving from Affluence to Generosity.* Nashville: Thomas Nelson, 2005.

Singer, Peter. *The Life You Can Save.* New York: Random House, 2009.

———. *The Life You Can Save.* The Why and How of Effective Altrusim. March, 2013. http://www.thelifeyoucansave.org/Learn-More/The-Why-and-How-of-Effective-Altruism-Peter-Singers-TED-Talk.

Skinner, Michael, et al. "Ancestral Dichlorodiphenyltrichloroethane (DDT) Exposure Promotes Epigenetic Transgenerational Inheritance of Obesity." BMC Medicine, *BioMedical Center Medicine* 11 (2013). http://www.biomedcentral.com/1741-7015/11/228.

Snoop Doggy Dogg. "Aint No Fun (If the Homies Can't Have None). *Doggystyle*, Death Row Records, 1993.

Spurgeon, Charles. "Christ Lifted Up." Sermon no. 139, delivered July 5, 1857 at London's Music Hall. *The Spurgeon Archive*, The New Park Street Pulpit. http://www.spurgeon.org/sermons/0139.htm.

Stanford, Dennis, et al. *Across Atlantic Ice: The Origin of America's Clovis Culture.* Berkeley: University of California Press, 2012.

Steinberg, Robert. *Successful Intelligence: How Practical and Creative Intelligence Determine Success in Life.* New York: Plume, 1977.

Stevenson, Mark. "Array of Toxic Chemicals in Humans 'Alarming.'" *The Globe and Mail,* March 8, 2005. http://www.advancedhealthplan.com/toxicbody.html.

Strauss, Chris. "Robin William's Inspiring Speech Won the ESPYS." *USA Today Sports*, July 18, 2013. http://ftw.usatoday.com/2013/07/robin-roberts-espys-classy-moment/.

Strayer, Robert W. *Ways of the World: A Brief Global History with Sources.* Boston: Bedford/St. Martin's, 2011.

Stossel, John, and Gina Binkley. "Are Americans Cheap? Or Charitable?" *20/20 News*, August 21, 2007. http://abcnews.go.com/2020/story?id=2682100&page=1.

Tal, Aner, et al.. "Eyes in the Aisles: Why Is Cap'N Crunch Looking Down at My Child?" *Environment & Behavior* (April 2, 2014). http://papers.ssrn.com/sol3/papers.cfm?abstract_id=2419182.

Tikhonov, Vladimir, and Torket Brekke, eds. *Buddhism and Violence: Militarism and Buddhism in Modern Asia*. New York: Routledge, 2013.

Teilhard de Chardin, Pierre. *The Divine Milieu*. New York & Evanston: Harper & Row, 1960.

Tennyson, Alfred. "In Memoriam A. H. H." London: Bankside, 1900. American Libraries. https://archive.org/details/inmemoriamahhootenng00g.

Torrance, Thomas F. *The Mediation of Christ*. Colorado Springs: Helmers and Howard, 1992.

Tucker, Abigail. "Are Babies Born Good?" *Smithsonian.com*, January, 2013. http://www.smithsonianmag.com/science-nature/Are-Babies-Born-Good-183837741.html.

Twain, Mark. ThinkExist. Mark Twain Quotes. http://thinkexist.com/quotation/the_human_race_%20has_only_one_%20really_effective/156393.html.

Tylor, Edward B. *Primitive Culture* [1871]. New York: J.P. Putnam's Sons, 1920.

University of Iowa. "Professor: profit motives behind sexualization of 'tween girls." News Release, April 25, 2008. http://www.news-releases.uiowa.edu/2008/april/042508lolita_effect.html.

Vallotton, Kris. Bethel School of Supernatural Ministry. Bethel Church, Redding, California. http://bssm.net.

Vanderzalm, Lynn. *Finding Strength in Weakness*. Grand Rapids: Zondervan, 1995.

Van de Vliert, Evert, and Onne Janssen. "Competitive Societies are Happy if the Women are less Competitive than the Men." *Cross-Cultural Research: The Journal of Comparative Social Science* 36 (2002) 321–37.

Varghese, Roy Abraham. *The Wonder of the World: A Journey from Modern Science to the Mind of God*. Fountain Hills, AZ: Tyr, 2003.

Veenhoven, Ruut. *World Database of Happiness*. Erasmus University Rotterdam. http://world databaseofhappiness.eur.nl/.

Voice of the Martyrs. http://persecution.com.

Wallis, Jim. *The Call to Conversion: Why Faith is Always Personal but Never Private*. New York: HarperOne, 2005.

Warren, Rick. *The Purpose Driven Life: What On Earth Am I Here For?* Grand Rapids: Zondervan, 2012.

Weiner, Eric. *The Geography of Bliss: One Grump's Search for the Happiest Places in the World*. New York: Twelve Books, 2009.

Wells, H. G. *The Country of the Blind and Other Stories by H.G. Wells*. Project Gutenberg. http://www.gutenberg.org/ebooks/11870.

Welton, Jonathon. *Normal Christianity*. Shippensburg, PA: Destiny Image, 2011.

Westminster Shorter Catechism Project. Westminster Shorter Catechism, Question 1. Bible Presbyterian Church. http://www.shortercatechism.com/resources/wsc/wsc_001.html.

Wiesel, Elie. Elie Wiesel Foundation for Humanity. http://www.eliewieselfoundation.org.

———. *Night*. New York: Steck-Vaughn, 2009.

Williams, Ray B. "Why Do We Have an Obsession with Winning?" *Psychology Today*, Wired for Success, Aug. 4, 2012. http://www.psychologytoday.com/blog/wired-success/201208/why-do-we-have-obsession-winning.

Wilson, E.O. *Consilience: The Unity of Knowledge*, New York: Vintage, 1999.

Wilson, Woodrow. "U.S. Declaration of War with Germany, 2 April 1917." FirstWorldWar.com: A Multimedia History of World War One. http://www.firstworldwar.com/source /usa wardeclaration.htm.

Wood, Allan. "Relativism," Stanford University webpapers. http://www.stanford.edu/~allenw/webpapers/Relativism.doc.

World Bank. "GDP per capita (Current US$)." Data. http://data.worldbank.org/indicator/NY.GDP.PCAP.CD?order=wbapi_data_value_2012+wbapi_data_value&sort=asc.

World Values Survey Association. Official Data File v.20090901, 2009. Aggregate File Producer: ASEP/JDS, Madrid. http://www.worldvaluessurvey.org/.

Yeats, William Butler. *Yeats, William Butler, 1865-1939: Autobiographies*. Chadwyck-Healey, 1999. http://www.scribd.com/doc/79247890/Autobiographies.

Yong, Ed. "There Is No 'Healthy' Microbiome." *The New York Times Sunday Review*. Opinion SR4, November 1, 2014. http://www.nytimes.com/2014/11/02/opinion/sunday/there-is-no-healthy-microbiome.html?ref=opinion&_r=0.

Young, Alexander. *Chronicles Of The Pilgrim Fathers Of The Colony Of Plymouth, From 1602 To 1625*, 2nd ed. Internet Archive, Openlibrary.org. https://openlibrary.org/books/OL7084938M/Chronicles_of_the_Pilgrim_Fathers_of_the_colony_of_Polymouth_from_1602_to_1625.

Zimmer, Carl. "Bringing Them Back To Life." *National Geographic* 223(2013) 28–41.

Index

A Contribution (Marx), 232–33n22
AARO (Association of Americans Resident Overseas), 174n22
Abby, Edward, 111
Abel, 280
aboriginal, 82, 169. *See* also Aborigines and Native People.
Aborigines, of Australia, 103, 187
Abraham, 125
　as Abram, 280
Adam, 238n29, 268, 272, 280, 281, 282
　and Eve, 82, 223, 279
adaptation
　cultural 4, 31, 75, 86, 87, 280
　and evolution, 21, 106, 112
　to the kingdom, 280, 281
　maladaptation, 36, 86
　to the natural environment, 31, 73, 75, 86, 112
　social, 82
　successful, 86, 87, 90
Aeschliman, Gordon, 254, 255
aesthetics, 46–47, 50
affluence, 50, 112, 122, 145, 147
　culture of, 50, 167
Afghanistan, 101, 123, 178, 179
Africa, 11, 37, 39, 78, 82, 89, 91, 117, 128, 163, 173, 176, 255, 256. *See* also Slavery.
African-Americans, 66, 75, 80, 123, 158
agape, 207, 222
ageism, 117, 118, 177
　and veneration of youth, 117–21. *See* also Youth.
agnostics, 67

Ainu, of Japan, 77
Alexander, Eben, 249n12
allergies, 106
　and autoimmune disease, 107
　and microbiomes, 106, 107
Always Enough (Baker), 245
Amazon, 105
Ambo Tibetans, 188, 189
　and "Son of God," 189
America
　and Christianity, 187–213
　false hopes in, 277
　as land of opportunity, 80, 138
　myths about, 161–84
　origins, 73–87
　as symbol, 276
Amish, 59, 123
　and Mennonites, 255
Amish Proverbs (Fisher), 59n7
angels, 82, 229n14, 262
Anglo-Americans, 7, 74, 75, 96, 100, 116, 131, 158, 165, 206
anorexia nervosa, 7, 63
anthropology, 17, 90, 189, 217
anthropomorphizing God, 262
anti-Christ, 278n15. *See* also Satan.
Antrosio, Jason, 21n1
Arab, 65, 128
Archimedes, 191
Aristotle, 30, 237
Armenians, 230
Asians
　Asian-Americans, 156
　and culture, 89
　region of Asia, 62

as U.S. immigrants, 77
atheism, 36, 39, 67, 177, 249n12, 279
    and atheists, 79, 190
athletes, 98, 132
Augé, Marc, 147
Augustine, Saint, 201
AWI (Animal Welfare Institute), 51n30
"Axis of Evil," 181

Baha'is, 79, 157
Bailyn, Bernard, 83, 84
Baker, Heidi, 7, 242, 246, 259, 264, 275
    and Roland, 245, 259n30
Barker, Kenneth, 8n4, 220n3
Bartholomew, Patriarch, 253
Beecher, Henry Ward, 50
Bellamy, Francis, 102
benevolence, 125–29
    as adaptive, 108, 172
    and altruism, 127
    as American myth, 172–73
    as cultural value, 126, 172
    divine, xiii, 27, 57, 160, 228, 244, 251, 253, 265, 279, 281
    self-serving, 257n27
Berry, Wendell, 238
Bethel School of Supernatural Ministry, 210, 211
Bhutan, 62, 110
    and Gross National Happiness, 110
Bible, xiii, xvi, 5, 18, 23, 39, 57, 65, 86, 103, 129, 146, 163, 179, 197, 212, 228, 247, 253, 271, 278
    as revelatory gift, 225
    as truth, 224
biodiversity, 223, 260. *See also* Ecotheology.
Bird-David, Nurit, 103, 104n15
Black Plague, 64, 65
Blake, William, 222
Blank Slate, The (Pinker), 21n4, 40
    and "blank slate" concept, 21, 40, 60
Bloch, Maurice, 21
Bloomberg Businessweek, 149n23
Bond, Mel, 204n15, 229, 229n14, 272
Bonhoeffer, Dietrich, 55, 101, 102
Bono, 73, 173
Boston, 84, 128

and Marathon, 127
Boyd, Gregory, 219
BPCO (Bible Presbyterian Church Online), 47n27
Bradford, William, 83
Brazil, 78, 176
Broca, Paul, 60
Brooks, Carol, 270n3
Brown, Donald, 63. *See also* Pancultural.
Brzezinski, Zbigniew, 175
Buber, Martin, 252n17
Buddhism, 62, 158
    and "969 Movement," 62
    and *nirvāna*, 62
    and Noble Eightfold Path, 62
    among Tibetans, 197
    See also Ambo Tibetans.
Butler, Samuel, 108
buzkashi, 123. *See* Afghanistan.
Byzantine Catholic Church, 262n34

Cage, John, 46
Cain, 223, 281
Call to Commitment (O'Conner), 244n6
Cambodia, 62
Cambrensis, Giraldus, 82
Cambridge Platform, 91
Campbell, Don, 272n9
Campbell, Joseph, 44. *See also* Symbols.
Canada, 77, 78, 147
capitalism
    free-market, 7, 42, 84, 140, 165
    myths about, 178, 245
    and "trickle-down economics," 166
Capon, Robert, 258n28
Caribbean, 78, 147, 179
Carter, Jimmy, 127
    and The Carter Center, 127
Casals, Pablo, 16
caste, 58, 66, 109, 176, 260n32
    in India, 58, 176, 260n32
Catholicism, 66, 79, 92, 192, 195, 197, 206, 209. *See also* Jesuits.
census, 80
    and U.S. Census Bureau, 118
chemicals, 27, 106, 106n17, 114, 115, 121, 167
Chesterton, G. K., 151

children, 4, 31, 56, 64, 91, 106, 238, 255,
    264, 270, 278
  of God, 65, 83, 267, 269, 271, 272,
    282
China, 46, 99, 111, 138, 152, 172, 179,
    188
  and Shang Dynasty, 170
CHRGJ (Center for Human Rights and
    Global Justice), 63n13
Christ and Culture (Niebuhr), 240n1
Christian Freedom International, 43n23
Christianity
  as counter-natural, 54–55
  attempt to define, 188–91
  and cults, 258–59
  culturalized, xiii, 91, 134, 193, 230
  as mere religion, 230, 267
  mystical nature of, 189–90, 206, 223
  as personalized faith, 193, 223
  and power, 198–200
  and public service, 207–8
  as reactionary religion, 199, 200–
    201
  and the supernatural, 209–11
  See also Christians and the Church.
Christians, 30, 38, 60, 65, 101, 121, 226,
    230, 243, 247, 268
  American, 7, 12, 101, 131, 154, 166,
    179, 187–213, 219, 245, 255,
    261, 266
  definition of, 12, 16, 22, 41, 44
  as distinctive, 49, 58, 76, 98, 131,
    142, 146, 172, 175, 241, 251,
    258, 271–75
  as elitist, 90, 93, 278
  and history, 43, 44, 68, 79, 85, 90
  numbers worldwide, 187
  persecution or martyrdom of, 42,
    180
  and post-Christian movement,
    208–11
  See also Christianity and the
    Church.
Christocentrism, 221, 261
*Chronic Fatigue Syndrome, Christianity,
    and Culture* (Rotholz), 98n10
chronos, 263
church, the, xi, 42, 131, 138, 142, 179
  in America, xv, 92, 93, 110, 124,
    129, 143–54, 161, 184, 187–213,
    276–79
  as culturally irrelevant, 117
  and denominationalism, 194–96
  as the early church, 58
  and ethnocentrism, 196
  and the kingdom, 217–67, 274, 275,
    280–82
  and the state, 79, 91.
  See also Christianity and Christians.
civil rights, 202, 207
  and Civil Rights Movement, 155
  See also Justice.
Civil War, 80, 122, 244
civilization, 82, 104, 105, 119, 137,
    167–72
  as industrial, 137, 169
  and wilderness, 84
Clark, Dennis and Jen, 244n7
Clark, Randy, 117
Clinton, Bill, 127
Clooney, George, 145
clothing, as symbol of culture, 273, 279,
    282
Colonial Period, 79, 87, 122
colonialism
  and Great Britain, 42, 79, 83, 100,
    101, 148, 171
  and Spain, 78, 85
  as way of life, 89, 91, 122, 148
Columbus, 77
Compelled by Love (Baker), 7
competition, 50, 15
  as American value, 131–33, 164, 197
  and Christianity, 203–5, 245
  versus cooperation, 133, 236
  in the marketplace, 7, 98, 132
  in nature 132–33
Congo, 61, 154
conquistadores, 78
conscience, 38–39, 50, 52, 60, 129, 155,
    172, 230
Consilience: The Unity of Knowledge
    (Wilson), 67
Constantine, 213
consumerism, 111, 137–38
  as an addiction, 138–39

and over-consumption, 137, 138, 141
conversion, 7, 203, 206, 210, 225n8. See also Salvation.
Cooke, Graham, 267n1
and spiritual "upgrade," 268
Coolidge, Calvin, 164
Copernicus, 68, 97
Coronado, 82
corporations, 203, 135
American enculturation to, 136
and dominant ideology, 135–36
Cosmos Reborn (Crowder), 198n11, 206n19, 249n11, 258n28
Country of the Blind, The (Wells), 175
coupling, 30–32
and homosexuality, 31
and polyandry, 31
and polygyny, 31
Covenant
New, 222, 280
Old, 38, 39
creationism, 67
Cross, of Christ, 44, 53, 203, 221, 235, 236, 241, 258n28, 259, 262, 263, 277, 280, 282
Crouch, Andy, 46n26, 221n4, 235, 257–58n28
cultural norms, 130–60. See also Culture.
cultural relativism, 17–19
Culture Making (Crouch), 257–58n27. See also Andy Crouch.
Culture Wars (Hunter), 76
culture
in adolescent stage, 265
change, 75, 76, 86, 211
dominant in America, 73, 278
and history, xiv, 18, 43, 62, 73, 86, 93, 107, 122, 264
indigenous, 17, 62, 78, 82, 211
and language, 74
religious, 193, 197, 243, 266
secular, 67, 94, 142
as survival mechanism, 280
and thriving, 10, 27, 129, 139, 272
urban, 74, 75

"culture wars," 76, 85, 143. See also James Hunter.
Cushman, Robert, 83
cynicism, 143–45
manifest as complaining, 143, 144

Danick, Andrew Stephen, 70n17
David, King 15, 273
Dawkins, Richard, 68, 190
DaySpring Church, 244n6
Declaration of Independence, 95, 183
dehumanization, 12, 141, 235, 250. See also Justice.
Deists, 85, 93
Democracy in America, vols. 1 & 2 (de Tocqueville), 93
democracy, 127, 175, 256, 260
and Christianity, 179, 180
desire to export, 42, 163, 177–80
demons, 229n14
the demonic, 66, 220, 229, 231, 248
demonizing others, 143
Denmark, 92
"deposed royalty," 24n8, 237, 269
Deprill, Katheryn, 251
developed world, 106, 174
developing countries, 97, 148, 156
development, as a function of scale, 169
diet, 66, 87, 121
Dietrich, Marlene 149
discrimination, 95, 199, 165, 177. See also Civil Rights, Justice, and Dehumanization.
Disneyworld, 123
diversity
in America, 91, 195, 212
in the church, 91, 212
as strength, 34, 155, 188, 260
divine wisdom, xvi, 5, 6, 7, 268. See also Solomon
Dominican Republic, 177
Don't Let the Goats Eat the Loquat Tree (Hale), 258n29
Douglas, Preston, 77n5
Dove, Michael, 169
drone strikes, 101, 116, 141, 159
dualism, 81, 156, 261
and the Bible, 261–62

and faith, 205, 236, 261–64
Duina, Francesco, 132n3
Durham, Gigi, 150
Dust Bowl, 84
Dutch, the 78
    and the East Indies Company, 78

Eastern Orthodox Church, 192, 195, 262n34
Eastern religions, 249
economics, 40, 85, 101, 114
    capitalist, 84, 98, 165, 205
    global, 62, 110
    "laissez-faire," 165
economy of inversion, 234–36, 259
ecotheology, 205, 233. *See also* Biodiversity.
Ecotourism Project, The, 256
Eden, 82, 169, 170, 223, 272, 279, 280, 281, 282
education, 40, 56, 74, 80, 96, 114, 116, 143, 154, 159, 164, 202, 205, 207
    Americans' self-assessment of, 174–75
    and Christian ministry, 175, 207, 210, 255, 265
egalitarianism, 93, 95–96, 114, 130, 148
    and spirituality, 158
Egypt, 35, 42, 80, 171, 173, 180, 226
Einstein, Albert, 52, 190
El Salvador, 77, 162
elderly, the, 25, 65, 99, 117, 118, 119
Eliot, T.S., 253
Elliot, Elizabeth, 243
Ellul, Jacques, 142
Emerging Church, the, 209, 211
Emerson, Ralph Waldo, 20
emic, 17
enculturation, 8, 44, 191, 196
England, and the English, 79, 83. *See also* Great Britain.
enlightenment, as awareness, 58, 62, 225, 235
Enlightenment, the, 23, 28, 97
entitlement, 112, 144, 246, 247
    and the language of rights, 248
entrepreneurialism, 98, 138–140
    as "get rich quick" ethic, 138

environment, 16, 23, 38, 48, 60, 75, 86, 90, 101, 117, 140, 145, 150, 191, 197, 270, 279
    effect on culture, 112
    effect on genes, 21, 30, 60, 270
    effect on health, 106n17, 107, 121, 12
    efforts to control, 4, 48, 150
    having confidence toward, 104
    natural, xiv, 26, 67, 76, 81–85, 103, 135, 145, 166, 172, 179, 202, 207, 253–56
    social, 81–85, 119, 122, 128, 129, 149
    spiritual, 281
environmentalism, 211
    and faith, 253–56, 257
    and the poor, 253–55
Enzensberger, Hans Magnus, 3
epigenetics, 269–71
Ethiopia, 11, 46, 164, 233n23, 254n23
ethnicity, 11, 156, 237, 260
ethnocentrism, 8–9, 21, 34, 113, 137, 196
etic, 17
Europe, and Europeans, 35, 36, 42, 61, 64, 73, 77–85, 91, 95, 96, 113, 117, 135, 148, 156, 168, 173, 176–78, 187, 210
events ("9-11"), 65, 101, 134
evil, 27, 42, 49, 52, 60, 90, 141, 146, 169, 180–82, 199, 205, 229–31, 237, 241, 261, 269, 278n15
evolution, 21, 22, 40, 50, 68, 169, 170, 198, 246
    as cultural evolution, 170–72
exclusion, of outsiders, 116, 153, 195, 196, 201, 235, 250, 251, 259, 260

faith, 49–50
    and culture, xi–xiv, 18, 43, 62, 92, 163, 196, 201, 243, 275
    as divine gift, 244
    as form versus substance, 5–8
    and human nature, 54–55
    in the impossible, 22, 204, 263
    and reason, 23, 49, 69, 190

as universally present, 24, 50, 135, 187
and worldview, 41, 179, 189
Falkland Islands, 101
Federal Reserve Board, 159
Finding Strength in Weakness (Vanderzalm), 98n10
Fisher, Suzanne, 59
Florida, 77, 78, 169
formulaic cultural orientation, 105, 205
and faith, 196–98
Foster, George, 167
Founding Fathers, 93, 213
Francis, Saint, of Assisi, 204, 253
Franklin, Benjamin, 126
free will, 29–30, 33, 39, 50, 175
Freidman, Kinky, 189
Freidman, Thomas, 140
fun and entertainment, 121–25
as survival mechanism, 122, 183–84

Gardner, Howard, 116
Gates, Henry Louis, 80, 260
gender, 11, 152–53
and language, 192–93
as self-determined, 153
traditional concepts of, 153
and women's movement, 152
generosity, 112, 125, 137, 172, 173, 264. *See* also Benevolence.
genetics, 21, 68, 269
and culture, 21, 29, 48, 68, 75, 105, 106, 139, 222
and the environment, 60, 260
and epigenetics, 269–71
and faith, 50
and gender, 31, 63, 153
and God, 22, 24
and human nature, 29, 69
and race, 75, 77, 80
Gentiles, 266
Geography of Bliss, The (Weiner), 124
Germany, and the Germans, 14, 78, 96, 113
Ghost Boy (Pistorius), 249n12
Girard, Réne, 64, 65. *See* also Scapegoat.
Giving: How Each of Us Can Change the World (Clinton), 127

Glacken, Clarence J., 82n8
Global Awakening, 210
and Global School of Supernatural Ministry, 210, 211
Gnosticism, 227, 274
hedonistic form of, 274n13
God
as cultural creation, xii, 2, 22, 35, 43, 67, 70, 94
goodness of, xiii, 9, 28, 37, 80, 193, 226–27, 244, 25, 279, 281
his calling, 15, 37, 47, 64, 76, 102, 113, 142, 200, 253, 266, 271, 275
his image in humans, 20, 24, 25, 46, 47, 85, 124, 250
his nature, 13, 25, 28, 48, 268
and the natural world, 20, 45, 81, 104, 252–55, 271
personal nature of, xi, 27, 32, 193, 225n9, 282
and the poor, 7, 125, 173, 235
resting in, 207, 243, 266, 281
as source of human dignity, xii, 14, 29, 267–82
as source of wisdom, 6, 7, 60, 268
God's Last Day's People (Bond), 229n14
Goldman, Jonathan, 33n15
Gospel, the
and culture, 15, 76, 179, 184, 193, 204
essence of, xii, 6, 191, 249
as divine invitation, 281
and the poor, 259
sharing of, xii, 83, 204
and the supernatural, 206, 209, 212
rationalized, 231
universal relevance of, 18, 65, 102
See also Christianity.
Gow, Peter, 103n14
Granada, 177
Gray, Robert, 82
Great Britain, and the British, 42, 100, 101, 113, 148, 178. *See* also England.
Great Commission, 219
Great Depression, 119
Greeks
ancient 12–15

city-states, 13
and mythology, 191
and philosophical inheritance, 82
See also Dualism.
Green Bible, The (Maudlin), 253n20, 254n22, 255n24–25
Greene, Brian, 262n36
Greenwald, Robert, 136
Groothius, Douglas, 24n8, 85n21, 190n2, 230n15. *See* also "Deposed Royalty."
Gross Domestic Product, 163, 165
Gross National Income, 173
Gross National Product, 163
Guantanamo Bay, 134
Gutierrez, Ramon, 82n10

Haiti, 177
Hale, Susan, 273n11
Hale, Tom and Cynthia, 258n29
hard work and progress
    effect upon nature, 107
    as an ideal 82, 95–99, 108, 131, 144, 170
    shortcomings of, 116, 118, 171, 180–82
    as spiritualized value, 82, 196, 221
    and technology, 140
Harrison, K. David, 75n1
Harvard University, 80, 116, 121, 164n4, 166, 202
    and School of Public Health, 121
Healing Sounds (Goldman), 33n15
Helbawy, Kamal, 42n22
Hemings, Sally, 95
heresy
    in the early church, 274
    as secular value, 177
Heschel, Abraham Joshua, 28, 217
Hewlett, Barry, xi
Hinduism, 158
Hindus, 17, 18, 66, 134
Hmong, 79
Hobbes, Thomas, 170
holism, 23, 40, 69, 70, 81, 117, 211, 236, 262
Hollywood, 122, 187, 211
Holmes, Oliver Wendell, 13

Holy Spirit
    and being fully human, 61, 205, 224, 269
    blaspheming the, 66, 121
    and culture, 201, 222, 225n9, 243, 27
    in healing, 209, 270
    and kingdom culture, 227, 228, 234, 242
homosexuality, 31, 65, 153
hospitality
    and *philoxenia*, 125, 126
    in the Middle East, 125
How Should We Then Live? (Schaeffer), 240n1
How to See in the Spirit World (Bond), 229n14
Howard, Thomas, 55n2
Hugenburger, Gordon, 247n9
human nature, 16
    biblical basis of, 23
    as dual nature, 85
    fallen side of, 9, 23, 52–70, 268
    good side of, 20–51
    location, 69
    as reflective of God, 24, 25, 46, 47, 85, 124, 223, 250
human universals, 63. *See* also Donald Brown.
humanism, 18, 61, 94, 172, 209, 212, 245, 258, 259, 266
humor
    as cultural value, 50–51
    and human nature, 122
Hunter, James, 48, 76, 142, 143, 198, 199, 200. *See* also "Culture Wars" and *Ressentiment*.
hupsoō, 277
hurricanes
    Katrina, 27, 101, 167
    Sandy, 167

I and Thou (Buber), 252–53n17
ICPS (International Centre for Prison Studies), 162
identity, xv
    in Christ, 202, 210, 266, 267–82

and culture, 4, 9, 10, 15, 43, 67, 89, 92, 109, 114, 128, 148, 181, 201, 242, 261
ecclesiastical, 194–96, 208
as humans, 39
and myths, 161, 169
and natural environment, 103
and privacy, 145–47
ideology
corporate, 135–37
and dominant culture, 167
and economics, 112, 166
and nature, 107, 111
and politics, 142, 178, 257
and religion, 79, 82, 199
and worldview, 41–43, 50, 141, 153
image
digital, 120, 140–41
and the divine, xii, 14, 20–51, 85, 159, 124, 226, 177, 236, 249, 263, 267–82
of "limited good," 167
need to control, 7, 99, 151–52, 232, 258
self-conscious of, 59, 99, 120, 150, 196
and symbols, 13
of "unlimited good," 265
as victim, 199
of the West, 84, 89
and youth, 117–21
Imago Dei, 25. *See also* Image.
"image of limited good," 167, 265
contrasted with "image of unlimited good," 167, 168, 268
imam, 66
immigrants
early French, 77
early Spanish and Portuguese, 77
Jewish, 81
Native American, 76
non-Anglo, 74, 117, 138, 155, 156, 162, 260
non-Christian, 91
residing in the U.S., 76, 79, 260, 277
Inca, 171
Incarnation, 32, 207, 236, 238n29, 262

inclusion, 6, 12, 116, 194, 201, 235, 256–61, 265, 280, 281
income inequality, 156, 163–64
India, 43, 58, 63, 111, 138, 152, 172, 176, 260n32
Indians, 41, 77, 82, 84, 88, 169, 176, 229n14, 253. *See also* Native Americans.
individualism, 10, 86, 88–91, 94, 122, 131, 139, 145, 148, 171, 195, 266
Industrial Revolution, xiv, 97, 108, 110, 118, 205
infidels, 14, 83
informal, 148–49, 209. *See also* Casual.
institutional complexity, 158–60
Inward-Outward, 242–44
Iran, 13, 79, 99, 100, 101, 135, 181
Islam, 42, 125, 181
  in America, 158
  and Jihad, 9, 14
  and peace, 43
  and *Sharia Law*, 42
Islamic State of Iraq and the Levant (ISIL), 181
Israel
  ancient, 11, 65, 92, 125, 226, 236, 260, 265, 280
  modern, 11, 12, 173
Italy, 92

Jamestown, 78
Japan, and the Japanese, 14, 15, 37, 63, 77, 96, 103, 126, 138
Jefferson, Thomas, 87, 95, 183
Jerryson, Michael K., 62n10–11
Jesuits, 83
Jesus Christ
  and the cross, 236, 263, 278
  cultural relevance of, 189, 194, 202, 207, 213, 232, 275, 277, 280, 282
  divinity of, 29, 32, 200, 237, 238, 261
  and healing, 27, 207, 234
  and his disciples, 6, 12, 54, 64, 129, 177, 194, 227, 228, 238, 267
  as humanity's inheritance, 198, 279
  faith in, 44, 187, 206, 269
  genealogy of, 260

and the kingdom, 49, 147, 219, 221, 227, 262, 265, 274
the message of, xii, 6, 223
the mind of, 70, 200, 268
as misrepresented, 7, 112, 188, 231
his presence within, 237, 268, 275
as seen in others, 125, 201, 251
as scapegoat, 65
teachings of, 14, 15, 34, 39, 43, 54, 57, 58, 61, 66, 90, 201, 218, 222, 234, 273
and the Trinity, 223, 226, 249n11
as truth and life, xv, 37, 205, 224–26, 272
Jews, 11, 12, 14, 53, 64, 79, 91, 220, 230, 233, 260
Orthodox, 66
See also Israel.
John Paul II, Pope, 163, 208
Johnson, Bill, 193, 209, 233, 241, 263, 279
Joplin, Janice, 145
Journey Inward, Journey Outward (O'Conner), 244n6. *See* also Inward-Outward.
Judaism, 236, 252n15. *See* also Jews and Israel.
Juergensmeyer, Mark, 62n10, 62n11. *See* also "969 Movement" under Buddhism.
justice, 53n1, 155, 165, 173, 207, 209, 232, 255, 276
the God of, 64
and the kingdom 227, 228, 234
for the poor, 166, 199, 233
See also Civil Rights.

kairos, 263
Keillor, Garrison, 253
Keith, Thomas, 82n11
Keller, Tim, 109, 110
Kenniwick Man, 77
Kepnes, Matthew, 147
Khmer Rouge, 62
Khoisan, 82. *See* also San Bushmen.
Khrushchev, Nikita, 69
King, Jr., Martin Luther, 90, 114, 283

kingdom culture, 240, 242, 250, 251, 254, 256–58, 261, 275, 276, 280, 281
kingdom of God, xv, 145
within culture, 241, 275
defined, 220–22
as emerging, 227–28, 264, 273
misconceptions about, 218–19
as now, 218
as present in believers, 228
redemptive nature of, 234, 235
Klineberg, Steven, 156
knowledge, xvi, 40, 70, 94, 115, 141, 155, 172, 174–75, 225, 246
culturally-derived, 105, 132, 189
experience-based, 34, 116, 220
faith-based, 35, 69, 190, 210n24, 234
of the natural world, 167
science-based, 7, 41, 45, 205, 209
and wisdom, 5
Kockalumchuvattil, Thomas, 89n2
Kohn, Alfie, 133
kosmos, 273
Ku Klux Klan, 90
Kurds, 99

language, 12, 82
and culture, 74, 75, 156, 189, 192
gender-neutral, 192–93
of the kingdom, 220, 247–49
and pornography, 150
Latinos, 79, 156, 176
law of love, 222–23
Law of Moses, 39, 57, 65, 66, 222
Leaf, Laura, 26–27
legalism, 198, 205
Jewish, 236
religious 245
Lemons, Elizabeth, 91–92
Lenin, Vladimir, 232–33
and Marxism-Leninism, 233n23
León, Ponce de, 77
Lewis, C.S., 94, 110n2, 254, 267
liberalism
political, 41, 154, 191
theological, 227, 257
Life, Inc: How Corporatism has Conquered the World, And How

We Can Take It Back (Ruskoff), 135
Lincoln, Bruce, 43
litigiousness, 142–43, 200
Locke, John, 183
logic
    and Christianity, xvi, 205, 267
    and culture, 17, 18, 20, 21
    and reason, 21, 39–41, 114–17
logos, 225n9
Lombardi, Vince, 98
Lord's Prayer, the, 239, 241
Loren, Sophia, 120
Lost Boys of Sudan, 155

Mac, Toby, 25
Mandela, Nelson, 175
Manifest Destiny, 41
    modern-day, 112, 163, 178
Manikkam, Mohan, 270n5b
Maori, 77
Marx, Karl, 232–33
    and Marxism-Leninism 233n23
mass media, 74, 110, 135n9, 143, 150, 151, 154, 157, 159, 177
materialism
    and happiness, 109, 183
    scientific and philosophical, 23, 36, 37, 49, 150
    as wealth and possessions, 109–12, 137, 172, 213, 245, 249, 274, 278
mathmatics, 24, 105, 114, 116, 174. *See also* Money.
Mayflower Compact, 91
McDonald's, 138
Me and Bobby Mcgee (Joplin), 143
Meadors, Gary T., 38
Mediation of Christ, The (Torrance), 225n8
medicine
    as allopathic, 48, 79, 105, 114, 115, 121, 139, 162, 181, 205
    as alternative, 115
    and smart drugs, 139
melanoma, 119
memes, 59, 67–69, 127, 212, 270
Mennonites, 255
Merchant, Carolyn, 83n13

Mercy Ships, 256
Mere Christianity (Lewis), 94
Merriman, David, 136
Metaphysics (Aristotle), 237, 238n28
Mexico, 41, 78, 100, 147
Microsoft, 149
Middle East, 43, 63, 68, 99, 125, 128, 131, 179
Miles, Nelson A., 88
military, 11, 63, 101
    American, 105, 134, 146, 155, 159, 173, 174, 179
    Christians and, 101, 134, 202
    and post-Vietnam initiatives, 178
Miller, Claudia, 106n17
miracles, xii, 193, 209, 210, 225, 234, 263, 278n15
mobility
    among Americans, 140, 147–48, 155
    upward or downward, 162, 164, 202, 260
Molle, Andrea, 37
money, xii, 99, 121 244
    and Christian ministry, 245, 246, 264
    and happiness, 124
    love of, 109, 110, 205
    and mentality of lack, 167, 245
    and power, 154, 198
    See also Materialism.
Morris, Henry, 24
Moses, 39, 57, 65, 125
Mother Teresa, 25, 114
Mozambique, 123, 245, 246, 259
Mpambara-Cox Foundation, 255
Mubarak, Hosni, 180
multicultural, 73
multi-generational housing, 119
music, 46, 50, 116, 122, 123, 249, 272, 282
Muslim, Brotherhood, 42, 180
    and Student Association, 42n22
Myanmar, 62
Myers, Bryant, 259n31
mysticism
    among Aborigines, 103
    Christian, 190, 206, 209, 212, 249n11

Eastern, 236
   as symbolized by hair, 152
Myth of a Christian Nation, The (Boyd), 219
myths, xiv, 68, 80
   among Americans, 44, 161–84
   biblical "look-alikes," 184
   impact upon church, 161
   oppositional, 171
   power of, 171

Nash, Roderick, 84, 168
National Center for Charitable Statistics, 127
Native Americans, 77, 80, 81, 83, 100, 116, 169, 229n14
   and Kenniwick Man, 77
   Muskogee Nation Creek Tribe, 126n20
   Narragansett, 83
   of the Pacific Northwest, 126
   Pueblo, 82
native peoples, 83, 103, 105, 169. *See also* Aboriginal, Aborigines, and Native Americans.
natural sciences, 20
nature, 22n7, 86
   as fallen, 253
   human attitude toward, 103–7
   as pristine, 169
   as sacred, 237–38
   as stable and bountiful, 167–68
   and wilderness, 169
Nazis, 12, 14, 53, 101, 102
NCES (National Center for Education Statistics), 174n21
Neimark, Jill 106n17b
neo-Anabaptists, 199
Nepal, 50, 58, 96, 126, 165, 254n23, 258n29
New Age, 58, 157, 158, 172
   and astrology, 229
   and karma, 229
New England, 83, 84, 96, 169
New Jerusalem, 218, 223, 265, 280
New Mexico, 78, 82, 172n15, 272n8
New Testament, 33, 38, 57, 125, 249n12, 274n12

New Zealand, 77
Nicene Creed. 197. *See also* Formulaic Orientation.
Niebuhr, H. Richard, 240n1
Night (Wiesel), 53n1
nihilism, 142, 143–45, 211
noble savage, 168–70, *See* also Indians, Native Americans and Primitivists.
Nolan, Albert, 240n1
non-governmental organizations, 204, 255
non-place, 147–48
non-Trinitarians, 157
North Africa, 128
North Korea, 13, 100, 102, 181
nostalgia, 170, 171
Nouwen, Henri, 202
NSAIDS (non-steroidal anti-inflammatory drugs), 115

O'Conner, Elizabeth, 244n6
O'Conner, Flannery, 55
Obama, Barack, 75n2, 160
OECD (Organization for Economic Co-Operation and Development), 173n17
Old Testament, 70
   as Hebrew Scriptures, 38, 125, 222
Opendoors, 43n23

Pacific Northwest, 126, 169
pacifism, 62
Pakistan, 5, 43, 169, 179, 187, 197
Panama, 177
pancultural, 189, 261. *See also* Transcultural and Panhuman.
panhuman, 8, 31, 37, 57, 58, 65, 196. *See also* Pancultural and Transcultural.
partnership
   with God, 29
   with humans, 32, 130
   with nature, 81, 104, 107, 252–56
Pascal, Blasé, 24n8, 37, 37n16
patriarch, 118, 153, 253
patriotism, 92, 99–103, 111, 162, 195

Paul, Apostle, xvi, 5, 6, 8, 15, 53, 111, 125, 200, 212, 226, 228, 230, 253
   on the conscience, 39
   on the Holy Spirit, 61, 222
   on human nature, 41, 57, 60, 87
   on money, 206
   on power, 200, 227
Penseés (Pascal), 37n16. *See* Blasé Pascal.
persecution, 79
   of Christians, 43, 43n23, 180
   political, 79
Persky, Joseph, 136
personalizing the world, 249–52
   of people, 250, 251
   of nature, 252–56
Peru, 103
Pew Research Center, 113, 156, 158n30
pharmaceutical companies, 30, 106, 115
Pilgrims, 79–80, 83, 85, 88, 89, 105
Pinker, Steven, 21, 40. *See also The Blank Slate.*
Piper, John, 273n12
Pistorius, 249n12
Plato, 81
Pledge of Allegiance, 42n22, 100, 102
Plotkin, Bill, 265n43
pluralism, 58
   as segmented, 155–57, 195
   See also Diversity.
Plymouth Colony, 83
pograms, 64
politicization, 142–43
   and faith, 230
politics, 42, 58, 63, 99, 114, 134, 142, 143, 197, 205, 235
   and the church, 199, 200, 219
   See also James Hunter and *Culture Wars.*
Ponce de León, 77
pornography, 47, 86, 149, 150
Porterfield, Amanda, 93n7
Portugal, 78
Postman, Neil, 141
potlatch, 126
Power and Love, 210n24
power
   and American Christians, 198–200, 243, 255
   of culture, 3–19, 44, 55, 67, 81, 93, 98, 103, 120, 141, 145, 188, 231
   and culture change, 41, 45, 154
   corporate and economic, 59, 115, 136, 156
   of God and the gospel, 44, 54, 182, 191, 201, 209, 226, 227, 234, 236, 238, 264, 269, 274, 277, 281, 282
   and human nature, 50, 53, 54, 146
   and language, 12–14, 59, 247
   malevolent, 182, 231, 247, 278
   and the media, 154
   of myths, 161, 165
   and powerlessness, xiv, 136, 163, 202, 210, 234, 235
   struggle to obtain, xiv, 35, 42, 69, 74, 126, 142–43, 153, 154–55, 158, 230, 233 and technology, 48, 141, 254
Practicing God's Presence (Clark), 244n7
prayer, 7, 15, 57, 201, 239, 241, 242, 244
predestination, 29, 198, 249n12
pride, 36, 49, 55, 58–61, 250, 259
primitivists, 138, 169
privacy, 146–48
progress, *See* Hard Work and Progress.
Proof of Heaven (Alexander), 249n12
Protagoras, 18
Protestant work ethic, 97, 206
Protestantism, 92, 131, 195, 197, 208
Psychology Today, 183
Puritans, 79, 83
Purpose Driven Life, The (Warren), 56
"push-pull" forces, 80, 277

Qur'ān, 125, 126n18
Quakers, 79
quantam physics, 190, 262n36

race
   and children, 176
   and language, 75
   and racism, 11
   as sociocultural construction, 75, 80
   as self-assessed, 175–77

INDEX

Reagan, Ronald, 92, 165
Reardon, Patrick, 263n39
redemption, 6, 140, 223, 232–33, 237, 240, 262, 263
  and nature, 237, 252–56, 262
Reformation, the 95, 197
  as new movement, 208
  and *sola scriptura*, 197
refugees, 79, 80
religion, xi, 28, 279
  as non-Christian, 9, 125, 157, 249
  as mere culture, 92, 96, 192–94, 198, 213, 230, 243, 266
  and religious majority, 11, 93, 96, 158, 219
Renaissance, the 97, 205
  and post-Renaissance, 36, 212
respectability, as Christian ideal, 201–3
ressentiment, 143. See also "Culture Wars" and James Hunter.
reverence, for God, 6, 8, 70
revival, 209–211. See also Christianity.
rhema, 225n9
Rich Christians in an Age of Hunger (Sider), 259n31
Rohr, Richard, 27, 60, 191, 197, 231, 234, 241, 251, 266, 271
Rolston III, Holmes, 252, 263
Roman Catholicism, 66, 79, 192, 195, 197, 206, 208, 209
  Jesuits, 82
Romani (Gypsies), 12
Roosevelt, Eleanor, 89
Rosenbaum, Ron, 83n14, 84n20
Roth, Sid, 231n17
Rotholz, Jim, 75n2, 98n10
Ruskoff, Douglas, 135
Russell, Bertrand, 57
Russell, Jeffery Burton, 240, 252n15
Russia, 107
Rutz, James, 187n1, 196n9
Rwanda, 61, 182, 230

Sachs, Jeffery, 166
sacred, the, 14, 17, 28, 66, 67, 150, 180, 197, 252, 274, 275, 278
  and culture, 5, 43, 100, 116, 134, 183, 261, 262
  nature as, 227, 236–38, 252, 253
  and the profane, 66, 81, 261, 262
sadhus, 126, 152
Sahlins, Marshal, 127
  on Nuer and Dinka, 127
salvation, 8, 197, 198, 206, 225, 258n28, 266. See also Conversion.
San Bushmen, 37. See also Khoisan, 82.
Sandy Hook, 241
Satan, 83, 229, 232, 262, 269, 278
  as anthropologist, 231
  in disguise, 230
  and God's kingdom, 228–32, 261
  and human distress, 229
  and human empowerment, 247
Scandinavia, 107
scapegoat
  concept of, 64–65
  scapegoating others, 64, 176, 180
Scapegoat, The (Girard), 64
Schaeffer, Francis, 240n1
science, 22, 23, 31, 60, 70, 116, 143, 154, 174, 226, 247, 262, 270, 271
  and culture, 41, 205, 271
  and faith, 45, 209, 269, 271
  and nature, 20, 105
  and social science, 17, 21, 22, 24, 35, 66, 97
  and technology, 104, 105, 140
segmentary lineage system, 127n24, 128. See also Marshal Sahlins.
segregation, 156, 195
self-centered, 56–58, 90, 129, 133, 147, 176, 181
Selfish Gene, The (Dawkins), 68. See also Richard Dawkins.
self-other divide, 9–12, 176, 177, 195, 200
self-preservation, 54–56, 133
sense of humor, 50–51, 122, 189
sentience, 28–29, 36, 50
seppuku, 63
Sermon on the Mount, 241, 260, 265
sex, 28, 31, 32, 119, 120, 152, 177, 188
  America's obsession with, 149–51, 245
  and evolutionary theory, 128

shalom, 109, 124, 125, 183, 265, 274, 276, 277, 279, 280
shamans, and shamanism, 27, 66, 182, 197, 229
Shaw, Charles, 137–38
Shaw, George Bernard, 81
Shekinah, 252n15
shibboleths, 15
Shiva, Vandana, 63n13
Sider, Ron, 259n31
Sikhs, 79
Singer, Peter, 129n26, 173. See also *The Life You Can Save*.
Skinner, Michael, 270n5
slavery, 43, 80–81, 97. See also Africa.
slogans, 42, 103, 134
Smith, Adam, 43, 165
Snoop Dog, 183
social capital, 96, 164, 166, 264
social construction, 26, 250
social science, See Science.
social shaming, 100, 149, 157, 163, 229, 231
sociobiology, 128
Socrates, 18
Sodom, 173
Solomon, King, 60, 99, 247
Solutreans, 77
sozo, 204, 266n44
South Korea, 177, 187
Spain, 77, 78, 85, 113
spirituality, 7, 37, 91, 94, 109, 231, 242
    among Christians, 211, 243–45, 255
    democratized, 157–58
    personalized, 43, 94, 95, 157
    among Puritans, 83
Spurgeon, Charles, 277n15
Stanford, Dennis, 77n4
Steinberg, Robert, 116
subcultures, 18, 68, 90, 130, 131, 171, 188, 193
    in America, 74, 75, 123, 158, 278
success, 5, 98, 203
    as culturally defined, 16, 47, 95, 98, 109, 132, 135, 139, 151, 202, 213
Surma, 11, 12, 46, 181
survival
    as adaptive benefit, 16, 68, 90, 119, 122, 133, 262
    as basic, 25, 48, 56, 262
    and culture 280, 282
Switzerland, 124
symbols, 44–45, 134
    and the symbolic, 55, 64, 65, 134, 148, 152, 235, 238n29, 276, 278, 279
Syria, 43, 99, 179, 230, 256

taboos, 66–67, 80, 157
Tal, Aner, 111
Tanzania, 111, 112
technology, 75, 80, 105, 141
    infatuation with, 140–42, 255
    and innovation, 48, 140
    as impersonal, 140
    and nature, 48, 104
Technopoly: The Surrender of Culture to Technology (Postman), 141
Teilhard de Chardin, Pierre, 262
Ten Commandments, 38, 39. See also Law of Moses.
Tennyson, Alfred, 133
Thailand, 62
The Life You Can Save (Singer), 129n26, 137n12, 172n16, 173n19
To Change the World (Hunter), 142. See also James Hunter.
Toby Mac, 25
Tocqueville, Alexis de, 93, 110
Torrance, Thomas F., 225
Tower of Babel, 36, 212
transcultural, 63, 90. See also Pancultural and Panhuman.
tribalism, 99, 128, 182, 265
Trinity, the, 25, 226
    believers' relationship to, 249
    Muslim view of, 188
Truman, Harry, 164
Tucker, Abigail, 57
Twain, Mark, 122, 161
Tyndale, William, 55

U.S. Supreme Court, 66, 80, 159
Ubuntu, 89–90
Uganda, 174, 255

INDEX

Unitarians, 91
unitive thinking, 218, 261
    as non-dualistic thought, 209, 218
universalism, 258
University of Iowa, 150
utopianism, 141

Vallotton, Kris, 211n27
values
    American cultural 88–129
    gospel-conflicting, 16, 68, 101, 131, 134, 225, 259
    of the kingdom, 240–66
    self-conflicting, 44, 85, 87, 93, 95, 109, 113, 122, 150
    See also Culture.
Vanderzalm, Lynn, 98n10a
Varghese, Roy Abraham, 22, 271n6
Veenhoven, Ruut, 124
Vietnam, 177
Vikings, 77
violence, 11, 13, 14, 27, 47, 52, 64, 65
    and human nature, 53, 61–64
    and men, 63
    See also Scapegoat.
Voice of the Martyrs, 43n23
Vonnegut, Kurt, 130

Walking with the Poor (Myers), 259n31
Wall Street, 159
Wallis, Jim, 7
Wal-mart, 136
Wal-mart: The High Cost of Low Price (Greenwald), 136
Warren, Rick, 56
wealth
    and favoritism, 166
    and the gospel, 204, 255
    and nation states, 165
    and tax rates, 126, 164, 257n27
Weiner, Eric, 124
Weisel, Elie, 53
Wells, H.G. 175
Welton, Jonathon, 187
Westminster Shorter Catechism, 47
What a Way to Go: Life at the End of Empire (Shaw), 137

When Heaven Invades Earth (Johnson), 194n5, 209n21, 210n25, 225n8, 227n10, 229n13, 231n16, 233n24, 241n3, 247n10, 257n26, 264n41
wilderness
    as anthropogenic landscape, 83, 84, 169
    as "howling wilderness," 83, 101, 104, 148
    and myth, 83, 168, 169
Williams, Bear Heart, 126n20
Williams, Ray B., 132n4
Williams, Robin, 263
Williams, Roger, 83
Wilson, E. O., 29, 67
Wilson, Woodrow, 177
Wonder of the World (Varghese), 22n5–7, 271n5
Wood, Allan, 18n10
World Bank, 165
World Database of Happiness, 124
World Trade Center, 12, 133
World Vision, 255
World War II, 53, 178
worldview, 4
    Christian, 190
    Hebraic, 236
    science-based, 22
    See also Ideology.

xenophobia, 55

Yale Cancer Center, 119
Yeats, William Butler, 238
Yemen, 141
Yong, Ed, 107n22
youth, 10, 43, 53n1, 66, 74, 103, 138, 147, 149, 160, 191, 204, 207, 245
    and image, 117–21
Yugoslavia, 61

Zephaniah, 282

www.ingramcontent.com/pod-product-compliance
Lightning Source LLC
Chambersburg PA
CBHW070231230426
43664CB00014B/2264